The
East Asian
Miracle

A World Bank Policy Research Report

The East Asian Miracle

Economic Growth
and Public Policy

Published for the World Bank
OXFORD UNIVERSITY PRESS

Oxford University Press

OXFORD NEW YORK TORONTO
DELHI BOMBAY CALCUTTA MADRAS KARACHI
KUALA LUMPUR SINGAPORE HONG KONG TOKYO
NAIROBI DAR ES SALAAM CAPE TOWN
MELBOURNE AUCKLAND

and associated companies in

BERLIN IBADAN

© 1993 *The International Bank for Reconstruction
and Development* / THE WORLD BANK
*1818 H Street, N.W.
Washington, D.C. 20433, U.S.A.*

*Published by Oxford University Press, Inc.
200 Madison Avenue, New York, N.Y. 10016*

*Manufactured in the United States of America
First printing September 1993*

*Cover photographs: At the top, a rice field in Java, Indonesia; courtesy of Maurice Asseo. At
the bottom, the port of Pusan, Republic of Korea; courtesy of Jitendra Bajpai.*

*The map that appears on the inside covers, which shows the eight economies discussed in this
book, was prepared solely for the convenience of the reader; the designations and presentation
of material in it do not imply the expression of any opinion whatsoever on the part of the
World Bank, its affiliates, or its Board or member countries concerning the legal status of any
economy, territory, city, or area, or of the authorities thereof, or concerning the delimitation
of its boundaries or its national affiliation.*

Library of Congress Cataloging-in-Publication Data

The East Asian miracle : economic growth and public policy.
    p. cm. — (World Bank policy research reports)
    Includes bibliographical references.
    ISBN *0-19-520993-1*
    1. East Asia—Economic policy. 2. East Asia—Economic conditions.
3. Asia, Southeastern—Economic policy. 4. Asia, Southeastern—Economic conditions.
I. World Bank. II. Series.
HC*460.5.E275 1993*
338.95—dc20   *93-30466*
                                                                                          CIP

ISSN *1020-0851*

*Text printed on paper that conforms to the American National Standard for Permanence of
Paper for Printed Library Materials, Z39.48-1984*

Foreword

DEBATES ON THE APPROPRIATE ROLE OF PUBLIC POLICY IN economic development have occupied policymakers and scholars since the study of developing economies began in earnest at the close of World War II. The success of many of the economies in East Asia in achieving rapid and equitable growth, often in the context of activist public policies, raises complex questions about the relationship between government, the private sector, and the market. Seemingly, the rapidly growing economies in East Asia used many of the same policy instruments as other developing economies, but with greater success. Understanding which policies contributed to their rapid growth, and how, is a major question for research on development policy. For these reasons I announced at the time of the 1991 Annual Meetings of the Board of Governors of the World Bank in Bangkok, Thailand, that our Development Economics Vice Presidency would undertake a comparative study of economic growth and public policy in East Asia.

This volume is the summary of that program of research. It appears as the first in a series of Policy Research Reports, which are intended to bring to a broad audience the results of research on development policy issues carried out by staff of the World Bank. As reports on policy issues, we intend that they should help us to take stock of what we know and clearly identify what we do not know; they should contribute to the debate in both the academic and policy communities on appropriate public policy objectives and instruments for developing economies; and they should be accessible to nonspecialists. Because they summarize research, we also anticipate that Policy Research Reports will provoke further debate, both within the Bank and outside, concerning the methods used and the conclusions drawn.

What does this report tell us about the East Asian miracle? The research shows that most of East Asia's extraordinary growth is due to superior accumulation of physical and human capital. But these economies were also better able than most to allocate physical and human resources to highly productive investments and to acquire and master technology. In this sense there is nothing "miraculous" about the East Asian economies' success; each has performed these essential functions of growth better than most other economies.

The eight economies studied used very different combinations of policies, from hands-off to highly interventionist. Thus, there is no single "East Asian model" of development. This diversity of experience reinforces the view that economic policies and policy advice must be country-specific, if they are to be effective. But there are also some common threads among the high-performing East Asian economies. The authors conclude that rapid growth in each economy was primarily due to the application of a set of common, market-friendly economic policies, leading to both higher accumulation and better allocation of resources. While this conclusion is not strikingly new, it reinforces other research that has stressed the essential need for developing economies to get the policy fundamentals right. The research also further supports the desirability of a two-track approach to development policy emphasizing macroeconomic stability on one hand and investments in people on the other. The importance of good macroeconomic management and broadly based educational systems for East Asia's rapid growth is abundantly demonstrated.

The report also breaks some new ground. It concludes that in some economies, mainly those in Northeast Asia, some selective interventions contributed to growth, and it advances our understanding of the conditions required for interventions to succeed. The authors argue that where selective interventions succeeded they did so because of three essential prerequisites. First, they addressed problems in the functioning of markets. Second, they took place within the context of good, fundamental policies. Third, their success depended on the ability of governments to establish and monitor appropriate economic-performance criteria related to the interventions—in the authors' terms, to create economic contests. These prerequisites suggest that the institutional context within which policies are implemented is as important to their success or failure as the policies themselves, and the report devotes substantial attention to the institutional bases for East Asia's rapid growth.

While these factors help to explain why apparently similar policies did not succeed in many other economies, the report also leaves unanswered many important questions. The market-oriented aspects of East Asia's policies can be recommended with few reservations, but the more institutionally demanding aspects, such as contest-based interventions, have not been successfully used in other settings. Noneconomic factors, including culture, politics, and history, are also important to the East Asian success story. Thus, there is still much to be learned about the interactions between policy choices and institutional capability and between economic and noneconomic factors in development. Work in these areas will continue beyond this report.

The support of the Government of Japan for the research program on the high-performing Asian economies is gratefully acknowledged. The report is a product of the staff of the World Bank, and the judgments made herein do not necessarily reflect the view of its Board of Directors or the governments they represent.

Lewis T. Preston
President
The World Bank

August 1993

Contents

The Research Team

THIS POLICY RESEARCH REPORT WAS PREPARED BY A TEAM LED by John Page and comprising Nancy Birdsall, Ed Campos, W. Max Corden, Chang-Shik Kim, Howard Pack, Richard Sabot, Joseph E. Stiglitz, and Marilou Uy. Robert Cassen, William Easterly, Robert Z. Lawrence, Peter Petri, and Lant Pritchett made major contributions. Lawrence MacDonald was the principal editor. Case studies of the seven developing high-performing Asian economies were undertaken under the direction of Danny Leipziger. The team was assisted by Maria Luisa Cicogniani, Varuni Dayaratna, Leora Friedberg, Jay Gonzalez, Jennifer Keller, May Khamis, Sonia Plaza, Myriam Quispe, Carol Strunk, and Ayako Yasuda. The work was initiated by Lawrence H. Summers and was carried out under the general direction of Nancy Birdsall.

The editorial-production team for the report was led by Alfred Imhoff. The support staff was headed by Sushma Rajan and included Milagros Divino, Jan-Marie Hopkins, Anna Marie Maranon, and Linda Oehler. Polly Means gave graphical assistance. Bruce Ross-Larson and Meta de Coquereaumont provided additional editorial support. The map was designed by Jeffrey N. Lecksell. Mika Iwasaki coordinated work in Japan.

Acknowledgments

PREPARATION OF THIS REPORT DREW ON SEVERAL OTHER RElated research projects. Studies of the Japanese main bank system and civil service were carried out under the direction of Hyung-Ki Kim. Yoon-Je Cho and Dimitri Vittas directed the project on the effectiveness of credit policies in East Asia. Brian Levy directed the project on support systems for small and medium-size enterprises in Asia, and John Page coordinated projects on Japanese perspectives on public policy during the rapid growth period, and tax policy and tax administration in East Asia.

Many individuals inside and outside the World Bank provided valuable contributions and comments. (Specific acknowledgment of their efforts is made in the Bibliographic Note at the end of the book.) Particular thanks are due to the following senior officials of the economies studied who reviewed and commented on an earlier draft: Seung-Chul Ahn, Isao Kubota, Shijuro Ogata, J. B. Sumarlin, Teh Kok Peng, Chikao Tsukuda, Tan Sri Dato Lin See Yan, and Cesar Virata. Vinod Thomas commented on several drafts and coordinated the comments of his colleagues in the East Asia and Pacific Region of the Bank. Comments by Carl Dahlman, Kemal Dervis, Mark Gersovitz, Ralph W. Harbison, Magdi Iskander, Hyung-Ki Kim, Danny Leipziger, Johannes Linn, Gobind Nankani, Mieko Nishimizu, Guy P. Pfeffermann, D. C. Rao, and Michael Walton contributed to the improvement of the book.

Preparation of the report was aided by seminars organized by the Indonesian Economists Association, the Economic Society of Singapore, the Monetary Authority of Singapore, Stanford University, and the World Institute for Development Economic Research. The financial assistance of the Government of Japan is gratefully acknowledged.

Definitions

Economy Groups

FOR OPERATIONAL AND ANALYTICAL PURPOSES, THE WORLD Bank's main criterion for classifying economies is gross national product (GNP) per capita. Every economy is classified as low-income, middle-income (subdivided into lower-middle and upper-middle), or high-income. Other analytical groups, based on regions, exports, and levels of external debt, are also used.

Because of changes in GNP per capita, the economy composition of each income group may change from one Bank publication to the next. Once the classification is fixed for any publication, all the historical data presented are based on the same economy grouping. The income-based economy groupings used in this study are defined as follows:

- *Low-income economies* are those with a GNP per capita of $635 or less in 1991.
- *Middle-income economies* are those with a GNP per capita of more than $635 but less than $7,911 in 1991. A further division, at GNP per capita of $2,555 in 1991, is made between *lower-middle-income* and *upper-middle-income* economies.
- *High-income economies* are those with a GNP per capita of $7,911 or more in 1991.
- *World* comprises all economies, including economies with sparse data and those with fewer than 1 million people.

Low-income and middle-income economies are sometimes referred to as developing economies. The use of the term is convenient; it is not intended to imply that all economies in the group are experiencing similar development or that other economies have reached a preferred or final stage of development. Classification by income does not necessarily reflect development status.

Analytical Groups

FOR ANALYTICAL PURPOSES, THIS STUDY GROUPS ECONOMIES into several regions, defined as follows:

- *High-performing Asian economies* (HPAEs), led by Japan, are identified by several common characteristics, such as very rapid export growth. The HPAEs are subclassified roughly according to the duration of their successful record of economic growth:

  - *The Four Tigers*, usually identified as Hong Kong, the Republic of Korea, Singapore, and Taiwan, China, have been growing rapidly for decades and have joined or approached the ranks of high-income economies.
  - *The newly industrializing economies* (NIEs) are Indonesia, Malaysia, and Thailand. They have joined the group of HPAEs more recently, within the last two decades.

- *East Asia* comprises all the low- and middle-income economies of East and Southeast Asia and the Pacific, east of and including China and Thailand.
- *South Asia* comprises Bangladesh, Bhutan, India, Myanmar, Nepal, Pakistan, and Sri Lanka.
- *Sub-Saharan Africa* comprises all economies south of the Sahara including South Africa but excluding Mauritius, Reunion, and Seychelles, which are in the Other Asia and Islands group.
- *Europe, Middle East, and North Africa* comprises the middle-income European economies of Bulgaria, the former Czechoslovakia, Greece, Hungary, Poland, Portugal, Romania, Turkey, and the former Yugoslavia, and all the economies of North Africa and the Middle East, and Afghanistan.
- *Latin America and the Caribbean* comprises all American and Caribbean economies south of the United States.

The regional grouping of economies in occasional parts of the text or tables may differ from that used in the main text of this study, described above. Such variations are noted where they occur.

Data Notes

- *Billion* is 1,000 million.
- *Trillion* is 1,000 billion.
- *Dollars* are current U.S. dollars unless otherwise specified.
- *Growth rates* are based on constant price data.

Historical data in this study may differ from those in other Bank publications because of continuous updating as better data become available, because of a change to a new base year for constant price data, or because of changes in economy composition of income and analytical groups.

Acronyms and Initials

CPI	Consumer price index
DFI	Direct foreign investment
GDP	Gross domestic product
GNP	Gross national product
HPAEs	High-performing Asian economies
IMF	International Monetary Fund
ISIC	International Standard Industrial Classification
MITI	Ministry of Trade and Industry, Japan
NIEs	Newly industrializing economies
OECD	Organization for Economic Cooperation and Development (Australia, Austria, Belgium, Canada, Denmark, Finland, France, Germany, Greece, Iceland, Ireland, Italy, Japan, Luxembourg, Netherlands, New Zealand, Norway, Portugal, Spain, Sweden, Switzerland, Turkey, United Kingdom, and United States)
PPP	Purchasing power parity
R&D	Research and development
TFP	Total factor productivity
UNDP	United Nations Development Programme
UNESCO	United Nations Educational, Scientific, and Cultural Organization

Overview: The Making of a Miracle

EAST ASIA HAS A REMARKABLE RECORD OF HIGH AND sustained economic growth. From 1965 to 1990 the twenty-three economies of East Asia grew faster than all other regions of the world (figure 1). Most of this achievement is attributable to seemingly miraculous growth in just eight economies: Japan; the "Four Tigers"—Hong Kong, the Republic of Korea, Singapore, and Taiwan, China; and the three newly industrializing economies (NIEs) of Southeast Asia, Indonesia, Malaysia, and Thailand. These eight high-performing Asian economies (HPAEs) are the subject of this study.*

Selecting any set of economies and attempting to understand the origins of their successful growth are necessarily arbitrary processes.[1] Botswana, Egypt, Gabon, and Lesotho in Sub-Saharan Africa have also been among the world's top growth performers in the past two decades, as have such diverse economies as Brazil, Cyprus, Greece, and Portugal (see figure 2). Why focus on eight economies in East Asia? In part the choice reflects popular interest; it has become common to see references to the "Asian Economic Miracle." In part it reflects recent attention by the academic and development policy communities to the relationship between public policies—which some authors have argued have a number of common threads in the eight economies, especially Japan, Korea,

*Recently China, particularly southern China, has recorded remarkably high growth rates using policies that in some ways resemble those of the HPAEs. This very significant development is beyond the scope of our study, mainly because China's ownership structure, methods of corporate and civil governance, and reliance on markets are so different from the those of the HPAEs, and in such rapid flux, that cross-economy comparison is problematic. We touch on China's recent development in chapters 1 and 3. The economic transition in China is the subject of current research by the Policy Research Department of the World Bank (see Bibliographic Note).

Figure 1 Average Growth of GNP per Capita, 1965–90

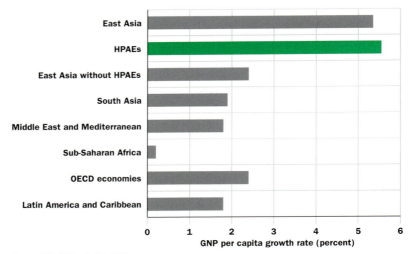

Source: World Bank (1992d).

Singapore, and Taiwan, China—and rapid growth. And in part it reflects the belief of those involved with this study that the eight economies do share some economic characteristics that set them apart from most other developing economies.

Since 1960, the HPAEs have grown more than twice as fast as the rest of East Asia, roughly three times as fast as Latin America and South Asia, and five times faster than Sub-Saharan Africa. They also significantly outperformed the industrial economies and the oil-rich Middle East–North Africa region. Between 1960 and 1985, real income per capita increased more than four times in Japan and the Four Tigers and more than doubled in the Southeast Asian NIEs (see figure 2). If growth were randomly distributed, there is roughly one chance in ten thousand that success would have been so regionally concentrated.

The HPAEs have also been unusually successful at sharing the fruits of growth. Figure 3 shows the relationship between the growth of gross domestic product (GPD) per capita between 1965 and 1990 and changes in the Gini coefficient, a statistical measure of the inequality of income distribution. The HPAEs enjoyed much higher per capita income growth at the same time that income distribution improved by as much or more than in other developing economies, with the exceptions of Korea and Taiwan, China, which began with highly equal income distributions. The HPAEs are the only economies that have high growth *and* declining

Figure 2 Change in GDP per Capita, 1960–85

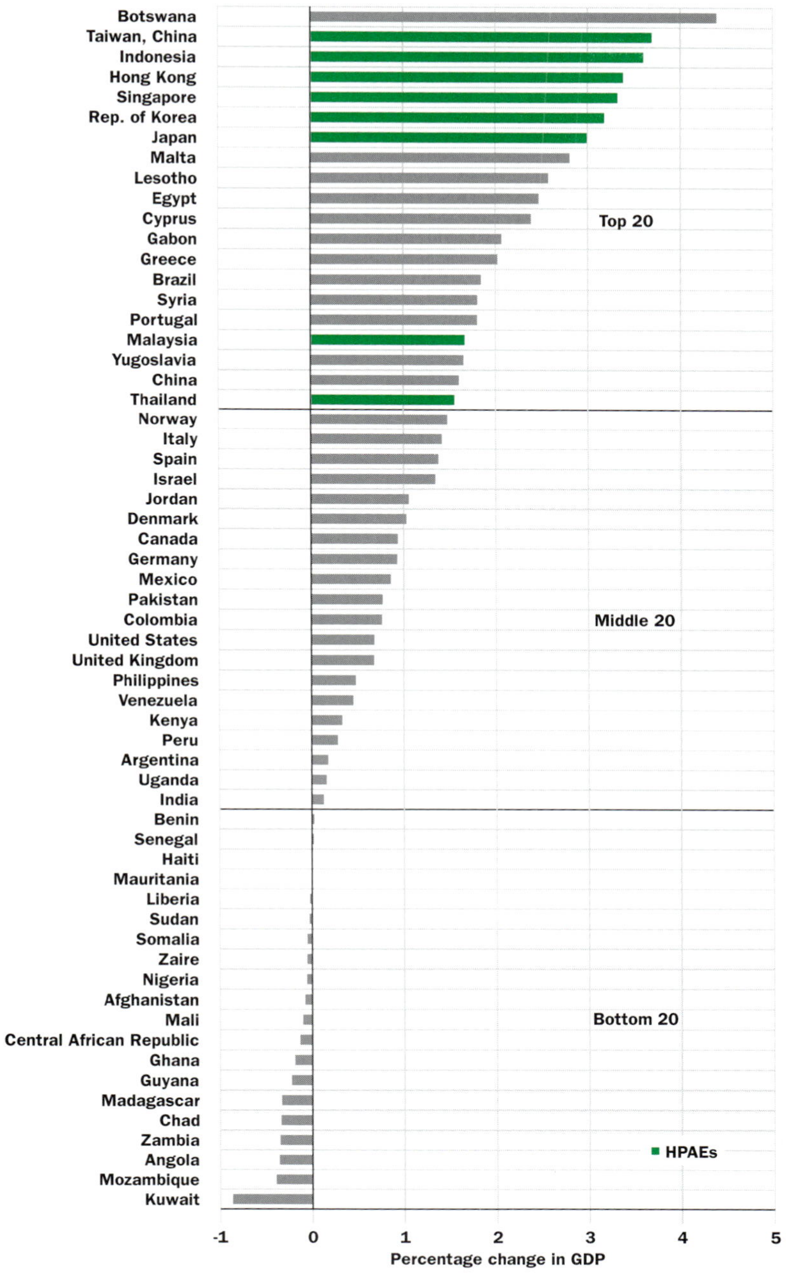

Source: Summers and Heston (1988).

Figure 3 Change in Inequity and the GDP per Capita Growth Rate

Change in average Gini coefficient (1980s minus 1960s)

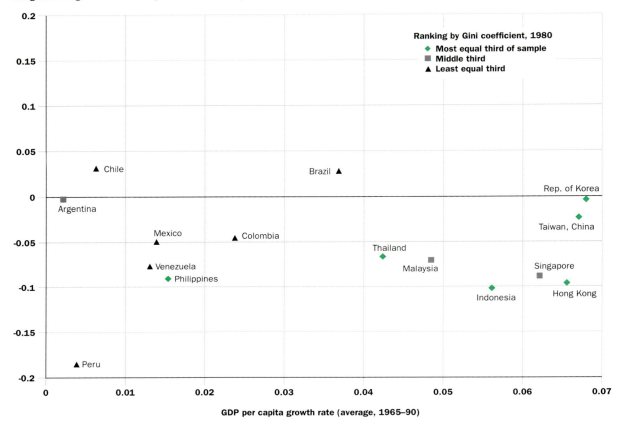

GDP per capita growth rate (average, 1965–90)

Note: Figure 3 plots the relationship between average per capita income growth and changes in the decade average of the Gini coefficient from the 1960s to the 1980s; a negative number indicates that income became less concentrated. The decade average is used because data are available for different years in different economies; the decade average for the 1960s begins with data from 1965.

Source: World Bank data.

inequality. Moreover, the fastest growing East Asian economies, Japan and the Four Tigers, are the most equal.

As a result of rapid, shared growth, human welfare has improved dramatically. Life expectancy in the developing HPAEs increased from 56 years in 1960 to 71 years in 1990. (In other low- and middle-income economies, life expectancy also rose considerably, from 36 and 49 to 62 and 66 years, respectively.) In the HPAEs, the proportion of people living in absolute poverty, lacking such basic necessities as clean water, food, and shelter, dropped—for example, from 58 percent in 1960 to 17 percent in 1990 in Indonesia, and from 37 percent to less than 5 percent in Malaysia during the same period. Absolute poverty also declined in other developing economies, but much less steeply, from 54 to 43 percent in India and from 50 to 21 percent in Brazil from 1960 to 1990. A host of other social and economic indicators, from education to appliance ownership, have also improved rapidly in the HPAEs and now are at levels that sometimes surpass those in industrial economies.

What caused East Asia's success? In large measure the HPAEs achieved high growth by getting the basics right. Private domestic investment and rapidly growing human capital were the principal engines of growth. High levels of domestic financial savings sustained the HPAEs' high investment levels. Agriculture, while declining in relative importance, experienced rapid growth and productivity improvement. Population growth rates declined more rapidly in the HPAEs than in other parts of the developing world. And some of these economies also got a head start because they had a better-educated labor force and a more effective system of public administration. In this sense there is little that is "miraculous" about the HPAEs' superior record of growth; it is largely due to superior accumulation of physical and human capital.

Fundamentally sound development policy was a major ingredient in achieving rapid growth. Macroeconomic management was unusually good and macroeconomic performance unusually stable, providing the essential framework for private investment. Policies to increase the integrity of the banking system, and to make it more accessible to nontraditional savers, raised the levels of financial savings. Education policies that focused on primary and secondary schools generated rapid increases in labor force skills. Agricultural policies stressed productivity and did not tax the rural economy excessively. All the HPAEs kept price distortions within reasonable bounds and were open to foreign ideas and technology.

But these fundamental policies do not tell the entire story. In most of these economies, in one form or another, the government intervened—systematically and through multiple channels—to foster development, and in some cases the development of specific industries. Policy interventions took many forms: targeting and subsidizing credit to selected industries, keeping deposit rates low and maintaining ceilings on borrowing rates to increase profits and retained earnings, protecting domestic import substitutes, subsidizing declining industries, establishing and financially supporting government banks, making public investments in applied research, establishing firm- and industry-specific export targets, developing export marketing institutions, and sharing information widely between public and private sectors. Some industries were promoted, while others were not.

At least some of these interventions violate the dictum of establishing for the private sector a level playing field, a neutral incentives regime. Yet these strategies of selective promotion were closely associated with high rates of private investment and, in the fastest-growing economies, high rates of productivity growth. Were some selective interventions, in fact, good for growth?

In addressing this question, we face a central methodological problem. Since we chose the HPAEs for their unusually rapid growth, we know already that their interventions did not significantly inhibit growth. But it is very difficult to establish statistical links between growth and a specific intervention and even more difficult to establish causality. Because we cannot know what would have happened in the absence of a specific policy, it is difficult to test whether interventions increased growth rates. Other economies attempted similar interventions without success, and on average they used them more pervasively than in the HPAEs. Because the HPAEs differed from less successful economies both in their closer adherence to policy fundamentals and in the manner in which they implemented interventions, it is virtually impossible to measure the relative impact of fundamentals and interventions on HPAE growth. Thus, in attempting to distinguish interventions that contributed to growth from those that were either growth-neutral or harmful to growth, we cannot offer a rigorous counterfactual scenario. Instead, we have had to be content with what Keynes called an "essay in persuasion," based on analytical and empirical judgments.

Our judgment is that in a few economies, mainly in Northeast Asia, in some instances, government interventions resulted in higher and more equal growth than otherwise would have occurred. However, the prerequisites for success were so rigorous that policymakers seeking to follow similar paths in other developing economies have often met with failure. What were these prerequisites? First, governments in Northeast Asia developed institutional mechanisms which allowed them to establish clear performance criteria for selective interventions and to monitor performance. Intervention has taken place in an unusually disciplined and performance-based manner (Amsden 1989). Second, the costs of interventions, both explicit and implicit, did not become excessive. When fiscal costs threatened the macroeconomic stability of Korea and

Malaysia during their heavy and chemical industries drives, governments pulled back. In Japan the Ministry of Finance acted as a check on the ability of the Ministry of International Trade and Industry to carry out subsidy policies, and in Indonesia and Thailand balanced budget laws and legislative procedures constrained the scope for subsidies. Indeed, when selective interventions have threatened macroeconomic stability, HPAE governments have consistently come down on the side of prudent macroeconomic management. Price distortions arising from selective interventions were also less extreme than in many developing economies.

In the newly industrializing economies of Southeast Asia, government interventions played a much less prominent and frequently less constructive role in economic success, while adherence to policy fundamentals remained important. These economies' capacity to administer and implement specific interventions may have been less than in Northeast Asia. Their rapid growth, moreover, has occurred in a very different international economic environment from the one that Japan, Korea, and Taiwan, China, encountered during their most rapid growth. Thus the problem is not only to try to understand which specific policies may have contributed to growth, but also to understand the institutional and economic circumstances that made them viable. Indeed, the experience of the Southeast Asian economies, whose initial conditions parallel those of many developing economies today, may prove to have more relevance outside the region than that of Northeast Asia.

The book is organized as follows: chapter 1 describes the distinguishing characteristics of the East Asian economic miracle, rapid growth with equity, and uses economic models to attempt to account for this growth. Chapter 2 reviews policy explanations for East Asia's economic success and introduces the framework that we will use throughout to explore the relationship between public policy and economic growth. Chapter 3 discusses pragmatism and flexibility in the formulation of policies that led to two important characteristics of the HPAEs' economic performance: macroeconomic stability and rapid growth of manufactured exports. Chapter 4 discusses the role of institutions. Chapter 5 looks at the role of public policy in the HPAEs' unusually rapid accumulation of physical and human capital, while chapter 6 analyzes the means used to achieve efficient allocation of resources and productivity growth. Chapter 7, in conclusion, assesses the success of East Asian polices and their applicability in a changing world economy. The remainder of this overview parallels the organization of the book, highlighting the central arguments and conclusions.

The Essence of the Miracle: Rapid Growth with Equity

THE EIGHT HPAEs ARE HIGHLY DIVERSE IN NATURAL RE-sources, population, culture, and economic policy. What shared characteristics cause them to be grouped together and set apart from other developing economies? First, as we noted above, they had rapid, sustained growth between 1960 and 1990. This in itself is unusual among developing economies; others have grown quickly for periods but not for decades at such high rates. The HPAEs are unique in that they combine this rapid, sustained growth with highly equal income distributions. They also all have been characterized by rapid demographic transitions, strong and dynamic agricultural sectors, and unusually rapid export growth (see chapter 1).

The HPAEs also differ from other developing economies in three factors that economists have traditionally associated with economic growth. High rates of investment, exceeding 20 percent of GDP on average between 1960 and 1990, including in particular unusually high rates of private investment, combined with high and rising endowments of human capital due to universal primary and secondary education, tell a large part of the growth story. These factors account for roughly two-thirds of the growth in the HPAEs. The remainder is attributable to improved productivity. Such high levels of productivity growth are quite unusual. In fact, productivity growth in the HPAEs exceeds that of most other developing and industrial economies. This superior productivity performance comes from the combination of unusual success at allocating capital to high-yielding investments and at catching up technologically to the industrial economies.

Public Policies and Growth

What was the role of public policy in helping the HPAEs to rapidly accumulate human and physical capital and to allocate those resources to high-yielding investments? Did policies assist in promoting rapid productivity growth? There are several explanations for East Asia's success. Geography and culture were clearly important; however, they do not entirely account for the high-performing economies' success, as the presence of unsuccessful economies in the same region attests. Among the variety of policy explanations, two broad views have emerged (see chapter 2).

Adherents of the *neoclassical view* stress the HPAEs' success in getting the basics right. They argue that the successful Asian economies have been better than others at providing a stable macroeconomic environment and a reliable legal framework to promote domestic and international competition. They also stress that the orientation of the HPAEs toward international trade and the absence of price controls and other distortionary policies have led to low relative price distortions. Investments in people, education, and health are legitimate roles for government in the neoclassical framework, and its adherents stress the importance of human capital in the HPAEs' success.

Adherents of the *revisionist view* have successfully shown that East Asia does not wholly conform to the neoclassical model. Industrial policy and interventions in financial markets are not easily reconciled within the neoclassical framework. Some policies in some economies are much more in accord with models of state-led development. Moreover, while the neoclassical model would explain growth with a standard set of relatively constant policies, the policy mixes used by East Asian economies were diverse and flexible. Revisionists argue that East Asian governments "led the market" in critical ways. In contrast to the neoclassical view, which acknowledges relatively few cases of market failure, revisionists contend that markets consistently fail to guide investment to industries that would generate the highest growth for the overall economy. In East Asia, the revisionists argue, governments remedied this by deliberately "getting the prices wrong"—altering the incentive structure—to boost industries that would not otherwise have thrived (Amsden 1989).

The revisionist school has provided valuable insights into the history, role, and extent of East Asian interventions, demonstrating convincingly the scope of government actions to promote industrial development in Japan, Korea, Singapore, and Taiwan, China. But, in general its proponents have not claimed to establish that interventions per se accelerated growth. Moreover, as we shall show, some important government interventions in East Asia, such as Korea's promotion of chemicals and heavy industries, have had little apparent impact on industrial structure.

In other instances, such as Singapore's effort to squeeze out labor-intensive industries by boosting wages, policies have clearly backfired. Thus neither view fully accounts for East Asia's phenomenal growth.

The Market-Friendly View. In describing the policies associated with rapid growth, *World Development Report 1991* (World Bank 1991b) expands on the neoclassical view, clarifying systematically how rapid growth in developing countries has been associated with effective but carefully limited government activism. In the "market-friendly" strategy it articulates, the appropriate role of government is to ensure adequate investments in people, provide a competitive climate for private enterprise, keep the economy open to international trade, and maintain a stable macroeconomy. Beyond these roles, the report argues, governments are likely to do more harm than good, unless interventions are market friendly. On the basis of an exhaustive review of the experience of developing economies during the last thirty years, it concludes that attempts to guide resource allocation with nonmarket mechanisms have generally failed to improve economic performance.

The market-friendly approach captures important aspects of East Asia's success. These economies are stable macroeconomically, have high shares of international trade in GDP, invest heavily in people, and have strong competition among firms. But these characteristics are the outcome of many different policy instruments. And the instruments chosen, particularly in the northeastern HPAEs, Japan, Korea, and Taiwan, China, sometimes included extensive government intervention in markets to guide private-sector resource allocation. The success of these northeastern economies, moreover, stands up well to the less interventionist paths taken by Hong Kong, Malaysia, and more recently Indonesia and Thailand.

A Functional Approach to Understanding Growth. To explore these varying paths to economic success, we have developed a framework that seeks to link rapid growth to the attainment of three functions. In this view, each of the HPAEs maintained macroeconomic stability *and* accomplished three functions of growth: accumulation, efficient allocation, and rapid technological catch-up. They did this with combinations of policies, ranging from market oriented to state led, that varied both across economies and over time.

We classify policies into two broad groups: fundamentals and selective interventions. Among the most important fundamental policies are those that encourage macroeconomic stability, high investments in human capital, stable and secure financial systems, limited price distortions, and openness to foreign technology. Selective interventions include mild financial repression (keeping interest rates positive but low), directed credit, selective industrial promotion, and trade policies that push nontraditional exports. We try to understand how government policies, both fundamental and interventionist, may have contributed to faster accumulation, more efficient allocation, and higher productivity growth.

We maintain as a guiding principle that for interventions that attempt to guide resource allocation to succeed, they must address failures in the working of markets. Otherwise, markets would perform the allocation function more efficiently. We identify a class of economic problems, coordination failures, which can lead markets to fail, especially in early stages of development. We then interpret some of the interventionist policies in East Asia as responses to these coordination problems—responses that emphasized cooperative behavior among private firms and clear performance-based standards of success.

Competitive discipline is crucial to efficient investment. Most economies employ only market-based competition. We argue that some HPAEs have gone a step further by creating contests that combine competition with the benefits of cooperation among firms and between government and the private sector. Such contests range from very simple nonmarket allocation rules, such as access to rationed credit for exporters, to very complex coordination of private investment in the government-business deliberation councils of Japan and Korea. The key feature of each contest, however, is that the government distributes rewards—often access to credit or foreign exchange—on the basis of performance, which the government and competing firms monitor. To succeed, selective interventions must be disciplined by competition via either markets or contests.

Economic contests, like all others, require competent and impartial referees—that is, strong institutions. Thus, a high-quality civil service that has the capacity to monitor performance and is insulated from political interference is essential to contest-based competition. Of course, a high-quality civil service also augments a government's ability to design and implement non-contest-based policies.

Our framework is an effort to order and interpret information. We are not suggesting that HPAE governments set out to achieve the functions of growth. Rather, they used multiple, shifting policy instruments in pursuit of more straightforward economic objectives such as macro-economic stability, rapid export growth, and high savings. Pragmatic flexibility in the pursuit of such objectives—the capacity and willingness to change policies—is as much a hallmark of the HPAEs as any single policy instrument. This is well illustrated by the great variety of ways in which the HPAEs achieved two important objectives: macroeconomic stability and rapid export growth (see chapter 3).

Achieving Macroeconomic Stability and Export Growth

More than most developing economies, the HPAEs were characterized by responsible macroeconomic management. In particular, they generally limited fiscal deficits to levels that could be prudently financed without increasing inflationary pressures and responded quickly when fiscal pressures were perceived to building up. During the past thirty years, annual inflation averaged approximately 9 percent in these economies, compared with 18 percent in other low- and middle-income economies. Because inflation was both moderate and predictable, real interest rates were far more stable than in other low- and middle-income economies. Macroeconomic stability encouraged long-term planning and private investment and, through its impact on real interest rates and the real value of financial assets, helped to increase financial savings. The HPAEs also adjusted their macroeconomic policies to terms of trade shocks more quickly and effectively than other low- and middle-income economies. As a result, they have enjoyed more robust recoveries of private investment.

Many of the policies that fostered macroeconomic stability also contributed to rapid export growth. Fiscal discipline and high public savings allowed Japan and Taiwan, China, to undertake extended periods of exchange rate protection. Adjustments to exchange rates in other HPAEs—validated by policies that reduced expenditures—kept them competitive, despite differential inflation with trading partners.

In addition to macroeconomic policies, the HPAEs used a variety of approaches to promoting exports. All (except Hong Kong) began with a period of import substitution, and a strong bias against exports. But each moved to establish a pro-export regime more quickly than other developing economies. First Japan, in the 1950s and early 1960s, and then the Four Tigers, in the late 1960s, shifted trade policies to encourage manufactured exports. In Japan, Korea, and Taiwan, China, governments established a pro-export incentive structure that coexisted with moderate but highly variable protection of the domestic market. A wide variety of instruments was used, including export credit, duty-free imports for exporters and their suppliers, export targets, and tax incentives. In the Southeast Asian NIEs the export push came later, in the early 1980s, and the instruments were different. Reductions in import protection were more generalized and were accompanied by export credit and supporting institutions. In these economies export development has relied less on highly selective interventions and more on broadly based market incentives and direct foreign investment.

Building the Institutional Basis for Growth

Some economists and political scientists have argued that the East Asian miracle is due to the high quality and authoritarian nature of the region's institutions. They describe East Asian political regimes as "developmental states" in which powerful technocratic bureaucracies, shielded from political pressure, devise and implement well-honed interventions. We believe developmental state models overlook the central role of government–private sector cooperation. While leaders of the HPAEs have tended to be either authoritarian or paternalistic, they have also been willing to grant a voice and genuine authority to a technocratic elite and key leaders of the private sector. Unlike authoritarian leaders in many other economies, leaders in the HPAEs realized that economic development was impossible without cooperation (see chapter 4).

The Principle of Shared Growth. To establish their legitimacy and win the support of the society at large, East Asian leaders established the principle of shared growth, promising that as the economy expanded all groups would benefit. But sharing growth raised complex coordination problems. First, leaders had to convince economic elites to support progrowth policies. Then they had to persuade the elites to share the benefits of growth with the middle class and the poor. Finally, to win the cooperation of the middle class and the poor, the leaders had to show them that they would indeed benefit from future growth.

Explicit mechanisms were used to demonstrate the intent that all would have a share of future wealth. Korea and Taiwan, China, carried out comprehensive land reform programs; Indonesia used rice and fertilizer price policies to raise rural incomes; Malaysia introduced explicit wealth-sharing programs to improve the lot of ethnic Malays relative to the better-off ethnic Chinese; Hong Kong and Singapore undertook massive public housing programs; and in several economies, governments assisted workers' cooperatives and established programs to encourage small and medium-size enterprises. Whatever the form, these programs demonstrated that the government intended for all to share the benefits of growth.

Creating a Business-Friendly Environment. To tackle coordination problems, leaders needed institutions and mechanisms to reassure competing groups that each would benefit from growth. The first step was to recruit a competent and relatively honest technocratic cadre and insulate it from day-to-day political interference. The power of these technocracies has varied greatly. In Japan, Korea, Singapore, and Taiwan, China, strong, well-organized bureaucracies wield substantial power. Other HPAEs have had small, general-purpose planning agencies. But in each economy, economic technocrats helped leaders devise a credible economic strategy.

Leaders in the HPAEs also built a business-friendly environment. A major element of that environment was a legal and regulatory structure that was generally hospitable to private investment. Beyond this the HPAEs have with varying degrees of success enhanced communication between business and government. Japan, Korea, Malaysia, and Singapore have established forums, which we call deliberation councils, in which private sector groups are invited to help shape and implement the government policies relevant to their interests. In contrast to lobbying, where rules are murky and groups seek secret advantage over one another, the deliberation councils are intended to make allocation rules clear to all participants.

Using Deliberation Councils. In Japan and Korea technocrats used deliberation councils to establish contests among firms. Because the private sector participated in drafting the rules, and because the process was transparent to all participants, private sector groups became more willing participants in the leadership's development efforts. One by-product of these contests was a tendency to reduce the private resources devoted to wasteful rent-seeking activities, thus making more available for productive endeavors. Deliberation councils also facilitated information exchanges between the private sector and government, among firms, and between management and labor. The councils thus supplemented the market's information transmission function, enabling the HPAEs to respond more quickly than other economies to changing markets.

Institutions of business-government communication have not been static in the HPAEs. The role of the deliberation council is changing in Japan and Korea to a more indicative and consensus-building role, along functional as opposed to industry-specific lines. In Malaysia the councils appear to be increasing in importance and scope. In Thailand the formal mechanisms of communication have generally been used to present businesses' positions to government and to reduce the private sector's suspicion of government. In institutional development, as in economic policymaking, East Asian governments have changed with changing circumstances.

Accumulating Human and Physical Capital

Drawing on the strength of their institutions, East Asian economies used a combination of fundamental and interventionist policies to achieve rapid accumulation of human and physical resources. Fundamentals included such traditional government obligations as providing adequate infrastructure, education, and secure financial institutions. Interventions included mild repression of interest rates, state capitalism, mandatory savings mechanisms, and socialization of risk (see chapter 5).

Building Human Capital. The East Asian economies had a head start in terms of human capital and have since widened their lead over other developing economies. In the 1960s, levels of human capital were already higher in the HPAEs than in other low- and middle-income economies. Governments built on this base by focusing education spending on the lower grades; first by providing universal primary education, later by increasing the availability of secondary education. Rapid demographic transitions facilitated these efforts by slowing the growth in the number of school-age children and in some cases causing an absolute decline. Declining fertility and rapid economic growth meant that, even when education investment as a share of GDP remained constant, more resources were available per child. Limited public funding of postsecondary education focused on technical skills, and some HPAEs imported educational services on a large scale, particularly in vocationally and technologically sophisticated disciplines. The result of these policies has been a broad, technically inclined human capital base well-suited to rapid economic development.

HPAE education policies also contributed to more equitable income distributions. To be sure, initial conditions helped to set up a virtuous circle: initial low inequality in income and education led to educational expansion, which reinforced low inequality. In addition, by focusing spending on primary and secondary education, and leaving demand for tertiary education to be largely met by a self-financed private system, governments served large segments of the population that otherwise would have lacked access to education.

Increasing Savings and Investment. The HPAEs increased savings and investment with a combination of fundamental and interventionist policies. Two fundamental policy areas provided a foundation for high and rising savings rates. First, by avoiding inflation, the HPAEs avoided volatility of real interest rates on deposits and ensured that rates were largely positive. As a result, the HPAEs have generally offered higher real interest rates on deposits in the financial system than other developing economies. Second, they ensured the security of banks and made them more convenient to small and rural savers. The major instruments used to build a secure, bank-based financial system were strong prudential regulation and supervision, limits on competition, and institutional reforms. In Japan, Korea, Malaysia, Singapore, and Taiwan, China, postal savings systems lowered transaction costs and increased the safety of saving while making substantial resources available to government. These initiatives promoted rapid growth of deposits in financial institutions (see figure 4).

Some governments also used a variety of more interventionist mechanisms to increase savings. Singapore and Taiwan, China, maintained unusually high public savings rates. Malaysia and Singapore compelled high private savings rates through mandatory provident fund contributions. Japan, Korea and Taiwan, China, all imposed stringent controls and high interest rates on loans for consumer items, and levied stiff taxes on so-called luxury consumption. Whether these more interventionist measures to increase savings improved welfare is open to debate. On one hand, making consumers save when they would not have otherwise imposes a welfare cost. On the other, the benefits are apparent in the rapid growth of these economies. Savings, forced or not, generated high payoffs based on consistently high rates of return to investments. In contrast to other economies that have used compulsory savings, such as the former Soviet Union, welfare costs were clearly offset by substantive benefits.

The HPAEs encouraged investment by several means. First, they did a better job than most developing economies at creating infrastructure that was complementary to private investment. Second, they created an investment-friendly environment through a combination of tax policies

Figure 4 Savings Rates of HPAEs and Selected Economies, 1970–88

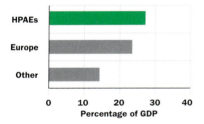

Percentage of GDP

Note: Europe includes Austria, Belgium, Denmark, Finland, France, the Federal Republic of Germany before reunification, Greece, Iceland, Ireland, Italy, Luxembourg, the Netherlands, Norway, Portugal, Spain, Sweden, Switzerland, and the United Kingdom. "Other" includes these developing economies: Argentina, Brazil, Chile, Colombia, Côte d'Ivoire, Egypt, Ghana, India, Mexico, Morocco, Nigeria, Pakistan, Peru, Sri Lanka, Turkey, Uruguay, Venezuela, the former Yugoslavia, and Zaire.

Source: Summers and Heston (1991).

favoring investment and of policies that kept the relative prices of capital goods low, largely by avoiding high tariffs on imported capital goods. These fundamental policies had an important impact on private investment. Third and more controversial, most HPAE governments held deposit and lending rates below market clearing levels—a practice termed financial repression.

Japan, Korea, Malaysia, Thailand, and Taiwan, China, had extended periods of mild financial repression. To be sure, increasing interest rates from negative to zero or mildly positive real rates and avoiding fluctuations (by avoiding unstable inflation) encourages financial savings. But because savings are not very responsive to marginal changes in positive real interest rates, HPAE governments were able to mildly repress interest rates on deposits with a minimal impact on savings and to pass the lower rates to final borrowers. Because savers were mostly households and borrowers were mostly firms, this resulted in a transfer of income from households to firms and in a change in the form in which savings were held, from debt to corporate equity.

Holding down interest rates on loans increases excess demand for credit, which in turn leads to rationing of credit by the government itself or by private sector banks working with government guidance. This heightens the risk that capital will be misallocated. Thus there is a trade-off between the possible increase in investment and the risk that the increased capital will be badly invested. There is some evidence that in Japan, Korea, and Taiwan, China, governments allocated credit to activities with high social returns, especially to exports. If this was the case, there may have been benefits from mild financial repression and government-guided allocation; microeconomic evidence from Japan supports the view that access to government credit increased investment (see chapter 6).

Generally, financial repression is associated with low economic growth, especially when real interest rates are strongly negative. But tests of the relationship between interest rates and growth in Japan, Korea, and Taiwan, China, do not show the negative relationship between interest rate repression and growth found in cross-economy comparative studies (see chapter 5). While we cannot establish conclusively that mild repression of interest rates at positive real levels enhanced growth in northeast Asia, it apparently did not inhibit it.

Finally, some governments, especially in the northeastern Asian tier, have encouraged investment by spreading private investment risks to the public. In some economies the government owned or controlled the institutions providing investment funds, in others it offered explicit credit guarantees, and in still others it implicitly guaranteed the financial viability of promoted projects. Relationship banking by a variety of public and private banking institutions in Hong Kong, Japan, Korea, Malaysia, Singapore, Thailand, and Taiwan, China, involved the banking sector in the management of troubled enterprises, increasing the likelihood of creditor workouts. Directed-credit programs in Japan, Korea, and Taiwan, China, signaled directions of government policy and provided implicit insurance to private banks.

Efficient Allocation and Productivity Change

Some policies that favored accumulation in the HPAEs, including financial repression and the socialization and bounding of risk, could have adversely affected the allocation of resources. Similarly, industrial targeting could have resulted in extensive rent-seeking and great inefficiency. Apparently they did not. The allocational rules followed by HPAE governments—particularly the devices used to shift market incentives—are therefore among the most controversial aspects of the East Asian success story (see chapter 6).

Like policies related to accumulation, policies affecting allocation and productivity change fall into fundamental and interventionist categories. Labor market policies tended to rely on fundamentals, using the market and reinforcing its flexibility. In capital markets, governments intervened systematically, both to control interest rates and to direct credit, but acted within a framework of careful monitoring and generally low subsidies to borrowers. Trade policies have included substantial protection of local manufacturers, but less than in most other developing countries; in addition, HPAE governments offset some disadvantages of protection by actively supporting exports. Finally, while interventions to support specific industries have generally not been successful, the export-push strategy—the mix of fundamental and interventionist policies used to encourage rapid manufactured export growth—has resulted in numerous benefits, including more efficient allocation, increased acquisition of foreign technology, and more rapid productivity growth.

Flexible Labor Markets. Government roles in labor markets in the successful Asian economies contrast sharply with the situation in most other developing economies. HPAE governments have generally been less vulnerable and less responsive than other developing-economy governments to organized labor's demands to legislate a minimum wage. Rather, they have focused their efforts on job generation, effectively boosting the demand for workers. As a result, employment levels have risen first, followed by market- and productivity-driven increases in wage levels. Because wages or at least wage rate increases have been downwardly flexible in response to changes in the demand for labor, adjustment to macroeconomic shocks has generally been quicker and less painful in East Asia than in other developing regions. Rapid adjustments helped to sustain growth, which in turn made more rapid real wage growth possible.

High productivity and income growth in agriculture helped to keep East Asian urban wages close to the supply price of labor. In contrast to many other developing economies, where the gap between urban and rural incomes has been large and growing, in the HPAEs the incomes of urban and rural workers with similar skill levels have risen roughly at the same pace; moreover, the overall gap between urban and rural incomes is smaller in the HPAEs than in other developing economies.

In Sub-Saharan Africa, Latin America, and South Asia, where wages in the urban formal sector are often pushed up by legislated minimum wages and other nonmarket forces, urban wage earners often have incomes twice their counterparts' in informal sectors. In contrast, the gap between the formal and informal sectors in East Asia is only about 20 percent. Smaller income gaps contribute to overall social stability, thus enhancing the environment for growth.

Capital Markets and Allocation. Most HPAEs influenced credit allocation in three ways: (i) by enforcing regulations to improve private banks' project selection; (ii) by creating financial institutions, especially long-term credit (development) banks; and (iii) by directing credit to specific sectors and firms through public and private banks. All three approaches can be justified in theory, and each has worked in some HPAEs. Yet each involves progressively more government intervention in credit markets and so carries a higher risk.

Government relationships with banks in the HPAEs have varied widely. In Hong Kong banks are private and regulated primarily to ensure their solvency. In Indonesia, Malaysia, Singapore, and Thailand, banks are privately owned and exercise independent authority over lending. While governments have broadly guided credit allocations through regulations and moral suasion, project selection is generally left to bankers. In other HPAEs, banks have been subject to direct state control or stringent credit allocation guidelines. For example, Indonesia, Korea, and Taiwan, China, tightly controlled the allocation of credit by public commercial banks.

Each of the HPAEs made some attempts to direct credit to priority activities. All East Asian economies except Hong Kong give automatic access to credit for exporters. Housing was a priority in Singapore and Hong Kong, while agriculture and small and medium-size enterprises were targeted sectors in Indonesia, Malaysia, and Thailand. Taiwan, China, has recently targeted technological development. Japan and Korea have used credit as a tool of industrial policy, organizing contests through deliberative councils to promote at various times the shipbuilding, chemical, and automobile industries.

The implicit subsidy of directed-credit programs in the HPAEs was generally small, especially in comparison to other developing economies, but access to credit and the signal of government support to favored sectors or enterprises were important. In Korea, the subsidy from preferential credit was large during the 1970s, resulting in a large gap between bank and curb market interest rates. This gap has declined sharply in recent years, as Korea has shifted away from heavy credit subsidies to selected sectors. In Japan implicit subsidies were small, and the direction of credit may have been more important as a signaling and insurance mechanism than as an incentive.

Although East Asia's directed-credit programs were designed to achieve policy objectives, they nevertheless included strict performance criteria. In Japan, public bank managers chose projects on basic economic criteria, employing rigorous credit evaluations to select among applicants that fell within government sectoral targets. In Korea, the government individually monitored the large conglomerates using market-oriented criteria such as exports and profitability. In some cases, major enterprises that failed to meet these tests were driven into bankruptcy. Recent assessments of the directed-credit programs in Japan and Korea provide microeconomic evidence that directed-credit programs in these economies increased investment, promoted new activities and borrowers, and were directed at firms with high potential for technological spillovers. Thus these performance-based directed-credit mechanisms appear to have improved credit allocation, especially during the early stages of rapid growth (see chapter 6).

Directed-credit programs in other HPAEs have usually lacked strong, per-formance-based allocation and monitoring and therefore have been largely unsuccessful. Even in the northern-tier economies, the increasing level of financial sector development and their increasing openness to international capital flows have meant that directed-credit programs have declined in im-portance, as the economies have liberalized their financial sectors.

Openness to Foreign Technology. The HPAEs have actively sought foreign technology through a variety of mechanisms. All welcomed technology transfers in the form of licenses, capital goods imports, and foreign training. Openness to direct foreign investment (DFI) has speeded tech-nology acquisition in Hong Kong, Malaysia, Singapore, and, more re-cently, Indonesia and Thailand. Japan, Korea and, to a lesser extent, Taiwan, China, restricted DFI but offset this disadvantage by aggressively acquiring foreign knowledge through licenses and other means.

In contrast, other low- and middle-income economies such as India and Argentina have adopted policies that hindered the acquisition of for-eign knowledge. Often they have been preoccupied with supposedly ex-cessive prices for licenses. They have refused to provide foreign exchange for trips to acquire knowledge, been restrictive of DFI, and have at-tempted prematurely to build up their machine-producing sectors, thus forgoing the advanced technology embodied in imported equipment.

Promoting Specific Industries. Most East Asian governments have pur-sued sector-specific industrial policies to some degree. The best-known instances include Japan's heavy industry promotion policies of the 1950s and the subsequent imitation of these policies in Korea. These policies included import protection as well as subsidies for capital and other im-ported inputs. Malaysia, Singapore, Taiwan, China, and even Hong Kong have also established programs—typically with more moderate incentives—to accelerate development of advanced industries. Despite these actions we find very little evidence that industrial policies have af-fected either the sectoral structure of industry or rates of productivity change. Indeed, industrial structures in Japan, Korea, and Taiwan, China, have evolved during the past thirty years as we would expect given factor-based comparative advantage and changing factor endowments.

It is not altogether surprising that industrial policy in Japan, Korea, and Taiwan, China, produced mainly market-conforming results. While these governments selectively promoted capital- and knowledge-intensive industries, they also took steps to ensure that they were foster-ing profitable, internationally competitive firms. Moreover, their industrial policies incorporated a large amount of market information and used performance, usually export performance, as a yardstick. Efforts elsewhere to promote specific industries without better information exchange and the discipline of international markets have not succeeded. This has been the case with the ambitious industrial policy programs in Brazil and India, and with the more limited but also disappointing efforts to build an aerospace industry in Indonesia and to promote heavy industries in Malaysia.

Export Push: A Winning Mix of Fundamentals and Interventions. One combination of fundamental and interventionist policies practiced in the HPAEs has been a significant source of rapid productivity growth: the active promotion of manufactured exports. Although all HPAEs except Hong Kong passed through an import-substitution phase, with high and variable protection of domestic import substitutes, these periods ended earlier than in other economies, typically because of a compelling need for foreign exchange. In contrast to many other economies, which tried to preserve foreign exchange with stricter import controls, the HPAEs set out to earn additional foreign exchange by increasing exports. Hong Kong and Singapore adopted trade regimes that were close to free trade; Japan, Korea, and Taiwan, China, adopted mixed regimes that were largely free for export industries. In the 1980s, Indonesia, Malaysia, and Thailand have adopted a wide variety of export incentives while gradually reducing protection. Exchange rate policies were liberalized, and currencies frequently devalued, to support export growth. Overall, these policies exposed much of the industrial sector to international competition and resulted in domestic relative prices that were closer to international prices than in most other developing economies.

The northern-tier economies—Japan, Korea, and Taiwan, China—halted the process of import liberalization, often for extended periods, and heavily promoted exports. Thus while incentives were largely equal between exports and imports, this was the result of countervailing subsidies rather than trade neutrality; the promotion of exports coexisted with protection of the domestic market. In the Southeast Asian HPAEs, conversely, governments used gradual but continuous liberalization of the trade regime, supplemented by institutional support for exporters, to achieve the export push. In both cases governments were credibly committed to the export-push strategy; producers, even those in the protected domestic market, knew that sooner or later their time to export would come.

East Asia's sectoral policies were usually geared toward export performance, in contrast to the inward-oriented policies of less successful developing economies. Japan, Korea, Singapore, and Taiwan, China, all relied on economic performance criteria, usually exports, to judge success. For example, in Taiwan, China, the government suspended domestic-content requirements that interfered with the exports of foreign investors. In addition, sectoral policies were closely monitored and frequently adjusted. Thus, many of East Asia's "industrial upgrading" programs of the late 1970s and early 1980s were substantially modified or abandoned when they failed to produce satisfactory results. Using the export rule meant that even programs of selective industrial promotion were indirectly export promoting.

Manufactured export growth also provided a powerful mechanism for technological upgrading in imperfect world technology markets. Because firms that export have greater access to best-practice technology, there are both benefits to the enterprise and spillovers to the rest of the economy that are not reflected in market transactions. These information-related externalities are an important source of rapid productivity growth. Both cross-economy evidence and more detailed studies at the industry level in Japan, Korea, and Taiwan, China, confirm the significance of exports to rapid productivity growth.

These experiences suggest that economies that are making the transition from highly protectionist import-substitution regimes to more balanced incentives would benefit from combining import liberalization with a strong commitment to exports and active export promotion, especially in those cases in which the pace of liberalization is moderate.

Policies for Rapid Growth in a Changing World Economy

WHAT ARE THE BROAD LESSONS OF SUCCESS IN THE HPAEs? Their rapid growth had two complementary elements. First, getting the fundamentals right was essential. Without high levels of domestic savings, broadly based human capital, good macroeconomic management, and limited price distortions, there would have been no basis for growth and no means by which the gains of rapid productivity change could have been realized. Policies to assist the financial sector capture nonfinancial savings and to increase household and corporate savings were central. Acquisition of technology through openness to direct foreign investment and licensing were crucial to rapid productivity growth. Public investment complemented private investment and increased its orientation to exports. Education policies stressed universal primary schooling and improvements in quality at primary and secondary levels.

Second, very rapid growth of the type experienced by Japan, the Four Tigers, and more recently the East Asian NIEs has at times benefited from careful policy interventions. All interventions carry costs, either in the direct fiscal costs of subsidies or forgone revenues, or the implicit taxation of households and firms, for example, through tariffs or interest rate controls. Unlike many other governments that attempted such interventions, HPAE governments generally held costs within well-defined limits. Thus, price distortions were mild, interest rate controls used international interest rates as a benchmark, and explicit subsidies were kept within fiscally manageable bounds. Given the overriding importance ascribed to macroeconomic stability, interventions that became too costly or otherwise threatened stability were quickly modified or abandoned.

Whether these interventions contributed to the rapid growth made possible by good fundamentals or detracted from it is the most difficult question we have attempted to answer. It is much easier to show that the HPAEs limited the costs and duration of inappropriately chosen interventions—itself an impressive achievement—than to demonstrate conclusively that those interventions maintained for a long time accelerated growth. Our assessment of three major uses of intervention is that promotion of specific industries generally did not work and therefore holds little promise for other developing economies. Mild financial repression combined with directed credit has worked in certain situations but carries high risk. Export-push strategies have been by far the most successful combination of fundamentals and policy interventions and hold the most promise for other developing economies (chapter 7).

But are these approaches feasible in the early 1990s? While limited repression of interest rates may have contributed to overall higher rates of investment in Japan, Korea, and Taiwan, China, these three northeastern economies undertook their initial growth spurts—and their most sustained and forceful repression of interest rates—during a period when it was possible for a developing economy to close its financial markets to the outside world. Furthermore, strong bureaucracies and a general climate of government-private sector cooperation meant that their restrictions on capital outflows were more effective than similar restrictions in many other economies. In today's increasingly global economic environment, few governments have the ability or desire to close their financial markets. Indeed, many East Asian governments are in the process of liberalizing restrictions on capital flows. In such circumstances, the scope for repressing interest rates without provoking capital flight is sharply narrowed. However, in some exceptional instances, very mild financial repression of short duration to increase corporate equity remains a viable option. This has been the case in Malaysia, which has wide open financial markets but nonetheless succeeded with very mild financial repression for more than a year.

The export-push strategy appears to hold great promise for other developing economies. But the conditions of market access under the General Agreement on Tariffs and Trade (GATT), and other trading arrangements, will hamper developing economies' use of policies viewed as unfair in major industrial-economy markets. Subsidies to exports and directed-credit programs linked to exports are not generally consistent with the GATT and may therefore invite retaliation from trading partners. Furthermore, like financial repression, these highly directed interventions require a high level of institutional capacity now lacking in most developing economies. Fortunately, many powerful instruments of export promotion are not only within the institutional capacity of many developing economies but remain viable in today's economic environment. Creating a free trade environment for exporters, providing finance and support services for small and medium-size exporters, improving trade-related aspects of the civil service, aggressively courting export-oriented direct foreign investment, and focusing infrastructure on areas that encourage exports are all attainable goals that are unlikely to provoke opposition from trading partners. Indeed, some or all of these have been part of the export push in Indonesia, Malaysia, and Thailand. These three economies, the most recent participants in the "economic miracle," may show the way for the next generation of developing economies to follow export-push strategies.

■ ■ ■

The phenomenal success of the HPAEs is already inspiring attempts at imitation. We have shown that the HPAEs used an immense variety of policies to achieve three critical functions of growth: accumulation, allocation, and productivity growth. The sheer diversity of these policies precludes drawing any simple lessons or making any simple recommendations, except perhaps that pragmatic adherence to the fundamentals is central to success. These market-oriented aspects of East Asia's experience can be recommended with few reservations. More institutionally demanding strategies have often failed in other settings and they clearly are not compatible with economic environments where the fundamentals are not securely in place. The use of contests in Japan and Korea required competent and insulated civil servants. In parts of Sub-Saharan Africa and Latin America, and elsewhere in Asia where such institutional conditions are lacking, activist government involvement in the economy has usually gone awry. So the fact that interventions were an element of some East Asian economies' success does not mean that they should be attempted everywhere, nor should it be taken as an excuse to postpone needed market-oriented reform.

The success of the HPAEs broadens our understanding of the range of policies that are consistent with rapid development. It also teaches us that willingness to experiment and to adapt policies to changing circumstances is a key element in economic success. In the following chapters we explore more fully the contribution of fundamental and interventionist policies to East Asia's remarkable growth, and the crucial role that institutions have played in their evolution and application. As we shall see, making a miracle is no simple matter.

Note

1. Japan, which has been firmly in the ranks of industrial economies arguably for all of this century, may at first seem to be an inappropriate subject for study. However many of the policy instruments used by the Japanese government during the period of rapid growth, 1950–73, have been used subsequently by developing economies. Thus, notwithstanding Japan's longer history of modern economic growth, it may provide some useful insights into the relationship between public policy and growth.

CHAPTER 1

Growth, Equity, and Economic Change

THE EIGHT ECONOMIES OF OUR STUDY ARE HIGHLY diverse in natural resources, culture, and political institutions. Japan, unlike the others, was already a relatively mature industrial economy at the beginning of the postwar period. Moreover, the eight differ in the degree of government intervention in the economy and the manner in which their leaders have shaped and implemented policies. Korean policymakers, for example, have intervened heavily in industrial, labor, and credit markets, while policymakers in Hong Kong have been consistently hands-off.

Despite many differences, however, the eight economies have much in common. In a number of ways, their postwar experience distinguishes them as a group. Their most obvious common characteristic is their high average rate of economic growth. During the same period, income inequality has declined, sometimes dramatically. These two outcomes—rapid growth and reduced inequality—are the defining characteristics of what has come to be known as the East Asian economic miracle.

The eight economies share six other characteristics that set them apart. Compared with most other developing economies, all have had:

- More rapid output and productivity growth in agriculture
- Higher rates of growth of manufactured exports
- Earlier and steeper declines in fertility
- Higher growth rates of physical capital, supported by higher rates of domestic savings
- Higher initial levels and growth rates of human capital
- Generally higher rates of productivity growth.

These characteristics are all related to their rapid, more equitable growth. Some are sources of growth, some are outcomes of growth, and some are unique features of HPAE growth, but most fall in more than one of these categories.

Rapid and Sustained Economic Growth

THE EIGHT HPAEs GREW MORE RAPIDLY AND MORE CONSIStently than any other group of economies in the world from 1960 to 1990. They averaged 5.5 percent annual per capita real income growth, outperforming every economy in Latin American and Sub-Saharan Africa (except diamond-rich Botswana). Another East Asian economy, China, has grown 5.8 percent a year since 1965 and could stake a claim to join the ranks of the HPAEs.[1]

Figure 1.1 shows the relationship between income level relative to the United States in 1960 and per capita income growth for 119 economies during the period 1960 to 1985. Developing economies were not catching up with the advanced economies; more than 70 percent of the developing economies grew more slowly than the high-income-economy average.[2] More disturbingly, in thirteen developing economies, per capita income actually fell. Growth among the eight HPAEs is quite different. Their growth rates are significantly above the high-income-economy average. Unlike most of the rest of the developing world, the HPAEs were catching up to the industrial economies. Hong Kong, Japan, the Republic of Korea, Singapore, and Taiwan, China, were particularly notable.

Other developing economies have grown fast for several years, particularly before the 1980s, but few others have sustained high growth rates for three decades.[3] Figure 1.2 shows the growth rates in per capita income for 119 economies in two periods, 1960–70 and 1970–85. The 11 that achieved rapid growth during both periods are in the northeast corner. Of these, five are East Asian success stories: Hong Kong, Japan, Korea, Singapore, and Taiwan, China. Japan's shift from extremely rapid growth in the 1960s to rates more typical of high-income economies in the 1970s is apparent. The other three HPAEs—Indonesia, Malaysia, and Thailand—all show accelerating growth, with higher growth rates in the second period than in the first. Indonesia is one of only three economies

Figure 1.1 GDP Growth Rate, 1960–85, and GDP per Capita Level, 1960

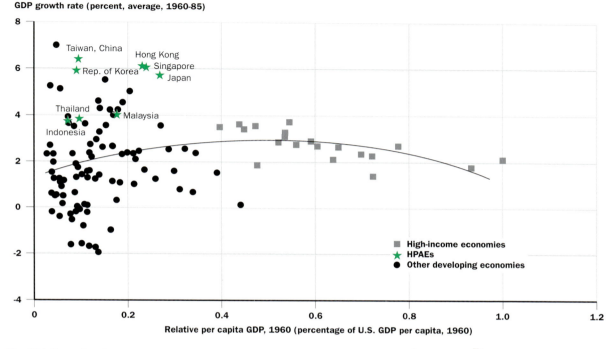

Note: This figure plots this regression equation: GDPG = 0.013 + 0.062RGDP60 - 0.061RGDP60^2. N = 119; $\bar{R}^2$ = 0.036.

(0.004)   (0.027)   (0.033)

Sources: Summers and Heston (1991); Barro (1989); World Bank data.

to move from the bottom to the top of the distribution of growth rates between the two periods.

Declining Income Inequality and Reduced Poverty

THE HPAEs HAVE ALSO ACHIEVED UNUSUALLY LOW AND DE-clining levels of inequality, contrary to historical experience and contemporary evidence in other regions (Kuznets 1955). The positive association between growth and low inequality in the HPAEs, and the contrast with other economies, is illustrated in figure 1.3. Forty economies are ranked by the ratio of the income share of the richest fifth of the population to the income share of the poorest fifth and per capita real GDP growth during 1965–89. The northwest corner of the figure

Figure 1.2 Growth Rate Persistence

GDP growth rate (percent), 1970-85

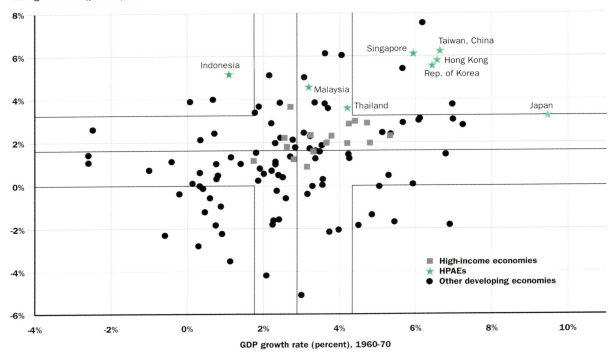

Note: Boxes are seventy-fifth percentile of growth rates in each period.
Sources: Summers and Heston (1991); Barro (1989); World Bank data.

identifies economies with high growth (GDP per capita greater than 4.0 percent) and low relative inequality (ratio of the income share of the top quintile to that of the bottom quintile less than 10). There are 7 high-growth, low-inequality economies. All of them are in East Asia; only Malaysia, which has an index of inequality above 15, is excluded.

When the East Asian economies are divided by speed of growth, the distribution of income is substantially more equal in the fast growers (Birdsall and Sabot 1993b). For the eight HPAEs, rapid growth and declining inequality have been shared virtues, as comparisons over time of equality and growth using Gini coefficients illustrate (see figure 3 in the Overview). The developing HPAEs clearly outperform other middle-income economies in that they have both lower levels of inequality and higher levels of growth. Moreover, as figures A1.7–A1.9 at the end of the chapter show, improvements in income distribution generally coincided with periods of rapid growth.

Figure 1.3 Income Inequality and Growth of GDP, 1965-89

GDP growth per capita (percent)

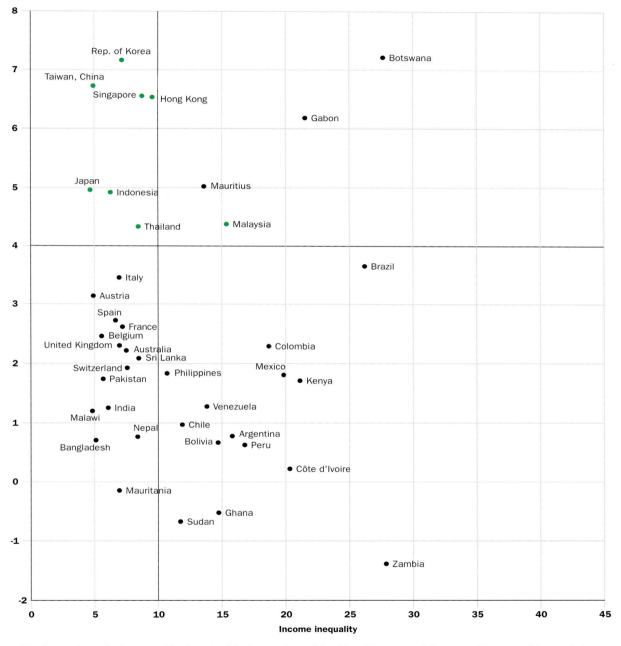

Income inequality

Note: Income inequality is measured by the ratio of the income shares of the richest 20 percent and the poorest 20 percent of the population.
Source: World Bank data.

Two qualifications should be noted here. First, some studies of Korea have shown increasing inequality in recent years; however, most of this is due to the rising value of assets, particularly land, rather than increased variation in incomes. Second, reductions in inequality in Thailand have been relatively minor compared with those in the other HPAEs, although Thailand's performance is still better than that of most developing economies.

Given rapid growth and declining inequality, these economies have of course been unusually successful in reducing poverty. Table 1.1 compares the declines in poverty, defined as the inability to attain a minimal standard of living (World Bank 1990b), in some HPAEs and other selected economies (the period varies depending on data available). Increases in life expectancy have also been larger than in any other region (see table 1.2).

Dynamic Agricultural Sectors

TYPICALLY, AS AN ECONOMY DEVELOPS, AGRICULTURE'S SHARE of the economy declines. The six HPAEs with substantial agricultural sectors—Indonesia, Japan, Korea, Malaysia, Thailand, and Taiwan, China—have been making this transition more rapidly than other developing economies.[4] But the decline in the relative importance of agriculture in the HPAEs is not because agriculture has lacked dynamism. Across developing regions, agriculture's share of output and employment has declined most and fastest where agricultural output and productivity have grown the most (see table 1.3). From 1965 to 1988, growth in both agricultural output and agricultural productivity was higher in East Asia than in other regions. Many factors contributed to the success of agriculture in these economies. Land reform (notably in Korea and Taiwan, China), agricultural extension services, reasonably good infrastructure (especially in the former Japanese colonies), and heavy investments in rural areas (notably in Indonesia) all helped.

East Asian governments have actively supported agricultural research and extension services to speed diffusion of Green Revolution technologies. Their substantial investments in irrigation and other rural infrastructure hastened adoption of high-yielding varieties, new crops, and the use of manufactured inputs, such as fertilizer and equipment, to cultivate them. In Taiwan, China, during the 1950s, 45 percent of the

Table 1.1 Changes in Selected Indicators of Poverty

Economy	Year	Percentage of population below the poverty line			Number of poor (millions)		
		First year	Last year	Change	First year	Last year	Percent change
HPAEs							
Indonesia	1972–82	58	17	-41	67.9	30.0	-56
Malaysia[a]	1973–87	37	14	-23	4.1	2.2	-46
Singapore	1972–82	31	10	-21	0.7	0.2	-71
Thailand[a,b]	1962–86	59	26	-30	16.7	13.6	-18
Others							
Brazil[a,b]	1960–80	50	21	-29	36.1	25.4	29.6
Colombia	1971–88	41	25	-16	8.9	7.5	-15.7
Costa Rica[a]	1971–86	45	24	-19	0.8	0.6	-25
Côte d'Ivoire	1985–86	30	31	1	3.1	3.3	6.4
India	1972–83	54	43	-9	311.4	315.0	1
Morocco	1970–84	43	34	-9	6.6	7.4	12
Pakistan	1962–84	54	23	-31	26.5	21.3	-19
Sri Lanka[a]	1963–82	37	27	-10	3.9	4.1	5

Note: This table uses economy-specific poverty lines. Official or commonly used poverty lines have been used when available. In other cases the poverty line has been set at 30 percent of mean income or expenditure. The range of poverty lines, expressed in terms of expenditure per household member and in terms of purchasing power parity (PPP) dollars, is approximately $300–$700 a year in 1985 except for Costa Rica ($960), Malaysia ($1,420), and Singapore ($860). Unless otherwise indicated, the table is based on expenditure per household member.

a. Measures for these entries use income rather than expenditure.

b. Measures for these entries are by household rather than by household member.

Source: World Bank (1990b, tables 3.2 and 3.3).

growth of agriculture was due to rising productivity, much of which resulted from government programs (see Ranis 1993).

Information on the allocation of public investment between rural and urban regions is limited, and it is difficult to make good comparisons among economies, but available data suggest that the HPAEs have allocated a larger share of their public investment to rural areas than did other low- and middle-income economies. Of critical importance in this respect has been the build-up of infrastructure—roads, bridges, transportation, electricity, water, and sanitation. Table 1.4 shows that there has been a more even balance between rural and urban public investment in sanitation and water facilities in Indonesia, Korea, and Thailand than in other developing economies. The data on rural electrification also suggest that the HPAEs with rural sectors have, on average, more effectively provided electricity to rural areas. Since the early 1980s, elec-

Table 1.2 Life Expectancy at Birth, 1960 and 1990

Economy/region	Life expectancy at birth (years)	
	1960	1990
HPAEs		
Hong Kong	64	78
Indonesia	46	59
Korea, Rep. of	53	72
Malaysia	58	71
Singapore	65	74
Thailand	52	68
Other Asia[a]	50	62
China	43	69
India	47	58
Sub-Saharan Africa	43	52
Latin America and Caribbean	54	70
Low-income economies	36	62
Middle-income economies	49	66
Industrial economies	70	77

Note: The regional averages are weighted.
a. Excludes China and India.
Source: World Bank data.

tricity has been universally available in the rural areas of Korea and Taiwan, China. Malaysia and Thailand have made great strides in rural electrification. Indonesia has not done as well, but even there the relative disparity between the urban and rural sectors is smaller than the disparity in economies with approximately the same per capita income (Bolivia and Liberia) or the same population (Brazil [see table 1.4]).

Table 1.3 Growth Rates of Agricultural Income, Labor Force, and Share in Output, 1965–88
(percent)

Region	Share of agriculture in output			Average annual growth rate of:		
	1965	1988	Decline, 1965–88 (percent)	Agricultural income	Agricultural labor force	Productivity
Asia						
South Asia	44	33	25	2.4	1.7	0.6
East Asia	41	22	46	3.2	1.0	2.2
Sub-Saharan Africa	43	34	21	1.9	1.6	0.3
Latin America	16	10	37	2.3	1.7	1.5

Sources: Turnham (1993). For measures of share of agricultural output: World Bank data.

Equally important, however, were the typically low levels of direct and indirect taxation on agriculture in East Asia. During the past three decades, dozens of governments in other regions, eager to promote industrial growth, have funneled surpluses from agriculture to industry through taxes, food price controls, and pro-industry allocations of public investment. Less overtly, governments have favored manufacturers, and hurt agriculture, by overvaluing currencies and protecting domestic industries that manufacture agricultural inputs and the goods purchased by rural households. The exchange rate that results from restrictions on

Table 1.4 Comparison of Rural and Urban Public Investment

Rural-urban disparities in access to services, 1987–90
(100 = rural-urban parity)

Economy	Water	Sanitation
HPAEs		
Korea, Rep. of	54	101
Thailand	126	102
Indonesia	168	113
Other Asia	64.6	38.6
Latin America	58	46.5
Sub-Saharan Africa	43	30

Percentage of rural and urban population served by electricity

Economy	Urban	Rural
HPAEs		
Indonesia, 1984	39	10
Malaysia, 1983	85	55
Thailand, 1984	78	40
Other Asia		
Bangladesh, 1981	20	2
India, 1981	< 25	15
Sri Lanka, 1982	35	8
Latin America		
Argentina, 1982	> 95	5
Bolivia, 1981	72	9
Brazil, 1981	> 95	19
East & West Africa		
Côte d'Ivoire, 1981	93	20
Liberia, 1982	86	4
Senegal, 1982	83	12

Sources: Top panel: UNDP (various years); Bottom panel: Munasinghe (1987).

manufactured imports reduces the domestic currency proceeds of agricultural exports. Industrial protection acts as a hidden tax on agriculture, raising the price of agricultural inputs to subsidize industry. Figure 1.4 illustrates the lower taxation of agriculture by contrasting three HPAEs with large rural economies with three South Asian economies. Direct interventions include export taxes and price controls, while indirect interventions also take account of industrial protection policies and real exchange rate overvaluation. Both Korea and Malaysia have substantially lower taxation of the agricultural sector than the comparators, and in Korea the

Figure 1.4 Intervention and Growth in the Agricultural Sector

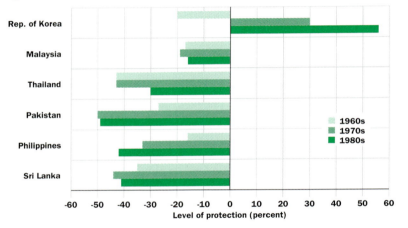

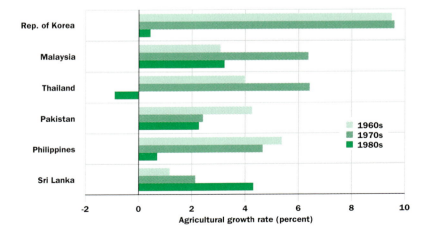

Source: Schiff (1993).

agricultural sector receives positive protection. Thailand's taxation of the agricultural sector was similar to South Asian levels in the 1960s and 1970s but fell in the 1980s while taxation in South Asia was rising.

We are not suggesting that the HPAEs avoided transferring any resources from agriculture to industry. Rather, in contrast to other developing economies, they transferred fewer resources. Moreover, transfers were often voluntary—financial savings, for example—and were nearly always limited to levels that did not choke off agricultural growth.

Rapid Growth of Exports

ANOTHER STRIKING FEATURE OF THE HPAEs HAS BEEN THEIR superior export performance. This is reflected in their steadily rising share of world exports (see table 1.5). As a group, the HPAEs increased their share in world exports from 8 percent in 1965 to 13 percent in 1980 and 18 percent in 1990. Manufactured exports have provided most of this growth. From 1965 to 1990, Japan emerged as the world's biggest exporter of manufactured goods, increasing its share of the world market from nearly 8 to almost 12 percent. In the 1970s and 1980s, the locus of growth shifted to the Four Tigers, whose share of manufactured exports grew nearly four times faster than Japan's (see table 1.5). Beginning around 1980, the three Southeast Asian HPAEs (Indonesia, Malaysia, and Thailand), which had been historically dependent on commodity exports, recorded a similar but so far smaller surge in manufactured exports.

Some analysts have, with hindsight, attributed these achievements to unique cultural and geographical circumstances. But there was little evidence at the outset that East Asian economies would achieve such spectacular results. In the 1950s even trade optimists were export pessimists and did not anticipate that Korea's exports would grow four times as fast as world trade during the next thirty years (see, for example, Little 1982).

One obvious effect of rapid export growth has been a marked increase in the openness of these economies, the share of exports plus imports in GDP (see table 1.6). Malaysia has been heavily trade oriented throughout its post-colonial history while Korea, Thailand, and Taiwan, China, had average trade propensities until 1965 but have since moved well above international norms. The trade orientation of Indonesia,

Table 1.5 Export Penetration, Selected East Asian Economies, 1965–90

Economy	Share in world exports			Share in developing-economy exports		
	1965	1980	1990	1965	1980	1990
Total exports						
Japan	5.0	7.0	9.0	—	—	—
Four Tigers[a]	1.5	3.8	6.7	6.0	13.3	33.9
Southeast Asian NIEs[b]	1.5	2.2	2.4	6.2	7.8	12.4
HPAE subtotal	7.9	13.1	18.2	12.2	21.1	56.3
All developing economies	24.2	28.7	19.8	100.0	100.0	100.0
World	100.0	100.0	100.0	N.A.	N.A.	N.A.
Exports of manufactures						
Japan	7.8	11.6	11.8	—	—	—
Four Tigers[a]	1.5	5.3	7.9	13.2	44.9	61.5
Southeast Asian NIEs[b]	0.1	0.4	1.5	1.1	3.8	12.0
HPAE subtotal	9.4	17.3	21.3	14.2	48.6	73.5
All developing economies	11.1	11.8	12.9	100.0	100.0	100.0
World	100.0	100.0	100.0	N.A.	N.A.	N.A.

—Not available.
N.A. Not applicable.
a. Republic of Korea, Hong Kong, Singapore, and Taiwan, China.
b. Indonesia, Malaysia, and Thailand.
Source: U.N. Trade Systems data.

with its vast economy and only relatively recent export drive, is only slightly above the world average but growing.

Rapid Demographic Transitions

THE DEMOGRAPHIC TRANSITION FROM HIGH TO LOW BIRTH and death rates began in Europe and North America with the Industrial Revolution, and it took nearly two centuries to complete. That same transition is occurring much faster in the developing world. In virtually all economies, death rates have fallen substantially in the postwar period; in all except Sub-Saharan Africa, birth rates have also fallen significantly (see table 1.7). However, compared with other developing regions, the transition to low fertility began sooner in East Asia (in the 1960s in the north and in the early 1970s in the south—and of course even earlier in Japan) and has gone farther.

Table 1.6 Ratio of Total Trade to GDP

Economy/region	1970	1980	1985	1988
HPAEs				
Hong Kong	1.50	1.52	1.78	2.82
Indonesia	0.25	0.46	0.38	0.42
Korea, Rep. of	0.32	0.63	0.66	0.66
Japan	0.19	0.25	0.23	0.11
Malaysia	0.89	1.00	0.85	1.09
Singapore	2.12	3.70	2.77	3.47
Taiwan, China	0.53	0.95	0.82	0.90
Thailand	0.28	0.49	0.44	0.35
Sub-Saharan Africa	0.24	0.30	0.27	0.45
South Asia	0.11	0.17	0.16	0.19
Latin America and Caribbean	0.20	0.25	0.22	0.23

Note: Total trade = value of exports and value of imports divided by gross domestic product.

Sources: World Bank data. Taiwan, China, various issues. National Accounts Statistics: Analysis of Main Aggregates, 1988–89 (United Nations).

During the period 1965–80, all the developing regions of the world experienced a marked decline in crude death rates (see table 1.7). The decline in most economies was 30–40 percent and did not vary much among regions. There was, however, substantial regional variation in the extent to which declines in birth rates held in check the potentially explosive growth in population from the rapid mortality decreases. In Sub-Saharan Africa during this period, the declines in birth rates were around 2–10 percent; in South Asia, 10–30 percent; and in Latin America, 30–40 percent. The sharpest declines were in East Asia: 40–50 percent.

As a result, the rate of population growth declined in all the East Asian economies, in some cases quite sharply. For example, in Korea it fell from 2.6 percent a year in 1960–70 to 1.1 percent in 1980–90; in Hong Kong, from 2.5 to 1.4 percent; and in Thailand, from 3.1 to 1.8 percent. In Latin America, fertility declines were also sufficient to reduce population growth rates, though generally not to the levels observed in East Asia. In South Asia the picture is mixed, with fertility declines sufficient to reduce the rate of population growth in Bangladesh but insufficient in Nepal or Pakistan. In Sub-Saharan Africa, the combination of sharp declines in death rates and modest declines in birth rates resulted in an acceleration of population growth—for example, in Ghana from 2.3 percent a year in 1960–70 to 3.4 percent in 1980–90, and in Kenya from 3.2 to 3.8 percent.

Table 1.7 The Demographic Transition
(percent)

Economy	Change in crude birth rate, 1965–80	Change in crude death rate, 1965–80	Average annual growth of population	
			1960–70	*1980–90*
East Asia				
Hong Kong	-52	-54	2.5	1.4
Indonesia	-40	-55	2.1	1.8
Korea, Rep. of	-54	—	2.6	1.1
Malaysia	-25	-58	2.8	2.6
Singapore	-45	-16	2.3	2.2
Thailand	-46	-30	3.1	1.8
Latin America				
Brazil	-31	-36	2.8	2.2
Mexico	-40	-55	3.3	2.0
Peru	-33	-50	2.9	2.3
Venezuela	-31	-38	3.8	2.7
Sub-Saharan Africa				
Ghana	-6	-28	2.3	3.4
Kenya	-13	-50	3.2	3.8
Sierra Leone	-2	-29	1.7	2.4
Tanzania	-2	-22	2.7	3.1
South Asia				
Bangladesh	-27	-33	2.5	2.3
India	-33	-45	2.3	2.1
Nepal	-13	-42	1.9	2.6
Pakistan	-13	-43	2.8	3.1

—Not available.
Source: World Bank data.

High Investment and Savings Rates

PHYSICAL INVESTMENT INCLUDES ALL OF THE ECONOMY'S OUT-put that is not either directly consumed or used up in the production of other goods. Machines, buildings, and infrastructure are physical capital, but elements of working capital, such as inventories, are also important. Economists traditionally have viewed investment as one of the driving forces of economic growth. In a closed economy, savings is the only source of investment, and the two, by definition, must be equal. But in an open economy, investment can be financed by borrowing from abroad as well, that is, with foreigners' savings. Even so, inadequate domestic savings will eventually pull down investment rates, either directly or through constraints on the continued build-up of foreign liabilities, which must eventually be repaid from domestic savings.

Between 1960 and 1990, both savings and investment increased markedly in the HPAEs, outstripping the performance of other developing regions (see figure 1.5). Savings rates in the developing HPAEs were lower than in Latin America in 1965, but by 1990 they exceeded Latin America's savings rates by almost 20 percentage points. Investment levels were about equal in Latin America and East Asia in 1965; by 1990 East Asia's investment rates were nearly double the average for Latin America and substantially exceeded the rates for South Asia and Sub-Saharan Africa. The HPAEs are the only group of developing economies in which savings exceeds investment, making them exporters of capital.

When we compare the HPAEs individually to all 118 economies for which investment data exist, the picture is more complex (see figure 1.6). During the period 1960–85, the HPAEs' investment levels were in

Figure 1.5 Savings and Investment as a Percentage of GDP

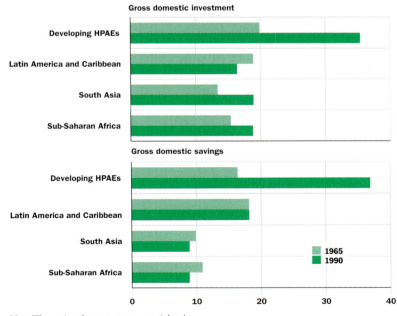

Note: The regional averages are unweighted.
Source: World Bank data.

Figure 1.6 Average Investment Rate as a Percentage of GDP, 1960–1985, and GDP per Capita Level, 1960

Average investment rate (percentage of GDP, 1960-85)

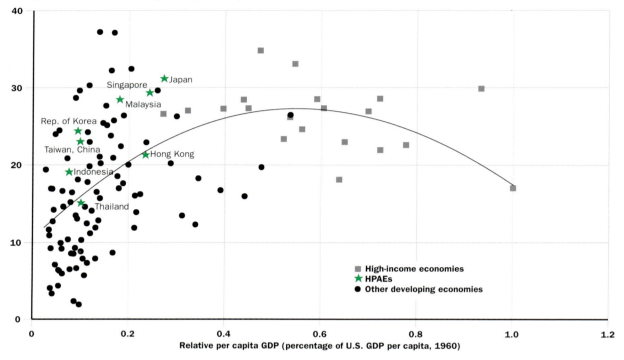

Note: Regression equation: $I6085 = 10.125 + 59.120RGDP60 - 51.881RGDP60^2$. N = 119; $\bar{R}^2 = 0.295$.
    (1.383)   (10.344)   (12.593)

Sources: Summers and Heston (1991); Barro (1989); World Bank data.

the top quartile of all low- and middle-income economies, but since investment generally rises with incomes, this is not remarkable.[5] What is remarkable is their high share of private investment. Figure 1.7 compares average private and public investment shares in GDP for 1970–89 in the developing HPAEs and other middle-income economies. Private investment is about 7 percentage points higher in the HPAEs than in other middle-income economies. It rose from about 15 percent of GDP in 1970 to nearly 22 percent in 1974, then declined and held at about 18 percent between 1975 and 1984. Private investment contracted sharply between 1984 to 1986, reflecting the global recession, then recovered by 1988.[6] In contrast, private investment in other low- and middle-income economies has remained relatively stable at about 11 percent of GDP.

The story is different with respect to public investment. In the 1970s overall levels of public investment did not differ markedly between the HPAEs and other developing economies; during the decade public investment rates in all economies rose from about 7 to 10 percent (see figure 1.7). But during the 1980s the HPAEs and other developing economies diverged. In other economies, the fiscal contraction of macroeconomic adjustment was reflected in lower public investment rates. In the HPAEs, conversely, public investment shares actually rose between 1979 and 1982 and then remained at a level nearly 4 percentage points above their 1970s average. Only after 1986 did they begin to decline toward historical levels. In short, in striking contrast to elsewhere, public investment in 1980–87 in these East Asian economies was counter-cyclical to the reduction in private investment.

Creating Human Capital

I N NEARLY ALL THE RAPIDLY GROWING EAST ASIAN ECONOMIES, the growth and transformation of systems of education and training during the past three decades has been dramatic. The quantity of education children received increased at the same time that the quality of schooling, and of training in the home, markedly improved. Today, the cognitive skill levels of secondary school graduates in some East Asian economies are comparable to, or higher than, those of graduates in high-income economies (see appendix 1.2).

Figures 1.8 and 1.9 present a stylized summary of the results of regressing primary and secondary enrollment rates on per capita national income for more than 90 developing economies for the years 1965 and 1987.[7] Enrollment rates are higher at higher levels of per capita income. But the HPAE's enrollment rates have tended to be higher than predicted for their level of income. At the primary level, this was most obvious in 1965, when Hong Kong, Korea, and Singapore had already achieved universal primary education, well ahead of other developing economies, and even Indonesia with its vast population had a primary enrollment rate above 70 percent.[8] By 1987, East Asia's superior education systems were evident at the secondary level. Indonesia had a secondary enrollment rate of 46 percent, well above other economies with roughly the same level of income, and Korea had moved from 35 to 88 percent,

Figure 1.7 Public and Private Investment

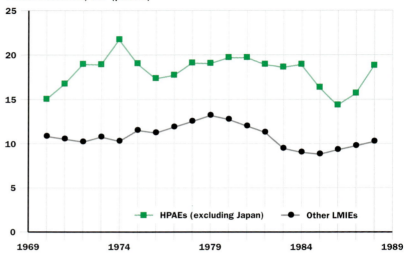

Private investment/GDP (percent)

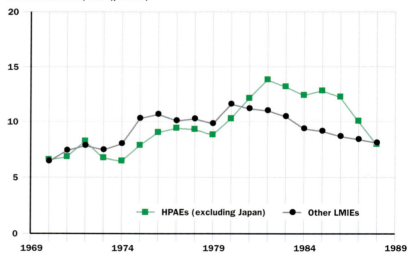

Public investment/GDP (percent)

Note: LMIEs = low- and middle-income economies.
Source: World Bank data.

maintaining its large lead in relative performance. Only in Thailand was the 28 percent secondary enrollment rate well below the income-predicted 36 percent and the 54 percent mean for middle-income economies.[9] In recent years Thailand's weak educational performance has been felt, as serious shortages of educated workers have begun to threaten

Figure 1.8 Cross-Economy Regression for Primary Enrollment Rates, 1965 and 1987

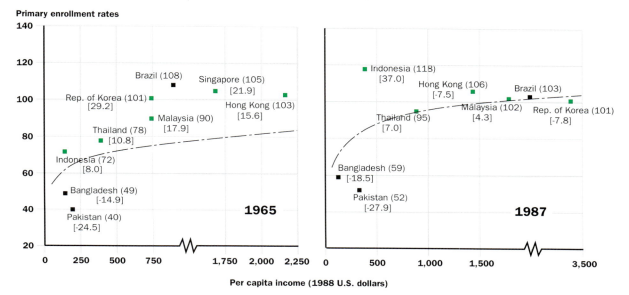

Note: Figures in parentheses are enrollment rates; bracketed numbers show residuals.
Source: Behrman and Schneider (1992).

continued very rapid growth. In part as a function of their success in increasing enrollment, the East Asian economies have also been faster to close the gap between male and female enrollments (see box 1.1).

A common, though imperfect measure of educational quality is expenditures per pupil. Between 1970 and 1989, real expenditures per pupil at the primary level rose by 355 percent in Korea. In Mexico and Kenya, expenditures rose by 64 and 38 percent, respectively, during the same period, and in Pakistan expenditures rose by only 13 percent between 1970 and 1985 (Birdsall and Sabot 1993b). These dramatic differences reflect mostly differential changes during the period in income growth and in the number of children entering schools, both of which favored the East Asian economies. A somewhat better measure of school quality is the performance of children on tests of cognitive skills, standardized across economies. In the relatively few international comparisons available from such tests, East Asian children tend to perform better than children from other developing regions—and even, recently, better than children from high-income economies.[10]

Figure 1.9 Cross-Economy Regression for Secondary Enrollment Rates, 1965 and 1987

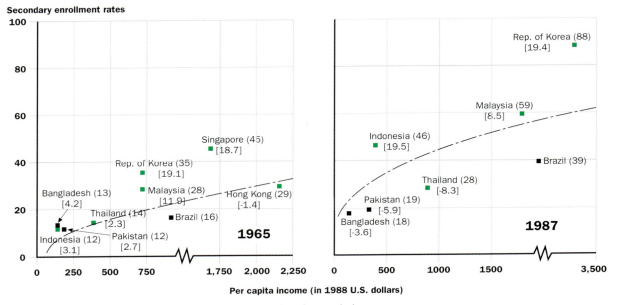

Note: Figures in parentheses are enrollment rates; bracketed numbers show residuals.
Source: Behrman and Schneider (1992).

How much a child learns is also influenced by the nature of the learning environment in the child's home. Again, children in the East Asian economies had advantages in the 1970s and 1980s. Using a simple index taking into account the mother's education and the number of children at home, we estimate that the learning environment in Korea during twenty years was enhanced 114 percent more than in Brazil and 147 percent more than in Pakistan (Birdsall and Sabot 1993b).

Rapid Productivity Growth

THE FINAL OUTSTANDING CHARACTERISTIC OF THE HPAEs IS their rapid productivity growth. That labor productivity in the HPAEs increased rapidly is self-evident: per capita GDP growth depends primarily on rising output per worker. Some of this increase in output per worker results from increases in physical capital per worker (for example, more machines) and some results from increases in human

Box 1.1 East Asia Was Faster in Eliminating Gender Gaps in Enrollment

NEARLY ALL SOCIETIES HAVE HISTORICALLY PRO-vided educational opportunities first to boys and only later, usually gradually, to girls. This gender gap in education may have far-reaching effects on development if, for example, the lower educational attainments of women reduce their ability to improve nutrition and sanitation at home or their productivity outside the home. The HPAEs narrowed the gender gap much more quickly than other developing economies, despite cultural norms that put greater value on the education of sons and, in some cases, actively discouraged the education of daughters (see box figure 1.1). In general the reduction of gender gaps resulted from a successful push for universal education rather than deliberate attention to the education of females. Nonetheless, as we argue below, the specific benefits of educating girls appear to have been substantial.

The gender gap (male minus female) in enrollment rates at the primary and secondary levels tends to decline as incomes increase (see figures A1.10 and A1.11 at the end of the chapter). In 1965, at the primary level, all the East Asian economies' gender gaps were smaller than expected. By 1987 the four East Asian economies for which data are available had all achieved universal primary education for girls, virtually eliminating the gender gap at that level. Substantial gender gaps in enrollment rates continue to be the rule, rather than the exception, in low-income countries and have persisted over the past three decades despite the rapid expansion of educational systems (Hill and King 1991). For example, in forty economies with GNP per capita below $500, the gap in primary school enrollment between boys and girls averages 20 percentage points and is not much less today than it was in 1960.

In 1965, the HPAEs (except for Thailand) had larger than predicted gender gaps at the secondary level. Indeed, increasing secondary school opportunities for girls in the HPAEs was as much of a challenge in the 1970s and early 1980s as it is elsewhere in the developing world today. Partly because the East Asian economies were more successful in raising enrollments overall, by 1987 the gender gaps had narrowed and were no longer larger than predicted by per capita income (figure A1.11). All of the East Asian economies in our study had secondary enrollment rates for girls that were as high, or even higher, than the rates for boys, except for Indonesia, although the gender gap was also much reduced.

Box Figure 1.1 Ratio of Female to Male Years of Education

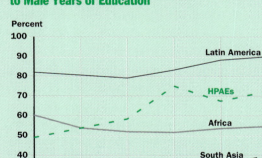

Source: Barro and Lee (1993).

capital (for example, better schooled workers). In addition, however, some may result from greater efficiency, from changes in production practices that result in greater output from the same stock of physical and human capital. We call the increase in productivity that cannot be accounted for by measured increases in inputs total factor productivity

(TFP) growth.[11] Among its sources are better technology, better organization, gains from specialization, and innovations on the shop floor.

As we demonstrate below, about two-thirds of East Asia's extraordinary growth is attributable to rapid accumulation; that is, to unusually rapid growth in physical and human capital. The remaining third of this growth cannot be explained by accumulation and is therefore attributable to increased efficiency or TFP. This is large relative to other economies, both absolutely and as a share of output growth, and therefore partly explains why these economies have been catching up with the industrial economies, while most other developing economies have not. In box 1.2 we review two broad interpretations of the relation between accumulation and output growth and the link between productivity change and technological catching up.

Evidence from Cross-Economy Regressions of per Capita Income Growth

In this section we use two statistical techniques to examine the relationship between accumulation and output growth. Our first model is a cross-economy regression in which we estimate the relationship between the rate of real per capita income growth and the share of investment in GDP, and two measures of educational attainment, controlling for the rate of growth of the economically active population, and the relative gap between per capita income and U.S. per capita income in 1960 at 1980 U.S. dollar prices.[12] Our measures of educational attainment are primary and secondary school enrollment rates in 1960, the area of human capital accumulation in which the HPAEs showed a substantial difference from other low- and middle-income economies.

The results of applying our statistical analysis to 113 economies are summarized in table 1.8. The estimates indicate that factor accumulation matters. Investment in both physical capital and schooling contribute significantly to economic growth.[13] An increase of 10 percentage points of GDP in the rate of investment—about the difference in private investment rates between HPAEs and other low- and middle-income economies—would raise the growth rate of GDP per capita by 0.5 percent. An increase of 10 percentage points in the primary or secondary school enrollment rate would raise per capita income growth by 0.3 percent.

Beyond accumulation of physical and human capital, initial income also has a significant relationship with per capita income growth.

Box 1.2 Modeling Economic Growth

ECONOMISTS HAVE PUT FORWARD TWO BROAD interpretations of the relationship between accumulation and output growth, the neoclassical view and the endogenous growth approach.

The older, neoclassical view is based on the assumption that as physical and human capital are accumulated their incremental contribution to output diminishes. If this is correct, poor economies, those with smaller endowments of physical and human capital per worker, will grow faster than rich economies for the same level of investment in physical and human assets. Economic growth is like a handicapped race; the returns to equal effort at accumulation are greater for the poor economy. If the rates of accumulation of all economies, rich and poor, are roughly similar, neoclassical growth models predict that poor economies will eventually catch up to the leaders. That is, per capita income will converge to roughly equal levels.

In general, rates of growth of income per capita in low- and middle-income economies do not exceed those for high-income economies; on average, poor economies are not catching up. This fact has led to an alternative view of economic growth: growth models in which increments to physical and human capital make either the same contribution or an *increasing* contribution to output as economies become richer. In this race the rules favor stronger economies. Endogenous growth theories generally do not predict that output per capita will eventually converge across all economies. Indeed, they suggest that dynamic economies of scale tend to favor the richer economies, which may grow faster than the poorer economies indefinitely.

Numerous studies have attempted to test which type of model could best predict the differences in economic growth during the past thirty years. Neither model has been consistently superior, but the controversy has highlighted two important determinants of growth performance among economies. First, both types of models predict that higher levels of investment in human and physical capital will result in higher rates of growth in per capita income, although they differ on whether higher growth can persist indefinitely. Nevertheless, some economies can grow faster than others for extended periods by investing more of their national income.

Second, accumulation does not explain all of economic growth, and differing rates of accumulation do not explain all of the differences in growth rates among economies. Other factors, such intangible elements as economic organization, innovation, and absorption of technology, are also at play. Economies with similar records of accumulation—for example, the HPAEs and the former Soviet Union—can have very different records of growth. In neoclassical growth theory, the component of economic growth that cannot be assigned to accumulation is termed "technical progress," or total factor productivity change. Early neoclassical models assumed that technical progress was exogenously given (Solow 1957), although empirical studies of TFP change using neoclassical assumptions revealed wide variations in estimated TFP growth rates, especially among developing countries (Nishimizu and Page 1987; Page 1990). In the newer endogenous growth theories, this component of growth is generally attributed to the interaction between "ideas" and accumulation, which results in increasing returns to scale to physical and human capital (Romer 1993).

Foreign knowledge and technology is a potentially important source of productivity change in low- and middle-income economies. By adapting technologies available in the high-income economies, low- and middle-income economies could move rapidly up the technological ladder (Gerschenkron 1962). Moreover, because developing economies can choose among a large inventory of existing technologies rather than developing new technologies, as economies close to the technological frontier must, less industrialized economies should

(Box continues on the following page.)

49

Box 1.2 *(continued)*

be able to acquire technology more cheaply, and progress more rapidly, than industrial economies. This is productivity-based catching up.

But international best practice is itself a moving target. Total factor productivity change in the high-income economies is an important source of their growth (Chenery 1986; Boskin and Lau 1992). Appendix 1.1 presents a formal analysis of the relationship between movements in international best practice, which we term "technological change," and movements *toward* best practice, which we call tech-

nical efficiency change. Both theory and empirical evidence lead us to conclude that total factor productivity growth in the industrial economies is largely due to technological change, the movement in international best practice, while in low- and middle-income economies most TFP change is due to changes in technical efficiency (Pack and Page 1993). For productivity-based catching up to occur, the low- and middle-income economies must be gaining on the moving target; that is, technical efficiency change must be positive.

Economies that were relatively poor in 1960 grew significantly faster than relatively rich ones, controlling for levels of education and investment. So although, as shown above, poor economies did not do better on average than the high-income economies—income levels were not converging—this was partially because poor economies invested less. But an economy at 50 percent of the level of U.S. per capita income in 1960, and at average levels of education and investment, would have grown about 2.1 percentage points more rapidly than the United States. We call this conditional convergence, because economies with low rates of investment and school enrollment would not catch up despite the "advantages" apparently offered by being relatively poor.

This conditional convergence can be interpreted as a measure of the gains realized as a consequence of moving from lower to higher technological levels, or "catching up" (see box 1.2). But the relative income variable may capture more than the productivity-based catch-up effect that some initially poor economies benefited from. One of the important empirical regularities found in the early literature on structural transformation (Kuznets 1959; Chenery 1960) is the discrepancy in the average product of labor between traditional (agriculture) and modern (industry) sectors at low income levels. A dominant share of productivity growth in low-income economies can be attributed to intersectoral reallocation of labor from agriculture to industry (Pack 1993c). Thus the initial income variable may also be capturing the reallocation effect of this structural change on per capita GDP growth.

Table 1.8 Basic Cross-Economy Regression Results
(dependent variable: average rate of real per capita income growth, 1960–85)

Variable	113 observations	113 observations	113 observations
Intercept	-0.0070 (0.0079)	-0.0034 (0.0075)	0.0042 (0.0081)
Relative GDP to U.S., 1960	-0.0430 ** (0.0118)	-0.0293 * (0.0115)	-0.0320 ** (0.0110)
Primary enrollment, 1960	0.0264 ** (0.0065)	0.0233 ** (0.0062)	0.0272 ** (0.0065)
Secondary enrollment, 1960	0.0262 (0.0139)	0.0160 (0.0132)	0.0069 (0.0131)
Growth of population, 1960–85	0.1015 (0.2235)	0.0201 (0.2095)	0.0998 (0.2023)
Average investment/GDP, 1960–85	0.0578 * (0.0224)	0.0455 * (0.0211)	0.0285 (0.0207)
HPAES		0.0230 ** (0.0056)	0.0171 ** (0.0056)
Latin America			-0.0131 ** (0.0039)
Sub-Saharan Africa[a]			-0.0099 * (0.0041)
Adjusted R^2	0.3480	0.4324	0.4821

** Statistically significant at the 0.01 level.
* Statistically significant at the 0.05 level.
Note: Coefficient is top number in each cell. Standard error is in parentheses.
a. Also includes Tunisia and South Africa.
Source: World Bank staff estimates.

Armed with these statistical results, we can examine two facts about the role of accumulation in growth in the HPAEs. First, our estimates of the parameters of the cross-economy growth equation enable us to do a simple "accounting for growth" in the HPAEs. Table 1.9 shows the predicted contribution to growth of investment, human capital, population growth, and relative income for each HPAE. It also shows the share of actual growth predicted by these variables. Except for Hong Kong (44 percent), 60 percent or more of the actual growth rate in the HPAEs is predicted by the accumulation of physical and human capital, initial income levels, and population growth, ranging as high as 87 percent for

Table 1.9 Contribution of Accumulation to the Growth of the HPAEs, 1960–85

Variable	Parameter estimate	Hong Kong Contribution to growth (percent)	Hong Kong Percentage of total predicted growth	Indonesia Contribution to growth (percent)	Indonesia Percentage of total predicted growth	Japan Contribution to growth (percent)	Japan Percentage of total predicted growth	Korea, Rep. of Contribution to growth (percent)	Korea, Rep. of Percentage of total predicted growth
Intercept	-0.0070	-0.70	(-26)	-0.70	(-31)	-0.70	(-15)	-0.70	(-19)
GDP relative to U.S., 1960	-0.0430	-1.00	(-37)	-0.32	(-14)	-1.16	(-25)	-0.40	(-11)
Primary enrollment, 1960	0.0264	2.30	(86)	1.77	(79)	2.72	(58)	2.48	(67)
Secondary enrollment, 1960	0.0262	0.63	(23)	0.16	(7)	1.94	(41)	0.71	(19)
Growth of population, 1960–85	0.1015	0.23	(9)	0.22	(10)	0.10	(2)	0.20	(5)
Average investment/GDP, 1960–85	0.0578	1.22	(46)	1.10	(49)	1.80	(38)	1.40	(38)
Actual growth		6.09		3.72		5.69		5.89	
Predicted growth		2.68		2.23		4.69		3.69	
(Percentage of actual growth predicted)		(44)		(60)		(82)		(63)	

Note: A variable's contribution to growth for economy X equals the variable value in economy X times the estimated coefficient on the variable from the basic regression. The predicted growth for economy X equals the sum of all contributions to growth by the basic regression variables.
Source: World Bank staff estimates.

Malaysia. On average, about two-thirds of the observed growth in the HPAEs is predicted by our model.

Primary education is by far the largest single contributor to the HPAEs' predicted growth rates. Between 58 percent (Japan) and 87 percent (Thailand) of predicted growth is due to primary school enrollment. Physical investment comes second (between 35 and 49 percent), followed by secondary school enrollment. Japan's high secondary school enrollment in 1960 makes a particularly strong contribution to its growth (41 percent), more than investment, while the laggards in secondary enrollment rates, Indonesia, Malaysia, and Thailand, have the smallest proportion of their predicted growth attributable to secondary enrollments (less than 15 percent). Investment, conversely, is most important in Hong Kong, Indonesia, Malaysia, and Singapore, where it accounts for more than 40 percent of explained growth.

Second, we are also able to look for regional patterns in growth rates that are unexplained by physical and human capital investment. Controlling for their performance in education and investment, and initial income, the HPAEs have a significantly higher rate of growth than all other economies. Latin America and Sub-Saharan Africa, in contrast, have significantly lower underlying growth rates (about 1 percent), controlling for the same variables. Thus, the expected growth rate differential between the high-performing East Asian economies and Sub-Saharan Africa or Latin America, even if they had the same accumulation and initial income, is nearly 3 percent.

To assess the contribution of the HPAEs' superior accumulation relative to other groups, we can predict growth rates in four groups of

| Parameter estimate | Malaysia | | Taiwan, China | | Singapore | | Thailand | |
	Contribution to growth (percent)	Percentage of total predicted growth	Contribution to growth (percent)	Percentage of total predicted growth	Contribution to growth (percent)	Percentage of total predicted growth	Contribution to growth (percent)	Percentage of total predicted growth
-0.0070	-0.70	(-20)	-0.70	(-19)	-0.70	(-18)	-0.70	(-28)
-0.0430	-0.77	(-22)	-0.42	(-11)	-1.04	(-27)	-0.42	(-17)
0.0264	2.53	(73)	2.53	(69)	2.93	(75)	2.19	(87)
0.0262	0.50	(14)	0.72	(19)	0.84	(22)	0.31	(13)
0.1015	0.26	(8)	0.24	(6)	0.18	(5)	0.26	(11)
0.0578	1.64	(47)	1.32	(36)	1.69	(43)	0.87	(35)
4.00		6.38		6.03		3.82		
3.46		3.70		3.90		2.51		
(87)		(58)		(65)		(66)		

economies based on level of investment, primary and secondary school enrollment, relative income in 1960, and population growth. The differences in actual growth rates between the HPAEs and other groups can be divided into the predicted differences (due to group differences in accumulation or initial income) and to an unexplained residual (see table 1.10). Accumulation explains only some of the difference in per capita income growth rates between the HPAEs and other groups. For example, between 1960 and 1985 average primary and secondary school enrollment rates and investment rates in the HPAEs were below those in the OECD, leading us to predict that growth would be lower by 0.68 percent. Offsetting this is a conditional convergence gain of 1.2 percent and the contribution of the HPAEs' higher rate of population growth, 0.1 percent. We would predict that the HPAEs would grow about .67 percent faster than the OECD, primarily due to their initially lower income level; in fact, they grew about 2.3 percent faster.

The effect of the HPAEs' higher rates of accumulation is more telling in the comparisons between East Asia and Latin America or Sub-Saharan Africa. Between the HPAEs and Latin America, 34 percent of the predicted difference in growth rates is due to higher investment levels and 38 percent to higher enrollment rates. Far and away the major difference in predicted growth rates between HPAEs and Sub-Saharan Africa derives from variations in primary school enrollment rates. Investment accounts for only about 20 percent of the difference and is offset by the conditional convergence advantage of Sub-Saharan Africa and its more rapid population growth. Education is the main theme of the story of

Table 1.10 Accounting for Differences in Growth Due to Differences in Accumulation: The HPAEs, Latin America, Africa, and the OECD Economies

| | | Differences in sample means | | |
| | | | | |
Variable	Parameter estimate	HPAEs–Latin America	HPAEs–Africa	HPAEs–OECD
Intercept	0.0042			
GDP relative to U.S., 1960	-0.0320	-0.0574	0.0707	-0.3831
Primary enrollment, 1960	0.0272	0.0612	0.4784	-0.1774
Secondary enrollment, 1960	0.0069	0.0823	0.2427	-0.2166
Growth of population, 1960–85	0.0998	-0.0015	-0.0056	0.0127
Average investment/GDP, 1960–85	0.0285	0.0713	0.1073	-0.0180
HPAEs	0.0171			
Latin America	-0.0131			
Sub-Saharan Africa[a]	-0.0099			
Total difference in predicted growth				
Difference in actual growth				

Note: The difference in the sample means of a variable between regions *X* and *Y* equals the average variable value in region *X* minus the average variable value in region *Y*. Differences in predicted growth are broken down by variable. The difference in predicted growth between region *X* and region *Y* attributable to a certain variable equals the difference in the sample means of that variable between regions *X* and *Y* times the estimated coefficient on that variable from the basic regression. The total difference in predicted growth between regions *X* and *Y* equals the sum of the differences in predicted growth attributable to the variables contained in the basic regression.
a. Also includes Tunisia and South Africa.
Source: World Bank staff estimates.

the differences in growth between Sub-Saharan Africa and the East Asian high performers.

What is most striking, however, is how little we are able to account for differences in growth rates between the HPAEs and other economies on the basis of conventional economic variables.[14] We are able, in the end, to predict only about 17 percent of the actual difference in growth rates between the HPAEs and Latin America. We do somewhat better between Sub-Saharan Africa and the HPAEs, predicting about 36 percent of the difference. Controlling for their superior rates of accumulation, the HPAEs still outperform while Sub-Saharan Africa or Latin America underperform the statistical relationship between accumulation and growth, leaving much of the regional difference in per capita income growth unexplained (even though a large fraction of HPAE success is explained).[15] They have been apparently more successful in allocating the resources that they have accumulated to high-productivity activities and in adopting and mastering catch up technologies.

Evidence from Estimates of TFP Growth

TFP change captures both of these important aspects of productivity growth. TFP is estimated in a neoclassical framework by subtracting from output growth the portion of growth due to capital accumulation, to human capital accumulation, and labor force growth. In keeping with this framework we estimate TFP change for eighty-seven economies

		Difference in predicted growth (percent)			
HPAEs– Latin America	Percentage of total	HPAEs– Africa	Percentage of total	HPAEs– OECD	Percentage of total
0.18	(31)	-0.23	(-15)	1.23	(184)
0.17	(28)	1.30	(87)	-0.48	(-72)
0.06	(10)	0.17	(11)	-0.15	(-22)
-0.01	(-2)	-0.06	(-4)	0.13	(19)
0.20	(34)	0.31	(20)	-0.05	(-8)
0.60	(100)	1.49	(100)	0.67	(100)
3.62		4.19		2.32	

using a production function estimated with cross-economy data. (The techniques are discussed in appendix 1.1.) Figure 1.10 plots the resulting TFP growth estimates for 1960–89 against relative income levels in 1960. There is great variance in the rates of TFP growth among low-income economies. A number of developing economies show higher rates of TFP growth than industrial economies, consistent with the possibility of large catching-up gains. Many others, however, have low or even negative rates of productivity change. The East Asian economies stand out sharply, with high absolute levels of TFP. Five HPAEs—Hong Kong, Japan, Korea, Thailand, and Taiwan, China—are in the top decile. The other three HPAEs—Indonesia, Malaysia, and Singapore—are closer to TFP growth rates in high-income economies (about 1.5 percent), but are still in the top third of all developing economies.

Presumably, in the high-income economies most of the estimated TFP growth is due to advances in best practice, which explains their relatively compact distribution of TFP growth rates around 1.5 percent a year, and the tendency for TFP growth to decline with rising income among the high-income economies (see figure 1.10). In low- and middle-income economies, however, changes in TFP must reflect more than technical progress, otherwise we would never find negative TFP growth rates. We have already argued that TFP growth for low- and middle-income economies contains an element of catching up to (or falling behind) best-practice technologies. (The relationship between technical change and catching up is discussed in appendix 1.1.) But TFP growth rates in a

Figure 1.10 Total Factor Productivity Growth, 1960–89, and GDP per Capita Relative to U.S. GDP, 1960

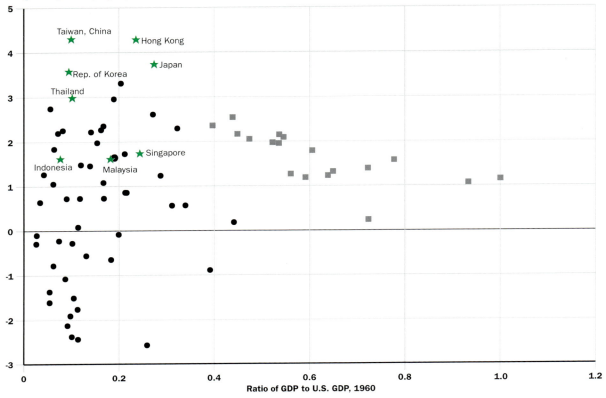

Source: World Bank data.

one-sector, cross-economy estimate will also contain an element of allocative efficiency; economies that allocate physical and human capital to low-yielding investments will have low or negative estimated TFP growth rates. The clearest demonstrations of this are the thirteen economies with negative output growth and positive accumulation. Thus our estimates of TFP growth answer the following question: on the basis of the average efficiency with which physical and human capital are used in the world economy, does accumulation over- or underpredict income growth? The answer is that for most low- and middle-income economies it overpredicts, while for the HPAEs it underpredicts.[16]

Under very restrictive assumptions (see appendix 1.1), we are able to offer some speculations concerning which of the HPAEs were catching up to best practice between 1960 and 1989. To do this we assume that the elasticities of output, which should be used to calculate TFP change, are those that apply to high-income economies only. These more allocatively efficient economies have elasticities of output with respect to both physical and human capital that are higher than those for the whole cross-economy sample. We subtract the average rate of TFP change for the high-income economies, which we have associated with movements in international best practice, from TFP change estimated using those higher elasticities to get an estimate of technical efficiency change. Using this method, Hong Kong (2.0 percent); Japan (1.0 percent); Taiwan, China (0.8 percent); and Thailand (0.1 percent) are the only HPAEs catching up to international best practice. Korea (-0.2 percent) was essentially just keeping pace with technological progress in the high-income economies, while the investment-driven economies of Indonesia, Malaysia, and Thailand were falling behind international best practice at rates of 1.2 percent (Indonesia) to 3.5 percent (Singapore) a year (see table A1.3 in appendix 1.1).

When the HPAEs are contrasted with other developing regions, however, their ability to keep pace with international best practice seems somewhat more remarkable. Using the same method, we have estimated the average rate of technical efficiency change for Latin America (-1.4 percent) and Sub-Saharan Africa (-3.5 percent). Against these benchmarks, all the HPAEs except Singapore stand up well in their ability to keep pace with the world's shifting technological frontier.[17]

Although the absolute magnitude of TFP in HPAEs is higher, so is growth. Is the proportion of growth due to TFP high? On the basis of an analysis of sources of growth for a sample of economies, Chenery (1986) developed a typology of the contribution of TFP growth to total output growth by income. A typical low- and middle-income economy had a relatively small contribution of TFP growth to total output growth, between 10 and 20 percent. High-income economies, conversely, derived about 30–50 percent of their total output growth from TFP growth.

Figure 1.11 largely confirms this pattern for low-, middle-, and high-income economies. Only seven of the fifty-nine non-HPAE low- and middle-income economies have contributions of TFP growth exceeding 33 percent, while for the high-income economies it was much higher. The HPAEs fall into two distinct groups: investment-driven and productivity-driven economies. The investment-driven economies—Indonesia, Malaysia, and Singapore—conform to the developing-econ-

Figure 1.11 Total Factor Productivity Growth and Part of Growth Due to Growth of Factor Inputs, 1960–89

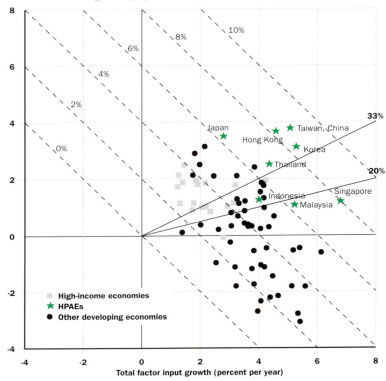

Note: Dashed lines represent total average GDP growth rates, 1960–89. Solid rays represent the contribution to total growth by TFP growth.

Sources: Nehru and Dhareshwar (1993); World Bank data.

omy pattern with a low TFP contribution. Conversely, the productivity-driven economies—Japan, Korea, Hong Kong, Thailand, and Taiwan, China—are more unusual and look more like industrial economies, with a high contribution of TFP (above 33 percent). China's recent growth (see box 1.3) shows some of these characteristics.

The HPAEs are unusual among developing economies because of the relatively important role of TFP growth. Even so, we find, consistent with our previous findings with cross-economy regressions, that between 60 and 90 percent of their output growth derives from accumulation of physical and human capital. Productivity change has been higher than in other developing economies and is important to the East Asian success story. But it is not the dominant factor.

Box 1.3 The Chinese Miracle

NO ASSESSMENT OF ECONOMIC GROWTH IN EAST Asia would be complete without consideration of China's performance. With a population 2.6 times the combined population of all eight economies in our study and a land area nearly three times as big, the Chinese mainland is Asia's second biggest economy, after Japan, in terms of total GNP. Indeed, East Asia could hardly be termed an economic miracle if China were not also growing extremely rapidly. While a detailed assessment of this performance is beyond the scope of this study, there are striking parallels in the general pattern of growth in China and the HPAEs.

Building on pre-reform achievements in education, health, and macroeconomic stability, China recorded average annual GNP growth of 9.4 percent from 1979 to 1989, with a surge to 11.4 percent from 1982 to 1988. Following a brief retrenchment that trimmed growth to 4.4 percent in 1989 and 4.1 percent in 1990, the economy has resumed very rapid growth, reaching a breakneck 12 percent in 1992. Aside from the HPAEs (and diamond-rich Botswana), no other economy in the world achieved such rapid and sustained growth during the 1980s.

China also broadly resembles the economies in our study in terms of declining poverty. While the vastness of China makes any generalization about income equality highly problematic, growth has been spread widely enough that an estimated 160 million people emerged from poverty since 1978. In contrast to the pre-reform period, when real incomes were flat or declining and the state squeezed consumption to invest an astounding 30 percent of GNP, development since 1978 has seen a marked improvement in living standards. Consumption of pork, the main source of animal protein in the Chinese diet, although still low compared with meat consumption in the HPAEs, doubled from 1978 to 1988 to nearly 15 kilograms per person annually. In the cities, the number of color televisions per 100 households increased from less than 1 in 1981 to 59 in 1990.

As with most of the HPAEs, rapid growth in China relied on a solid agricultural foundation and a government-fostered export push. Reforms giving farmers greater control over the land they tilled, together with a 25 percent real increase in crop prices, boosted agricultural productivity, generating large cash savings that farmers invested in township and village enterprises. China's export push (see chapter 3) has included currency devaluations and such export incentives as tax breaks, foreign exchange retention privileges, and duty-free imports, all utilized by the HPAEs.

Finally, like most of the economies in our study, China has achieved very rapid productivity growth. These productivity gains contrast sharply with the pre-reform period, when productivity was nearly stagnant and growth resulted entirely from increasing inputs. Not surprisingly, growth and productivity are highest in the export-oriented southern provinces that have attracted heavy investment flows from Hong Kong and Taiwan, China.

Source: World Bank (1992a).

• • •

We have described the East Asian economies' success in achieving high rates of growth and reductions in inequality. These were accompanied by agricultural transformations, rapid fertility decline, and manufactured export growth; and accounted for by rapid accumulation of physical and human capital and by productivity growth. What policies lie behind this success? In the next chapter, we examine alternative explanations of the relationship between public policies and economic success and particularly the ways that public policy can lead to improved economic outcomes. In subsequent chapters, we explore the relevant policies and their apparent links to the inputs and outcomes we have described in this chapter.

Appendix 1.1: Accounting for Growth

IN THIS APPENDIX WE BRIEFLY DESCRIBE THE METHODS USED TO estimate the relationship between accumulation and growth using both cross-economy and production function methods. We also compare our results with other results available.

Cross-Economy Regressions

The cross-economy regressions employ the basic specification of other cross-economy growth studies (Barro 1991; De Long and Summers 1991; Dollar 1992):

(1.1) $GDPG = f(INV, ED, LFG, RGDP60)$

where GDPG is the average rate of real per capita income growth using Heston-Summers' measures from 1960 to 1985; INV is the average share of investment in GDP for the period 1960–85; ED is a measure of educational attainment; LFG is the rate of growth of the economically active population, and RGDP60 is the relative gap between per capita income in 1960 (at 1980 U.S. dollar prices) and U.S. per capita income in 1960.[18] Mankiw, Romer, and Weil (1992) have recently demonstrated that this specification corresponds to the transitional dynamics of an enhanced neoclassical growth model with human capital.

Table A1.1 below reports our basic results on the relationship between accumulation and growth. The estimated equations compare favorably with other studies using similar specifications. The overall fit of the regressions is good, and the coefficients of the variables are of the expected sign and are significant at conventional levels (0.05 level).[19] We have also estimated the basic relationship for two subperiods, 1960–70 and 1970–85. The fit of the regression is markedly better in the earlier

Table A1.1 Determinants of Growth
(dependent variable: per capita GDP growth)

Sample period: Number of observations:	1960–85 113	1960–70 113	1970–85 113	1960–85 61	1960–85 98	1960–85 54
Intercept	-0.0070 (0.0079)	0.0064 (0.0092)	-0.0156 (0.0109)	-0.0034 (0.0113)	0.0141 (0.0084)	0.0243* (0.0094)
GDP relative to U.S., 1960	-0.0430** (0.0118)	-0.0444** (0.0137)	-0.0422* (0.0163)	-0.0408** (0.0146)	-0.0292* (0.0133)	-0.0251 (0.0160)
Primary enrollment, 1960	0.0264** (0.0065)	0.0169* (0.0076)	0.0324** (0.0090)	0.0247** (0.0082)		
Secondary enrollment, 1960	0.0262 (0.0139)	0.0192 (0.0162)	0.0309 (0.0192)	0.0078 (0.0180)		
Educational attainment, 1960					0.0013 (0.0010)	-0.0002 (0.0013)
Growth of population, 1960–85	0.1015 (0.2235)	-0.1638 (0.2592)	0.2738 (0.3083)	-0.0450 (0.2891)	-0.3135 (0.2351)	-0.4290 (0.2654)
Average investment/GDP, 1960–85	0.0578* (0.0224)	0.1153** (0.0260)	0.0201 (0.0309)		0.0864** (0.0245)	
Average equipment investment/ GDP, 1960–85				0.3050** (0.0721)		0.3100** (0.0743)
Adjusted R^2	0.3480	0.3424	0.1921	0.3646	0.1893	0.2614

** Statistically significant at the 0.01 level.
 * Statistically significant at the 0.05 level.
Note: Coefficient is top number in each cell. Standard error is in parentheses.
Source: World Bank staff estimates.

two periods, but in most respects the parameter estimates have similar values and significance. The major exception is the coefficient estimate on investment, which becomes insignificant in the period 1970–85.

Table A1.1 also reports on two efforts to examine the impact of changing the basic specification. DeLong and Summers (1991, 1993) have argued that equipment investment, rather than total investment, is a superior explanatory variable for per capita income growth. When the investment share in GDP is replaced with the share of equipment investment, the explanatory power of the regression is improved, and the coefficient on the share of equipment investment is highly significant. Our sample size is much reduced, however, and we conclude that the reduction in residual variance is not sufficient to justify a change in our basic specification. Because school enrollment may not be a good indicator of human capital accumulation, Barro and Lee's (1993) measure of education stock, based on population censuses, can be used in an alternative specification.

Deviations from the regression are estimates of labor productivity change that cannot be attributed to accumulation—investment in physical or human capital or to the component of TFP change associated with relative income levels. The patterns of productivity change resulting from the basic specification of the cross-economy growth regressions can be seen in figure A1.1. The figure plots the partial scatter of the relationship between growth of output per capita and investment, controlling for human capital and the component of TFP change related to relative backwardness. Per capita income is an increasing function of the share of investment. Observations are plotted relative to the estimated regression line, and the HPAEs are identified. The estimated productivity performance of the HPAEs is remarkably similar to the pattern derived from the

Figure A1.1 GDP Growth Rate and Average Investment

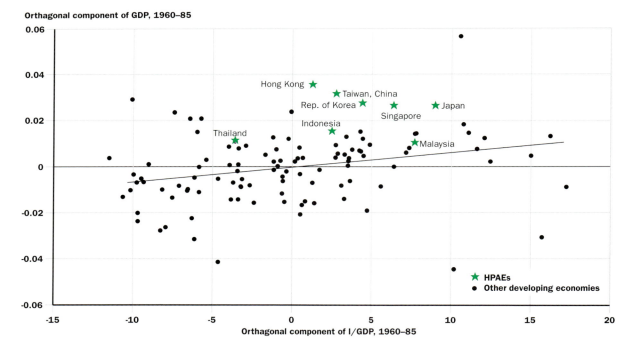

Note: The *X* and *Y* components are orthagonal on RGDP60, PRIM60, and GPOP6085, where RGDP = real GDP per capita relative to U.S. GDP per capita, 1960; PRIM60 = primary school enrollment rate, 1960; GPOP6085 = growth rate of population, 1960–85.
Source: World Bank data.

TFP estimates. All seven of the economies are positive outliers. A dummy variable taking on the value of 1 for HPAEs is positive and significant.

How We Estimate TFP Change

Suppose that every economy has access to an international cross-economy production function of the form:

$$(1.2) \quad Q = AF(K,E,L)$$

where A is total factor productivity, K is a measure of capital services, E is a measure of human capital endowments, and L is a measure of labor services in natural units. Then growth of output per head can be represented as:

$$(1.3) \quad (q\text{-}l) = a + s_K (k\text{-}l) + s_E (e\text{-}l)$$

where lowercase letters indicate rates of change and s_K and s_E are the elasticities of output with respect to physical and human capital. The share-weighted growth rates of physical and human capital per head give the contribution of accumulation to growth in output per worker. TFP change can be then found as the residual of growth of output per worker after deducting the contributions of human and physical capital accumulation:

$$(1.4) \quad a = (q\text{-}l) - s_K (k\text{-}l) - s_E (e\text{-}l).$$

Under assumptions of competitive factor markets and constant returns to scale, s_K and s_E are equal to the income shares of factors. Thus most empirical applications of equation 1.4 estimate the output elasticity coefficients with income shares.[20]

Since income share data are not available for most economies in our sample, we instead estimate s_K and s_E directly using a simple, cross-economy production function. The data for this analysis include a new constant price capital stock data set (Nehru and Dhareshwar 1993). Measures of human capital are incorporated in the specification using Barro and Lee's (1993) measure of educational attainment. We regress annual log output growth on log capital growth, log human capital growth, and log labor growth during the 1960 to 1990 period, constraining their coefficients to sum to unity (that is, specifying the production function to be Cobb-Douglas). We also include economy-specific dummy variables to estimate individual rates of TFP change for each of the sample's 87 economies.

Table A1.2 reports the production function parameters and the estimated TFP growth rates. One striking finding of our analysis is the low elasticity of output with respect to capital from the whole cross-economy sample. This is not altogether surprising. As we pointed out in chapter 1, there is a subset of developing economies that has positive net investment and human capital growth rates but negative output growth rates. In effect, the marginal product of both physical and human capital was negative in these economies, reducing the elasticity of output of both physical and human capital in the production function based on the whole sample. We have reestimated the production function on the basis of only high-income-economy input-output relationships. These results and the estimated TFP growth rates are displayed in table A1.2. The elasticity of output with respect to capital in the high-income-economy production function rises to more conventional levels. TFP estimates, particularly for those economies with rapidly growing capital stocks, are

Table A1.2 Elasticity of Output with Respect to Capital (SK), Labor (SL), and Human Capital (SH): Full Sample and High-Income Economies

	Observations	SK	(t-stat)	SL	(t-stat)	SH	(t-stat)
Full sample	2,093	0.178	10.895	0.669	6.411	0.154	1.49
High-income economies	460	0.399	10.237	0.332	1.679	0.269	1.476

Resulting total factor productivity growth estimates for the HPAEs

Economy/region	TFP growth (full sample, parameter estimates)	TFP growth (high-income only, parameter estimates)
Hong Kong	3.6470	2.4113
Indonesia	1.2543	-0.7953
Japan	3.4776	1.4274
Korea, Rep. of	3.1021	0.2355
Malaysia	1.0755	-1.3369
Singapore	1.1911	-3.0112
Taiwan, China	3.7604	1.2829
Thailand	2.4960	0.5466
Latin America	0.1274	-0.9819
Sub-Saharan Africa[a]	-0.9978	-3.0140

a. Also includes Tunisia and South Africa.
Source: World Bank data.

correspondingly reduced. The pattern of productivity change, however, with the five productivity-driven HPAEs falling as outliers in the distribution of developing economies is maintained. (See figure A1.2.)

It is possible to compare the consistency of the TFP estimates presented above with other independent estimates of TFP growth in a large sample of economies to test their robustness. Using a data base derived from World Bank real product data and alternative estimates of constant price capital stock, Elias (1990) calculates economywide TFP growth rates for a subset of 73 economies using standard growth accounting assumptions. The relationship between his results and those presented above are summarized in figure A1.3, which plots the scatter of Elias's estimate of average TFP growth during 1950–87 against our estimates. Fischer (1993) has also presented a set of TFP growth rates for a large sample of economies. A similar plot of his results against ours is shown in figure A1.4.

Figure A1.2 Per Capita Output Growth and Capital Stock Growth, 1960–89

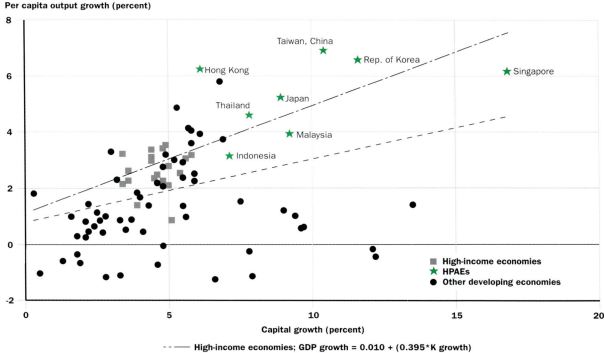

Per capita output growth (percent)

Taiwan, China
★Hong Kong
Thailand
★Japan
★ Rep. of Korea
★ Singapore
★ Malaysia
★ Indonesia

■ High-income economies
★ HPAEs
● Other developing economies

Capital growth (percent)

– – – High-income economies; GDP growth = 0.010 + (0.395*K growth)
– – – Full sample; GDP growth = 0.0076 + (0.23*K growth)

Source: World Bank data.

Figure A1.3 Comparison of Total Factor Productivity Growth Estimates

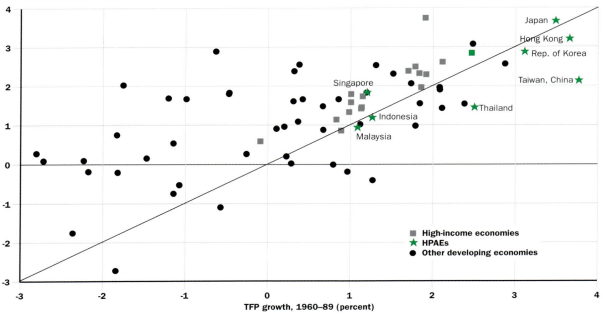

Sources: Elias (1990a); World Bank data.

Both samples show similarly great variance in rates of TFP growth among low-income economies, while the high-income economies are rather closely distributed around a mean TFP growth rate of about 1.5 percent a year. There is also great consistency between the relative ranking of TFP growth rates for the HPAEs. The same productivity-driven economies—Japan, Korea, Thailand, and Taiwan, China (Hong Kong is absent from Fischer's TFP estimates)—are in the upper quintile of both distributions, with the exception of Thailand, which under the Fischer estimate is still in the upper half of the distribution but is not in the upper half under the Elias estimate.

Technical Progress and Technical Efficiency Change

As we pointed out in the concluding section of chapter 1, it is difficult to disentangle the relative contributions of allocative mistakes, technical progress, and technological catch-up to TFP growth, especially in a cross-economy, one-sector setting. One way of separating the concepts of tech-

Figure A1.4 Comparison of Total Factor Productivity Growth Estimates

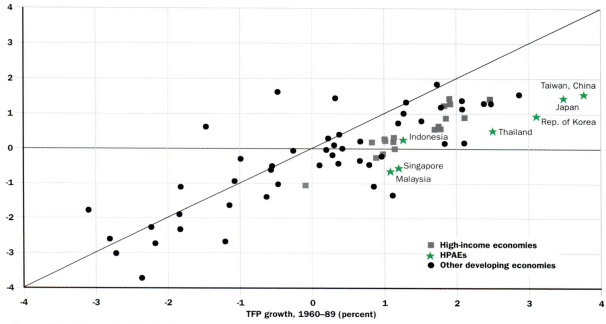

TFP growth comparator (percent) (Fischer)

Sources: Fischer (1993); World Bank data.

nological progress and changing efficiency in the use of technology is to model formally the relationship between observed output and best-practice technology. We address the relationship between accumulation, productivity change, and growth using a simple neoclassical model.

Following Nishimizu and Page (1982), we define an internationally accessible best-practice production function of the form

$$(1.5) \qquad Q^f(t) = F[Z(t);t]$$

where $Q^f(t)$ is potential output at best practice, and $Z(t)$ is a vector of inputs in natural units at time t. We assume that the function F(.) satisfies the usual neoclassical properties and that an appropriate aggregate index of output exists.

The best-practice function defines the "state of the art" in the sense that further increases in output at given levels of inputs cannot be achieved without the introduction of new techniques. Firms can move along the best-practice function, increasing output as the result of accumulation of inputs. The introduction and dissemination of new techniques move the best-practice frontier and is technological progress as defined by Solow (1956). Observed performance in a sample of economies or firms reveals that few are at best practice.[21] Rather, most lie below the production frontier due to use of dominated techniques or to inefficient use of best-practice techniques. Observed output $Q(t)$ for a vector of inputs $Z(t)$ can be expressed as

(1.6) $Q(t) = Q^f(t)e^{u(t)} = F(Z(t);t)e^{u(t)}$

where $u(t)$ is the level of technical efficiency $[0 < e^{u(t)} = Q(t)/Q^f(t) < 1]$ corresponding to observed output $Q(t)$.

The derivative in logarithms of equation 1.6 with respect to time yields:

(1.7) $Q\cdot(t)/Q(t) = F_z Z(t)/Z(t) + F_t + u\cdot(t)(t)$

where F_z and F_t are the output elasticities of $F(Z(t);t)$ with respect to inputs $Z(t)$ and time t, and dotted variables indicate time derivatives.

Output changes in equation 1.7 are decomposed into three main elements. The first one gives output changes due to input changes, weighted by the elasticity of output with respect to each input. This is the component of growth due to accumulation. The second element is the rate of technological progress of the best-practice frontier, and the last element, $u\cdot(t)$, is technical efficiency change during period t. While F_t is always non-negative, $u\cdot(t)$ can be either positive or negative.

We define the rate of total factor productivity change as the variation in output not explained by input changes. Thus for any observation, i:

(1.8) $\text{TFP}_i(t) = F_t + u\cdot_i(t),$

is the sum of technological progress, measured at the frontier, and the change in efficiency observed at the individual level.

These concepts are represented in figure A1.5.[22] We assume constant returns to scale in capital and labor. The international best-practice production function, f_1, relates output per worker to capital (including human capital) input per worker. Economies that are technically inefficient operate along functional relationships such as f_0 in

Figure A1.5 The Growth of Inputs and Outputs

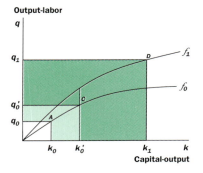

figure A1.5.[23] Catch-up can be achieved by moving from a point such as A to D, combining accumulation with a movement toward best practice.

This reinterpretation of TFP change is useful in understanding the sources of rapid catch-up in technologically backward economies. Industrial economies, which employ international best practice, are limited to rates of TFP change determined by the rate of technological progress, $u_i(t) = 0$. Economies that do not employ best practice can have TFP growth rates exceeding the rate of technological progress if technical efficiency change is positive, $u_i(t) > 0$. It is also possible for TFP change to be negative, if technical efficiency change is negative and greater in absolute value than technological progress. A rapid shift from average practice to best practice—positive technical efficiency change—can provide a powerful engine of growth that is recorded as high rates of (TFP) change.

There are two possible approaches to the estimation of the model outlined above. One would be to estimate the best-practice production function and derive estimates of both the rate of technological change and the rate of technical efficiency change.[24] This approach is not suited to the cross-economy data available, and we do not employ it. An alternative is to measure TFP change directly by growth accounting. Since measured TFP change consists of both technological progress and technical efficiency change, we impose the strong assumption that technological change, the movement of best practice, is constant and does not vary across economies.[25] Under this assumption all of the variance in rates of TFP change derives from variance in the rate of technical efficiency change.

We have argued, however, that allocative mistakes were partly responsible for the low output elasticities in the cross-economy production function estimates. Hence the high estimated TFP growth rates of those economies with rapid factor accumulation may represent allocative efficiency more than either technical progress and technical efficiency change. To address this we use the parameter estimates of the high-income economy production function on the grounds that these economies are the most allocatively efficient. We then subtract from the estimated TFP growth rate the average TFP growth for the high-income economies, our estimate of technical change. The residual estimate of technical efficiency change is presented for the HPAEs and other regional groupings in table A1.3.

Table A1.3 Technical Efficiency Change Estimates for the HPAEs

Economy/region	Technical efficiency change, 1960–89
Hong Kong	1.9714
Indonesia	-1.2352
Japan	0.9876
Korea, Rep. of	-0.2044
Malaysia	-1.7767
Singapore	-3.4510
Taiwan, China	0.8431
Thailand	0.1067
Latin America	-1.4217
Sub-Saharan Africa[a]	-3.4539

a. Also includes Tunisia and South Africa.
Source: World Bank data.

Appendix 1.2: What Do Tests of Cognitive Skills Show?

Tests provide a convenient quantitative measure of differences in performance. By providing a consistent instrument, it is possible to compare the performance of students in different learning environments. The key is objective versus subjective assessment. It is important, however, to recognize the weaknesses of standardized tests. First, tests evaluate only a limited range of skills, and there is no reason to be confident that the mastery of skills tested is highly correlated with the mastery of other skills that may also have an important influence on subsequent productivity in the labor market. Second, testing skills, not just cognitive skills, may influence performance; if there is significant "teaching to the test," both the predictive ability of test scores and levels of skill in areas not tested may fall. Differences in the curriculum may also account for some of the observed differences in performance (see Hanushek and Sabot 1991).

These criticisms suggest that, whenever possible, evidence from a variety of tests should be reviewed before reaching a general conclusion. While internationally comparable test data are not abundant, they are, however, consistent with the results already noted. Table A1.4 shows the performance of thirteen-year-old students on a standardized test of

Table A1.4 Percentage of Children Performing at or above Each Level of the Mathematics Scale, Age 13 Years

Economy/province	Can add and subtract	Can solve simple problems	Can solve two-step problems	Understands concepts	Can interpret data
British Columbia	100	96	69	24	2
Ireland	98	86	55	14	<1
Korea, Rep. of	100	95	78	40	5
New Brunswick (English)	100	95	65	18	1
New Brunswick (French)	100	95	58	12	<1
Ontario (English)	99	92	58	16	1
Ontario (French)	99	85	40	7	0
Quebec (French)	100	97	73	22	2
Quebec (English)	100	97	67	20	1
Spain	99	91	57	14	1
United Kingdom	98	87	55	18	2
United States	97	78	40	9	1

Source: Birdsall and Sabot (1993). Based on scores from the Educational Testing Service.

mathematics administered by the Educational Testing Service in a number of different economies, including Korea.[26] Students from Korea ranked first in each of the five categories of problems. The performance gap between Korean students and the others, all of whom were from high-income economies, was greater for higher-order skills.

The International Association for the Evaluation of Educational Achievement also administered mathematics tests to thirteen-year-olds in 1980–82 and included children from Hong Kong, Japan, and Thailand among the children from twenty economies in the sample. Figure A1.6 summarizes the results for algebra, which are very similar to those for arithmetic, geometry, and measurement. Japanese students ranked first, students from Hong Kong were in the top half of the distribution, and students from Thailand were near the bottom, at about the same level of performance as students from Nigeria.

Figure A1.6 Test Scores on Algebra Tests: Selected Economies

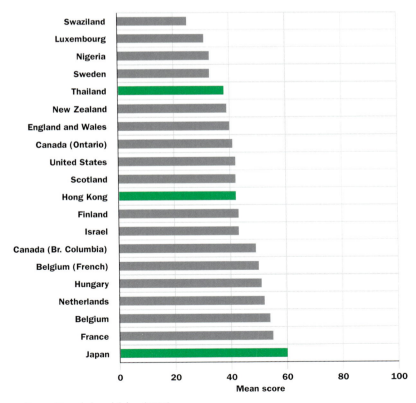

Source: Hauvsheh and Sabot (1991).

These results reinforce the conclusion that in some East Asian economies cognitive achievement levels exceed those in other developing economies and match, or exceed, those in high-income economies. The results also suggest that just as Thailand has lagged the rest of East Asia with respect to rates of enrollment in basic education, Thai children also lag with respect to levels of cognitive achievement.

Figure A1.7 Gini Coefficient and GDP per Capita Growth Rate, 1965–70

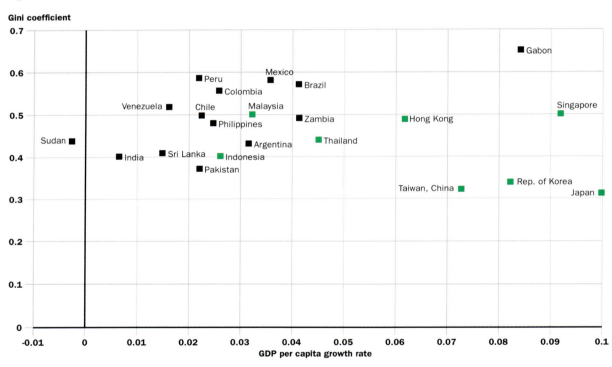

Source: World Bank data.

Figure A1.8 Gini Coefficient and GDP per Capita Growth Rate, 1971–80

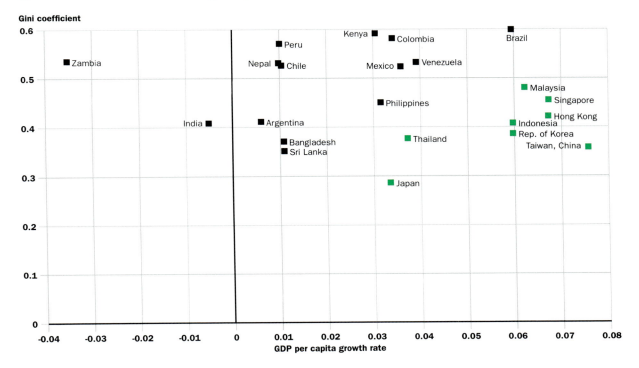

Source: World Bank data.

Figure A1.9 Gini Coefficient and GDP per Capita Growth Rate, 1981–90

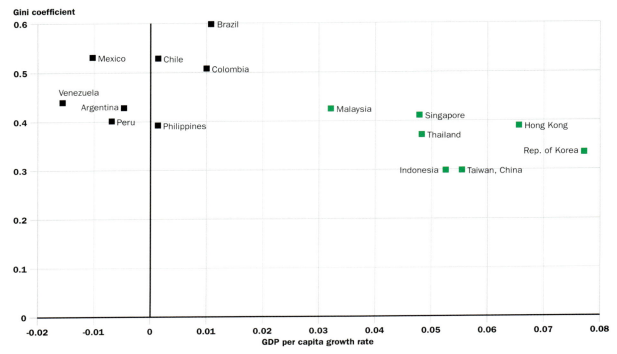

Source: World Bank data.

Figure A1.10 Cross-Economy Regression for Gender Gap in Primary Enrollment Rates, 1965 and 1987

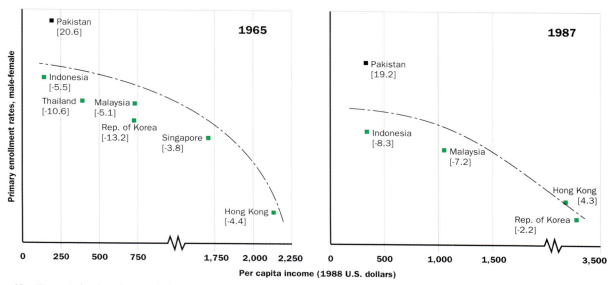

Note: Figures in brackets show residuals.
Source: Behrman and Schneider (1992).

Figure A1.11 Cross-Economy Regression for Gender Gap in Secondary Enrollment Rates, 1965 and 1987

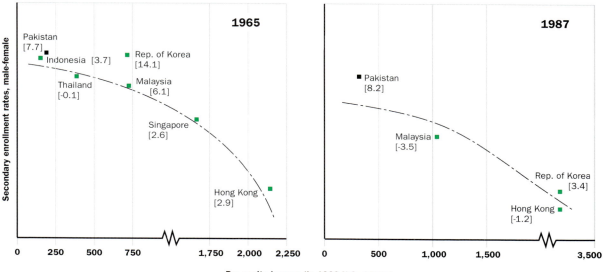

Note: Figures in brackets show residuals.
Source: Behrman and Schneider (1992).

Notes

1. As we pointed out in the Overview, a strong argument could be made for including China among the "miracle" economies of East Asia. We have not done so for three reasons: (a) China's recent very rapid growth has been highly regionally concentrated; (b) the experience of very rapid growth is more recent than in Japan and the Four Tigers and than that of Malaysia and Thailand among the southeast Asian NIEs; and (c)—and most important—the nature of the economic policy framework in China is sufficiently different from that of the other eight economies, and is in such rapid flux, that it makes attempts to understand the links between public policy and growth on a cross-economy basis even more problematic. We look at some aspects of China's rapid growth in the remainder of the book but have not treated it as systematically as the other economies.

2. High-income economies are defined according to relative income to the United States in 1960. They include: Australia, Austria, Belgium, Canada, Denmark, Finland, France, Germany, Iceland, Israel, Italy, Luxembourg, Netherlands, Norway, New Zealand, Sweden, Switzerland, Trinidad and Tobago, United Kingdom, and United States. Simple catching up by low-income economies, with growth rates exceeding those in industrial economies, is defined as "unconditional convergence" in the new literature on growth theory (see box 1.2) and would be expected to occur only under very restrictive assumptions, for example, equal savings rates and technological levels. Below we examine the concept of "conditional convergence," catch-up controlling for differences in variables contributing to growth.

3. This issue, termed "persistence," is explored by Easterly and others (1993), who find even more striking evidence of the uniqueness of persistent growth among the HPAEs.

4. Hong Kong and Singapore, which almost entirely lack agricultural sectors, are excluded from this discussion.

5. Statistical analysis indicates no significant (in the statistical sense) difference of these eight economies from other economies in their share of total investment, controlling for relative income levels.

6. This basic pattern is observed in four individual economies—Korea, Malaysia, Singapore, and Thailand. The pattern for Indonesia differs; real private investment declined continuously during the 1980s from a peak of 20 percent of GDP to a low of 13 percent in 1989.

7. Behrman and Schneider (1992). The regressions control for a polynomial in average per capita income in the relevant year. The authors used per capita GNP at official exchange rates as the measure of income.

8. The residuals for Sri Lanka and Egypt are also above the line in 1965.

9. Despite increasing its secondary enrollment rate from 29 to 74 percent, Hong Kong also fell well below the predicted level in 1987. This is because, at $15,000, the per capita income of Hong Kong was so high that the OECD economies were now its comparators.

10. Birdsall and Sabot (1993b) cite Stevenson and Stigler (1992), among others, who report results of tests in cities of Japan, the United States, and Taiwan, China. Appendix 1.2 reviews the results of other tests comparing the cognitive skills levels of East Asian children to other students.

11. See appendix 1.1 for a formal definition of TFP growth.

12. This specification is the simplest of a group of cross-economy regressions that have been used in recent years. These studies have also introduced other variables to address different questions—equipment investment, De Long and Summers (1991); trade orientation, Dollar (1992); endogenous investment, Barro (1990). We have not included these variables because they are not central to our theme. This approach, while generally associated with tests of endogenous growth theory, is also consistent with neoclassical assumptions (Mankiw, Romer, and Weil 1992). A recent conference, How Do National Policies Affect Long-Run Growth, summarizes the state of the art in this field (Easterly and Schmidt-Hebbel, forthcoming).

13. We have also estimated the basic relationship for two subperiods, 1960–70 and 1970–85. The fit of the regression is markedly better in the earlier period, but in most respects the parameter estimates have similar values and significance. The major exception is the coefficient estimate on investment/GDP, which becomes insignificant in the period 1970–85.

14. Easterly (1993) finds similar results for the Four Tigers.

15. Use of a variable measuring equipment investment (DeLong and Summers 1991, 1993) enhances somewhat the explanatory power of the regression, though in a smaller sample. An alternative education variable (Barro and Lee 1993), measure of education stock, based on population censuses, fails to perform better than the primary enrollment rate.

16. Figures A1.8 and A1.9 (in the appendixes to this chapter) compare our estimates of TFP growth with two other independently derived estimates for a large sample of countries (Elias 1990; Fischer 1993). The pattern of productivity growth rates in figure 1.10 is remarkably robust to the specification of the growth accounting equation and to the capital stock series used. IMF (1993), contrasting Asia with other developing economies, reaches similar conclusions, both with respect to the estimated magnitudes of TFP change and the relative contribution of TFP change to output growth. Thomas and Wang (1993) and S. Edwards (1992) also reach broadly similar results concerning the pattern of productivity change in the HPAEs compared with other economies.

17. Young (1992) finds similarly disappointing results with respect to Singapore's TFP performance. Some caution is needed in interpreting these results, however. Much of Singapore's investment between 1960 and 1990 was in housing and social infrastructure, outputs of which are notoriously difficult to measure. It is possible that we have therefore undervalued the rate of growth of output and hence the rate of TFP change. Similar detailed criticisms could be made for other economies, both HPAE and non-HPAE, and our TFP results are therefore best regarded (as indeed are the cross-economy regression results) as indicative of broad international trends. (On problems of estimates of cross-economy regressions, see Srinivasan 1992).

18. The studies cited are listed in note 13 above. We have not included these variables because they are not central to our theme.

19. The magnitude of the coefficient on investment is lower than that reported in Dollar (1992) for his sample of 114 economies (0.113). The magnitude of the coefficient for education is about that given in Dollar's results, and the coefficient for RGDP60 is essentially similar to the results obtained by Dollar and by De Long and Summers (1991).

20. This literature is briefly surveyed in Nishimizu and Page (1987).

21. Farrell (1957) was one of the first to note the divergence between observed behavior and best practice, which he called technical inefficiency. There is by now a large literature on technical inefficiency. Pack (1988) summarizes much of this literature as it applies to developing countries.

22. Mankiw, Romer, and Weil (1992) also employ a Solow-type neoclassical model. Proponents of endogenous growth theory would not accept the depiction of the production function with diminishing returns to capital.

23. A comprehensive review of the large literature on the measurement of best-practice or frontier production functions and their relationship to traditional estimates of the production function is contained in Aigner and Schmidt (1980).

24. This is the approach adopted by Nishimizu and Page (1982) and recently applied to high-income economies by Fecher and Perelman (1992).

25. This assumption, while strong, may not be far from the truth. Industrial sector estimates of TFP change in industrial economies generally yield a compact distribution of rates with a mean value near 1.5 percent a year, both within and across economies. This may therefore be a good first approximation of the rate of technological change.

26. The tests were administered to a random sample of 2,000 students in each country. The test questions were drawn from the National Assessment of Educational Progress, a test designed for U.S. students. See Hanushek and Sabot (1991).

CHAPTER 2

Public Policy and Growth

WHAT ACCOUNTS FOR THE REMARKABLE record of rapid income growth and declining inequality described in chapter 1? Some observers attribute success to geography and culture rather than economic or other policies. But geography and culture cannot explain it all; East Asia includes Myanmar and the Philippines as well as the Republic of Korea and Malaysia. Nor is there a simple policy story. Of the successful East Asian economies, Hong Kong and Thailand have had relatively little activist intervention in economic sectors by their governments, while Korea and Malaysia have had a lot.

In this chapter, after examining the significance of geography and culture, we suggest a simple framework for understanding growth in the eight HPAEs. This framework explicitly allows for different, but potentially successful, mixes of policies across time and across economies. To set the stage for later chapters, we then show how very different policies can be used, if circumstances are propitious, to address the three critical functions of economic management mentioned in chapter 1—accumulation of resources, efficient allocation of those resources, and productivity growth, that is, increasingly greater output for given resources.

How much of East Asia's success is due to geography, common cultural characteristics, and historical accident? Certainly some—but definitely not all. Ready access to common sea lanes and relative geographical proximity are the most obvious shared characteristics of the successful Asian economies. East Asian economies have clearly benefited from the kind of informal economic linkages geographic proximity encourages, including trade and investment flows. For example, throughout Southeast Asia, ethnic Chinese drawing on a common cultural heritage have been active in trade and investment. Intraregional economic relationships date back many centuries to China's relations with the kingdoms that became Cambodia, Japan, Korea, Laos, Myanmar, and Viet Nam.

In South and Southeast Asia, Muslim traders sailed from India to Java, landing to trade at points in between, for several hundred years before the arrival of European ships. Thus tribute missions and traditional trade networks, reinforced in the nineteenth and twentieth centuries by surges of emigration, have fostered elements of a common trading culture, including two lingua francas, Malay and Hokein Chinese, that remain important in the region today.

In our own century, key Asian ports were integrated into the emerging world economic system as the result of European military and trade expansion. Cheap ocean transport and shared historical experiences further knit together a far-flung, culturally disparate region. U.S. assistance in rebuilding Japan after World War II, followed by massive U.S. economic assistance and military spending in the region throughout the cold war, also helped to set the stage for rapid growth. Positive impacts included enhanced security, which enabled governments not directly involved in the combat to focus on economic development. Perhaps as important, the U.S. military's extensive purchases in Asia provided a ready market for emerging export industries. Japanese industry received a substantial boost from the provisioning of U.S. troops in Korea; just as some of Korea's biggest conglomerates got their start selling goods and services to the U.S. military during the war in Vietnam.

Regional linkages facilitated the adoption of imitative strategies, in both public and private sector activity. Policy imitation—specifically of Japan's industrial strategy—was an explicit objective in Korea and Malaysia. Korea borrowed Japanese techniques for building large trading companies and directing the structure of industry; Malaysia focused first on developing heavy industry and more recently on building business-government relationships. Furthermore, the general model of Japanese success undoubtedly impressed policymakers throughout East Asia, engendering a sense of confidence as well as providing models of potential instruments of growth.

Finally, geographical proximity has facilitated capital flows, particularly in the past decade, as Northeast Asian manufacturers of labor-intensive exports moved their factories south to take advantage of lower wages. A surge of investment (since the real appreciation of the Japanese yen following the Plaza Accord)—flowing first from Japan and later from Hong Kong, Korea, Singapore, and Taiwan, China—has contributed significantly to the dynamism of Indonesia, Malaysia, and Thailand. From the policy viewpoint, these linkages have been encouraged by the generally liberal treatment of foreign investment. But even where foreign investment policies have been restrictive, informal credit and information networks have helped investors to move capital relatively freely.

In addition to direct linkages and imitation, East Asian economies may have benefited from positive regional externalities. Through their earlier trade with Japan, Western importers had become familiar with Asian business, established networks for sourcing East Asian products, and gained respect for East Asian quality. Later, U.S. trade policies imposed quantitative restrictions on Japanese products and created rare opportunities for other East Asian producers to enter international markets. Producers of garments, shoes, television sets, automobiles, and other products in Korea and Taiwan, China, took advantage of these episodes to establish lucrative market positions (Petri 1988).

Of course, regional characteristics alone cannot account for East Asia's remarkable success. If geography, history, and culture were an adequate explanation, other economies would have little to learn from Asia's success stories. Fortunately evidence suggests that this is not the case. Indeed, economies that are part of the same matrix of geography, culture, and history as the HPAEs but followed different economic policies—the Democratic People's Republic of Korea and the Philippines are two widely divergent examples—have yet to share in the East Asian miracle. We turn, then, to the heart of this book, an examination of the policies that have shaped East Asia's success.

Policy Explanations

ATTEMPTS TO IDENTIFY THE POLICIES THAT HAVE CREATED the East Asian economic miracle fall into several broad categories. Below we present a summary of these, focusing on the differences in interpretation that have arisen among observers confronted with the same set of economic facts.

The Neoclassical View

In the neoclassical interpretation of East Asia's success, the market takes center stage in economic life and governments play a minor role. For example, Wolf (1988, p. 27) found it "a striking fact that the few relatively successful developing [economies]—Hong Kong, Malaysia, Singapore, the Republic of Korea and Taiwan, China—have greatly benefited from decisions and policies that limit government's role in economic decision making, and instead allow markets—notwithstanding their imperfections and shortcomings—to exercise a decisive role in determining resource allocation." Similarly, Chen (1979, pp. 183–84) argued that in Japan and the Four Tigers (Hong Kong, Korea, Singapore, and Taiwan, China) state intervention was largely absent. "What the state has provided is simply a suitable environment for the entrepreneurs to perform their functions."

The neoclassical interpretation of the experience of the HPAEs, and especially of Korea and Taiwan, China, presents a coherent and powerful view of one path to successful industrialization.[1] In this view, governments in all of the HPAEs provided a relatively stable macroeconomic environment, characterized by limited inflation (except at times in Korea). Real effective exchange rates rarely appreciated, and such episodes were quickly corrected (S. Edwards 1988). Interludes of intensive import-substituting industrialization in Korea and Taiwan, China, were brief. Manufacturers were thus able to concentrate on improving productivity performance rather than coping with rapidly changing relative prices of inputs and outputs.

Although neoclassical interpretations of the success of Hong Kong, Japan, Korea, Singapore, and Taiwan, China, are often nuanced—and advocates offer them with varying levels of consumer warnings—they stress the benefits to the HPAEs of limited policy distortions in the foreign trade regime and domestic factor markets. In the neoclassical view, East Asia's export success is due to similar rewards for selling in the domestic and foreign markets. Because variation in incentives across sectors, as measured by the effective rate of protection of value added, has been limited, inputs have flowed to sectors roughly on the basis of static comparative advantage, and international competition has provided the impetus for cost discipline and technological upgrading. Traded inputs have been made available to exporters at international prices, and exporters have faced an international price regime in making their decisions. Finally, factor markets have been roughly competitive, so positive real rates of interest have prevailed, and there has been an absence of duality in the wage structure by size of firm or sector of production.

The Revisionist View

In the past six years, the neoclassical interpretation of the sources of rapid growth has been criticized for its lack of factual validity, at least as it applies to Japan, Korea, and Taiwan, China (Pack and Westphal 1986; Amsden 1989; Wade 1990). Advocates of this new view, sometimes dubbed revisionist, have systematically documented that governments in these three economies extensively and selectively promoted individual sectors. They have convincingly shown that levels of protection and the variation of protection across sectors has been greater than recognized in the neoclassical interpretations.[2]

Indeed, governments in each of these three economies at times intervened forcefully in markets. Korea, for example, strongly encouraged heavy and chemical industries by setting targets and offering a variety of financial incentives (Pack and Westphal 1986; Westphal, Rhee, and Pursell 1988). Japan promoted the development of several weak industries in the first fifteen years after World War II, offering protective tariffs and financial incentives to encourage the introduction of advanced technology and establishing rationalization cartels to facilitate the exit of inefficient firms.[3] Taiwan, China, used public investment in large-scale manufacturing enterprises to ensure inputs for predominantly small and medium-scale exporting industries.

Moreover, capital markets were not free in these three economies. Proponents of the neoclassical view have focused on the reduced intervention, particularly in the 1960s, that allowed real interest rates to shift from negative to positive levels (McKinnon 1973). But while intervention declined, it nonetheless continued. In fact, Japan, Korea, and to a lesser extent Taiwan, China, did not rely solely on markets to allocate savings. Rather, they repressed interest rates and directed credit in order to guide investments.

The revisionist view, proposed by Amsden (1989), Wade (1989, 1990), and others, sees market failures as pervasive and a justification for governments to lead the market in critical ways. In this view, the experiences of Japan, Korea, and Taiwan, China, provide evidence that governments can foster growth by "governing markets" and "getting prices wrong" and by systematically distorting incentives in order to accelerate catching up—that is, to facilitate the establishment and growth of industrial sectors that would not have thrived under the workings of comparative advantage. Amsden (1989, p. 14), for example, asserts that all "economic expansion depends on state intervention to create price distortions that direct economic activity toward greater investment. State intervention is necessary even in the most plausible cases of comparative advantage, because the chief asset of backwardness—low wages—is counterbalanced by heavy liabilities."

The Market-Friendly View

World Development Report 1991 (World Bank 1991b), in a comprehensive attempt to describe the policies needed for rapid growth, falls in the middle ground between the neoclassical and revisionist views. It concludes that rapid growth is associated with effective but carefully delimited government activism. In the "market-friendly" strategy it articulates (see box 2.1), not only do governments "need to do less in those areas where markets work," namely the production sector, they also "need to do more in those areas where markets cannot be relied upon" (p. 9). The appropriate role of government in a market-friendly strategy is to ensure adequate investments in people, provision of a competitive climate for enterprise, openness to international trade, and stable macroeconomic management.

But beyond these roles, governments are likely to do more harm than good. On the basis of an exhaustive review of the experience of most developing economies, *World Development Report 1991* concludes that in general governments have been unsuccessful in improving economic performance through attempts to guide resource allocations by other than market mechanisms. Attempts to guide resource allocation in international trade, financial markets and labor markets have reduced competitive discipline, guided resources into low-productivity and internationally uncompetitive sectors, and resulted in widespread rent-seeking. In short, though market failure is an important impediment to rapid growth, so is government failure—and government failure can have high costs.

A central contribution of *World Development Report 1991* is the argument that sustained growth results from the positive interaction of four critical aspects of economic policy: macroeconomic stability,

Box 2.1 Making the Most of Markets

IN THE PAST TWENTY YEARS, A CONSENSUS HAS emerged among economists on the best approach to economic development. This consensus was discussed at length in *World Development Report 1991: The Challenge of Development* (World Bank 1991b). The Report highlighted the importance of a healthy private sector, which results from investments in people, a much reduced role for government, openness to (and so competitiveness with) the rest of the world, and macroeconomic stability. These ideas have crystallized into what is now called the "market-friendly" approach.

The Report noted that the economic returns from investing in people can be high, but many governments spend too little on human development or do not target their spending appropriately. As a result, in Brazil and Pakistan, for instance, growth alone did little to improve the social indicators; in Chile and Jamaica, however, those indicators improved even in times of slow growth. Governments must also improve the quality of human capital investment. Too often, provisions for recurrent spending are inadequate, resulting in wasteful underutilization.

Most successful economies, including Japan, Singapore, and Korea, have established their global competitive advantage through the rigors of the marketplace. Conversely, restrictions on competition (for example, industrial licensing or inappropriate legal codes of employment or bankruptcy) hold back

technological change and productivity. The Report stressed that domestic policy should expose entrepreneurs to the information embodied in prices and provide the infrastructure and institutions that will help them respond.

Openness to international trade, investment, and ideas has been critical in encouraging domestic producers to cut costs by introducing new technologies and developing new and better products. By the same token, protection for domestic industry can hold back development for decades. Here, government can play a positive role. In Japan and Korea, for instance, government agencies and industry associations collaborate to gather and disseminate information on technology and develop quality control for exports.

A stable macroeconomic foundation is one of the most important public goods that governments can provide, as the Report pointed out. When government overspends, the result is often overborrowing, monetary expansion, and financial sector difficulties, quickly followed by inflation, chronic overvaluation of the currency, and loss of export competitiveness. The economies with a history of macroeconomic instability are legion and include Argentina, Bolivia, Côte d'Ivoire, and Ghana. Others, including Indonesia, Korea, Malaysia, and Thailand, have managed to keep their macroeconomic policies on course, and their broad economic performance has benefited accordingly.

---

human capital formation, openness to international trade, and an environment that encourages private investment and competition. Effective policy in one dimension (such as human capital formation) improves the results from effective policies in others (such as openness or macroeconomic stability). In this view, the success of many economies in East Asia has been due to reinforcing policy feedbacks. No single policy has ensured success; strong and effective policies in all four critical areas, and over a sustained period, have been key.

The market-friendly approach captures important aspects of East Asia's success. These economies are macroeconomically stable, have very high levels of human capital, are thoroughly integrated into the world economy, and have very high levels of competition among firms. Moreover, East Asian success sometimes occurred *in spite of* rather than *because of* market interventions. Korea's heavy and chemical industries (HCI) drive and Japan's computer chip push did not live up to expectations. Even so, other interventions combined with export targets apparently *were* consistent with rapid growth: quota-based protection of domestic industries in Japan and Korea; targeted industrial policies including directed credit in Japan, Korea, Singapore, and Taiwan, China; heavy reliance on large state enterprises in Japan, Korea, and Taiwan, China; and so on. Furthermore, the successes of these three northeastern economies compares favorably with the successes of Hong Kong, Malaysia, and more recently Indonesia and Thailand, where policy choices have been less interventionist.

Multiple Paths to Growth

As these three views show, while it is easy to see how elements of East Asian experience contributed to rapid growth, it is not easy to identify a single recipe followed across the region. An alternative approach is to recognize this diversity of policies and to assess whether and how various mixes of policies contributed to successful implementation of three central functions of economic management: accumulation, allocation, and productivity growth.[4] This approach recognizes that policies, like tactics, can and should vary depending on the situation, while the central functions, which are crucial to development, must always be addressed.

One of the hallmarks of economic policymaking in the HPAEs was the pragmatic flexibility with which governments tried policy instruments in pursuit of economic objectives. Instruments that worked were retained. Instruments that failed or impeded other policy objectives were abandoned. Thus, the Korean and Malaysian governments reduced intensive promotion of heavy and chemical industries when the fiscal costs and strains on the financial system threatened macroeconomic stability. Indonesia abandoned capital market controls and attempts to control interest rates when they were found to be ineffective. Japan shifted from highly selective interventions to promote exports in the 1950s and 1960s to industrial policies designed to reduce trade friction in the 1980s (see box 2.4 later in the chapter). Taiwan, China, gradually privatized key public sector investments made to support the rapid growth of exports by small and medium-size firms. Singapore shifted from a policy of repressing wages to one of promoting rapid wage growth, finally concluding by coordinating the increase in wages with rising productivity. And Malaysia shifted from policies that resulted in business-government conflict to highly structured mechanisms to encourage business-government cooperation. Chapter 3 discusses the pragmatic flexibility of HPAE governments in pursuing two goals, macroeconomic stability and growth of manufactured exports.

Obviously, our three functions of growth-oriented economic management were not objectives in themselves for policymakers in the rapidly growing East Asian economies. Instead, they are simply a framework for analyzing how the varying mix of policies and instruments chosen by HPAE governments contributed to or detracted from rapid growth. At the same time, we do not want to imply that growth was due to mere luck in the HPAEs. Though policies varied over time and place, the formulation and implementation of policies were purposeful, with an overriding objective of "shared growth." (This term is described and discussed in chapter 4.)

In contrast to the diverse, changing, but purposeful mix of policies in the HPAEs, other economies have either rigidly adhered to policies that were demonstrably unsuccessful—for example, extended periods of import substitution in Latin America and Sub-Saharan Africa, policies to develop domestic technology in India, and state-led industrialization in Eastern Europe—or have lacked a purposeful direction, as the history of adjustment programs in some economies in other regions attests. Indeed, as we illustrate in the next chapter, the flexibility and pragmatism of policymaking in most of the HPAEs reflected governments' willingness to try new approaches to achieve particular purposes, discard unsuccessful ones, and keep those perceived as successful.

The Functional Growth Framework

FIGURE 2.1 PORTRAYS THE FUNCTIONAL APPROACH TO UNDER-standing growth in the HPAEs. The figure shows, in four columns, the interaction among two sets of policy choices (fundamentals and selective interventions); two methods of competitive discipline (market and contest based); the three central functions of economic

Figure 2.1 A Functional Approach to Growth

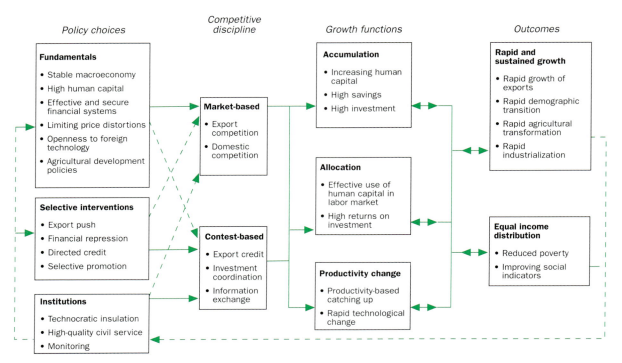

management; and the outcomes of growth and equity discussed in chapter 1. Institutions are also shown as critical to the successful definition and implementation of policies and to supporting high levels of competitive discipline.

The solid lines in the figure show how policy choices contributed to outcomes via attainment of the three functions. Many policies, such as high human capital and openness, contributed simultaneously to two or three functions. For example, stable macroeconomic management contributed to vigorous accumulation through higher rates of investment and to improved allocation by reducing instability in relative prices. High and growing investments in human capital contributed both to accumulation, since human capital is an essential input to economic growth, and to productivity-based catching up by permitting better mastery of technology. Effective and secure financial systems helped to increase the level of financial savings (accumulation) and channel it to high-productivity investments (allocation). Limited price distortions, by keeping domestic relative prices relatively close to international prices, were good for allocation and may have provided incentives for firms to adopt technologies and innovate. Openness to foreign technology was a major vehicle for productivity-based catching up, and agricultural sector policies that promoted rural development were central to both growth and improved distribution of income.

The arrows indicate that the system has numerous self-reinforcing feedbacks. For example, rapid growth and relatively equal income distributions contributed to the HPAEs' superior accumulation by increasing savings rates and generating larger and more effective investments in human capital; they also contributed to superior allocation of human capital by fostering labor mobility and market determination of wages. Similarly, they helped in the creation and protection of institutions, particularly the civil service, by reducing incentives for corruption.

The six policies listed as fundamentals are so defined in the sense that they affect the attainment of growth functions primarily through market-based mechanisms of competitive discipline. Three—macroeconomic stability, effective financial systems, and limited price distortions—assist markets. The two others—high investment in human capital and openness to foreign technology—require efficient markets to operate.

But the HPAEs also went beyond the fundamentals, intervening with varying degrees of intensity to alter market incentives. The broadest interventions were generous incentives for manufactured exports. (These are discussed in some detail in chapter 3.) As part of this export push, all the HPAEs permitted exporters automatic access to imported intermediate inputs at international prices. Most also offered subsidized credit, often performance-based, for exporters. In Hong Kong and Singapore, where international prices guided the domestic economy, massive public housing programs helped to keep down labor costs. In Japan, Korea, and Thailand, implicit or explicit export targets were used as the basis for awarding access to foreign exchange, investment licenses, or credit. In Taiwan, China, large-scale public investments, including in public enterprises, along with extensive support services to small and medium-size exporters, were used to support the export drive.

Most HPAEs also controlled interest rates on deposits and bank lending. These financially repressive policies enabled governments to ration credit, favoring some would-be borrowers over others. In addition to the importance of these directed-credit schemes to export promotion, some governments also directed credit to other activities, including agriculture, small and medium-size enterprises, and, in Japan and Korea, large-scale investments. By intervening in credit markets, governments selectively promoted industries, ownership groups, and, in some instances, individual firms. (These issues are analyzed in detail in chapters 5 and 6.) Some HPAEs chose very narrow promotion targets, selectively assisting knowledge- and capital-intensive industries and firms in hopes of upgrading the economy's overall level of industrial technology. In Japan and Korea the governments at times concentrated on promoting private domestic investment in heavy and chemical industries (HCIs). In Taiwan, China (and to some extent in Indonesia), the public sector invested directly in technologically sophisticated industries. Singapore and Thailand have attempted to attract foreign investment in capital- and knowledge-intensive sectors. Malaysia initially undertook public investments in HCI firms but has recently shifted to a strategy of promoting private investment more akin to that of Japan and Korea.

Some selective interventions went beyond helping markets perform better. Rather, they guided and in some cases even bypassed markets. In the following section of this chapter, we explain why, in light of market failures, some interventions make sense even within the neoclassical framework. We then describe how some of the interventions undertaken by HPAE governments addressed these market failures, effectively (if not necessarily intentionally) reducing the gap between social and private gains.

Market Failures: The Coordination Problem

A primary function of markets is coordination. The price system is a mechanism by which the production decisions of the myriad firms that make up the economy are coordinated; for instance, they signal to intermediate goods producers what outputs are required by final goods producers. When markets are incomplete or missing, they cannot perform this signaling function. Since the prices of outputs and inputs (including wages) depend critically on what other firms are doing, there are great potential benefits of sharing information. Even in well-developed market economies, information is conveyed in many ways other than prices. Trade journals, trade association meetings, and information newsletters are all important institutions for the transmission of information.

Adam Smith's invisible hand paradigm argues that each individual, in pursuing his or her self-interest, also maximizes the common welfare; cooperation is therefore unnecessary. In reality, modern economies are characterized by extensive cooperation. Among firms in economies that belong to the Organization for Economic Cooperation and Development (OECD), for example, formal and informal sharing of information is common. Cooperation among firms is maintained whenever the gains from cooperating outweigh the gains from cheating. Cooperative relations are ensured because of benefits from maintaining a good reputation. If a firm fails to cooperate, its reputation will be damaged, and future business that depends on its reputation will be lost.

Institutional arrangements for cooperation and information exchange in developing economies are weaker than in industrial economies, yet the needs for these forms of coordination are undoubtedly greater. When economic change is slow, making predictions about future prices is relatively easy: a simple projection of the recent past will do. But when economic change is rapid, predicting the future is much more difficult. There is often need for coordination beyond what markets can provide; hence there may be a greater role for government to create institutions and facilitate coordination.

Missing Information and Credit Markets. Among the markets most affected by information problems are capital markets. Even in industrial economies, equity markets generally do not finance much new investment, largely because of information asymmetries (Stiglitz 1993a). In economies where equity markets are weak or absent, credit mechanisms become the primary vehicle for raising capital and diversifying and spreading risk. But credit markets—even those free of interest rate controls—are often characterized by credit rationing. Credit is seldom allocated to the highest bidder. This is for an obvious reason: bidders are bidding promises; those who bid the most may not be able to fulfill their promises. Lenders are concerned not with the promised return but the actual return. As a result, capital is allocated by a screening and evaluation process that is quite different from the anonymity that characterizes resource allocation in an idealized market.

In some of the HPAEs, governments intervened aggressively to address this problem in the credit market, going beyond the normal regulatory functions and prudential supervision that help ensure consumer confidence. For example, in Japan, Korea, and Taiwan, China, government helped establish and aggressively supported development banks and other financial institutions—and only later encouraged equity and bond markets. In Japan and Korea, government set up and managed directed-credit programs, and through explicit and implicit guarantees or other forms of interventions, reduced the risks borne by investors.

Scale Economies, Externalities, and Cooperation. Coordination may yield substantial benefits when large indivisibilities in investment lead to economies of scale. One such case arises when investments are interdependent. For example, if a steel plant and a steel-using industry are needed concurrently, it does not pay to develop the plant unless there is a steel-using industry, and it does not pay to develop the steel-using industry unless there is a plant. If each awaits the other, nothing happens. Market failures due to incomplete markets, such as the absence of capital and risk markets, exacerbate this situation. With such large-scale investments, no single entrepreneur could amass the capital required for both investments, and capital market imperfections mean that investors have difficulty obtaining the funds required. Moreover, there are likely to be large risks, and the market provides no mechanisms by which these risks can be divested.

Economists have traditionally found externalities a persuasive argument for intervention in market allocation. Many of these externalities are related to learning: spillovers associated with developing markets, spillovers associated with discovering what goods can be produced, and spillovers associated with the incomplete appropriability of technological knowledge. In each case, firms undertaking a new activity face long-term, noncollateralizable investments that are difficult to finance. Coordination failures loom especially large where "diffuse externalities" exist and there are multiple linkages between firms (Stiglitz 1993a). It is precisely in situations where there are many participants that markets are particularly useful and where the absence of markets is particularly costly. Examples of these diffuse externalities include, for instance, the development of high-technology services and nontraded intermediate goods.

In the earlier development literature, the coordination problem arising from interdependent investments, economies of scale, and externalities was given a great deal of prominence. This was the argument for planning in the 1950s and 1960s. Such planning failed in part because it attempted to concentrate all relevant information in the government planning bureau. This was simply impossible; information is too diffuse, too complex. Planning ministries were not adept at generating the information needed to support investment decisions; as a result many planned investments failed. Moreover, because many of the planned investments were in monopolistic public sector companies, severe problems of economic performance arose related to corporate governance and market power.

Some HPAEs tackled problems of scale and externalities by setting up mechanisms through which business and government could exchange information and coordinate investment decisions. Japan and Korea, and later Singapore and Malaysia, developed institutions and market relationships that facilitated this process. In doing so, however, these governments did not attempt to supplant existing information networks. Rather, they built on the superior information that firms had as decisionmakers. Their approach to these problems, emphasizing information and cooperation through formal and informal interactions, is discussed in chapter 4.[5]

Creating Contests

Cooperation raises several problems, however. First, cooperative behavior may become collusion, if firms act together to raise prices. Second, cooperation may inhibit competition, leading to managerial slack or a more general loss of efficiency. Third, business-government cooperation may encourage firms to seek favors from government.

How did the East Asian economies that encouraged cooperation avoid these problems? They combined cooperative behavior—including sharing of information among firms and between the private and public sectors, coordination of investment plans, and promotion of interdependent investments—with competition by firms to meet well-defined economic performance criteria. They developed institutional structures in which firms competed for valued economic prizes, such as access to credit, in some dimensions while actively cooperating in others; in short, they created contests (see box 2.2). Market-based competition and contest-based competition both included prohibition of monopolies, although the number of competing firms was sometimes small. Even though Japan and Korea have tended to have high levels of concentration in their manufacturing sector (see table 2.1), domestic competition has usually been vigorous. The Japanese government has proceeded on the assumption that competition among fewer, more evenly matched firms is preferable to having one large firm competing with many smaller rivals, a principle that is well-recognized in athletic competitions (Nalebuff and Stiglitz 1983).

Contest-based competition included clear, well-enforced rules, and prizes for winners. Table 2.2 briefly describes some of the contests organized by HPAE governments.[6] The simplest and most widely used were

Table 2.1 Concentration Ratios in Manufacturing

Economy	Share
Three-firm concentration ratios	
Japan, 1980	56
Korea, Rep. of, 1981	62
Taiwan, China, 1981	49
Four-firm concentration ratios	
Argentina, 1984	43
Brazil, 1980	51
Chile, 1979	50
India, 1984	46
Indonesia, 1985	56
Mexico, 1980	48
Pakistan, 1985	68
Turkey, 1976	67
United States, 1972	40

Sources: Amsden (1989); Frischtak (1989).

Box 2.2 Running a Contest: Rewards, Rules, and Referees

THE ECONOMIC CONTESTS THAT GOVERNMENTS in Japan, Korea, and Taiwan, China, set up among firms to combine the benefits of competition and cooperation are complex endeavors that last many months and sometimes years. At base, however, these contests and their role in the economy resemble children's party games.

Organizing contests is a more complicated way to run an economy than relying on laissez-faire, just as organizing party games is more complicated than providing a level playing field and letting children do as they please. Laissez-faire and free play both work. But a well-run contest, like a well-run party game, can generate even better results, by providing a focus for competition and inducing participants to cooperate as they compete.

In both instances there are three prerequisites for success: rewards, rules, and referees. Rewards must be substantial enough to elicit broad participation and energetic competition. Rules must be clear-cut so that contestants know which behavior will be rewarded—and which will be punished. Finally, as anybody who has organized children's party games knows, competent, impartial referees are crucial. If children think parents running the game are incompetent or—heaven forbid—favoring their own child, the game quickly falls apart.

Contests in Northeast Asian economies have succeeded partly because the prerequisites were right. Preferential access to credit and foreign exchange have been extremely attractive rewards. Rules have centered on economic performance, primarily a well-understood imperative to export. Referees, the government officials who have designed and supervised the contests, have been generally competent and fair.

At the same time, participation has not been mandatory: firms that preferred to sit out a contest have not been punished for doing so. In some instances, such as Honda's shift from motorcycle to automobile manufacturing at a time when Japanese officials considered the automotive field saturated, this tolerance of nonconformists has paid off handsomely.

Contests won't work everywhere, as the preponderance of unproductive subsidies in developing economies that proffer rewards but lack adequate rules and referees makes clear. Moreover, even in economies with strong government institutions, running contests becomes harder as firms grow and their power increases in relation to that of the bureaucracy. As Japanese officials who are now moving away from contests toward a more functional approach to incentives have discovered, running a party game for children is one thing, and doing it for professional wrestlers is quite another.

export contests for access to credit and sometimes foreign exchange. While export credit schemes varied widely, all made credit available to firms with confirmed export orders. For many small and medium-scale enterprises, export credits were their only access to the formal financial sector (Levy 1993). Monitoring performance was simple; firms were required to show evidence of export orders to receive credit.

In Korea and Taiwan, China, export contests were more elaborate. Not only did export projects get easier access to funds, but firms that exported successfully had an easier time getting future loans. Because such credit was fungible and credit generally was tight, firms sometimes diverted export financing to higher-yielding nonexport investments. Thus exports became a performance criterion for projects that were not directly aimed at serving the export market. In these cases monitoring problems were greater, since both export performance and the related projects needed to be monitored.

A second type of contest used the power of government to grant licenses. Table 2.2 shows two of these contests, based on Japanese experience. In the first, the Bank of Japan created a contest in which commercial banks competed to provide financial services in line with government policy—for example, by opening rural branches—in hopes of winning highly sought-after urban branch licenses. The contest also gave banks a strong incentive to comply with technically nonbinding

Table 2.2 Examples of Contests

Economy	Rules	Rewards	Referees
Export credit			
Japan Korea, Rep. of Taiwan, China Malaysia	Firms have to have an export order, often verified through a letter of credit (LC). In Korea and Malaysia, indirect exporters (or suppliers to exporters) may present a domestic LC.	Automatic access to postshipment and, in some cases (Korea and Malaysia), longer-term pre-shipment export credit for all exporters. The Central Bank automatically rediscounts export bills (often based on LCs) at concessional rates of interest. In Korea, export credits were generous and were often used to fund other activities.	Central banks, commercial banks, and eligible financial institutions.
Japan Korea, Rep. of Taiwan, China	Firms have to demonstrate good sustained export performance. In Korea, past export performance was a major criterion in obtaining government licenses to produce priority products.	(a) Access to concessional credit, over and above export credit. (b) In Korea, incentives (for example, concessional credit, exemptions from import duties, tax exemptions) provided to producers of priority products.	Ministry of finance, central bank.
Korea, Rep. of Singapore Hong Kong	Firms have to have an export order, often verified by an LC.	An export credit corporation (often government-created) provides export credit insurance at subsidized rates.	Ministry of finance, export credit corporation.
Rationalization programs			
Japan	One of the objectives of the First Temporary Measure for the Machine Industry Promotion Law (1956–60) was to raise the quality of machine tools and to lower production costs by 20 percent. Another objective of the measure was to raise the quality of locally produced auto parts to international standards and to lower the 60 percent cost disadvantage of Japanese auto parts (vis-à-vis international competitors) in 1955 by 12.5 percent in 1960 and by an additional 15–30 percent in 1963. Another target was to double the volume of production of autoparts between 1960 and 1963.	Mainly preferential credit from government financial institutions, such as the Japan Development Bank (JDB) and the concomitant ready access to credit from private financial institutions.	Agencies of the Ministry of Finance and MITI, government financial institutions, and the relevant deliberation council.
	The goal of the First Steel Industry Rationalization Program was to shift capital investments toward rolled steel, with priority to modernizing rolling equipment. Another goal was to build integrated and modern steel factories.	Preferential credit from government financial institutions, and in addition, access to special depreciation schemes, exemptions of tariffs on important machines, deduction from taxes of export-related income, and approval of technology licenses (plus priority allocation for foreign currency).	Bank of Japan, Ministry of Finance

(Table continues on the following page.)

Table 2.2 (continued)

Economy	Rules	Rewards	Referees
	Bank licensing		
	City banks did not dispense subsidized long-term credit but often co-financed many of the loans packaged by the JDB, as well as purchased the financial debentures issued by long-term credit banks. City banks were also often involved in financial workouts during crisis situations. For prudence and other objectives, central banks and the Ministry of Finance impose regulations (formal and informal) on lending of city banks.	City Banks that co-financed with JDB or bought long-term debentures gained access to the preferential loans by the Bank of Japan (and could use the debentures as collateral). The Bank of Japan often provided more lenient treatment (for example, in granting applications for branch expansion) to city banks that it perceived as cooperative in co-financing loans as well as in following regulations.	Japan Development Bank, Ministry of Finance
	In the 1980s, firms receiving credit for JDB demonstrated higher R&D investments and better sales records in the past.	Access to cheaper credit by JDB.	Japan Development Bank
	Research and development		
Korea, Rep. of	During the HCI period: When the government initiated a large project or granted a license (for example, to produce television sets), it chose entrepreneurs to undertake the investment on the basis of past business performance often using as proxy their previous exports). The government exercised more discretion than in automatic export credit schemes since it had room to make choices based on more arbitrary criteria. But since past performance was used, this rule set a contest among successful incumbents and favored the expansion of successful conglomerates into other activities. Small exporters had the opportunity to build a reputation through exporting and thereby become one of the contest participants.	Subsidized credit, technology import licenses, etc. (Bad performers found their short-term credit not rolled over or their managements changed by government).	Ministry of finance, Bank of Korea, and commercial banks
	Financial institutions were subject to policy loans, or loans to the government's priority activities.	Financial institutions that complied found easier access to central bank rediscount facilities.	Bank of Korea, Ministry of finance

Sources: For information on export credit systems, see various Central Bank reports of the respective economies. For Japan: (a) Rationalization programs, JDB/JERI (1993); (b) bank licensing, Yoshino (1993); (c) research and development, Calomiris and Himmelberg (1993). For Korea, interviews.

administrative guidance of their lending: banks that failed to comply with guidance about the spread between deposit and lending rates were not permitted to expand their branch networks (Yoshino 1993).

During the rapid growth period, the Ministry of International Trade and Industry (MITI) licensed capacity expansion in several key industries—usually heavy and chemical industries. In the 1950s and 1960s, MITI limited entry and restricted competing imports. Firms in the protected industry were required to coordinate investments to prevent excessive expansion of capacity, but they were also required to compete. Firms that received "extra profits due to regulation" (quasi-rents) were required to reinvest these profits in activities that would result in economies of scale or learning (Ito 1993). These in turn contributed to declining real product prices and increasing market shares. Thus, firms competed for domestic market share within a framework of "orderly capacity expansion." Success was further judged by the extent to which economies of scale or learning permitted industries to expand export market shares.

Our final example is that of the coordination of investments in Korea under the HCI drive. This is the most complex example we have of a contest, one that combined licensing of capacity, access to credit, and protection against competing imports with both physical and economic targets for performance. Its economic success is still not clearly established, and many observers have judged it a failure, but it illustrates very well the use of contests.[7]

At the heart of the HCI drive was the goal of changing industrial structure toward more capital- and knowledge-intensive industries through coordinating public and private investments. Large private companies, the "chaebol," bid on individual, large-scale investments—for example, electronics, shipbuilding, and machinery—for which they received exclusive licenses combined with generous access to credit. The rewards consisted of quasi-rents due to import restrictions and restrictions on entry, access to credit in a highly credit-constrained system, and government support during business cycle downturns.

These incentives have been the source of disastrous economic performance in other economies. The check on poor performance in Korea was the result of two performance-based rules. First, government established a timetable for the attainment of international competitiveness in each industrial sector. Firms that failed to maintain the pace of cost reductions in line with the international norms faced both political and economic sanctions (Kim and Leipziger 1993). Second, because access to credit, even at early nonexporting stages of the development of HCI investments, was linked to the export performance of other products produced by the chaebol, efforts to maintain export competitiveness across a wide range of products were encouraged.

The Rules of the Game: Exports as a Yardstick. Contests are only as beneficial as their rules. If performance criteria channel effort into unproductive activities, there will be little benefit to the economy.[8] If rewards are unrelated to effort, contests will not increase competition. There is one common thread among all of the contests outlined above. Exports, and especially manufactured, nontraditional exports, were the yardstick against which the success of other allocation decisions—for example, credit allocation, domestic content requirements, and industrial licensing—were judged. Accordingly, there was a high degree of competition among firms, in spite of the fact that in certain domains and at certain times they acted cooperatively. The export performance rule was broadly shared among HPAE governments and is almost unique to the East Asian economies. Chapter 3 illustrates how each of the HPAEs used shifting combinations of fundamental policies and selective interventions to maintain the pro-export orientation. Box 2.3 describes how some HPAEs used apparent constraints on their ability to export to create export contests to new markets.

Using exports as a performance yardstick generated substantial economic benefits. A firm's success in the export market is a good indicator of economic efficiency—a much better indicator, in fact, than success in a domestic market. Export markets are likely to be much more competitive than domestic markets. Even if the firm's success is based on finding a niche in a foreign market, its contribution to the domestic economy is still as large as if it had succeeded by developing new production processes or otherwise boosting efficiency.[9]

Box 2.3 Turning a Constraint into a Contest

AS A CONSEQUENCE OF THEIR RAPID EXPORT GROWTH (OUT-lined in chapter 1), many of the HPAEs encountered so-called voluntary export restraints (VERs), limits on their exports negotiated with trading partners in the face of threatened unilateral ceilings. Some of the HPAEs' governments turned this apparent constraint into another contest.

Approaches to allocating VER quotas among exporters vary. Most developing-economy governments distribute quotas to established exporters according to their market share prior to the imposition of VERs. But Korea, Malaysia, Singapore, and Taiwan, China, have used a two-tier system, allocating part of the quota according to prior market share and the remainder as rewards to those who export successfully to unrestricted markets. They created a contest for the privilege of selling in the higher-priced markets subject to VERs.

Such contests are useful to the exporting economy in several ways. In addition to boosting overall exports and foreign exchange earnings, they encourage exporters to establish new market positions. Moreover, quota contests force firms to compete for access to protected markets by selling in more competitive, unrestricted markets, giving firms a strong incentive to maintain and upgrade their productivity. Quota contests are not an unmitigated good, however. They can provide incentives for selling below cost in unrestricted markets and may trigger antidumping actions or the imposition of VERs in previously open markets.

There are, of course, other advantages associated with exports. In the process of entering international markets, firms learn a great deal and not only about the particular markets they are entering. There are spill-overs related both to marketing know-how and to production know-how, topics to which we shall return in chapter 6. For instance, success in the production of intermediate goods requires producing to standards that are typically higher than those that prevail within developing economies. The contacts made in the process of exports may also be of value when the firm decides to enter related markets. It will know to whom to turn to acquire advanced technology.

While from a social perspective, success in exporting may be a better indicator of whether a firm merits additional funds than success in selling domestically, banks have (in the absence of government prodding) typically preferred domestic lending to foreign lending, and for a simple reason (Stiglitz 1993b). Banks are likely to be less informed concerning external markets than they are concerning internal markets, and from the bank's perspective, there is greater risk associated with lending for export-oriented projects than with lending for products for the domestic market.

HPAE governments were also less heavy-handed than some others that have attempted selective interventions. Though they made mistakes of judgment, they generally did not force decisions on others who were willing to risk their own capital. (The creation of the Mitsubishi Automobile Company in 1965, rejecting MITI's guidance to refrain from entering the production of automobiles, is a case in point.) This is one of the strengths of decentralized decisionmaking: it provides insurance against mistaken views being given too much dominance.

Running the Game: The Role of Referees. Referees are also fundamental to contests. Someone must enforce the rules, administer the rewards, and discourage cheating. If one group of participants in a contest captures it and turns it to their advantage, they will reap rewards without the necessary effort. If some participants feel that others are excessively favored, they will refuse to abide by the rules.

In the contests described above, the referees varied. For export credit, the contest was largely self-enforcing. Banks had the incentive to monitor export performance, since execution of the export order was essential to repayment. Banking supervisors and customs authorities could also use their coercive power to enforce the rules. In the case of banking in Japan, the supervisory authorities of the Bank of Japan were responsible for running the contest. The officials of MITI were the arbiters of industrial policy in Japan, and in Korea during the HCI drive both the political leadership and the economic administration monitored performance.

The Limits and Constraints of Contests

What determines whether contests can be effectively used to promote better allocation and faster growth? There appear to be two important elements: the relative benefits of coordinated behavior and the institutional costs of implementing nonmarket, contest-based competitive discipline.

Where the benefits of coordinated behavior are not great—for example, in small, highly open economies with good entrepreneurial skills and small nontraded goods sectors—the benefits of coordination of investment decisions or sharing of information are likely to be small. International prices convey sufficient information for markets to be efficient, and social and private returns will coincide. This may explain why HPAEs such as Hong Kong and Singapore have not found it worthwhile to run contests and establish the types of highly structured information-sharing mechanisms (deliberative councils) found in Japan and Korea, despite the high quality of their bureaucracies.

Even in cases where coordination benefits are potentially large—in nontraded goods, externalities, or interdependent investments—governments may not be able to enforce performance-based coordination rules. Taiwan, China, is an example. Despite benefits from coordinated behavior that were presumably potentially as large as in Korea, and the presence of a high-quality civil service, contests of the types employed in Japan and Korea were not used. This may have been due to Taiwan, China's, different industrial structure. With a large number of small and medium-scale firms, in contrast to Japan's and Korea's relatively small number of major industrial groups, the institutional costs of attempting to coordinate all but the simplest activities were prohibitive. Instead, Taiwan, China, addressed the coordination problem through public investment in large, indivisible industries.

The absence of effective contests—except for the export contest—in the Southeast Asian economies, Indonesia, Malaysia, and Thailand, can also be interpreted as a case of high institutional costs. Civil services in these economies are not well insulated from political or economic interference. It is not surprising, then, that efforts to coordinate economic activity through selective interventions have been less successful. The contests either have had poorly defined rules or have been hijacked by their participants.

These two factors may also explain why the reliance on contest-based competition may change over time in the same economy. Box 2.4 documents the changing nature of industrial policy in Japan, from selective to functional incentives and from extensive reliance on contests during the rapid growth period to market-based competition in the 1990s. In large measure this is due to perceptions among policymakers that the large benefits from coordination characteristic of the rapid growth pe-

---

Box 2.4 The Shifting Goals of Industrial Policy in Japan

JAPAN'S MINISTRY OF INTERNATIONAL TRADE AND Industry has employed industrial policy in various forms since the end of World War II, adapting its strategy as required by the changing external environment and the growing complexity of the economy. As policy goals and the tools to achieve them changed over time so, too, did the industries and firms that benefited.

Throughout, industrial policy has sought to protect infant industries from foreign competition while using various measures to increase exports. To meet these goals, MITI has focused on four major areas: creating infrastructure for all industries, allocating resources among industries, restructuring individual industries, and helping small and medium-size firms.

In the immediate postwar period, Japan's industrial policy was akin to socialist economic planning. The economy was devastated, and industries suffered from chronic shortages of productive capacity. Targeted for special government assistance were coal and steel. Preferential loans, price controls and subsidies, and import restrictions all played a role.

In the 1950s, with reconstruction largely complete and the economy facing new challenges, the government gave markets much greater leeway, attempting to shape the economy through extensive tax incentives. Favored industries included shipbuilding, electric power, synthetic fibers, chemical fertilizers, petrochemicals, machine tools, and electronics, as well as steel and coal. In general, industrial policies

succeeded for industries with scale economies (steel, for instance) and failed for those without (such as coal). MITI, believing that Japanese companies could not withstand foreign competition, set about strengthening industry. The ministry organized megamergers, coordinated investment to avoid overcapacity, coordinated the specialization of small and medium-size companies, and established a comprehensive energy policy.

In the 1970s, Japan began its integration into the international economic system. To qualify for membership in international organizations such as the General Agreement on Tariffs and Trade, the International Monetary Fund, and the Organization for Economic Cooperation and Development, Japan had to show a schedule for liberalizing import quotas, tariffs, and capital controls. MITI shifted industrial policy to pursue objectives other than growth, including pollution control and other environmental aims, and shifted to more functionally based and less selective incentives. But Japan was bedeviled by its success. The rapid expansion of its exports stirred protests. In the late 1970s and 1980s, and continuing in the early 1990s, it faced increasing conflict with its major trading partners. Ever resourceful and flexible, Japan's industrial policy came to include measures to prevent trade conflicts and to control and limit the damage from those that occurred.

Source: Ito (1992).

riod had diminished as the economy grew and became more complex, and that the institutional costs of administering contests had increased as power shifted from government administrators to enterprises. Similar concerns appear to be driving recent changes in Korean industrial policies (Kim and Leipziger 1993).

■ ■ ■

The search for policy explanations for East Asia's success has not been completely successful. Each of the broad views of the relationship between public policy and rapid growth—neoclassical, revisionist, and market-friendly—adds important elements to our understanding, but none fully captures the complexity of public policy and rapid growth in the HPAEs. We have proposed using a functional approach to understanding the relationship between policies and growth. In this view, policies contribute to the attainment of three central functions: accumulation, allocation, and productivity growth. Market-oriented policies, the fundamentals, were widely used by all the HPAEs and formed the basis for their rapid growth. More interventionist policies have the potential to contribute to growth in cases where they address economic coordination problems, but to succeed they must combine the benefits of cooperation with competitive discipline by creating contests.

Effective implementation of contests depended on two sets of factors almost unique to the northern HPAEs. The first is the competence, insulation, and relative lack of corruptibility of the public administrations in Japan and Korea. The historical origins of these economies' high-quality economic administrations and the mechanisms that they used to maintain quality and limit political influence and corruption are the subject of chapter 4. The second is the pragmatism and flexibility of governments in the high-performing East Asian economies where contests were tried and abandoned or continued depending on their results. We examine this flexibility in policy formulation in two important areas, macroeconomic management and promotion of exports, in the next chapter.

Notes

1. For good examples, see Balassa (1982), Bhagwati (1978), Krueger (1978), and Little, Scitovsky, and Scott (1970).

2. Moreover, some of the measures presented, such as those of Itoh and Kiyono (1988) for Japan, are probably minimum estimates insofar as their calculations of effective rates of protection (ERPs) are based on tariff data, not on estimates of nominal levels of protection derived from comparisons of domestic and international prices. On Korea, see Pack and Westphal (1986) and the references cited therein. On Taiwan, China, see Wade (1990). On Japan, see Itoh and Kiyono (1988). Wade does not present or cite estimates of effective rates of protection in Taiwan, China, for the period after 1969, while the other two present evidence on ERPs for Japan and Korea. Conversely, Wade does offer carefully documented qualitative evidence of the extent of selective intervention. Despite the frequent use of Taiwan, China, as a model of limited intervention, there are no estimates of which we are aware of effective rates of protection or domestic resource cost for the period after 1970.

3. See Yamawaki (1988) on the steel industry, Mutoh (1988) on cars, Yamazawa (1988) on textiles, Yonezawa (1988) on shipbuilding, and Tanaka (1988) on aluminum refining.

4. A formal exposition of this concept is contained in Page and Petri (1993).

5. Popular discussions of the success of Japan and several other economies of East Asia have stressed the cooperative relations between government and business, between workers and employers, and among businesses. This phenomenon is sometimes referred to as "Japan, Inc." or "Malaysia, Inc.," conveying an impression of a single-minded direction to economic activity, promoting the collective interests of the economy. Clearly, this popular image exaggerates. Like all governments, governments in East Asia lack the control to enforce a common set of goals.

6. The list is by no means exhaustive, nor does it include examples of failed contests, of which there are many.

7. See, for example, Kim and Leipziger (1993) for a discussion of the institutional features of the HCI drive and an evaluation of the success of the program.

8. Amsden (1989) in a seminal work outlines the nature of performance criteria used in Japan and Korea to discipline interventionist policies.

9. Again, this is perhaps not quite accurate; there may be spillovers from learning how to produce some commodity more cheaply.

CHAPTER 3

Macroeconomic Stability and Export Growth

MACROECONOMIC STABILITY AND RAPID EXport growth were two key elements in starting the virtuous circles of high rates of accumulation, efficient allocation, and strong productivity growth that formed the basis for East Asia's success. Governments achieved macroeconomic stability by adhering to orthodox policy prescriptions—in particular, by holding budget deficits to levels that could be prudently financed. They achieved rapid export growth through an export push—a combination of orthodox, market-oriented mechanisms, many linked to macroeconomic stability, and complementary pro-export incentives.[1]

Policy initiatives in these two areas shared two features that further illustrate the framework outlined in chapter 2: respect for certain fundamentals—for example, fiscal prudence and avoidance of exchange rate overvaluation; and quick and flexible responses to changing economic circumstances. Policies to achieve macroeconomic stability and rapid export growth differed over time and across economies, partly because governments were responding to a changing economic environment and partly because they were seeking efficient policy packages through trial and error.

We define macroeconomic stability to mean that inflation was kept under control, internal and external debt remained manageable, and macroeconomic crises that emerged were resolved quickly, usually within a year or two. Short recessions and policy adjustments to macroeconomic stress sometimes squeezed the private sector. But these were transitional periods to new episodes of rapid growth, quite unlike the years of recession and uncertainty that have plagued many other developing economies, particularly in Sub-Saharan Africa and Latin America.

Export push is a more complex phenomenon than macroeconomic stability and the variety of policies used is greater. Mechanisms range from broad, export-friendly measures such as avoiding an appreciated exchange rate, which are employed in all the HPAEs, to government-run export contests, which have been used primarily in Japan, the Republic of Korea, and Taiwan, China. Universal export incentives, such as tax breaks and credit guarantees for all exporters, have been the main instruments in Hong Kong, Indonesia, Malaysia, Singapore, and Thailand. Despite this diversity of approach, as a group the HPAEs are unique among developing countries in the attention they have devoted to export promotion and the success they have achieved. The second half of this chapter reviews the evolution of export-push policies in each of the HPAEs.

Pragmatic Orthodoxy in Macroeconomic Management

THE HPAEs WERE MORE SUCCESSFUL THAN MOST OTHER DEveloping economies in keeping public deficits within the limits the economy could absorb; as a result, they were better able to restrain inflation and manage both internal and external debt. Low inflation and manageable debt in turn facilitated realistic exchange rates and the avoidance of the appreciation that elsewhere undermined export performance. When the macroeconomy did go awry, usually due to external shocks, governments quickly implemented orthodox solutions, reducing the fiscal deficit and, when necessary, devaluating the currency. In contrast, many other developing economies have been less successful in keeping deficits within bounds and have therefore had more trouble managing inflation, debt, and exchange rates. As a result, policymakers in these economies have often had less room to maneuver when confronted with a macroeconomic shock; perhaps partly because of this, their response has often been hesitant and ineffective. The HPAEs macroeconomic management superior is reflected in less severe imbalances and generally lower variance in key indicators, including real exchange rates, real interest rates, and inflation.

To be sure, macroeconomic conditions vary widely among the HPAEs. Malaysia and Singapore have long-run inflation rates comparable to Switzerland's, at below 4 percent, while inflation in Indonesia and Korea exceeds the South Asian average of around 8 percent. Singapore has consistently avoided fiscal deficits, while Malaysia's fiscal deficit peaked at 18 percent of GDP in 1982. Hong Kong, Singapore, and Taiwan, China, do not borrow abroad, while Korea was the world's fourth biggest debtor in 1980 and Indonesia's foreign debt tripled during the 1980s. Exchange rate regimes have varied from rigidly fixed to managed floats.

Amid the diversity, however, are some common themes. While some governments have run substantial deficits, none has financed a deficit in a manner that destabilized the economy. The level of the deficit that is affordable, and hence not destabilizing, is specific to each economy. It is generally larger the faster the rate of growth and the larger the pool of private savings (both at home and abroad) relative to private investment. In both these dimensions, the HPAEs have performed better than many of their developing-economy counterparts during the past thirty years. Because of this, while some economies have had higher inflation than others, none has had to endure the very high, debilitating inflation that has troubled other developing economies.

The HPAEs chose a variety of macroeconomic policy paths because of different economic conditions and preferences. All lay within the bounds of prudent stability, and whenever the macroeconomy appeared to be in danger of moving out of control, swift action was taken to restore stability. This was true even when the source of macroeconomic instability was policies intended to promote growth in the real economy. For example, the heavy and chemical industries drive in Korea, to which we shall return below, was modified when its adverse impact on the key indicators of macroeconomic stability, inflation, and the real exchange rate became excessive.

In the following section we discuss how low deficits enabled the successful Asian economies to keep key macroeconomic indicators relatively stable, and we contrast their performance with the macroeconomic instability that plagues many other developing economies. We then turn briefly to four HPAE case studies that illustrate the variety of rapid and effective responses to macroeconomic shocks.

Adhering to Macroeconomic Fundamentals

In contrast with many other developing economies, where boom-and-bust cycles have caused wild swings in macroeconomic indicators, the HPAEs have been remarkably successful in creating and sustaining macroeconomic stability. This has been a potent encouragement for private savings, investment, exports, and growth, since the private sector could count on relatively constant prices and interest rates. Here we consider the HPAE's successful management of four macroeconomic fundamentals: budget deficits, inflation, external debt, and exchange rates.

Keeping Budget Deficits Manageable. The HPAEs' budget deficits are not dramatically better as a group than other developing economies'. But there are two distinctive things about the HPAEs. First, they almost always kept the deficit within the limits that could be financed without macroeconomic destabilization. Second, these limits were higher than in other developing economies because of the beneficial feedback from other good policies.

International experience suggests that the macroeconomic consequences of public sector deficits depend on how they are financed.[2] Excessive monetary financing of deficits leads to inflation; heavy government domestic borrowing drives up interest rates and crowds out private borrowing; large external financing of the deficit leads to debt crises. The HPAEs kept each type of financing within bounds, avoiding the corresponding macroeconomic disease.

The means for restraining deficit financing have varied widely. Some governments established institutional watchdogs, such as the currency board in Singapore. Others took rule-based approaches, such as Indonesia's balanced budget law and Thailand's exchange rate management framework, which until the early 1980s resembled a gold standard. Still others relied on the discretion of economic policymakers, as evidenced by the macroeconomic adjustment process in Korea and Malaysia.

Table 3.1 shows consolidated public sector deficits for the 1980s for three HPAEs for which there are good data compared with a sample of OECD and developing economies. As a percentage of GDP, Korea's budget deficits were below even the OECD average. This helps explain why Korea was able to keep inflation, external borrowing, and interest rates within bounds. Malaysia and Thailand are more complicated. Thailand's budget deficits were about average for developing economies in the 1980s, while Malaysia's were substantially bigger than average. Both ran bigger budget deficits than such troubled economies as Argentina, Brazil, Mexico, and the Philippines. Unlike these and other economies that encountered difficulties, however, Malaysia and Thailand successfully financed their deficits. This was possible for the following reasons:

Table 3.1 Consolidated Public Sector Deficits, Selected East Asian and Other Economies

Economy/region	Average public deficit, percentage of GDP, 1980–88	Rank among 40 developing countries (1 = highest deficit)
HPAEs		
Korea, Rep. of	1.89	34
Malaysia	10.80	6
Thailand	5.80	23
Average, 40 developing economies	6.39	
Average, OECD economies	2.82	
Other economies		
Argentina	9.62	
Brazil	4.02	
Mexico	6.73	
Philippines	4.30	

Source: Easterly, Rodriguez, and Schmidt-Hebbel (forthcoming).

- First, there was *feedback from high growth.* Since growth was higher in Malaysia and Thailand than in less successful economies, a higher budget deficit could be financed. Because high growth increases the demand for financial assets, Malaysia and Thailand were able to absorb higher levels of monetary financing without a rapid rise in inflation. Moreover, their rapid GDP growth raised the level of sustainable domestic and external borrowing (an economy can borrow more for a given debt to GDP ratio when GDP is rising rapidly). In contrast, many Latin American economies fell into a vicious cycle of low growth and unsustainable deficits.

- Second, there was *feedback from high financial savings.* Savings rates were high in Malaysia and Thailand, and much of this savings went into the domestic financial system (as opposed to real assets or capital flight as in Latin America) due to the pro-savings financial policies described in chapter 5. This further increased the demand for money and other domestic financial assets, making increased domestic financing of the deficit possible without resorting to inflationary financing. In Malaysia, the government's Provident Fund mobilized domestic savings for the government's use in noninflationary financing of the deficit.

■ Third, there were *low initial debt ratios*. In Thailand, the initial level of external debt to GDP was very low, which meant that external financing was available when needed.

Because of this, the HPAEs have avoided the inflation-inducing bursts of money creation that afflict other developing economies. Figure 3.1 shows money creation as a ratio to GDP in Korea, Malaysia, and Thailand and in three unstable comparators—Argentina, Mexico, and Zaire. The contrast is striking: while money creation has been relatively constant among the HPAEs, each of the comparators experienced two episodes of rapid money creation when fiscal balances deteriorated or external financing dried up. The impact on inflation has been equally dramatic.

Maintaining Moderate to Low Inflation. Unlike many Latin American economies, the HPAEs kept inflation from spinning out of control. Table 3.2 shows the low inflation in Malaysia, Singapore, Thailand, and Taiwan, China. Indonesia and Korea have higher inflation but still far below Latin America. International experience suggests inflation below 20 percent, a level not breached by any of the HPAEs during their rapid growth periods, can be maintained for long periods without generating macroeconomic instability (Dornbusch and Fischer 1993). Low inflation is a corollary of fiscal prudence: East Asian governments never had to rely heavily on the inflation tax because their deficits were within financeable limits.

Several East Asian governments have made formal commitments to low inflation that constrained their options for activism. Historically, the most important of these was the commitment to a fixed exchange rate; however, all but Hong Kong have since abandoned this mechanism. Other self-imposed constraints on fiscal policies and borrowing, including balanced budget laws and various institutional checks, remain in place and have generally contributed to fiscal discipline and low inflation. (We discuss these in chapter 4.) In general, HPAE governments have been strong enough to alter public spending and foreign borrowing as needed, although in Thailand this has been a continuous struggle (Warr and Nadhiprabha 1993).

Reasons for the commitment to low inflation vary widely but are rooted in the recent economic history of each of the HPAEs. In Indonesia and Taiwan, China (and to a lesser extent Korea), aversion to inflation grew out of traumatic inflationary spirals that accompanied economic and political crises. In Malaysia and Singapore, the success of colonial-era fiscal conservatism seems to have helped shape postcolonial policies. In

Table 3.2 Inflation Rates

Economy/region	Average CPI, 1961–91
HPAE[a]	7.5
Hong Kong[b]	8.8
Indonesia[c]	12.4
Korea, Rep. of	12.2
Malaysia	3.4
Singapore	3.6
Taiwan, China	6.2
Thailand	5.6
All low- and middle-income economies	61.8
South Asia	8.0
Sub-Saharan Africa	20.0
Latin America and Caribbean	192.1

a. Averages are unweighted.
b. 1972–91 only.
c. 1969–91 only.
Sources: World Bank data; World Bank (1992d); Taiwan, China (1992).

Figure 3.1 Revenues from Money Creation as a Percentage of GDP: Examples from East Asia and Other Selected Economies

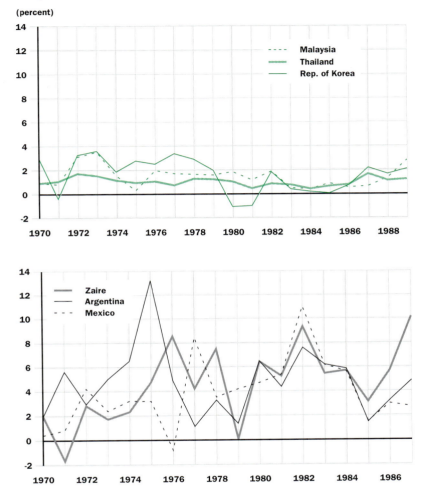

Note: Revenues from money creation as a percentage of GDP is defined as ratio of nominal change in high-powered money to nominal GDP.
Source: World Bank data.

Thailand, the tradition of responsible fiscal policies dates from the nineteenth century, when a strong currency helped the kingdom retain its independence. In Hong Kong, colonial rule has insulated the government from demands for increased government spending.

One result of low to moderate inflation rates particularly welcome to business is stable real interest rates. Figure 3.2 shows real interest rates in

Korea, Malaysia, and Thailand, compared with Argentina, Ghana, and Mexico. As with money creation, the contrast is remarkable. In the East Asian cases, low inflation and flexible financial policies kept real interest rates within a narrow range. For the comparators, the combination of nominal interest rate controls with high and unstable inflation was deadly: wild gyrations in real interest rates created severe uncertainty for investors.

Figure 3.2 Real Interest Rates: Examples from East Asia and Other Selected Economies

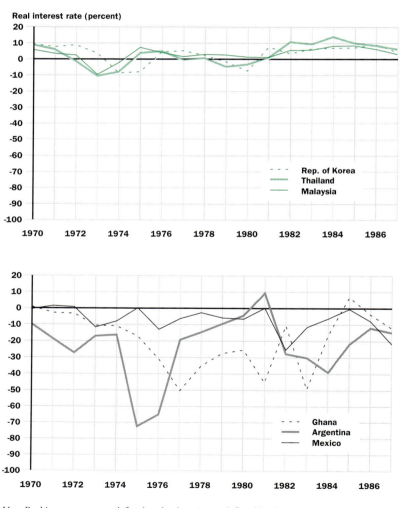

Note: Real interest rates are defined as the deposit rate deflated by the consumer price index.
Source: World Bank data.

Keeping External Debt under Control. Of the seven developing HPAEs, only Indonesia, Korea, Malaysia, and Thailand have public or publicly guaranteed foreign debt. The governments of the others—Hong Kong, Singapore, and Taiwan, China—have not borrowed abroad. None of the four with foreign debt has faced a crisis, in the sense of having to reschedule debt; but sharp increases in debt have led to rapid adjustment. In some economies during some periods—for example, Korea in 1980–85, Malaysia in 1982–88, and Indonesia since 1987—debt-GNP ratios have been quite high compared with other indebted economies (see table 3.3). As with fiscal deficits, however, favorable feedback from other policies enabled the HPAE debtors to sustain higher external debt to GDP than other economies. High levels of exports meant that foreign exchange was readily available to service the foreign debt. Similarly, high growth implied that returns on borrowed capital were sufficient to pay the interest.

Korea's successful handling of a very high foreign debt illustrates these trends. Beginning in the early 1970s, Korea borrowed heavily to finance private sector investment and build up foreign exchange reserves. By 1984 Korea's foreign debt was fourth largest in the world; by 1985 it equaled more than half its GNP. Yet because of its high export-GNP ratio and rapid overall growth, Korea never lost creditworthiness. From 1986 the government pursued an active debt-reduction policy, drawing on

Table 3.3 International Indebtedness

Economy/region	Ratio of total debt to GNP		Ratio of total debt to exported goods and services	
	Peak year[a]	1991	Peak year[a]	1991
HPAEs				
Indonesia	69.0	66.4	263.5	225.6
Korea, Rep. of	52.5	15.0	142.4	45.2
Malaysia	86.5	47.6	138.4	54.2
Thailand	47.8	39.0	171.7	94.8
All low- and middle-income				
economies		38.4		176.2
South Asia		29.6		293.3
Sub-Saharan Africa		106.1		340.8
Latin America and Caribbean		37.4		268.0

a. 1987 for Indonesia, and 1985 or 1986 for the other three countries.
Source: World Bank data.

burgeoning international reserves generated by exports to make payments ahead of schedule; by 1990 the debt-GNP ratio was down to 14 percent. (In contrast, when Mexico faced severe problems with its creditors in 1982, it had a much *lower* debt to GNP ratio than Korea in 1984 but a much *higher* debt to export ratio.)

Keeping the Exchange Rate in Line. The HPAEs avoided the severe appreciation that beset Sub-Saharan Africa and Latin America (see table 3.4). In contrast to such economies as Bolivia and Ghana, the East Asian economies did not cling to a given nominal exchange rate (or inadequate rate of nominal depreciation) in the face of continuing inflation but depreciated when necessary, sometimes quite sharply. Fiscal prudence prevented the excessive demand pressures that appreciated the real exchange rate in such economies as Côte d'Ivoire and Nigeria.

The evolution of exchange rate regimes in the HPAEs has been broadly similar. Hong Kong, Malaysia, and Singapore pegged their currencies to the British pound during the Bretton Woods period, then floated them in 1973 or 1974. The Taiwan, China, dollar was pegged to the U.S. dol-

Table 3.4 Average Appreciation Index, 1976–85

Economy	Index (higher value means more appreciated)[a]	Percentage rank (100 means most appreciated, 0 least)
HPAEs		
Hong Kong	64	1
Indonesia	98	25
Korea, Rep. of	110	41
Malaysia	88	12
Singapore	87	11
Taiwan, China	116	47
Thailand	75	5
Other selected economies		
Argentina	113	45
Bolivia	181	89
Côte d'Ivoire	185	90
Ghana	248	99
Nigeria	277	100
Zaire	201	95

a. Dollar's index is based on Summers-Heston purchasing power parity (PPP) comparisons. An index value of 100 signifies that the economy's deviation from PPP is where it should be, given its per capita income.
Source: Dollar (1992).

lar from 1960 to 1973, then appreciated twice, and was floated in 1979. Thailand had the longest fixed rate regime: the baht was fixed to the dollar during 1954–84, with a single small devaluation in 1981. In 1984 the baht was devalued and floated as part of an adjustment program. Indonesia fixed the rupiah to the U.S. dollar from 1971 to 1978. Because inflation was higher in Indonesia than the United States, the rupiah appreciated vis-à-vis the dollar, necessitating major devaluations in 1978 (51 percent), 1983 (38 percent), and 1986 (45 percent), after which Indonesia shifted to a managed float. Korea, too, tried to tie its currency to the dollar but resorted to four major devaluations between 1961 and the start of a managed float in 1980.

Most moved from long-term fixed rate regimes, to fixed-but-adjustable rate regimes with occasional steep devaluations, to managed floating rate regimes. Hong Kong, the single exception, reintroduced a fixed (linked) rate regime in 1983 in the face of fierce speculation against the currency prompted by political uncertainty. Under the managed floating regimes that began in the early 1980s, policymakers no longer set rates but attempt to influence them at the margin, generally to move in parallel to the U.S. dollar. Because the United States has been the region's major export market, maintaining a stable and at times slightly undervalued exchange rate vis-à-vis the U.S. dollar has assisted exporters.

The HPAEs' success at maintaining stable exchange rates is apparent in figure 3.3, which contrasts the remarkable stability of real exchange rates since 1970 in Korea, Malaysia, and Thailand with the severe exchange rate instability in Argentina, Peru, and Sri Lanka. Argentina repeatedly attempted to use the exchange rate as a nominal anchor against high inflation (for example, in 1973–74 and 1980–81). But failure to keep other macroeconomic fundamentals in line led to the collapse of the real exchange rate and sharp real devaluations. In contrast, the East Asian economies' pragmatic macroeconomic management enabled them to avoid swings of the real exchange rate, even in the face of major external shocks (see box 3.1).

Responding Quickly to Macroeconomic Shocks

The HPAEs' rapid response to macroeconomic shocks has been greatly facilitated by two characteristics. First, by limiting distortions and tightly supervising banks, governments reduced the spillover from the

Figure 3.3 Examples of Real Exchange Rate Variability in East Asia and Other Selected Economies

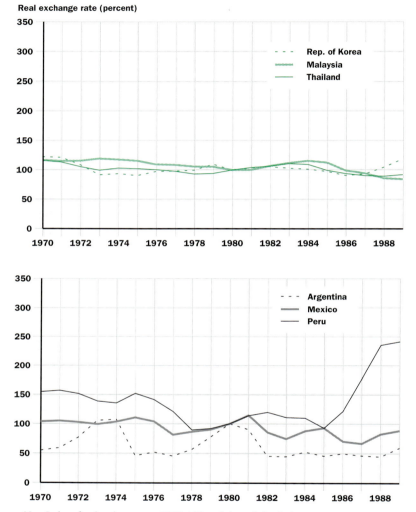

Note: Index of real exchange rate: 1980=100; real depreciation is down.
Source: World Bank data.

real sector into the financial sector that in other economies exacerbated fiscal woes. Second, flexible labor and capital markets enabled the real sector to react quickly to government initiatives, setting off new growth cycles that eased the recessionary impact of stabilization measures. Thus the HPAEs recovered quickly from macroeconomic shocks. Box 3.2 describes two more typical developing economies, Côte d'Ivoire and Mex-

Box 3.1 East Asia Was Agile, Not Lucky

ONE EXPLANATION FOR THE HPAEs' RELATIVELY RAPID REBOUND from external shocks is that the shocks were smaller in Asia than in other developing regions. According to this view, adverse shocks from declining terms of trade and rising interest rates were less severe for the HPAEs than for other developing economies. Put simply, the successful East Asian economies were lucky rather than agile.

But the East Asian economies have been buffeted by the same external shocks that hit other regions. As oil importers, Korea, Thailand, and Taiwan, China, faced sharp declines in their terms of trade during the oil price rise shocks of 1974–75 and 1980–81. Indonesia and Malaysia, being oil exporters, benefited from the oil price rises but faced severe adverse shocks in 1986 due to sagging oil and commodity prices and rising interest rates. Oil price hikes had little direct impact on Hong Kong and Singapore, which depend primarily on manufactured exports, but both suffered from the ensuing world recessions.

Available data indicate that while the shocks to East Asian economies were sometimes smaller than shocks to other developing economies, more often they were about the same or larger. For example, a 1993 World Bank study of eighteen economies that ranked external shocks as a proportion of GDP found that the 1974–75 shocks for Korea and Thailand (the two HPAEs it studied) were smaller than those faced by Chile, Costa Rica, Pakistan, and three Sub-Saharan African economies; about the same as for Brazil and Sri Lanka; and greater than those faced by Argentina, Colombia, India, Mexico, and Turkey. For 1979–81, the study found that the adverse shock from terms of trade deterioration and rising interest rates was about 6 percent of GDP for Korea and Thailand. This was less than for Chile, Côte d'Ivoire, and Sri Lanka; a little more than for Brazil (5 percent); and much more than for all the others, notably Argentina (2 percent) and India (less than 1 percent).

Source: Little and others, forthcoming.

ico, that failed to take timely action in response to such shocks and suffered from prolonged recessions and uncertainty as a result.

Some observers have argued that East Asia has been lucky rather than agile. We examine this argument in box 3.1 and find that the terms of trade for the East Asian economies have been at least as unfavorable as those facing other developing economies. Below we examine four cases in which the HPAEs responded successfully to a variety of macroeconomic shocks: Indonesia, Korea, Singapore, and Thailand.

Box 3.2 The High Cost of Delay in Mexico and Côte d'Ivoire

WHAT IF THE SUCCESSFUL EAST ASIAN ECONOMIES had failed to deal quickly with macroeconomic dislocations? The experience of nations that responded to external shocks inadequately suggests that delays can be very costly indeed. These problems have been particularly severe in Latin America and Sub-Saharan Africa, as the cases of Mexico and Côte d'Ivoire illustrate.

Flush with cash from the 1979 oil boom, Mexico increased public spending sharply, then failed to cut back when oil revenues fell. By early 1981 the need for currency devaluation was obvious. While the government hesitated, investors worried about the coming devaluation and pulled $20 billion to $30 billion out of the economy. Lacking foreign exchange to make regular payments on its foreign debt, Mexico instituted capital controls and nationalized the banks in late 1982, exacerbating the crisis. Fiscal adjustment in the mid-1980s was strong but erratic and failed to tame inflation or restore business confidence. Only in the late 1980s and early 1990s did a further stabilization program finally take hold and bring down inflation.

Problems have been similar in Côte d'Ivoire, which embarked on a huge public investment program in the mid-1970s when world prices of cocoa and coffee soared. Some of the investment was of dubious economic value, like the expansion of the showcase city of Yamassoukro. Public investment remained high even after coffee and cocoa prices collapsed. The resulting huge deficits led to heavy external borrowing, a full-blown debt crisis, real exchange rate appreciation, and the collapse of investment and growth. Côte d'Ivoire, which had been a Sub-Saharan African success story, entered into a vicious cycle of unsustainable budget deficits, failed adjustment attempts, and shrinking per capita GDP from which it has yet to emerge.

The contrast between the experiences of Mexico and Côte d'Ivoire and that of the HPAEs shows how valuable a reputation for macroeconomic stability is and how costly it is to lose it. Some HPAEs got away with brief episodes of mismanagement because they had a well-earned reputation for prudence and because they corrected the mismanagement quickly. Mexico and Côte d'Ivoire lastingly damaged their reputation by not correcting the macroeconomic imbalances in the late 1970s and early 1980s quickly enough. The differences between success and failure can turn on a couple of years' delay in adjustment; in Mexico, two "lost years" of adjustment resulted in a "lost decade" of growth.

Declining Oil Prices in Indonesia. From 1982 to 1986, Indonesia faced rapidly worsening terms of trade caused primarily by declining oil prices. Starting in 1983, the government responded with a remarkably comprehensive and successful adjustment program. It devalued the rupiah in 1983 and 1986 and cut expenditures, mainly by rescheduling capital-intensive projects. The need to reduce a current account deficit without creating a recession was straightforward; the orthodox solutions were effective.

A measure of the achievement from 1985 is illustrated by the following calculation (from Little and others, forthcoming). The excess of imports of goods and nonfactor services over non-oil exports fell from

15 percent of GDP in 1984 to 7 percent in 1988. This shift of 8 percent of GDP measures the extent by which absorption had to be reduced—the effects of increased principal repayments of long-term debt, higher interest payments, and reduced income from oil and gas imports. This massive resource shift, also associated with trade liberalization, was brought about without increased inflation.

Adjustment was not painless. Growth initially fell due to lower export incomes and a tight 1983 budget; by 1985 the economy had slipped into a recession, with only 1 percent growth. Even so the government pushed ahead with the adjustment process, which actually accelerated in 1986. In the later half of the 1980s, perseverance paid off in a boom of manufactured exports that pushed the export growth rate to 25 percent a year for the period 1985–91. Since then Indonesia has chalked up average annual growth of about 7.1 percent.

Responding to Macroeconomic Crisis in Korea. In 1979, Korea encountered a variety of problems that threatened to undercut the 1970s' impressive growth. Rising oil prices battered Korea's terms of trade, the world recession dampened export demand, and high interest rates boosted debt service costs. Korea was not unique in these troubles, of course; these were the same woes that led to debt crises in many economies outside of East Asia.

Korea had plenty of specific problems besides. Real appreciation during the 1974–79 fixed exchange rate regime had made exports less competitive, the rice crop had failed, and the assassination of President Park Chung-Hee had exacerbated political uncertainty (Collins and Park 1989).

Korea had a few structural advantages, however. Unlike economies that quickly fell into debt crises, Korea was not running large and growing budget deficits. And while private savings had dropped due to declining output and incomes, investment remained high. More important, Korea responded quickly to its troubles with an aggressive January 1980 stabilization package backed by IMF standby credits. The government ended the fixed exchange rate regime, devalued the won by 17 percent, and tightened monetary and fiscal policy.

Things got worse before they got better. In 1980, output fell 5 percent, inflation soared to more than 25 percent, and the current account deficit approached 9 percent of GDP. The strong medicine was partly responsible for the economy's worsening symptoms: the devaluation spurred inflation, while tighter aggregate demand policies exacerbated the drop in output. Even so, and despite political outcries over Korea's rising foreign debt, it continued foreign borrowing throughout the crisis, thus maintaining high investment levels.

Within two years, the medicine had begun to take the desired effect. In 1982 inflation dropped to 7 percent and in 1983 to 3.4 percent. The current account deficit fell to 2 percent of GDP in 1983. Overall, the government's prompt and effective response to a potential crisis strengthened the economy, preparing it for rapid growth in the 1980s.

Adjusting to Oil Shocks in Thailand. Thailand only partially adjusted to the first oil shock and in the late 1970s engaged in a mild private and public spending boom. Then came the second oil shock and the rise in world interest rates. By 1980–81, the consolidated public sector deficit was 7 percent of GDP, nearly half of which was the deficit of nonfinancial public enterprises. The current account deficit was also about 7 percent. Because foreign borrowing had been moderate—the debt-GDP ratio was only 35 percent in 1982—Thailand was not facing a debt crisis and continued to borrow. Even so, the new government that took over in 1980 perceived that macroeconomic adjustment was needed. Monetary policy options were limited by the fixed exchange rate and the relatively open capital market. The government therefore took the alternative path, fiscal contraction, moving gradually but consistently during the next several years to cut expenditures and boost revenues.

Policymakers steeply cut deficits of the nonfinancial public enterprises, then gradually reduced the central government deficit. As a result, the consolidated government deficit declined from 8 percent of GDP in 1981–82 to 1.6 percent in 1986–87, when adjustment was essentially complete. Meanwhile, steeper tax rates and tougher collection efforts boosted central government tax revenue from 13 percent of GDP in 1982 to 16 percent in 1988. The adjustment process was facilitated by a 1984 devaluation.

Thai gradualism was possible because foreign borrowing had been moderate and the economy did not yet face a crisis. But gradualism was not hesitancy; conservative fiscal policies were consistent and were sustained into the late 1980s amid an export and foreign investment boom. Since 1987–88 Thailand has been accumulating foreign exchange reserves, and the government has regularly recorded a fiscal surplus.

Correcting Policy Failures in Singapore. Singapore escaped the 1980–81 world recession with scarcely a dip in its robust growth. But in 1985 the economy encountered a sudden and severe recession: growth fell from

8.3 percent in 1984 to -1.6 percent in 1985. Reasons for this unusual episode included government encouragement of high wages between 1979 and 1981, which was intended to speed the decline of labor-intensive production but backfired by eroding competitiveness, and the appreciation of the Singapore dollar's trade-weighted exchange rate. These were exacerbated by a sharp decline in public investment due to the simultaneous completion of several major projects. Private investment, which had been declining gradually for several years, also dropped in 1985, apparently because of falling external demand resulting from Singapore's declining competitiveness.

Recognizing the problems, the government devised an integrated policy package that reversed the high wage policy to restore Singapore's competitiveness and stimulated domestic demand. The government also cut the employers' compulsory contribution to the Central Provident Fund from 25 percent of wages to 10 percent, reduced corporate taxes, and introduced accelerated depreciation. Income taxes were cut and development expenditure was boosted by 21 percent. These policy responses and a fortuitous depreciation in the Singapore dollar, due to the global depreciation of the U.S. dollar, contributed to a rapid recovery. In 1986 growth recovered to 2 percent, and by 1987 it had reached 9.5 percent, a level maintained through 1990.

How Macroeconomic Stability Contributed to Growth

It cannot be a coincidence that all of these seven economies have had exceptionally high growth by world standards, and all have had unusual success managing their macroeconomies over the long run. All but Indonesia and Korea have also been long-term low-inflation economies, while Indonesia and Korea fall into the moderately low-inflation category. Low or moderate inflation for long periods provides a favorable environment for growth.

There are four main reasons why high inflation is likely to be adverse for growth and why the conservative policies followed in the HPAEs are likely to have been favorable for growth. First, economies that are not fully adjusted to a given rate of inflation usually suffer from relative price distortions caused by inflation. Nominal interest rates are often controlled, and hence real interest rates become negative and volatile; depreciations of the exchange rate lag behind inflation, so that real appreciations and exchange rate variability result. As we saw, the real interest rate and the real exchange rate were unusually stable in most HPAEs, compared with other developing economies, which meant that these crucial relative prices were more effective at guiding resource allocation (a topic to which we shall return in chapter 6).

Second, real tax collections lag inflation, because collections are based on nominal incomes of an earlier year (the Tanzi effect), and public utility prices are not raised in line with inflation. For both reasons the fiscal problem is intensified by inflation, and public savings may be reduced. Public savings have been an important component of the unusually high levels of total savings in the HPAEs, compared with other low- and middle-income economies (see chapter 5).

Third, high inflation is inevitably unstable. There is uncertainty about future rates of inflation, and this both reduces the efficiency of investment and discourages it. If the inflation rate were high and stable, there would, in theory, be no problem on this account. But in reality the higher the inflation, the more likely are measures to reduce it. These in turn have a contractionary impact on private investment in the short run. Finally, high and variable inflation imposes substantial institutional costs in many economies. During periods of price volatility, scarce managerial resources in the economy are drawn into financial as opposed to real sector management, as was the case in Latin America in the 1980s.

How important to growth is macroeconomic stability? Cross-economy, econometric studies generally find that higher inflation reduces growth (Fischer 1993). But the relationship is not robust for small changes; an economy with a slightly lower-than-average inflation rate for a longer period does not necessarily have a somewhat higher growth rate. For example, Thailand's long-term growth rate is well below that of Korea, even though Korea's average inflation rate has been higher. Furthermore, there are many economies that have, at various times, had low inflation rates and low growth. The most important case is that of India. There are also cases of high inflation associated with high growth. The most important example is Brazil from 1968 to 1980. More recently, Turkey's growth rate from 1981 to 1990 averaged 5.4 percent, while its inflation rate averaged 46 percent (Little and others, forthcoming). Low to moderate inflation may be a necessary condition for growth, but it clearly is not sufficient.

Relatively cautious fiscal and foreign borrowing policies meant that serious debt crises were avoided, which reduced the stop-go pattern of crisis and response that characterized many developing economies in the

1980s. As noted above, there have been problems, notably in Korea and Malaysia, but they were dealt with swiftly. The Indonesian and, even more, Thai reactions were more gradual but also effective. Avoiding crises and the need for rescheduling meant that creditworthiness was maintained, and it was easier to borrow in the short term and to avoid very deep cuts, especially in investment. Sudden reductions in aggregate demand and in investment compelled by debt crises were major causes of the sharp declines in growth rates in many of the heavily indebted economies of Latin America and elsewhere.

Although macroeconomic stability and prompt responses to macroeconomic shocks were not the whole story of the HPAEs' success, these factors created a basis from which policies intended to affect the real economy—the supply side—could be launched in an environment of stable real interest and exchange rates. We now turn to the most broadly shared of these supply side policy initiatives: creating an export push.

Creating an Export Push

THE GOVERNMENTS OF THE HPAEs HAVE ENCOURAGED exports by fostering a supportive macroeconomic climate and by providing suitable microeconomic incentives. Macroeconomic stability helped exports by easing the liberalization of restraints on trade and by facilitating realistic and, in some cases, undervalued exchange rates. We discuss these issues below. Few generalizations can be made about microeconomic incentives, however, since these economies differed in the degree and selectivity of promotion, and each economy passed through several stages. Because of this and because export promotion has played such an important role in the East Asian miracle, we conclude this chapter with a survey of the evolution of export-push policies in all seven developing HPAEs (these are summarized in table 3.5). Appendix 3.1 gives brief policy histories of each economy in the form of timelines.

Macroeconomic Stability Facilitated More Open Economies

The success of the HPAEs rests partly on what they have done and partly on what they have not done. One thing they have not done is to

Table 3.5 Phases in HPAE Trade Regimes

Indonesia	Korea, Rep. of	Malaysia	Taiwan, China	Thailand
Nationalism and guided development, 1948–66	War and construction, 1950–60	Market-led development, 1950–70	Land reform and reconstruction, 1949–52	Natural-resource-based exports, 1950–70
			Import-substituting industrialization, 1953–57	
			Export promotion, 1958–72	
	Tilting toward exports—industrial takeoff, 1961–73			
Outward-oriented new-order government, 1967–73				
	Selective intervention through heavy and chemical industries drive, 1973–79	Export promotion and import substitution, 1971–85	Industrial consolidation and export growth, 1973–80	Favoring import substitution, 1971–80
Oil and commodity boom, 1974–81				
	Functional incentives and liberalization, 1980–90			
Adjustment to external shocks, 1982–85				Reform and export incentives, 1980–present
Deregulation and outward orientation, 1986–present		Adjustment and liberalization, 1986–90	High technology and modernization, 1981–present	
	Financial sector liberalization, 1990–present			

impose general import restrictions to redress balance of payments deficits. Hong Kong, Malaysia, Singapore, Thailand, and Taiwan, China, had no cause to impose such restrictions, since their current account balances never faced serious long-term deficits. Indonesia and Korea, with more troubled current accounts, might have imposed restrictions but did not.

The benefit of avoiding import restrictions is widely understood. Such measures starve enterprises of imported inputs and are particularly hard on exporters, who tend to depend heavily on imported materials and capital goods. But easing import restrictions without accommodating macroeconomic or exchange rate policy can worsen current account problems, as consumers and firms buy imported goods not previously available. The trade regimes of the eight HPAEs have differed widely, but each has gradually liberalized without incurring a serious current account deficit. Often trade liberalization has been part of a policy package that included devaluation (usually to cushion the blow to import substitution industries), exchange rate unification, fiscal reform, and foreign aid or concessional loans to offset a temporarily deteriorating current account.

The close link between successful macroeconomic policies and trade liberalization can be seen in the experiences of Indonesia, Korea, and Taiwan, China. Taiwan, China, took its first big step toward trade liberalization in 1958 with a policy package that included a 25 percent devaluation, a unified exchange rate, export incentives, and the widespread removal of quantitative import restrictions. In Korea, devaluations and trade liberalization have gone hand in hand, beginning with a drastic devaluation in 1961 (Collins and Park 1989). Indonesia began trade liberalization in the late 1960s, together with the stabilization efforts that marked the start of the Suharto era. The new government abolished comprehensive import licensing and in 1970 united and devalued the exchange rate. After an inward-looking period in the mid-1970s, trade liberalization resumed in the 1980s and has since proceeded together with an export boom.

Exchange Rates and Exports

As we have seen, several HPAE governments used exchange rate policies to offset the adverse impact of trade liberalizations on producers of import substitutes. A few went beyond this objective, however, and used deliberately undervalued exchange rates to assist exporters. In these instances, exchange rate policy and the fiscal and monetary tools to carry it out became a part of an overall export-push strategy. Taiwan, China, is the most notable example of this, but Korea and Indonesia also deliberately undervalued their currencies to boost exports. We briefly discuss all three below:

- The very large current account surpluses that Taiwan, China, ran in the 1980s, especially from 1984 to 1987 (when the surpluses averaged 16 percent of GDP, with an extraordinary peak of 20 percent in 1986), resulted from government efforts to manage the exchange rate. What would have happened if the New Taiwan, China, dollar had been allowed to appreciate more rapidly? Exports would have become less competitive, reduced export growth would probably have had a deflationary effect, and this in turn could have reduced savings. Alternatively—and more realistically—the potential deflationary effect would have been offset by increased public expenditure, leading to a budget deficit.

- Korea used exchange rate protection from 1986 to 1989 when it ran a current account surplus (which peaked at 8 percent of GDP in 1988). A desire to protect the export industries was certainly a factor in Korean exchange rate policy, but the main concern was to reduce the debt ratio and build up reserves to avoid repeating the close brush with a foreign debt crisis in 1984–85.

- The Indonesian devaluation of 1978 can be classified largely as anticipatory exchange rate protection. No immediate balance of payments problem existed, as the adverse effect of the previous real appreciation of the rupiah on non-oil exports had been offset by the rise in the quantity and value of oil and natural gas exports. Rather, the aim of devaluation was to encourage non-oil exports and slow import growth. By 1982, when the balance of payments had sharply deteriorated, the wisdom of the 1978 devaluation was clear.

One can see a fairly clear relationship between devaluations and export growth in the 1980s. Taiwan, China's, real exchange rate relative to the United States depreciated sharply from 1980 to 1985 (the period of general dollar appreciation), and the result can be clearly seen in an export boom to the United States. The Korean real exchange rate was kept fairly stable by numerous nominal devaluations during the period of the first great Korean export boom, 1963–72. The effects on exports of real devaluation from 1982 to 1988 can also be seen very clearly. The Malaysian real exchange rate steadily depreciated from 1987 to 1990, and this must have been one factor in rapid export growth.

The effects of Thailand's real devaluation in 1984–88 on export growth were quite dramatic, even though there were also external factors explaining export growth, notably the availability of capital from Japan and Taiwan, China, for developing export industries. From 1986 to 1989 the dollar value of exports rose 12 percent. All three of Indonesia's devaluations had clear effects on exports of manufactures, and this was particularly true of the 1986 devaluation. From 1986 to 1988 the volume of exports of manufactures rose 80 percent (from a fairly low base), and growth continued right through 1990.

We now turn to our survey of the evolution of export-push strategies in the seven developing HPAEs.

Korea Pushes Exports and Industrialization

Korea's development has passed through three stages and is currently in the midst of a fourth. Unlike several of the larger economies in East Asia, which evolved from protectionist, inward-looking trade regimes toward relatively open economies, Korea did not have a sufficiently large domestic population to contemplate a strategy other than export-led development. Its performance may be described as forced growth, because it did not stem from exploitation of natural resources, an influx of labor, flows of speculative capital, or the adoption of new means of production. Rather, growth resulted from a systematic program of importing raw materials and intermediate goods for processing and export with added value.

War, Reconstruction, and Land Reform (1950–60). Korea had a relatively well-developed infrastructure at the end of World War II, but the partitioning of the peninsula by U.S. and Soviet forces severed economic links between the heavily industrial north and agricultural south. The war took a heavy toll, taking 1.5 million lives and destroying two-thirds of the south's industrial capacity. With a poor natural resource base and one of the world's highest population densities, the south was almost entirely dependent on U.S. aid after the war. For all its devastation, the war may have helped to prepare Korea for an industrial takeoff by loosening a rigid social structure, opening the way for fundamental changes in outlook. While development efforts in the 1950s included several false starts, progress was made in reconstruction, including the restoration of transportation and communication networks. The government also completed a land reform program that had stalled before the war.

Export Takeoff (1961–73). Under President Park, aggressive promotion of exports was combined with classic import protection at home. Korean policymakers maintained close control over trade, exchange, and financial policy, as well as aspects of industrial decisionmaking. In contrast to other controlled economies, they used these instruments to pursue the primary objective of export growth. The trade regime was biased in favor of exports as a whole but essentially neutral with respect to the composition of exports.

Even so, the first instruments of export promotion were highly discretionary. Exporters were supported with multiple exchange rates, direct cash payments (see table 3.6), permission to retain foreign exchange earnings to import restricted commodities, and permission to borrow in foreign currencies. This system not only avoided hampering exporters with restrictions on capital and intermediate inputs for their own use, but it also gave access to the favorable exchange rates determined by scarcity rents in heavily protected domestic markets. Even as discretionary incentives were gradually replaced by more automatic instruments, exporters received significant exemptions from import controls.

Table 3.6 Effective Exchange Rates for Imports and Exports, Republic of Korea

Year	Ratio of EERX to EERM[a]	Differences due to: Exchange premiums plus direct cash subsidies (percent)	Direct tax plus interest subsidies (percent)	Indirect tax and tariff equivalents (percent)
1958	1.79	97	3	0
1959	—	—	—	—
1960	—	—	—	—
1961	—	—	—	—
1962	1.03	-167	33	233
1963	1.28	64	7	29
1964	1.14	29	21	50
1965	1.04	-225	75	250
1966	1.09	-89	44	144
1967	1.13	-69	54	115
1968	1.17	-53	35	118
1969	1.18	-44	33	111
1970	1.18	-44	33	111
1971	1.22	-27	27	100
1972	1.20	-25	15	110
1973	1.19	-21	11	111
1974	1.17	-18	6	112
1975	1.12	-33	25	108

a. EERX: Effective exchange rate for exports; EERM: Effective exchange rate for imports.
Source: Westphal (1978, table 2).

Tariff exemptions were given to indirect as well as direct exporters, and generous wastage allowances on imported intermediates allowed some resale (table 3.6). These enabled exporters to avoid distortions from protection and in some cases to benefit from the protection of the domestic market.

Support for exports was also channeled through the state-controlled banking system. Objectives were implemented through bank loans explicitly earmarked by the government for particular activities or industries, lent passively by banks at preferential interest rates. Following explicit government directives, banks increasingly used export performance as the criterion of creditworthiness.

Heavy and Chemical Industries Drive (1973–79). The heavy and chemical industries (HCI) drive was a major policy shift, away from the neutral incentives of the takeoff period to a commitment by government to use all its levers to steer resources into specific sectors to rapidly alter the industrial structure. Special legislation singled out six strategic industries—steel, petrochemicals, nonferrous metals, shipbuilding, electronics, and machinery—to receive support, including tax incentives, detailed engineering, subsidized public services, and preferential financing. The government chose the first three sectors to enhance self-sufficiency in industrial raw materials, while the latter three were meant to be groomed into technology-intensive export industries.

Unlike other governments that have attempted to build a heavy-industry sector, Korea was at least partly successful. One reason is that the government made clear from the outset that these industries were expected to become internationally competitive. As a result, projects tended to be forward-looking—only current technology was imported, and U.S.-trained Korean scientists and engineers were recruited. (See box 3.3.)

However, interventions were so pervasive that bottlenecks emerged, large-scale debts were incurred, and labor-intensive industries were starved of credit. When the second oil shock hit, inflation was already high, and the exchange rate had appreciated; capacity utilization in the HCI sector was low, and exports were faltering. The government switched course.

Functional Incentives and Liberalization (1980–90). Support for strategic industries was curtailed and abruptly reversed. The currency was devalued, and credit allocation policies switched, with a termination of large-scale preferences to the HCI sector. The five-year economic plan

Box 3.3 Samsung Industries Battles for the Microwave Market

KOREAN MANUFACTURING GIANT SAMSUNG IN-dustries began making microwave ovens in the early 1970s in a cramped old laboratory, turning out a few hundred overpriced ovens annually for the heavily protected domestic market. Today, Samsung makes 80,000 microwave ovens a week and ranks as the world's biggest producer. How did a Korean company with almost no experience manufacturing complex ovens beat better financed and more experienced U.S. and Japanese companies?

The government's Economic Development Board was a key player in Samsung's success. Government officials were keenly aware that the Republic of Korea could not rely forever on low-wage manufacturing. Just as the United States had lost countless textile industry jobs to Korea, they reasoned, so Korea would one day find it could no longer compete for labor-intensive manufacturing jobs with lower-wage neighbors such as China and Indonesia. To prepare for that day, government officials, working in consultation with the private sector, developed incentives for new knowledge- and capital-intensive industries. Incentives varied widely and included the government's

building industrial parks, subsidizing utilities, giving tax rebates for exports, and making cheap loans for investment in new products. By 1980, urged forward by subsidies and incentives, Korean industry had moved into steel, ships, and even cars and was about to leap into world-class electronics.

Samsung made good use of these measures; company managers met frequently with government officials to trade ideas and projects. Even so, penetrating the world microwave market dominated by Japan was no easy task. By the late 1970s, when global production hit 5 million a year, Samsung had made a total of only 1,460 microwave ovens. The company's first break came in 1980, when a U.S. department store, looking for cheaper substitutes, ordered several thousand ovens. Soon production had risen to 100,000. When General Electric, unable to keep pace with the Japanese competition, decided to stop manufacturing microwaves itself and import the ovens under its own label instead, Samsung was a logical choice. The company has never looked back, and it now exports the ovens under its own name as well as buyers' labels.

---

drafted in 1979 recognized that the complexity of the economy was exceeding the government's management capacities. The plan's emphasis on indicative planning and a greater role for the market was eventually translated into a range of financial and import-liberalization programs. Intervention since 1979 has focused on the restructuring of distressed industries, support for the development of technology, and the promotion of competition.

Financial Sector Liberalization (1990–). The key to Korea's future industrial policy lies in its approach to financial sector reform. The government has been coping with the residue of the excesses of the 1970s and has been particularly active in bailouts of sunset and overleveraged industries. The remnants of past policies are part of the price Korea is paying for prior intervention policies and for the failure to establish an independent financial sector.

The Evolution of Export Push in Taiwan, China

Development policy in Taiwan, China, has consisted of five stages in which the government has implemented comprehensive but changing policy packages. Throughout, low inflation and macroeconomic stability have been a foundation for growth-enhancing policy initiatives, and since the late 1950s, export growth has also been a fundamental goal.

Land Reform and Reconstruction (1949–52). When the Taiwanese authorities took over in 1949, one of their first initiatives was an ambitious land reform program. The program fostered social and political stability and increased agricultural production. Greater agricultural output provided raw materials for exports and earned foreign exchange to fund imports of machinery, equipment, and industrial raw materials. These in turn helped to make possible subsequent export-led rapid development.

Import-Substituting Industrialization (1953–57). During the second stage, the government attempted to develop industry as the base for economic self-sufficiency. The government invested heavily in infrastructure, expanding transportation and power networks built by the Japanese; U.S. aid was an important source of finance, funding 49 percent of public investment in infrastructure. Extensive quantitative restrictions and high tariff rates shielded domestic consumer goods from foreign competition. To take advantage of abundant labor, the government subsidized some light industries, particularly textiles. Consumer goods industries such as textiles, apparel, wood and leather products, and bicycles developed very rapidly. By the end of the 1950s, industrial production had doubled. However, the costs of import substitution increased over time. By stimulating the import of capital and intermediate goods while penalizing exports, import substitution contributed to a growing trade deficit, financed largely by U.S. aid. As the small domestic market became saturated, overall growth declined, from 9 percent in the early 1950s to 6.5 percent in the mid-1950s.

Export Promotion (1958–72). Anticipating the termination of U.S. aid and hence a need to obtain foreign exchange, the government shifted to a policy of outward orientation and export promotion. Starting in 1958 it adopted a series of measures aimed at promoting exports and foreign investment. A multiple exchange rate system was replaced with a unitary rate, and appreciation was avoided. Tariffs and import controls were gradually reduced, especially for inputs to export. In addition, the Bank of Taiwan, China, offered low-interest loans to exporters. The government also hired the Stanford Research Institute to identify promising industries for export promotion and development. On the basis of Taiwan, China's, comparative advantage in low-cost labor and existing technical capabilities, the institute chose plastics, synthetic fibers, and electronic components. Other industries subsequently promoted included apparel, consumer electronics, home appliances, watches, and clocks. Direct foreign investment (DFI) played a catalytic role during this period and replaced U.S. aid as the main source of foreign capital. Although DFI was only 6 percent of gross capital formation in the 1960s, nearly 80 percent of it went into manufacturing. More important, DFI facilitated technology and skill transfers, leading to much improvement in quality and the diversification of industries.

The impact of these measures was dramatic. Exports, which had grown less than 12 percent annually between 1953–62, grew 28 percent a year between 1963–72, rising from 123 million to almost 3 billion dollars. The transition from import substitution to export promotion was the most important policy change in Taiwan, China's, economic development. It shifted the economy from a relatively closed to an open economic system and exposed it to the forces of international competition and technological change.

Industrial Consolidation and New Export Growth (1973–80). As the 1970s progressed, internal and external challenges threatened the continuation of export-led growth. The rapid manufacturing increases of the 1960s strained transportation, electricity, and communications systems. The island suffered profound external setbacks. More important, Taiwan, China's, light manufacturing industries faced new competition from lower-wage producers abroad. As foreign investors rushed to the newly opened mainland Chinese market, international confidence in Taiwan, China's, economy declined. The 1973–74 oil crisis had dramatic repercussions for the Taiwanese economy. Real GNP grew only 1.2 percent in 1974 and inflation climbed to 47 percent, while exports declined in real terms by about 7 percent.

Beginning in 1973, the government chose a more self-reliant development strategy based on industrial consolidation and renewed export growth. Once again, it turned to foreign experts and commissioned the U.S. management firm of Arthur D. Little to find solutions to the economic crisis. Based on Taiwan, China's, economic needs and capabilities, the Americans recommended heavy investments in infrastructure, industrial upgrading, and secondary import substitution. A government plan incorporating the recommendations focused on development of capital-intensive, heavy, and petrochemical industries to increase production of raw materials and intermediates for the use of export industries. The government also launched ten major public sector projects, at a total cost of 8 billion dollars, to revitalize the economy and remove bottlenecks to economic growth. These included highways, railroads, airports, and construction of nuclear power plants.

High Technology and Modernization (1981–). As it entered its fourth decade, Taiwan, China, confronted a challenging domestic and international environment. The spectacular growth of the 1960s and early 1970s sputtered to just below 7 percent in the late 1970s. Taiwan, China's, continued integration into the world economy revealed structural weaknesses, particularly the financial system's inability to match the increasing demands of industrialization and external trade. Externally, Taiwan, China's, persistent trade surpluses with major trading partners led to growing protectionism. In the later half of the 1980s, Taiwan's exports faced an additional loss of competitiveness due to the appreciation of the Taiwan, China, dollar and rapidly rising wages. Manufacturing wages rose, undercutting Taiwan, China's, advantage, and local firms moved production overseas. As in other first-generation East Asian NIEs, Taiwan, China, manufacturers were squeezed between lower-wage NIEs in traditional, labor-intensive manufacturing on the one hand, and high-technology products from industrial economies on the other.

Once again, the government moved to restructure the economy. After extensive consultations with domestic and foreign advisers, the government decided to focus on high-technology industries: information, biotechnology, electro-optics, machinery and precision instruments, and environmental technology industries. The shift to a high-technology economy has necessitated the close coordination of industrial, financial, science and technology, and human resources policies. In 1984, the government revised laws to provide tax incentives for manufacturers who allocate a percentage of their revenues to research and development (R&D). Incentives were given to industry to diversify and improve production techniques. The government encouraged the establishment of venture-capital firms and revised university curricula to strengthen science, mathematics, engineering, and computer education. It began to recruit technical manpower from abroad by offering competitive salaries to former Taiwan, China, residents living overseas.

In addition, in 1985 the government launched fourteen major infrastructure projects, including expansion of the energy, telecommunications, and transportation networks and development of water resources and national parks. The government's development plan for 1991–96 calls for 330 billion dollars in public sector projects. To support these efforts, the government has adopted an overall strategy of economic liberalization and internationalization, including the lifting of foreign exchange controls.

While it is too early to assess these policies fully, a few observations are possible. A growing number of small, high-technology firms produce increasingly sophisticated and higher-value-added products. For most firms, however, the transition to hi-tech industries has been difficult. On one hand, the rapid rate of technological change and rising protectionism in industrial economies make it increasingly difficult to obtain advanced technology. On the other, the small-scale structure of industry is not conducive to the costly investments in R&D and skills-training needed to shift toward high technology. As a result, most Taiwan, China, manufacturers are still assembling imported high-tech components.

Malaysia's Shift from Resource-Based to Manufactured Exports

During the first twenty years after independence, Malaysia continued the essentially free market trade and industrial policies of the colonial government, although it intervened extensively to promote rural development and provide social and physical infrastructure. While the government protected import-competing industries, protection was generally less strong than in other developing economies. Government was restrained from heavily biasing incentives against agriculture by the economic and political importance of the plantation and mining sector. In 1957, Malaysia's exports of tin and natural rubber accounted for a third of GDP (Bruton and others 1993).

Import Substitution (1950–70). The objective of Malaysia's limited import substitution was the same as that in other developing economies: reducing imports of consumer goods and increasing processing of natural resources to create industrial employment opportunities. The government did not promote individual sectors, and effective rates of protection were very low, averaging 7 percent, compared with a range of 25 percent to 92 percent in other economies at similar levels of income.[3]

Nevertheless, between 1960 and 1980 import substitution combined with domestic demand expansion accounted for virtually all of Malaysia's growth of manufacturing output (Salleh, Yeah, and Meyanathan 1993).

Combining Export Promotion and Import Substitution (1971–85). Malaysia's 1969 ethnic conflicts triggered a reexamination of development policy. The New Economic Policy (NEP) launched in 1971 had many dimensions intended to promote growth with equity. In trade policy, the government began more active promotion of natural resource exports, particularly rubber, timber, palm oil, and petroleum, and light manufactured exports, particularly textiles, footwear, and garments. During the 1970s, export-promotion efforts were designed to complement the modest import-substitution regime inherited from the 1960s. Major NEP export incentives included taxable income deductions linked to export performance and domestic input content, tax allowances for export-related promotional expenses, and accelerated depreciation for firms exporting more than 20 percent of their output. Credit policies promoted exports through guarantees and automatic rediscounting of export financing at low interest rates.

Export-processing zones, free trade zones, and licensed manufacturing warehouses that permitted duty-free import of materials to be assembled or processed for export were crucial to the successful combination of import substitution and export promotion. Foreign investment, particularly from Japan and elsewhere in Northeast Asia, poured in. By 1980, about 70 percent of manufactured exports originated in the export-processing zones, primarily from foreign-owned firms. As the economy has developed, the proportion of exports from the zones declined to about 40 percent in 1989.

Adjustment and Liberalization (1986–). A combination of terms of trade shocks and fiscal imbalances (described above) prompted the government to move in 1986 away from state-led industrialization. Promotion of private investment across a broad range of sectors was combined with macroeconomic adjustment and continued efforts to increase manufactured exports.[4] Tax incentives for exporters were increased and imports were liberalized. As a result, the average effective protection to industry declined from 31 percent in 1979–80 (an internal World Bank report) to 17 percent in 1987 (C. Edwards 1990). At the same time, tariff reductions and changes in export incentives increased the variation in effective protection across sectors.

Indonesia Tries It Both Ways and Opts for Export Push

Indonesian trade policies have swung from protectionism to openness. The current open phase has gone further than any earlier efforts and obtained the most impressive results.

Nationalism and Guided Development (1948–66). Following independence in 1948, economic policy was shaped by a strong sense of nationalism flavored with anticolonial and anti-Chinese sentiment. Despite several early attempts at liberalization, the policy regime became increasingly inward oriented and interventionist. A pervasive and complex regime of import and investment licenses fostered a new group of Indonesian importers and traders who earned substantial rents and became a powerful lobby for trade restrictions. Following a centralization of political power in 1958, President Sukarno expounded a populist platform of "Guided Democracy and Guided Economy," and the economy entered a period of more direct state control of production and trade. Dutch enterprises were nationalized, and state enterprises took over all aspects of the economy—including the recently emerged import monopolies.

Growing mismanagement resulted in chaotic economic conditions. Inflation accelerated to 1,000 percent by 1965. Exports and foreign exchange reserves dwindled, and debt service exceeded foreign exchange earnings. Economic growth stagnated. By 1965 per capita income was 15 percent lower than in 1958. Widespread social unrest and violence set the stage for a change in leadership.

Outward-Oriented New Order Government (1967–73). The new government of President Suharto moved quickly to restore macroeconomic stability and adopted a more favorable stance toward domestic and foreign private investment. Some nationalized enterprises were returned to previous owners, and a new Foreign Investment Law that provided a thirty-year guarantee of nonnationalization was enacted. The exchange rate was adjusted through large devaluations. In 1970, the government established the mechanism for a market-driven unified exchange rate and abolished controls on capital movements. Sweeping changes were introduced in the trade and incentive regimes, including the abolition of import licensing, although little change was made to tariffs. As a result, non-oil exports increased at an annual rate of nearly 26 percent from 1967 to 1973, compared with annual increases of barely 2 percent during the previous seven years.

Oil and Commodity Boom (1974–81). Indonesia benefited from the sudden surges in oil prices in the 1970s, and the boom in primary commodity prices. The surge in revenue gave the government an opportunity to intensify development efforts, but it also posed the problem of how to protect the competitiveness of the non-oil economy from the adverse consequences of oil-windfall spending. While Indonesia was relatively successful in moderating exchange rate appreciation, the appreciation that did occur increased pressures to protect domestic industry from imports.

Compared with many oil exporters, Indonesia used its enhanced resources well. During the 1970s, about 40 percent of the government budget went to infrastructure for the economy. The government also placed strong emphasis on improving the availability of education, health services, and family planning. As a result of these physical and social investments, Indonesia was able to make extremely rapid progress during the 1970s in reducing poverty and improving social conditions.

Economic growth averaged close to 8 percent through the 1970s and early 1980s, as a result of strong expansion of public and private investment. Non-oil activities remained buoyant, especially agriculture and manufacturing. The government maintained good macroeconomic management and, following a debt crisis with the state oil firm Pertamina in the mid-1970s, a conservative foreign borrowing strategy. By 1980, the current account of the balance of payments was in surplus, and debt service payments were less than 13 percent of exports.

Despite these achievements, the trade and investment regime became increasingly state dominated and inward oriented. Flush with cash from oil and commodities, the government invested heavily in such capital- and resource-intensive sectors as oil refining, liquid natural gas, chemicals, pulp and paper, fertilizer, cement, and steel. As the state's role in the economy grew, the government tightened regulations on foreign and domestic private investment. Meanwhile, gradual appreciation of the exchange rate eroded the competitiveness of non-oil exports, and pressure from domestic interests caused the trade regime to become more protectionist and variable.

Adjustment to External Shocks (1982–85). The high-cost nature of the industrial sector and the end of the oil boom sparked a debate and reassessment of industrial strategy in the early 1980s. The government initiated a broadly based adjustment program designed to maintain balance of payments and fiscal stability while reducing the economy's dependence on oil revenue. As with previous macroeconomic imbalances, the government responded with a combination of fiscal, monetary, and exchange rate policy adjustments. It also initiated comprehensive financial and tax reforms, and made major improvements in customs, ports, and shipping.

As we discuss elsewhere in this chapter, the macroeconomic measures successfully restored financial stability. The current account deficit declined, and inflation was brought to below 5 percent, from 7.6 percent in 1982. But trade and industrial policies gradually became even more inward oriented and subject to government intervention. In addition, the adjustment resulted in slower growth of output and incomes, reduced public and private investment, low rates of capacity utilization, and the emergence of financial problems among industrial enterprises. Moreover, although textiles and plywood both emerged as important exports during this period, overall manufacturing growth slowed in the face of weak non-oil exports and weak domestic demand.

By 1985, a plethora of decrees had brought a wide range of products under different forms of import control. Overall, the production regime favored import substitution relative to exports. As a result, domestic resources were drawn into relatively inefficient capital-intensive activities supplying the domestic market. This disadvantaged the more labor-intensive, efficient downstream producers and reduced export growth.

Deregulation and Outward Orientation (1986–). In 1986, the economy suffered further shocks, as declining oil and commodity prices led to a steep deterioration in the terms of trade and a jump in the debt-service ratio. This time, however, in addition to successful efforts to restore macroeconomic stability, the government launched a program of broad trade and regulatory reforms that opened the way for a decisive shift to export promotion. Export-oriented deregulation has gathered momentum since 1986–87, culminating in a series of major reforms in trade policy, investment licensing, and transport regulations.

The first step toward trade reform had actually been taken in 1985 with steep tariff cuts. In 1986, pushed forward by external shocks, the process gathered momentum. Between May and October, the government announced a package of export incentives, a major devaluation, and the first of several programs to simplify import and export procedures. Major exporters were given unrestricted, duty-free access to imports (see figure 3.4). Later the government deregulated domestic and foreign private investment, and for the first time permitted the private sector to invest in power, telecommunications, ports, and roads. It also further deregulated the financial sector.

Figure 3.4 Effective Rates of Protection

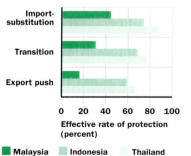

Effective rate of protection (percent)

■ Malaysia   Indonesia   Thailand

Sources: Salleh, Yeah, and Meyanathan (1993); Bhattacharya and Pangestu (1992); Brimble (1993).

The economy responded rapidly as manufacturing output, exports, and investment all increased. Growth accelerated from 1988 onward as a resurgence in domestic demand accompanied the continued growth of non-oil exports. Plywood and textiles remained the largest manufactured export items, but other manufactured exports such as shoes, apparel, and electronics began to grow very rapidly. Foreign investment projects approved by the government increased tenfold between 1986 and 1991, to more than $8 billion, and domestic investment rose by a similar proportion, to $30 billion. Perhaps more important, 70 percent of the foreign investment approved was export oriented, compared with 38 percent in 1986. Since 1986, GDP growth has averaged 9.3 percent annually, the highest sustained growth rate since independence.

Indonesia continues to encounter occasional difficulties. In 1990 and 1991, the economy experienced an import surge and deceleration of export growth due to increased aggregate demand prompted by a prior easing of monetary policies. This led to a widening current account deficit and a surge in foreign borrowing. As with previous macroeconomic distortions, the government responded by tightening monetary policy and curbing borrowing. Meanwhile, the obvious success of export-push policies can be expected to generate momentum for further export-oriented reform. If this is the case, future swings toward protectionism, should they occur, are likely to be less pronounced and less damaging than those of the past.

Thailand's Shift from Resource-Based Exports to Manufacturing

Like Indonesia and Malaysia, Thailand historically exported primary and agricultural products derived from its rich natural resources. Early trade policies emphasized taxation of the resource-based rent associated with the production of these exportable commodities. Trade was heavily controlled. Rice exports, Thailand's major commodity export, were controlled by a state marketing monopoly, export taxes on other commodities were heavy, and a multiple exchange rate regime discouraged export production (Jitsuchon 1991).

Natural-Resource-Based Exports (1955–70). In 1955 the exchange rate was unified, and the state marketing monopoly on rice exports was abolished. Although these policy reforms encouraged natural-resource-based and agricultural exports, Thailand maintained substantial import protection for specific industries. As late as the mid-1960s, however, overall levels of effective protection to industry were modest by developing-economy standards. This was especially notable in consumer goods manufacturing, where nominal tariffs were in the range of 25–30 percent ad valorem. Tariffs on machinery and intermediate inputs were in the range of 15–20 percent.

Favoring Import Substitution (1971–80). In the 1970s Thailand, following the import-substitution strategies favored by many other developing economies, raised tariffs on consumer goods to a range of 30–55 percent. Capital and intermediate goods continued to enter at low duty rates, leading to an increase in the effective protection to value added in import-substituting industries and to declines in the effective protection to agriculture and traditional exports (figure 3.4). The bias against agricultural and export production increased.

Textiles, pharmaceuticals, and automobile assembly were particularly favored. At times, vehicle imports were banned, which resulted in limitless protection for domestic manufacturers. But there was a quid pro quo. Domestic content requirements were established to promote upstream suppliers of components and parts. These nontariff barriers to competing imports of components and parts raised production costs in the assembly sector while subsidizing the producers of inputs. Consumers were in effect taxed to promote an intermediate goods sector.

Reform and Export Incentives (1980–). As was noted in our discussion of macroeconomic policy, the second oil shock exposed weaknesses in the Thai economy that were the result of the import-substitution policies of the 1970s. In 1981 Thailand's trade policy shifted explicitly in the direction of export promotion. Remaining export taxes were reduced, and as described above, the exchange rate was devalued and subsequently moved to a managed float. The government also began reducing protection of local industries and making tariffs lower and more uniform. The maximum duty rate was reduced from 100 to 60 percent, and the average rate was reduced. The tariff reductions were almost immediately offset, however, by the government's decision to impose a tariff surcharge to raise revenue for macroeconomic stabilization objectives. Effective protection remained high into the mid-1980s at 52 percent of value added, higher than other East Asian economies such as Korea (28 percent) and Malaysia (23 percent).

During these early stages of the export-push period, the government Board of Investment (BOI) played an important role in promoting export growth. The BOI, which had been established in 1960 to supervise the application of investment incentives, had long been a tool for implementing the import-substitution strategy. One of its key roles was to distribute (and often increase) the incentives for firms operating in protected domestic market niches through waivers of tariffs, import surcharges, and occasionally bans on competing imports.[5]

The shift to export promotion brought a different role to the BOI. A major study of the export-promotion system was carried out under a UNDP–World Bank technical assistance project. The study recommended radical reforms in the way in which the BOI did business. It advocated using more automatic, sectorally based incentives (in contrast to the firm-specific discretional incentives of the past two decades) and shifting the target of incentives to labor-intensive, export-oriented, geographically dispersed activities. In 1983 the BOI announced new promotional criteria that favored, among other objectives, exports and labor intensity. Box 3.4 describes the impact of this shift on direct tariff investment. Other incentives for exporters included tax exemptions and rebates, reductions in electricity tariffs, automatic access to credit, marketing assistance, and promotion of trading companies. The government also streamlined customs procedures and abolished unnecessary regulations to expedite export shipments.[6]

Automatic and concessionary credit was another major element in the export-push strategy. The Bank of Thailand had traditionally extended refinancing facilities (RFFs), through the commercial banks, to key economic sectors.[7] These RFFs were mostly used to rediscount export bills of large exporters handling traditional products. As part of the export incentives package, the Bank of Thailand revised its rediscount rules to focus more explicitly on small, nontraditional exporters and on other productive activities.

Many of the export-push incentives were specifically designed to offset remaining distortions from Thailand's import-substitution era. Tax rebates, duty-free imports, and export-processing zones corrected partially for existing distortions. In this sense, Thailand's experience is similar to that of the northeastern HPAEs; the initial surge of export promotion took place in the context of a domestic market that remained moderately protected from the rigors of foreign competition. Thailand has recently begun a more broadly based liberalization of imports. In 1990 tariffs on capital goods were reduced, and in 1991 large reductions were made in tariffs on automobiles and computers.

Box 3.4 Direct Foreign Investment Spurs Exports in Thailand

THAILAND'S EXPERIENCE WITH FOREIGN INVEST-ment shows how openness toward foreign invest-ment, combined with export orientation, can contribute to a dynamic export-push strategy. The Thai government has traditionally displayed a liberal and open attitude toward direct foreign investment (DFI). Every development plan since the early 1960s has targeted promotion of DFI, and restrictions and regulations in Thailand have always been minor com-pared with those imposed by other developing economies. Special promotional privileges from the Board of Investment (BOI) made Thailand even more attractive to foreign investors.

In keeping with Thailand's import-substitution strategies, most direct foreign investment in the 1960s and early 1970s was concentrated in production for a protected domestic market. The accompanying heavy dependence on imported machinery and inputs made the balance of payments contributions of DFI at the time minimal, if not negative. However, as the gov-ernment shifted its focus from import substitution to export orientation, the exports produced by foreign investors increased.

The promotional activities of the BOI shifted focus to complement the export push. Previous BOI policies that favored import-substituting projects changed, and the promotion of export-oriented foreign invest-ment became the new policy focus. In 1983 the BOI criteria on foreign ownership of business ventures changed to facilitate export-oriented investment. While the new criteria require majority local owner-ship for firms producing in the domestic market, they permit majority foreign ownership of export-oriented firms; plants whose output is wholly exported are per-mitted to be owned 100 percent by foreigners. The late 1980s saw the Board aggressively solicit export-oriented foreign investment by conducting overseas investment missions and making direct approaches to selected foreign firms.

By selectively granting promotional privileges to export-oriented foreign firms, the BOI created a con-test for foreign investors; exports were the perfor-mance criterion and BOI promotion was the reward. Foreign companies that are promoted by the BOI are exempt from even the modest restrictions that non-promoted DFI faces; these firms are permitted to own land in Thailand, and they may also bring in foreign technicians and managers to oversee and work on in-vestment projects. Moreover, export-oriented firms receive both full tax exemptions on imported machin-ery, equipment, and raw materials, and refunds on all taxes paid in the process of export production.

In part because of the changing focus of foreign in-vestment promotion, Thailand has experienced a boom in both foreign investment and in manufac-tured exports. Between 1980 and 1988, direct foreign investment more than tripled. (Between 1970 and 1988 it increased an astonishing 41 times.) The aver-age export propensity of foreign firms rose from 10 percent in 1971 to 33 percent in 1984 and to more than 50 percent by 1988. Now, more than half of Thailand's total exports are manufactures, which in-clude electrical appliances, machinery, transportation parts, and chemicals; most are produced by foreign investors or joint ventures.
Sources: Christensen and others (1992); Dahlman and Brimble (1990); Lim and Fong (1991).

The outcome of these policy changes was dramatic. By 1986 light manufactures represented 30.6 percent of a growing volume of Thai ex-ports. Leading sectors included clothing, footwear, artificial flowers, jew-elry, and integrated circuits. Direct foreign investment played a major role in the export boom, as firms from the northeastern HPAEs moved more labor-intensive manufacturing processes offshore (see table 3.7).

Table 3.7 Distribution of Manufacturing, Thailand

(percentage of gross domestic product)

Sector	1970	1979	1986
Heavy industries	31.9	42.6	36.7
High-skill, labor-intensive industries	9.7	11.1	13.8
Traditional light industries	19.2	20.1	23.3
Food and related industries	39.3	26.2	26.0
Total	100	100	100

Source: Bank of Thailand data.

The Elements of a Successful Export Push

These summaries of the evolution of export push reveal the plethora of policies consistent with export promotion. (China's recent policies favoring manufactured exports are outlined in box 3.5.) Assistance to exports varied over time and across economies and included preferential financing, promotion subsidies, tax incentives, subsidized infrastructure, and foreign investment incentives. Moreover, at any given time and in any particular economy, the magnitude of the incentives varied across activities. Some governments favored nontraditional exports, some favored particular types of manufactured exports. Even so, there are significant commonalities among these policies. Each contributed to one or more of the four elements of a successful export push: access for exporters to imports at world prices; access for exporters to long- and short-term financing; government assistance in penetrating markets; and flexibility in policy implementation.

Access to Imports at World Prices. When imports are restricted or taxed, exporters are disadvantaged vis-à-vis exporters from other economies who do not face similarly expensive imports. To combine import protection with export promotion, these ill effects must be mitigated. HPAE governments have found myriad ways to grant exporters access to imports at world prices: free trade zones, export-processing zones, bonded warehouses, duty drawbacks, or exemptions from tariffs. However, the higher the level of import-substitution protection, the greater the level of administrative competence needed to create countervailing incentives for exporters. Perhaps because of these difficulties and the declining benefits of import-substitution protection in successful export-oriented economies, each of these economies has gradually liberalized its trade regime.

143

Box 3.5 China's Export Push

AN EXPORT-PUSH STRATEGY HAS BEEN CENTRAL to China's rapid development since the government opened the economy to the outside world in 1978. Mechanisms have included export-oriented special economic zones (SEZs) and open cities; export incentives for domestic enterprises and foreign investors in targeted sectors; and, for some firms, mandatory export targets. Success has been spectacular: in five years, exports grew nearly tenfold to $72 billion in 1991.

Geographical targeting of specific areas as export bases and foreign investment magnets began in 1979 with four SEZs: Shenzhan, Zhuhai, and Shantou in Guangdong Province facing Hong Kong; and Xiamen in Fujian Province facing Taiwan, China. The zones, and fourteen open cities designated in 1984, offer domestic and foreign-backed exporters tax breaks, lower tariffs, better infrastructure, more flexible labor markets, and a minimum of red tape.

The SEZs have been particularly successful in attracting investment in labor-intensive exports from Hong Kong and Taiwan, China. These investors brought new technology and links to world markets, as did investors from North America and Europe. By clustering such investments, the zones generated economies of scale in the provision of infrastructure, and economies of agglomeration, such as opportunities for investors to draw on a common labor pool. These benefits in turn helped to attract more export-oriented investors. In the period 1979–89, direct foreign investment in the zones reached $4.1 billion. Spillover from the zones has boosted growth in the provinces that host them: in 1980–85, industrial output grew at an annual rate of 16 percent in Guangdong and 14.7 percent in Fujian, compared with 6.9 percent nationwide.

China has also attempted broad *sectoral targeting*. Starting in the early 1980s, the government favored light industrial products, textiles, and machinery and electronics by raising foreign exchange retention rights on export earnings. From 1985, the government also guaranteed firms participating in a government export network electrical power, raw materials, tax reductions on inputs, and attractive purchase prices. It is difficult to judge the impact of these efforts, partly because they have been broadly based. The share of labor-intensive products in total exports expanded significantly after 1985. But the effect on machinery sector, which rose sharply and then declined, is less clear.

Finally, China has also imposed *mandatory export targets*, primarily on state-owned firms, through the state-run foreign trade corporations that handle 90 percent of China's exports. These corporations usually guarantee raw material and other supplies to firms subjected to targets. Threatened punishments for failure to meet targets are implicit rather than explicit, but the potential for withdrawal of preferential treatment clearly gives officials powerful leverage. Although data are limited, this carrot-and-stick approach appears to be effective in prodding state firms to confront international markets.

Source: Panagariya (1993).

Export Financing. Expansion into new export activities often requires financing, both long- and short-term. Nearly every HPAE has had some program to ensure access to credit, often at subsidized prices. But again we observe the impressive variety of the types of credit (long-term versus short-term), the degree of subsidization (guaranteed access versus subsidized rates), the selectivity (all exports versus targeted export activities) and the means of delivery (specialized state-controlled financial institutions versus market subsidies).

Market Penetration. Nearly all governments recognized the difficulty exporters face in cracking foreign markets but again chose various means to encourage exporters to overcome these hurdles. Some directly subsidized export activity (direct income tax incentives), some subsidized market penetration (through exporter associations), some subsidized small and medium-size exporters to offset their difficulties in market penetration, and some promoted the creation of international trading companies.

Flexibility. Pragmatism and a commitment to results mark the HPAE governments' approach to export policy. Policy flexibility proved important because hitting the right strategy is not easy, for three reasons. The right strategy depends on the circumstances. It changes as the economy changes. And it is not always obvious. Making mistakes is not necessarily bad, as long as the mistakes are reversed. The classic example of policy flexibility is Korea's reversal of the HCI drive. After a large commitment to promoting heavy and chemical industries, the Korean government nevertheless changed course when circumstances changed and the policy threatened exports. But Korea was not unique in this regard. In each of the HPAEs, policies evolved over time and often required major revisions.

In chapter 1 we showed the impact of the HPAEs' export-push strategy on the rapid growth of manufactured exports. Another outcome of the export push can be seen in their changing composition of exports (see figure 3.5). With the exception of Indonesia (whose exports of refined petroleum products are included under chemicals) all of the HPAEs dramatically increased the share of exports in machinery and equipment at the expense of such traditional manufactures as food products and textiles. In 1991 the share of machinery exports in total manufactured exports for the developing HPAEs was about double that for other developing economies. This shift clearly shows the response of exporters to changing market opportunities, rising labor force skills, increasing technological capability, and changing comparative costs.

What is surprising, however, is the extent to which textiles and apparel remained important exports in the face of shifting comparative advantage. As late as 1991 most of the developing HPAEs had shares of textiles in manufactured exports which exceeded the average for other developing economies, suggesting that these sectors retained substantial cost competitiveness despite rapid capital deepening and rising real wages (a phenomonon to which we shall return in chapter 6).

Figure 3.5 Composition of Manufactured Exports, 1970 and 1991

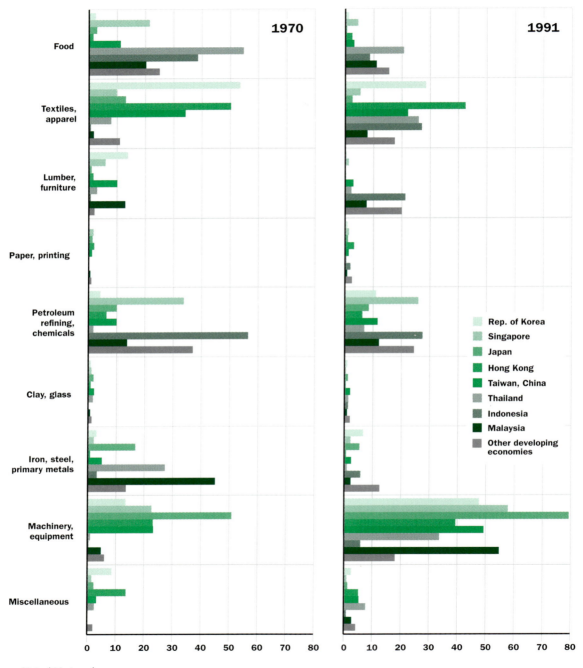

Source: United Nations data.

■ ■ ■

The successful East Asian economies have had much greater macroeconomic stability and much more rapid export growth than most other developing economies. They achieved macroeconomic stability by adhering to macroeconomic fundamentals—particularly by keeping fiscal deficits within the limits of prudent financing—and by rapidly and effectively correcting major macroeconomic imbalances that emerged. They achieved rapid export growth by fostering a favorable environment through macroeconomic stability and by applying on a trial-and-error basis a vast array of market interventions and microeconomic incentives. In contrast to the many less successful economies that have clung to failed policies, the HPAEs have pragmatically chosen and assessed policies according to their impact on macroeconomic stability and export growth. They have adapted policies as necessary, kept those that worked, and dropped those that failed or outlived their usefulness.

Why did the East Asian economies choose macroeconomic stability and exports as their policy yardsticks? And why have they been more successful than other economies in selecting, implementing, and altering policies as necessary to attain these goals? We turn to these questions of political economy in the next chapter.

Appendix 3.1 Economic and Political Timelines

Indonesia

						Pre-oil period					*Oil and commodity boom*	

Operation of subsidiary branches of foreign banks — Ban on entry of foreign banks

Guided economy; direct state control of production and trade nationalization of Dutch enterprises

Reincorporation to IMF and World Bank

Some nationalized firms returned to previous owners

Debt rescheduling

Growing inward orientation

Food crisis

Repelita 1

Hyperinflation

Program of direct credit control and allocation

New foreign investment law; balanced-budget law

Adjustments in tariffs; abolition of import licensing system

Unification of exchange rates

More devaluation liberalization of capital account

State dominance of the financial sector

Pertamina crisis

1948	1958	1965	1966	1967	1968	1969	1970	1971	1973	1974	1976

Sukarno era

Independence

Guided democracy — Coup attempt

Centralization of power after regions' unsuccessful attempts to secede

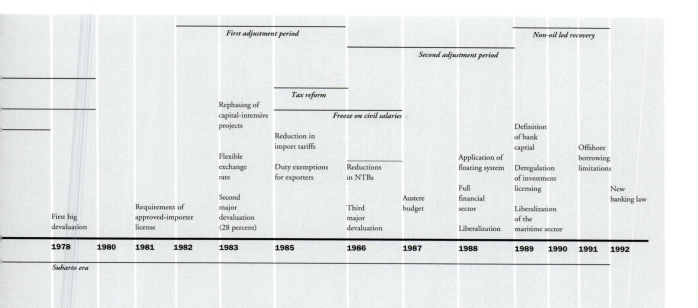

First adjustment period

Second adjustment period

Non-oil led recovery

Tax reform

Rephasing of capital-intensive projects

Freeze on civil salaries

Reduction in import tariffs

Definition of bank capital

Offshore borrowing limitations

Flexible exchange rate

Duty exemptions for exporters

Reductions in NTBs

Application of floating system

Deregulation of investment licensing

New banking law

Second major devaluation (28 percent)

Third major devaluation

Austere budget

Full financial sector

Liberalization of the maritime sector

First big devaluation

Requirement of approved-importer license

Liberalization

Liberalization

| 1978 | 1980 | 1981 | 1982 | 1983 | 1985 | 1986 | 1987 | 1988 | 1989 | 1990 | 1991 | 1992 |

Suharto era

149

Malaysia

		First Malaysia Plan				*Second Malaysia Five-Year Plan*						*Second Malaysia Plan*
									Promulgation of Investment Incentive Act			Creation of Credit Guarantee Enterprise
		Pioneer Industries Ordinance						Establishment of Action Committee on Tariff and Industrial Development	Formation of Federal Industrial Development Authority			Adoption of U.S. dollar as intervention currency
		Establishment of Central Bank	Establishment of Tariff Advisory Council								Free Trade Zone Act	

Market-led development ... *State-led development* / *New Economic Policy* / *Export-oriented policies* / *First Malaysia Plan*

1956	1957	1958	1959	1960	1961	1963	1965	1966	1968	1969	1970	1971	1972

						Inclusion of Sabah and Sarawak				Ethnic conflict			
	Independence												
	Coalition of the leading Malay, Chinese, and Indian political parties, which has remained in power since independence												

Heavy industralization push   Adjustment and liberalization

                                                                    New Development Policy

Third Malaysia Plan   *Fourth Malaysia Plan*   *Fifth Malaysia Plan*   Sixth
                                                                                         Malaysia
                                                                                         Plan

Conversion from a fixed to a flexible exchange rate regime	Investment Coalition Act / Amendment of Customs Act	Financial reform / Commercial banks were allowed to set their own interest rates	Creation of Heavy Industries Corporation of Malaysia / "Look East" Policy	Medium-term adjustment program	Introduction of base lending rate / Privatization Policy	Severe recession	Promulgation of Investments Act			Removal of the base lending rate			
1973	**1975**	**1976**	**1978**	**1980**	**1981**	**1982**	**1983**	**1985**	**1986**	**1988**	**1990**	**1991**	**1995**	**1996**	**2000**

Singapore

	Labor-intensive import substitution					Labor-intensive export-oriented manufacturing			First attempts to upgrade
		State of Singapore development plan				*Unemployment crisis*			

Above the timeline:

1959	1960	1961	1963	1965	1967	1968	1972	1973
Five-year tax holiday for labor-intensive industries	Five-year plan in education; Establishment of Housing and Development Board	Establishment of Economic Development Board; Five-year tax exemption for new industries		Signature of Productivity Code of Practice; Export promotion; Preferential loans to a set of industries	Economic Expansion Incentives Act; Promotion of export-oriented industries; 90 percent remission of tax profits	Industrial Relations Act; Employment Act	National Wages Council	Program to upgrade skill and technological level of manufacturing sector; Open door policy for foreign professionals and skilled workers

Timeline years: 1959   1960   1961   1963   1964   1965   1967   1968   1972   1973

Below the timeline:

1959	1961	1965	1968
Self-government under political leadership of the People's Action Party; Opening of the political study center to train civil servants	Singapore joins Malaysia	Independence from Federation of Malaysia	General elections; PAP wins all 58 parliamentary seats

				Economic restructuring				Retrenchment and further diversification				
				Joint industrial training scheme				*"High" wages policy*			*Promotion of higher-value-added, technology-based industries*		
									Promotion of investment in service industries			

| Strong construction and financial sectors | Capital assistance scheme and EDB loans for specialized projects of industries

Tariff protection fully removed | | Policy adjustments

Expansion of trade into financial and specialized services | Foreign companies were allowed 100 percent ownership

Fiscal incentives to enhance R&D activities

Economic development plan for 1980s | | Reorganization of Monetary Authority | | First severe recession | Light industries updating program | Creation of Economic Committee | Small and medium-size enterprises master plan | Strategic Economic Plan |
|---|---|---|---|---|---|---|---|---|---|---|---|---|
| **1974** | **1975** | **1978** | **1979** | **1980** | **1981** | **1984** | **1985** | **1986** | **1988** | **1989** | **1991** |

153

Taiwan, China

			Import substitution								*Export promotion*		
Land reform and reconstruction										Third Four-Year Economic Development Plan			
			High rates of interest on savings deposits										
			High tariff rates and non-tariff barriers								Require-ment for cement factories to export 100 percent of their pro-duction	Statute for establishment and manage-ment of export-processing zones	
			Multiple exchange rate			Nineteen-Point Program of Economic and Financial Reform							
Introduction of new Taiwan Dollar		Land to Tiller Act		Exchange surrender certificates	Low-interest export loans			Statutes for Encourage-ment of Investment	Single Uniform Exchange Rate				National Science Council
1949	**1950**	**1952**	**1953**	**1955**	**1957**	**1958**	**1959**	**1960**	**1961**	**1964**	**1965**	**1968**	**1969**
Nationalist Party takes power													
Authorities nationalize Japanese assets													

U.S. foreign aid

Industrial consolidation

High-technology industrialization

Direct public ownership and trade protection

R&D subsidies, brand development subsidies

Expansion of China productivity center with automation task force

Launching of ten major public sector projects

Eighth Four-Year Development Plan

Liberalization of foreign capital account

Foreign exchange liberalization

Investment in fourteen additional infrastructure projects

Establishment of standard labor laws

Regulatory controls on bank loan rates and deposits are abolished

Establishment of Industrial Technology Research Institute

Adjustment Period

Establishment of Hsinchu Science-Based Industrial Park

Government targeted strategic industries

Appreciation of exchange rate

Sixth National Development Plan

1971	1972	1973	1974	1975	1976	1980	1981	1982	1984	1985	1986	1987	1989	1990	1991	1996

United Nations votes to expel Taiwan, China

Taiwan, China, is forced out World Bank and International Monetary Fund

Creation of opposition parties

Lifting of martial law

Notes

1. Bradford is among the first to categorize a combination of functional and selective interventions that result in the effective exchange rate for exports exceeding that for imports as an export push. By this definition the Southeast Asian NIEs would not qualify (Bradford 1986, 1990). We use the term somewhat more broadly to include sustained movement toward parity of incentives between export and import substitutes, combined with institutional support for exporters.

2. The analysis in this section draws on Easterly and Schmidt-Hebbel (forthcoming). The data on consolidated public deficits, as well as the rest of the data in this section except where otherwise indicated, are from the same source. Consolidated public deficits, though less widely available than central government deficits, are a much more reliable indicator of fiscal management because they include operating deficits of public enterprises that have played a critical role in some macroeconomic crises.

3. Although the mean level of effective protection was low, variance among sectors was high.

4. The Promotion of Investments Act of 1986 provided incentives for investments in agriculture, industry, and tourism.

5. The BOI's policies of selective intervention to promote firms and specific sectors are discussed more fully in chapter 6.

6. One important example of these efforts was the establishment of export-processing zones (EPZs) and bonded warehouses. Drawing on Korea's and Taiwan, China's, experience, Thailand used the EPZs to streamline temporary admission of inputs for exporters in the zones. The zones also offered lower-cost electricity, freedom of immigration for managers and technicians, and common-facility bonded warehouses to reduce customs and storage costs for enterprises located in the zone. In general these incentives also favored large and often foreign-owned firms.

7. A firm wishing to obtain access to the scheme issued a promissory note, which was discounted by its commercial bank and further rediscounted by the central bank, both at subsidized interest rates.

CHAPTER 4

An Institutional Basis for Shared Growth

I N EACH HPAE EXCEPT JAPAN, NEW LEADERS FACED AN URGENT need to establish their political viability before the economic takeoff. The Republic of Korea was threatened by invasion from the North; Taiwan, China, from China; and Thailand, from Viet Nam and Cambodia. In Indonesia, Malaysia, Singapore, and Thailand, leaders faced formidable communist threats. In addition, leaders in Indonesia, Korea, and Taiwan, China, having taken power, needed to prove their ability to govern. Leaders in Malaysia and Singapore had to contend with ethnic diversity and attendant questions of political representation. Even in Japan, where the competition was less immediate, leaders had to earn public confidence after the debacle of World War II. In all cases then, leaders desperately needed to answer a basic question: why should they lead and not others?

Whatever strategy the leaders of the HPAE governments selected to answer the basic challenge of legitimacy, they included a *principle of shared growth*. The leaders hoped that rapid, widely shared improvements in economic welfare would bring legitimacy.

Of course, few political leaders anywhere would reject, on principle, either the desirability of growth or that the benefits of growth should be shared. What distinguished the HPAEs' leadership was the extent to which they adopted specific institutional mechanisms tailored to these goals, and that worked. In this chapter we briefly review the history of the adoption of an explicit commitment to shared growth. We then discuss the main institutional mechanisms adopted to achieve this goal and how they were created and maintained:

- Wealth-sharing programs designed to include non-elites in economic growth

- A cadre of economic technocrats insulated from narrow political pressures
- Institutions and mechanisms to share information and win the support of business elites.

Achieving Legitimacy through Shared Growth

THE PRINCIPLE OF SHARED GROWTH ASSUMED DIFFERENT forms in each HPAE. It was most explicit in Malaysia. In response to racial riots in 1969, three dominant parties, each representing a major ethnic group, widened their coalition to include other parties under a national front. The coalition's goal was to share wealth more equitably without stifling growth. The coalition's solution was the New Economic Policy (NEP), an attempt to improve the lot of the Bumiputera, the largest but poorest ethnic group. The coalition's own early description of the NEP is quite explicit:

> The NEP has as its overriding objective the promotion of national unity through the two pronged strategy of: (i) eradicating poverty by raising the income levels and increasing employment opportunities for all Malaysians, irrespective of race and (ii) accelerating the process of restructuring Malaysian society to correct economic imbalance, so as to reduce and eventually eliminate the identification of race with economic function. . . . The efforts to attain these objectives were, in turn, to be undertaken in the context of rapid structural change and expansion of the economy so as to ensure that no particular group experiences any loss or feels any sense of deprivation. [Salleh, Yeah, and Meyanathan 1993]

The principle of shared growth is also explicit in Indonesia, where President Suharto advocates "economic democracy." For example, in 1990 President Suharto himself strongly endorsed research results of the Indonesian Economists Association stressing the importance of sharing the benefits of growth. "I hope that ISEI's findings on the system of Economic Democracy receives as much public exposure as possible and that all levels of society become involved in the discussion of this vital issue. This will enable us to reach national consensus as we strive forward toward the full implementation of Economic Democracy" (ISEI 1990). Economic democracy advocates reliance on the free market to stimulate growth. But it also explicitly acknowledges the market system's inadequacies in distribution and actively seeks to redress them.

In Taiwan, China, commitment to shared growth grew out of the Taiwanese authorities' searching analysis of their failure in mainland China. The leaders' five-point diagnosis included three equity issues: agricultural tenants had rebelled against exploitation while the party continued to identify with the landlords; labor unions had run out of control; and government was beholden to vested interests (Wade 1990). These realizations, combined with pressure from the United States to undertake social and economic restructuring, led the Kuomintang to adopt shared growth as the formula for its rule in Taiwan, China.

Unlike the Taiwanese authorities, Korea's post–World War II leadership lacked a synchronized view of growth and distribution. Even so, the sequence of policies it pursued, and the flattening of wealth resulting from the Korean War, effectively produced egalitarian growth. Partly by accident and partly by trial and error, the leadership gradually adopted the principle of shared growth.

In both postwar Japan and post-independence Singapore, growth with equity was the leaders' primary concern. In Japan, the war's destruction of landed wealth actually helped the leadership to implement its redistributive goals. In Singapore lack of a significant rural sector and the absence of a landlord elite also made pursuing equity goals easier. But neither set of leaders was complacent; both adopted effective consultative arrangements between labor, government, and business.[1]

Chapter 1 presents evidence that the leaders of the HPAEs have been unusually successful in achieving shared growth. Growth-rate and income-distribution performance measures show that the HPAEs significantly outperformed other low- and middle-income economies. How did they do this? If adopting the principles were sufficient, certainly achievement would be widespread. The answer must partially lie in the institutions and mechanisms and in how they worked.

To win the support of non-elites, the leaders of the HPAEs introduced mechanisms that drastically increased opportunities to share the benefits of growth. These mechanisms varied from economy to economy but included education (in all the HPAEs); land reform (in Japan, Korea, and Taiwan, China); support for small and medium-size industries (Hong Kong, Japan, Korea, and Taiwan, China); and government provision of such basic amenities as housing and public health services (Hong Kong and Singapore). Nearly all HPAE governments walked a delicate line regarding labor by limiting the power of unions and intervening to check labor radicalism, while at the same time encouraging a cooperative climate in which labor was rewarded for increases in productivity.

These wealth-sharing measures have differed from the typical redistributive approach of most developing economies. Instead of granting direct income transfers or subsidizing specific commodities (for example, food or fuel), HPAE leaders have favored mechanisms that increase opportunities for upward mobility. The frequent result is that individuals and families, provided the opportunity and convinced that efforts will be rewarded, study more, work harder, and save more.

Universal Education

Education is arguably the most important of these wealth-sharing, opportunity-creating mechanisms. The provision of universal primary education and wide access to secondary and higher education contributed substantially to opportunities for upward mobility. This mobility in turn mitigated the feeling of non-elites that society is unjust and made them more accepting of the market-oriented policies needed to foster growth.

In Korea, for example, the government invested heavily in the expansion of education at the primary and secondary levels soon after the war. In the mid-1960s, Park Chung Hee's export-promotion drive boosted demand for educated labor, providing jobs for the first crop of graduates to benefit from the postwar education push.

Equitable Land Holding and Land Reform

Theory and empirical evidence suggest that widespread ownership of land not only improves equity but also improves land productivity (Berry and Cline 1979). All the HPAEs with substantial agrarian sectors have widespread land holding, resulting from either traditional ownership patterns (Indonesia and Thailand) or land reform (Japan, Korea, and Taiwan, China). In Malaysia, corporate-owned plantations have dominated agriculture since the colonial era. But with a relatively small population and ample land, it has avoided equity problems common to other developing economies with highly unequal land distributions. Hong Kong and Singapore have almost no agricultural sector.

Korea and Taiwan, China, began land reform under broadly similar circumstances. In both cases, authoritarian governments facing a communist threat were dependent on the assistance of the United States, whose advisers urged them to adopt more egalitarian land holding. In Taiwan, China, the government seized land from the landlords, compensating them with shares in state enterprises. It then sold the land to the tillers at favorable credit terms and favorable prices. The government then helped the tillers upgrade production for domestic and export markets. The program worked, economically and politically. Land reform helped Taiwan, China, achieve one of the world's most equitable income distributions (Kuo 1976). Political stability benefited in two ways. Newly landed farmers, focused on boosting production, had little interest in radical activities. Former landlords, as new shareholders in state enterprises, had a vested interest in the success of the Taiwanese authorities' economic program.

In Korea, land reform occurred in two stages. The first, initiated by U.S. forces in 1947, distributed the land confiscated from the Japanese at the end of World War II to the tillers and put a ceiling on rents of other land. The second, begun in 1950 and completed after the Korean War, was undertaken by the Korean government after a lengthy debate in the legislature. The government took over landlord properties, paid the latter nominal compensation, and distributed the land to 900,000 tenants, effectively eliminating tenancy.

Enterprises: Small and Medium-Size Are Beautiful

Just as numerous small land holdings improved equity and efficiency, the HPAEs benefited from a profusion of small and medium-size enterprises (SMEs). The large number of SMEs generally reflected market forces rather than government intervention. But several of these economies supported SMEs with preferential credits and specific support services. Rapid growth of labor-intensive manufacturing in these firms absorbed large numbers of workers, reducing unemployment and attracting rural labor. As firms shifted to more sophisticated production, efficiency rose and workers' real incomes increased.

Support for SMEs has been most explicit and successful in Taiwan, China. As shown in table 4.1, SMEs comprise at least 90 percent of enterprises in each sector. Not surprisingly, the SMEs also dominate the export sector, producing about 60 percent of the total value of exports

Table 4.1 Small and Medium-Size Businesses in Taiwan, China

Category	Total enterprises	Small and medium-size businesses	
		Number	Percentage of total enterprises
Agriculture, fishing, livestock, forestry	3,256	3,171	97.39
Mining and quarrying	1,390	1,360	97.84
Manufacturing	157,965	155,263	98.29
Electric, gas, and water	186	168	90.32
Construction	28,419	26,456	93.09
Commerce	489,864	475,106	96.99
Transport, storage, and communications	36,897	35,818	97.08
Finance, insurance, real estate business services	30,534	28,263	92.56
Community, social, and personal service	69,550	69,229	99.54
Total	818,061	794,834	97.16

Source: Taiwan, China (1992b).

(see table 4.2). Other HPAEs have also encouraged small and medium-size industries. Japan has directed enormous financial resources toward developing small and medium-size enterprises. Public financial institutions have allocated an average of 10 percent of lending toward SMEs. During the rapid growth period of the 1950s, as much as 30 percent of their total lending for fixed investments went to SMEs. The various government-supported directed-credit programs have proven particularly helpful during times of transition and rapid change (Itoh and Urata 1993). Although there are mixed evaluations of the success of these programs, one thing is clear. The SME sector has become an important cornerstone of Japan's economy. In 1989, SMEs accounted for about 52 percent of both manufacturing value added and sales, and their share of employment in various manufacturing subsectors

Table 4.2 The Export Value of Small and Medium-Size Businesses in Taiwan, China
(millions of U.S. dollars)

Category	Value of exports, all enterprises	Small and medium-size businesses	
		Export value	Percentage of value of all exports
Manufacturing	436.89	264.26	60.49
Trade	235.25	120.96	51.42
Total	672.14	385.22	57.31

Source: Taiwan, China (1992b).

ranged from a low of 41 percent in transport machinery to a high of 100 percent in silverware.

Korean development has been largely driven by the expansion of conglomerates, the so-called chaebols. But beginning in the early 1980s, the SME sector began to grow rapidly.[2] SMEs' share in total manufacturing employment rose from 37.6 percent in 1976 to 51.2 percent in 1988; while at the same time the SME share in manufacturing value added rose from 23.7 percent to 34.9 percent (Kim and Nugent 1993). Korea established an extensive support system for SMEs. And, as in Japan, financial support systems, such as export financing and credit guarantee programs, have been the most important.

Housing: Successfully Targeting Low-Income Households

Two HPAEs, Hong Kong and Singapore, intervened heavily in housing markets to win the support and cooperation of non-elites. By providing low-cost housing for the majority of residents, both programs have helped to decrease inequality and minimize social unrest, thus providing the long-term stability attractive to investors. Moreover, the massive construction effort created jobs when both economies faced high unemployment; subsequently, the wide availability of low-cost housing for workers helped to hold down wage demands, subsidizing labor-intensive manufacturing.

In Hong Kong, which has generally followed a laissez-faire approach to the economy, mass housing programs were a response to a massive influx of refugees and migrants from China. The rapid increase in Hong Kong's population from 600,000 in 1945 to 2.4 million in 1950 spawned slum areas, high unemployment, and poverty. These led to social disturbances, which culminated in riots in 1967. To diffuse the tension and improve living conditions of the general public, in 1972 the government launched a fast- track public housing program that has since expanded to include the construction of entire new towns outside the city proper. By 1987, more than 40 percent of the population lived in public housing.

Like Hong Kong, Singapore experienced a dramatic influx of migrants in the late 1950s and early 1960s and faced similar problems. Its expulsion from the Malayan Federation made matters worse. The government responded by creating the Housing Development Board (HDB) in 1960 to provide public housing to low-income families. As these needs were met, the HDB has turned to development of middle-income public housing and self-sufficient new towns similar to those in Hong Kong. Today 80 percent of the population lives in public housing, and more than 90 percent of the families in public housing own their units. While success in Hong Kong and Singapore has been aided by small territories and populations, the experience of Indonesia suggests that public housing carefully targeted toward low-income groups may have benefits in larger economies as well (see box 4.1).

The Labor Trade-Off: Cooperative Unions Get a Bigger Slice

In Japan, Korea, Singapore, and Taiwan, China (and to a lesser extent Malaysia), governments restructured the labor sector to suppress radical ac-

---

Box 4.1 Giving Workers a Stake in the Economy

LIKE OTHER DEVELOPING ECONOMIES WHERE URBAN POPULA-tions are growing rapidly, Indonesia faces tremendous demand for new urban housing, particularly in Jakarta. Workers unable to afford proper housing have settled in slums, creating many social, political, and economic problems.

To respond to this potential crisis, the Indonesian Workers' Co-operative Alliance, a ruling party–backed union, launched a low-cost housing program for workers in industrial areas. The association builds basic houses of very simple construction and sells them to workers at terms they can afford. Each house occupies 21 square meters on a 66 square meter lot, has electricity and clean water, and can be improved and expanded later, when the owner can afford it. The last characteristic parallels the tradition in rural communities of building houses step by step as resources become available. Each house costs about $2,000, payable with a 10 percent down payment and monthly installments from $16 to $35. The association makes a profit of 1–5 percent, which it reinvests.

The government has helped the cooperative by opening a loan facility at the State Savings Bank, facilitating land acquisition and preparation and providing basic infrastructure. Since its launch in 1990, the cooperative has built and sold about 8,000 units. It plans to build another 30,000 units in the next five years. As in Hong Kong and Singapore, where the programs are much larger, the program in Indonesia is an effort to give workers a stake in the economy.

tivity in an effort to ensure political stability. Governments abolished trade-based labor unions and pushed the creation of company- or enterprise-based unions. Management and company union representatives were then required to jointly formulate and implement work-related policies.

Labor movements in Indonesia and Thailand, while not subjected to systematic restructuring, were nonetheless routinely suppressed at the first sign of radicalism, primarily because of the governments' fear of communism. In Hong Kong, conversely, union radicalism has been held in check by a steady supply of new labor from China and by the influence of Beijing, which has encouraged moderation in the unions under its Hong Kong umbrella organization.

Governments in several Asian NIEs, particularly in Malaysia and Singapore, have modeled their systems of labor relations after Japan, where labor radicalism was quickly suppressed after World War II and labor-management consultations were gradually institutionalized. In Japan, these consultations have led workers to expect that adjustments in their wages will correspond to trends in the national economy despite the unions' lack of political weight. "Labor has been compensated for its decreased political role through wage policies tied to increases in productivity" (Johnson 1982, p. 151).

Like the government in postwar Japan, the government in Singapore sharply limited union autonomy soon after independence due to fears of political instability. Lacking natural resources following the separation from Malaysia, Singapore courted foreign investment in labor-intensive manufacturing by suppressing independent unions and assuring investors industrial peace. To meet workers' rising expectations, the government in 1969 instructed the National Trade Union Congress (NTUC), the officially recognized labor umbrella organization, to suggest new directions for the union movement.

The NTUC, which is in effect a branch of the ruling People's Action Party (PAP), made two recommendations: government, management, and labor should work together to avoid antagonistic wage negotiations; and workers should organize into cooperatives with a stake in the economy. To further cooperation, the NTUC established the tripartite National Wages Council (NWC). Each year, the NWC reviews wage and economic trends before advising the government on wage adjustment guidelines. Although recommendations are officially nonbinding, the government usually endorses them wholesale, and business and labor use them as wage settlement benchmarks. The NWC's effectiveness was evident during the 1985–86 recession, when it persuaded labor to accept wage cuts of about 12 percent. The PAP also reorganized the NTUC itself, transforming it from a negotiating agent to a provider of goods and services. The NTUC has since established a number of worker cooperatives, ranging from the Fairprice Supermarket Cooperative, with more than 240,000 members, to the Comfort Taxi Service, with 5,500 members (see box 4.2).

Box 4.2 Riding in Comfort

ONE OF THE FIRST COOPERATIVES ORGANIZED BY SINGAPORE'S National Trade Union Congress was the Comfort Taxi Service in 1970. It was part of a broader plan by the NTUC (itself a branch of the ruling People's Action Party) to give workers a stake in a growing economy and to transform the NTUC from an organizer of labor into a provider of goods and services.

Before the cooperative was launched, 3,800 registered Yellow Top cabs provided much of Singapore's taxi service. These cabs belonged to fleet owners and financiers and were hired out to more than 13,500 licensed taxi drivers. Because there was a limit on the number of registered taxis, owners were able to charge cab drivers high rents. The result: many drivers resorted to driving pirate taxis, which were mostly ill-maintained, uninsured, and a threat to the safety of the traveling public.

Comfort's start-up capital, a government loan, enabled the cooperative to buy large numbers of taxis at a discount. Under a vehicle ownership scheme, drivers obtained a taxi through balloting. Winners paid an initial deposit and, thereafter, weekly payments to cover the cost of the cab, insurance, road and diesel tax, and administrative costs. Total weekly payments were substantially less than the cost of hiring a Yellow Top. Small wonder that most unlicensed drivers joined Comfort. Pirate taxi services have all but disappeared, and the quality of Singapore's taxi service has improved markedly.

By the end of 1991, Comfort had accumulated a surplus nearly five times its initial government loan. Much of that goes to buy new cabs and other capital equipment to upgrade service. The rest goes to dividends (10 percent) and to fund educational, social, cultural, and safety net programs for the benefit of Comfort's members and their families. Comfort's next step? A share issue on Singapore's stock market. Recently, Comfort announced plans to issue shares to increase its capital base and expand operations. Most of the proceeds will be used to expand a new joint venture in China.

Other economies have forestalled development of large and politically powerful unions with less formal arrangements. In Taiwan, China, for example, close management-labor contact in small and medium-size enterprises reduced workers' interest in union representation (see table 4.3). Moreover, the emphasis on labor-intensive manufacturing generated rapid increases in the demand for labor. Consequently, as figure 4.1 illustrates, from 1952 to 1979, inflation-adjusted basic wages increased more than sixfold in manufacturing and more than fourfold in agriculture. The total increase in compensation has actually been higher, since basic wages are supplemented twice annually with profit-sharing bonuses.

Insulating the Economic Technocracy

IMPLEMENTING SHARED GROWTH TO SOLVE THE PROBLEM OF political legitimacy requires sharing, but it also requires growth. We now discuss HPAE institutional traits that have been critical to achieving both these goals. Foremost among them is technocratic insulation—the ability of economic technocrats to formulate and implement policies in keeping with politically formulated national goals with a minimum of lobbying for special favors from politicians and interest groups. Without it, technocrats in the high-performing Asian economies would have been unable to introduce and sustain rational economic policies, and some vital wealth-sharing mechanisms would have been neutralized soon after their inception, as was land reform in the Philippines (see box 4.3).

Table 4.3 Labor Union Activity by Scale of Business in Taiwan, China
(percent)

Number of employees	Labor union			
	Yes	*No*	*Unwilling to join*	*No response*
50–99	4.98	94.30	0.64	0.08
100–199	29.85	67.62	2.38	0.15
200–499	51.05	45.44	3.51	0
500 and more	72.32	19.05	6.26	2.37

Source: Taiwan, China, Social Bureau of the Taiwan Provincial Government, Annual Survey data, 1980–84.

Figure 4.1 Index of Real Wages, 1952–79

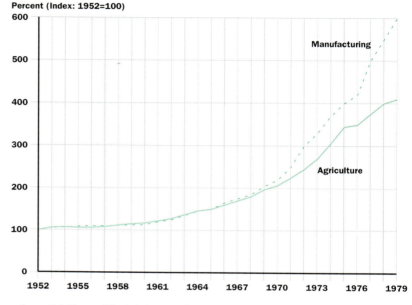

Source: Fei, Kuo, and Ranis (1981, p. 21).

Direct Insulation Mechanisms

Hong Kong offers the clearest case of insulation, since the colonial government, which has been strongly committed to free market forces, need not depend on the political support of private interests to maintain power. But insulation does not necessarily diminish as democratic institutions proliferate. Indeed, the technocracy in authoritarian societies may be utterly without insulation, while those in some democracies are heavily insulated from outside pressures.

In Japan, insulation characterizes not only the economic technocracy but nearly the entire bureaucracy. Japanese bureaucrats draft laws in consultation with the policy committees of the ruling Liberal Democratic Party and private sector representatives; the diet (parliament) merely ratifies what the bureaucracy has prepared. Because the bureaucracy has independent power, it can often ignore pressure from individual actors in the private sector. Moreover, the bureaucracy can achieve policy goals through *administrative guidance*—nonbinding recommendations. Guidelines are enforced with generous incentives—such as licenses and

Box 4.3 Vested Interests Doom Philippine Land Reform

PHILIPPINE POLICYMAKING HAS HISTORICALLY BEEN CAPTIVE TO powerful vested interests that have shaped economic policy to protect and enhance their privileged position, often to the detriment of national well-being. The difficulty of reforming the economy in the face of their opposition was especially evident after the 1986 "People Power" revolt that toppled Ferdinand Marcos and swept Corazon Aquino to power.

Aquino, herself a member of a prominent plantation-owning clan, had pledged during her campaign to carry out land reform, and the promise had wide public support. She did not do so while she had emergency powers at the start of her term, however. When the new congress, dominated by landlord interests, finally passed a land reform law, it was riddled with loopholes. Moreover, although some bureaucrats were dedicated to reform, they lacked the cohesion to implement such a complex undertaking. Like previous attempts at land reform in the Philippines, the program attempted under Aquino achieved little.

The many loopholes in the land reform law illustrate the hazards of a weak bureaucracy, which can easily permit vested interests to shape key economic policies. While the ostensible goal of the reform was redistribution, enforcement was nearly impossible. The law set an ownership ceiling of five hectares, but landowners were permitted to pass up to three hectares to each child older than fifteen years and had ten years to comply. In practice, many landowners nominally distributed their land to distant offspring while retaining control. Alternatively, they kept title to the land, confident that they had plenty of time to lobby a future administration for more favorable provisions. Penalties for noncompliance were negligible: a standard fine equal to half a hectare regardless of the size of the evasion attempted.

The failure of the Philippine program is a sharp contrast to the highly successful land reform programs in Japan, Korea, and Taiwan, China. In each of those instances, land reform was backed and in some cases actively guided by U.S. officials who had little interest in protecting the landed elites. As a result, land retention limits were lower, compensation formulas were straightforward, and the pace of reform was too rapid to permit delaying tactics and widespread evasion. In each of these economies, successful land reform helped to lay the foundation for the rapid, shared growth that has continued to elude the Philippines.

foreign exchange allocations—and the implicit threat to withhold them from companies that refuse to cooperate.

One of the distinct features of the budgetary process in all the HPAEs is the primacy given to the bureaucracy over the legislature in drafting laws. Though the legislature must approve the laws, the bureaucracy studies, analyzes, and drafts the bills. It has considerable control over the agenda and can use this to minimize political pressure.

The Japanese bureaucracy is further protected from political pressure by the National Personnel Authority, an independent body that sets the bureaucracy's pay scales and promotion policies, administers civil service exams, and makes most appointments. Japan's prime minister names only his ministers and, except in a few cases, one of the two vice-ministers in each ministry; the National Personnel Authority is responsible for the rest.[3]

As in Japan, the bureaucracy in Korea has a long tradition of independent policymaking. This was boosted in 1961, when army General Park Chung Hee seized power and reorganized the government to promote rapid development. He created a powerful Economic Planning Board that has had broad budgetary authority. Administrative control over the banking system has given the bureaucracy strong leverage over big business, which relies on government-backed financing to fund rapid expansion.[4] The partnership has generally been uneven, with the bureaucracy dominating the relationship.

While few of the HPAEs have such thoroughly insulated bureaucracies as Japan and Korea, each boasts at least a small, ideologically consistent technocratic core that answers directly to the top leaders and therefore has some independence from the legislature and other sources of political pressure. Indonesia and Thailand, where bureaucratic traditions more closely resemble those in other developing economies, are instructive on this score.

Inflation Control and Debt Management in Thailand and Indonesia

For historical reasons, Thailand and Indonesia have been profoundly concerned with low inflation and debt management. Thailand is unique in Southeast Asia for being the only economy in that region not to have been colonized, in fact one of the few in the developing world. One reason for this remarkable achievement was the openness of the Thai Kingdom to trade with foreigners. Another was the monarchy's concern with avoiding indebtedness to foreigners. And a third, and perhaps the most important, was the establishment of a bureaucracy in 1892 that enabled the monarchy to centralize political control over the kingdom's many regions. Historically, then, the bureaucracy in Thailand has always had a powerful influence over public administration and policymaking. But it was not until 1957, when General Sarit took over the reins of government, that bureaucratic reforms were introduced to address macroeconomic imbalances. Since then, keeping inflation low and efficiently managing debt have been among the government's key concerns.

These same issues have been extremely important to the Indonesian government since President Suharto took power in 1967. The previous Guided Democracy regime of President Sukarno had let government spending run out of control, leading to annual inflation rates of 1,000 percent and other serious economic problems including a rapidly deteriorating infrastructure. Suharto's New Order government ascended to power with an explicit commitment to fight inflation and develop infrastructure, particularly in the rural areas. This led to passage of a balanced budget law and to financial controls that addressed infrastructure development.

To achieve the twin objectives of low inflation and prudent debt management, both governments created mechanisms to insulate their economic technocracies. In Thailand, the government's Budget Bureau has tight control of the budget drafting process and has maintained a stable exchange rate and low inflation. To draft the budget, the Budget Bureau consults with the National Economic and Social Development Board about proposed public investments and with the Finance Ministry about expected revenues. It then determines together with the Central Bank how much deficit financing the economy can tolerate without increasing inflation. Having determined aggregate allowable expenditure, it calculates how much each government agency may spend and forwards a broad outline of proposed expenditures to the cabinet.

The cabinet may propose changes to the outline before forwarding it to a parliamentary budget committee for evaluation. But since neither the cabinet nor the committee receives budget details, the bureau's proposals usually survive with few alterations. After approval by the committee, the budget outline is submitted to the entire parliament for routine passage.

Throughout, the bureau draws support from budgetary laws that limit the government deficit to a small percentage of the year's total expenditures and that cap the percentage of the budget that can be spent servicing the foreign public debt (the current cap is 13 percent). Parliamentary rules offer a further unusual guarantee against runaway deficit spending: nonministerial members of parliament on the budget committee may propose only minimal changes and in any event may not revise the budget upward. The results have been impressive (see figure 4.2). Except for the disruptions caused by the 1972 and 1979 oil shocks, the annual inflation rate has been close to 5 percent. Few developing economies can lay claim to such an achievement, and even more advanced HPAEs such as Hong Kong and Korea have had higher rates. This demonstrates how a small technocratic core, insulated from politics, can set a positive tone for an entire economy.

In Indonesia, too, technocrats keep a tight rein on the budget. Under Suharto, a balanced budget has been the cornerstone of government financial policy. In 1967, the legislature approved a law limiting expenditures to domestic revenues plus foreign assistance. Since then, the finance ministry has institutionalized a review that requires each ministry to justify proposed expenditures on a line-by-line basis. In addi-

Figure 4.2 Thailand Consumer Price Index
(percentage change from previous year)

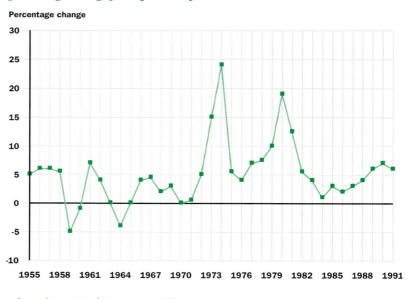

Source: International Monetary Fund data.

tion, parliamentary rules restrict the legislature's discussion of the budget to broad policy issues. Armed with these instruments, the finance ministry has established a macroeconomic environment favorable to growth. Inflation has dropped since the 1960s and has generally remained low and stable (see figure 4.3).

Indirect Insulation Mechanisms

Some HPAEs have enhanced bureaucratic insulation indirectly and generally inadvertently. For example, wealth-sharing mechanisms reduce the potential gain to interest groups of intervening in policymaking and implementation, since some share of the fruits of growth has already been assured. In addition, when wealth-sharing mechanisms reduce the size of production units, as with land reform and support for small and medium-size industries, the marginal cost of organizing and lobbying increases. With the benefits of lobbying down, and the costs up, interest groups tend to be more willing to leave the policy process to the technocrats.

Reorganization of labor from industrywide unions into company unions, along with labor federation provision of goods and services, has

Figure 4.3 Indonesia Consumer Price Index
(percentage change from previous year)

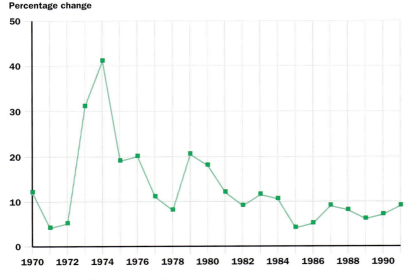

Percentage change

Source: International Monetary Fund data.

similarly reduced the marginal benefit and increased the marginal cost of collective action. Thus, in contrast with workers in many other developing economies, workers in the HPAEs are more likely to refrain from work stoppages and other disruptions and from lobbying the government for mandated wage increases. Because employers faced fewer demands from labor they, too, have had less incentive to press demands on the technocracy.

Of course a powerful bureaucracy insulated from external pressure can also be dangerous. Indeed, the description of Japan's bureaucracy—an independent force that controls generous incentives and issues vague guidelines—is not unlike that of bureaucracies in other economies that engage in corruption and malfeasance on a vast scale. In Japan, itself, some ministries are perceived to be captured by the interests they regulate. These ministries enjoy less power and prestige than those that resist politicization.[5] Even well-intentioned bureaucrats may become counterproductive or lose sight of the goals they are supposed to pursue if bureaucratic insulation means that they are not held accountable for their decisions. How have the HPAEs kept insulated bureaucracies honest and responsive to legitimate private concerns? The next two sections address these perennial problems of bureaucracy: honesty and responsiveness.

Building a Reputable Civil Service

While insulation of the technocracy may be necessary, it is hardly sufficient in the long term. To sustain growth, a bureaucracy must have the competence to formulate effective policies and the integrity to implement them fairly. The more policymakers attempt to fine tune the economy, the greater the need for competence and honesty. Among the HPAEs, Hong Kong, Japan, Korea, Singapore, and Taiwan, China, have been successful in building relatively competent and honest bureaucracies. The Southeast Asian NIEs, Indonesia, Malaysia, and Thailand, have gradually introduced measures to upgrade theirs, with Malaysia in the forefront of the process, but they still clearly lag behind more industrialized economies.

Despite the stress on culture in much popular writing about the Asian miracle, the most successful bureaucracies have not relied on culture alone. HPAE bureaucracies have employed numerous mechanisms to increase the appeal of a public service career, thereby heightening competition and improving the pool of applicants. The overall principles of these mechanisms, readily applicable to any society, are:

- Recruitment and promotion must be merit based and highly competitive.
- Total compensation, including pay, perks, and prestige, must be competitive with the private sector.
- Those who make it to the top should be amply rewarded.

Merit-Based Recruitment and Promotion. Recruitment in Japan revolves around highly competitive civil service examinations administered each year by the National Personnel Authority. For the higher-level exams, the rate of success has been less than 8 percent. Indeed, in 1980 the average rate of success was 2.7 percent (Kim 1988). Promotion within the bureaucracy is based on a combination of seniority and a host of performance indicators that differ across the ministries. Because the number of personnel in the bureaucracy is fixed by law, competition for promotion can be intense (see Pempel 1984).[6]

Korea also relies on exams and performance but has supplemented these filters by recruiting heavily among academics with advanced degrees. (Box 4.4 describes the turnaround in the Korean civil service in the 1960s.) This has resulted in a proliferation of research institutes associated with ministries. Since the Economic Planning Board established the Korea Development Institute in 1971, most other ministries have followed suit. Most institute researchers have a Ph.D., many from a respected foreign university (Kim and Leipziger 1993). Like Korea, Taiwan, China, recruits heavily from academia, primarily to offset weaknesses in the civil service exam system. Academics are recruited from major universities, usually for fixed periods ranging from three to six years.

In Malaysia, civil service exam results are subject to affirmative action guidelines meant to increase the number of Malays in government. Because this reduces the pool of eligible applicants, it probably hinders development of the bureaucracy.

Incentive-Based Compensation. In bureaucracies, as in nearly everything else, you get what you pay for. Table 4.4 suggests that relative pay is significantly better in the Four Tigers than in other economies. Relative pay in Malaysia and Thailand is about the same as the average for other low- and middle-income economies but is still significantly higher than in the Philippines, which is widely perceived to have one of the weakest bureaucracies in Southeast Asia. In general, the more favorably the total public sector compensation package compares to compensation in the private sector, the better the quality of the bureaucracy.

Box 4.4 The Turnaround of Korea's Civil Service

AS LATE AS 1960, THE KOREAN CIVIL SERVICE WAS WIDELY VIEWED as a corrupt and inept institution. In less than two decades, this view has been dramatically altered. By the late 1970s, the bureaucracy had become one of the most reputable in the developing world. How did this come about?

First, Korea has been heavily influenced by the Confucian tradition. More than six hundred years of that tradition has imbued respect for scholars above all others. To become a scholar, one had to take the examinations administered by the king. Successful candidates generally became teachers or "advisers" to the king. This tradition has continued till the present. Hence, there has always been some prestige associated with public service.

But this did not stop widespread corruption during the postwar years. It was not till General Park Chung Hee's takeover in 1961 that the turnaround began. Realizing the need for a competent and honest bureaucracy to help him achieve his goal of bringing Korea into the ranks of the industrialized world, Park reorganized the civil service and replaced the spoils system, which had governed personnel management, with a merit-based system. Monitoring of the activities of civil servants was improved, and recruitment and promotion became based more on capabilities and performance. A retirement system patterned after Japan's was introduced to encourage bright individuals to remain in the bureaucracy. This plan induced stiff competition among bureaucrats and improved the work ethic.

Not surprisingly, Singapore, which is widely perceived to have the region's most competent and upright bureaucracy, pays its bureaucrats best. The monthly base salary of a full minister in Singapore ranges from S$22,100 to S$27,825 (about US$13,812 to US$17,390), while a minister of state receives the equivalent of US$5,625 to US$7,688.

Japan and Korea also make a deliberate effort to match the private sector. In Japan, the National Personnel Authority annually surveys thousands of companies to determine job pay rates (Kim 1988, p.9). In Korea, base salaries are lower than salaries in large private companies, but fifty-nine allowances help to narrow the difference. Taking account of salary plus bonuses in the private sector and salary plus allowances in the public sector for entry-level, mid-level, and senior positions, differences in total compensation appear to be smaller than in most

Table 4.4 ICP Estimates of Per Capita GDP and Ratio of Public to Private Sector Salaries, 1992
(percent)

Economy/region	Senior level A	Senior level B	Mid-level A	Mid-level B	Entry level	GDP per capita (I$)
HPAEs						
Singapore	114.0[b]	114.0	115.0[b]	115.0	107.0	14,920
Korea, Rep. of [a]	98.8[b]	98.8	81.3	82.2	83.6	7,190
Taiwan, China	65.2	60.3	63.5	65.8	60.0	7,954
Malaysia	40	33.3	34.3	50.0	—	5,900
Thailand	47.6	27.5	33.6	43.0	78.9	4,610
Other Asia						
Philippines	27.7	24.3	25.0	32.5	62.5	2,320
Latin America						
Chile	70.4	63.2	—	—	—	6,190
Trinidad and Tobago	63.5[b]	63.5	76.9	77.9	—	8,510
Venezuela	29.5	42.4	53.4[b]	53.4	—	6,740
Uruguay	—	—	37.1[b]	37.1	—	6,000
Argentina	24.1[b]	24.1	28.6[b]	28.6	—	4,680
Sub-Saharan Africa						
Somalia	—	—	11.2[b]	11.2	12.2	540

— Not available.

Note: ICP refers to the U.N. International Comparison Project. I$ refers to "international dollars."

a. Estimates include allowances and bonuses. Data for private sector compensation are based on a survey of companies with 500 or more employees.

b. Average is used for both sub levels A and B.

Sources: World Bank (1992c); Taiwan, China (1992a). Salaries for the HPAEs and the Philippines were provided by local consultants and are based on latest available information. Salary data on Latin American economies were extracted from Reid (1992); data on Somalia, from Lindauer and Nunberg (1993).

economies for which data are available. Given that salaries tend to be lower in smaller firms, average compensation is probably higher in the public sector.

In other HPAEs, public sector base salaries are consistently lower than their private sector counterparts (table 4.4).[7] While figures were not available for Indonesia, anecdotal evidence suggests that the private-public wage gap there is the largest among HPAEs. A student graduating from an Indonesian university can expect to earn two to four times as much in the private sector as in a government job. Not surprisingly, aside from the technocratic core, Indonesia's bureaucracy is perhaps the least well regarded among HPAEs.

In economies where public sector wages are at least decent, prestige, job security, and other advantages of public employment will persuade some talented individuals to forgo higher earnings in the private sector. The trick for governments is to hit on a combination that will attract competent individuals to the civil service.

Prestige is of course partly a function of culture; thus East Asian cultures that regard civil servants highly have an advantage in building bureaucracies. Confucian thought, with its veneration of scholars and preoccupation with written tests, especially civil service exams, remains a powerful force in Hong Kong, Japan, Korea, Singapore, and Taiwan, China. Not surprisingly, these societies have produced strong bureaucracies.

But bureaucracy building need not be culturally constrained. Merit-based screening with economic incentives to attract a large pool of applicants can produce high status for civil servants in any society. Provided that the exams are sufficiently competitive, individuals who pass them will be relatively rare. Thus passing the exam or winning a competitive civil service promotion becomes similar to being inducted into a hall of fame; it signals the public that an individual is special. While the value of prestige cannot normally be quantified, the monetary value accorded to some Thai royal decorations, described in box 4.5, suggests that the value of such prestige can be very high indeed.

Job security can also offset slightly lower pay. In most HPAE bureaucracies, dismissal is unlikely unless the bureaucrat commits a serious mistake. Security of tenure translates into lower income variability, which in turn provides incentives for public employees to accept a lower salary. Furthermore, in many economies a public employee can look forward to a retirement pension, a benefit not normally available in the private sector except in large corporations.

A Clear Path to the Top. A final requirement for a successful bureaucracy is a well-defined, competitive career path with a substantial prize for those who make it to the top. In Japan and some other HPAEs, retirement comes early, and the rewards to a successful bureaucrat are substantial, extending beyond the pay, perks, and prestige to include a golden parachute. The Japanese have a special word for it: *amakudari*, which means "descent from Heaven" and connotes a lucrative job in a public or private corporation or occasionally election to political office. Similar practices exist in Korea, Malaysia, Singapore, and Taiwan, China, in differing degrees.

Unlike the much-criticized revolving-door, which whisks bureaucrats in other economies from the public sector to the private sector and back again, descent from Heaven is a one-way trip. Moreover, retiring bureaucrats in Japan do not choose their sinecures but are assigned them

Box 4.5 The Value of Prestige: Thai Royal Decorations

HIGHLY COMPETITIVE, MERIT-BASED RECRUITMENT TO A BU-reaucracy creates value for successful entrants, endowing them with a recognition that the private sector cannot generally provide. Merit-based recruitment and promotion have another positive feature. Because such a system attracts the cream of the crop and most of the cream comes from highly selective universities, it creates an esprit de corps among bureaucrats. This strengthens the bureaucracy and helps to insulate it from external pressures. The value of this prestige is evident in Thailand, where the king has for centuries granted highly coveted awards to individuals who have rendered extraordinary service to the kingdom. In modern times royal decorations have been awarded mostly to exemplary public servants.

On occasion, a business person who has contributed greatly to the betterment of the kingdom may qualify for an award. In order to receive it, however, that person must make a substantial donation to the kingdom. At the current exchange rate, the donations range from $12,000 to more than $1.2 million, depending on the class of the award.

That business people willingly pay such amounts to receive a royal award for service suggests that the prestige of the awards has a very high monetary equivalent. By implication, the prestige of excelling in public service and acquiring an award without making a donation carries substantial, if unrealizable, monetary value.

---

by a committee within their ministry. These features, combined with an intensely competitive environment within and between ministries, guard against firms offering post-retirement jobs in exchange for special favors. While there is no denying that firms welcome retired senior bureaucrats, partly to strengthen useful ties with government, the merito-cratic nature of the bureaucracy means that the retirees are often exceptional managers, valuable in their own right.

Competency Breeds Integrity

Mechanisms that induce competency can also enhance honesty. Competition discourages dishonesty, since discovery of a corrupt or dishonest act would disqualify an applicant. In societies that value public service, dismissal brings disgrace on the entire family; hence family members have an incentive to discourage corrupt activities. This mechanism appears to be especially effective in Korea, where tradition has placed a high premium on government service.

Strictly enforced dismissal policies also help reduce graft. In Singapore, large or small corruption is penalized by expulsion from the civil service and withdrawal of one's pension. In addition, dismissed public employees are unwelcome in the private sector. Under such circumstances, the cost of engaging in corrupt acts becomes nearly prohibitive. Other economies in the region have government anticorruption squads that focus on enforcement and punishment.

As Japan and Singapore in the early 1990s illustrate, rich economies have an advantage in building honest and competent bureaucracies that further the creation of wealth. For example, economies with higher per capita GDP can afford to pay bureaucrats better and to fund the high-quality education that results in a better pool of applicants. The challenge for developing economies is to concentrate available resources where they can most effectively replicate the advantages of the industrial economies. This is not to say that corruption and bribery do not occur in those HPAEs with reputable bureaucracies. These social evils exist in Japan, Korea, and Taiwan, China, and even in Singapore. The critical point is that they have occurred less frequently and in smaller magnitudes than in other low- and middle-income economies. Indeed, most of the HPAEs scored significantly better than other newly industrializing economies in survey rankings of the prevalence of improper practices and special interest group lobbying contained in the 1992 *World Competitiveness Report* (World Economic Forum 1992).

Developing Better Business-Government Relations

Whereas most other low- and middle-income economies have only recently turned to the private sector to stimulate growth, the HPAEs have done so for many years, often decades. They have done this by providing a legal and regulatory environment for private investment, by creating support systems for SMEs, and by establishing cooperative relations with big business and in some cases labor.

The Legal and Regulatory Environment. Compared with other developing economies, the HPAEs have been more successful in creating a legal and regulatory environment conducive to private sector development. Based on selected criteria of fourteen newly industrializing economies in the 1992 *World Competitiveness Report*, in which lower scores indicate a better environment, the HPAEs had an average overall score of 32.3 (with a standard deviation of 18.4) compared with an average of 56.9 (with a standard deviation of 13.3) for the other economies.[8]

Encouraging Small and Medium-Size Enterprises. Small and medium-size enterprises generally have difficulty getting credit to finance capital improvements, obtain better technology, and break into markets, particularly export markets. Hence, a nontrivial SME sector cannot be established without external assistance. Studies indicate that the northern-tier HPAEs—Japan, Korea, and Taiwan, China—have been able to develop relatively effective financial support programs (Itoh and Urata 1993; Kim and Nugent 1993; Wade 1990). Largely because of weak institutional capabilities, Indonesia has not had much success with its support programs (Berry and Levy 1993); however, the private banking system appears to have been helpful in developing some SMEs. Both Malaysia and Thailand have active support programs, but not much is known about their effectiveness.

Wooing Big Business

THE HIGH-PERFORMING ASIAN ECONOMIES TEND TO HAVE formal institutions that facilitate communication and cooperation between the private and public sectors, whereby rent-sharing rules can be made transparent and whereby each participant can be assured of a share of rents. These are, in effect, an institutionalized form of wealth sharing aimed primarily at winning the support and cooperation of business elites.

East Asia's Deliberation Councils

Japan's efforts to establish such institutions are the most widely recognized and have been the most thorough. Since the beginning of the postwar period, the Japanese government and private industry have engaged in serious policy deliberations though *deliberation councils* of two types. The first is organized along functional or thematic lines, such as pollution or finance; the second is organized according to industry, for example, automobiles or chemicals. Government ministries establish the councils, which are generally associated with a specific bureau within the establishing ministry.

Each council provides a forum for government officials and representatives from the private sector—business, labor, consumers, academia, and the press—to discuss policy and market trends and generally to exchange information. Consensus is encouraged. Figure 4.4 shows the process of formulating a policy at the Ministry of Trade and Industry. MITI officials first invite interested parties to a series of hearings, the results of which are forwarded to a MITI research group. The research group prepares a report for the appropriate deliberative council, where policy negotiations may take place. On the basis of feedback from the council, the group revises the report and releases it to the public to explain the objectives of the new policy. Final approval by the diet is usually routine. Without consensus from the relevant deliberative council, however, a MITI policy stands little chance of success.[9]

Figure 4.4 Industrial Vision Formulation Process

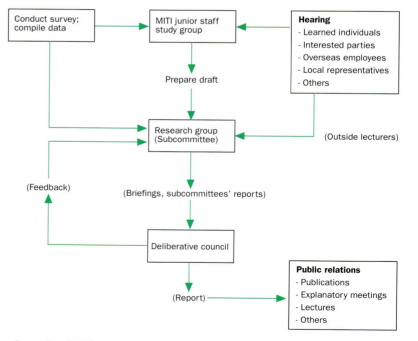

Source: Ono (1992).

In Korea, from the mid-1960s to the early 1980s, government and private sector relations were also close and cooperative, although some in the private sector argue that government was too strong handed and dictatorial.[10] Government and business leaders met often and regularly although less formally than in Japan. Government solicited businesses' views and included them as a critical policy component.

Until the early 1980s, the most important communication channels were monthly export-promotion meetings, at which the president of Korea himself presided over discussions between the economic ministers and top business leaders. Businessmen expressed their views about markets, regulations, and potential plans. The president then instructed specific ministers to attend to each important issue; at the next meeting, ministers delivered a progress report on their assigned tasks.

These meetings were supplemented by government-initiated discussion groups involving company managers, middle-level government officials, and experts or scholars. As in Japan, there were basically two types: functional (for example, taxation) and sectoral (usually focused on a particular industry). In both, bureaucrats invited interested parties and experts to present their views. The focus was on information gathering; bureaucrats made the final decision. Even so, officials tried to incorporate all viewpoints in policies.

With Korea's gradual democratization since the mid-1980s, relations between government and business have become more distant and the meetings less frequent. Recently, however, as the economy has slowed, there is a growing consensus that monthly meetings should resume.

Similar consultative mechanisms appear to be evolving in Malaysia. From independence until 1970, the government focused on infrastructure and generally left the private sector to function freely. From 1972 to 1985, as the government responded to the racial riots of 1969 with the New Economic Policy, relations between government and business tended to be contentious, in part because of the requirement that all enterprises have at least 30 percent Malay participation. Since 1986 business-government relations have gradually improved, culminating in 1991 in the New Development Policy (NDP), which has struck a more even balance between growth and distribution. For example, under the NEP, all firms with more than M$250,000 (US$104,167) capitalization were required to comply with ethnicity-based shareholding regulations. Under the NDP, the cut-off point has been raised to M$2.5 million (US$1.04 million).

The NDP specifically seeks to emulate Japan's government-business consultative mechanisms, a determination reflected in Prime Minister Mahathir Bin Mohamad's "Look East Policy." Formal consultations began in 1991, when the government invited captains of industry to discuss the national budget with finance officials in a much publicized budget dialogue. In the same year, Mahathir created the pinnacle of the consultative structure, the Malaysian Business Council, which is chaired by the prime minister and includes more than sixty members from industry, labor, and government.

Thailand has been slower to develop consultative mechanisms. In 1983, the government established the National Joint Public and Private Consultative Committee (NJPPCC) with the prime minister as chairman and the head of the planning agency as secretary general. Other members are top government officials, particularly from the economic agencies, and nine private sector representatives drawn from the Thai Chamber of Commerce, the Association of Thai Industries, and the Thai Bankers Association. Provincial consultative committees have been established to supplement the NJPPCC (Samudavanija 1992, p. 26). Views about the effectiveness of the committee differ widely.

Public-private consultation is most explicit in Singapore. The private sector participates in policymaking in many ways. For example, private citizens serve as directors on government statutory boards and as members of ad hoc government advisory committees. In both capacities, they review policies and programs and make recommendations for official consideration. In addition, the government regularly invites chambers of commerce, trade associations, and professional societies to submit their views on specific issues (Chia 1992, p. 11).

The Singapore government's efforts to manage the economy are most fully apparent in the National Wages Council, which includes representatives from government, business, and labor. Because of this tripartite structure, the NWC fulfills several coordination functions, simultaneously furthering the government's guidance of business and of labor, as well as business-labor cooperation. Having rejected more typical democratic forms as too adversarial, the PAP has also established a wide variety of citizen associations to provide channels of communication with the government.

Formal mechanisms for business-government interface are almost entirely lacking in Taiwan, China. Instead, coordination is handled through large public enterprises that provide basic inputs to manufacturers and through enterprises owned by the Kuomintang, the dominant political party.[11] Indeed, public enterprises, broadly defined, account for a larger share of GDP in Taiwan, China, than in Korea or even India, where central planning plays a key role. These public, quasi-public, and party-owned firms give the government a high degree of control over large-scale sensitive investments and a means to influence the generally smaller firms that comprise the private sector. Over the years, the large role of the public sector has become less obvious, as some party and government firms were sold to cooperative private interests. Coordination is also facilitated by middle- and lower-level officials of the Industrial Development Board, who make routine, informal visits to thousands of small and medium-size enterprises within their jurisdictions.

Like Taiwan, China, Indonesia lacks the formal government-business coordinating links of other HPAEs; this may be partly explained by the weakness of its bureaucracy. Coordination appears to be handled by informal networks linking senior officials with major enterprises.[12] Little is known about these networks, but they appear to have produced a high degree of cooperation in the economy. In contrast to the deliberation councils, where rules are more transparent, these networks are more susceptible to capture by participants and to corruption.

Deliberation councils naturally reflect the history and culture of the society in which they operate. Even so, the experience in the HPAEs suggests that their applicability is not limited, as some analysts may suggest, to the Confucian cultures of Northeast Asia. Because the operation of deliberation councils has been so important in winning the support of business elites, we now look in greater detail at the operation of these councils in two very different economies, Japan and Malaysia.

Japan's Councils: The Forerunners. The concept of deliberation councils in Japan is most closely associated with MITI. Because of MITI's role in developing and implementing the economy's industrial policy, the public-private consultative process was most clearly manifested in the councils attached to it.

Government-business collaboration has long been a hallmark of the Japanese economy. The *zaibatsu*—Japan's large corporate holding groups—were closely linked with the military-bureaucratic complex of the 1920s and 1930s and were a key element in building the economy's industrial and military base. At that time, the influence of big business matched and sometimes exceeded that of the bureaucracy.

The U.S. occupation forces, identifying the *zaibatsu* as a key element in the build-up of Japan's wartime machinery tried to limit their power, in part by conferring more power on the politically independent bureaucracy. Ironically, this not only strengthened the bureaucracy—particularly MITI, which became the center of development policy formulation—but also facilitated the resurrection of industrial holding groups, organized this time around banks (the so-called *keiretsu* system). These new groups became the main players in the government-initiated consultation process.

The principal instrument of the bureaucracy in managing this process has been administrative guidance, the use of threats and rewards to induce private parties to follow or implement measures suggested by the bureaucracy. Administrative guidance does not depend on any law or regulation. Rather, it employs either threats of adverse consequences should a private party refuse to conform to a "suggestion or recommendation" or, alternatively, rewards that can be granted should the party concede.[13] MITI is well known for having employed this with great skill.

Until the mid-1960s, administrative guidance was a powerful tool for MITI bureaucrats. MITI had firm control over the allocation of foreign exchange and over importation through the Foreign Exchange and Trade Control Law. But international pressure, combined with the need to maintain an export-based economy, led the government to gradually liberalize the trade and investment regime. The process began in the mid-1960s and continued till 1979, when the Foreign Exchange and Control Law was dismantled and the Foreign Capital Law liberalized. Of course this meant that MITI was losing key components of administrative guidance. By the late 1970s, guidance had taken a distinctively different form—mergers of industries spiced with financial support from the government—and coercion declined.

Malaysia's Councils: Emulating Japan and Korea. Malaysia's experience with public-private cooperation through deliberation councils has particular relevance for developing economies. Unlike Japan or Korea, Malaysia is a multiethnic society, and unlike Singapore it has a relatively large population and land area. Thus Malaysia is in many ways more typical of a developing economy than are the high-performing economies of Northeast Asia.

When the Malaysian government introduced formal public-private cooperation in 1983, it embodied the concept in the slogan "Malaysia Inc.," an overt attempt to emulate Japan Inc., particularly the close relationship between Japanese ministries (especially MITI) and big business. In Malaysia, officials have applied this concept to their quest for growth with equity, a particularly important goal in a multiethnic society.

Before 1983, Malaysia had some consultative panels within ministries that dealt with specialized issues and were concerned mainly with cutting red tape. Many had little private sector participation; those that did, however, produced concrete results. Since then, more deliberation councils have been formed, dealing with broader and more complicated issues (the budget and trade, for instance). One of the most ambitious, the Malaysian Business Council, which was formed in 1991, resembles Korea's highly successful Export Promotion Council.

Although it is too early to know how effective these new councils will be, they would be hamstrung without an efficient and reputable civil service bureaucracy. The government recognizes this and is trying to increase the bureaucracy's efficiency, eliminate corruption, and educate civil servants on the value of cooperating with the private sector.

Why Deliberation Councils Assist Growth

From an economic standpoint, deliberative councils facilitate information transmission. They enable the bureaucracy to gather information about world markets, technology trends, and the impact of regulations domestically and abroad, synthesize the information into an action plan, and communicate the plan back to the private sector. Self-interested behavior is more or less constrained by the repeated nature of the collaboration. This in part helps establish credibility—private sector participants believe cheating and reneging are less likely. Politically, these councils serve as proto-democratic institutions, providing direct channels for big business, labor, and academia to the seat of power. Finally, because the rules that govern an industry are effectively established within the council, every member is assured that the rules cannot be altered arbitrarily. With clear rules established, members can concentrate on market competition and not worry about others trying to curry special favors from the government. In effect, their share of industry profits is determined more through competition than through rent-seeking. In this sense, a deliberation council can be viewed as a wealth-sharing mechanism.

■ ■ ■

Studies of the successful Asian economies have frequently emphasized the authoritarian nature of their leadership. Leaders of these societies are described as benevolent dictators who, in contrast to most other dictators, used their authority to muscle businessmen, workers, and bureaucrats into a single-minded pursuit of development. This chapter offers a different interpretation. Leaders need the active cooperation of their people to stimulate and sustain growth. Heavy-handed treatment might subjugate the ruled, but it would also increase the perceived risk of expropriation, driving away capital. Lack of capital would slow growth, in turn driving away skilled workers and entrepreneurs. Thus, even authoritarian leaders cannot rely on coercion alone. Rather, all leaders need a strategy that will induce people to participate willingly in growth. Whether by design or accident, the leaders of the HPAEs have to various degrees devised mechanisms that effectively deliver the promise of shared growth.

Although policies to promote growth are generally well known, they tend to be either difficult to initiate and/or to sustain over time. Growth makes those at the top of the economic pyramid uncertain about the future of their wealth. It introduces changes that are likely to open avenues for fellow elites and new competitors to contest control of their economic fiefdoms. Elite groups therefore generally find it in their interest to try and maintain the status quo unless they are assured that they will benefit from rapid growth. Furthermore, the initial stages of growth often require that the general population make sacrifices. Hence, even if growth can be initiated it may be interrupted by social and political unrest, unless its fruits are shared by the non-elites.

The task of initiating and sustaining growth thus presents a very difficult coordination problem. Leaders must persuade elite groups to share the growth dividend. They must demonstrate to non-elites that part of the dividend will indeed accrue to them. Governments must create credible means to persuade everyone that their plans are not all rhetoric. The governments in the HPAEs all established mechanisms that operationalized the principle of shared growth. The NEP in Malaysia, deliberation councils in Japan, public housing in Hong Kong and Singapore, and small enterprise promotion in Korea and Taiwan, China—all helped to demonstrate the reality of shared growth.

Finally, governments must foster the conditions in which the bureaucracy, or at least a dedicated technocratic core, can design and implement effective policies. To varying degrees, and with a variety of mechanisms, the HPAEs have performed these tasks unusually well. In the next two chapters, we examine the policies and instruments that HPAE governments used in their effort to realize the promise of shared growth.

Notes

1. For example, the National Wages Council in Singapore has helped coordinate wage rises with increasing productivity. In Japan, the establishment of the Japan Productivity Center helped institutionalize labor-management consultations.

2. In fact, the SME sector declined only when the HCI push was initiated in the mid-1970s.

3. In those cases where the prime minister appoints both vice ministers, he is constrained by custom to appoint a career bureaucrat from the ministry to the post of administrative vice minister.

4. The debt-equity ratio has been inordinately high in Korea. Official statistics indicate that this is in the range 310–80, although the "true" figures are said to be lower, at about 160–80 (Wade 1990). Nevertheless, this is still high compared with the ratio in the United States and the United Kingdom, where the range is 50–90.

5. Okimoto (1989) ranks the power and prestige of ministries as the inverse of their degree of politicization. The heavily politicized construction ministry ranks lowest and the relatively nonpoliticized MITI the highest.

6. Seniority bears heavily on promotion decisions. It is assumed that, once one has successfully hurdled the difficult entrance exams, she or he is capable of doing (efficiently and effectively) what is asked of her or him. This is not to say that performance does not count. The pyramidlike structure of the bureaucracy guarantees some degree of competition. "An entering class works together to ensure that its members prosper. . . . Who becomes a bureau chief, a director-general, or ultimately the (administrative) vice minister is a source of intense competition among the classes in a ministry" (Johnson 1982, p. 62).

7. Finance-related agencies in Thailand, for example, the Bank of Thailand and the Budget Bureau, have their own personnel and recruitment programs. There, salaries are said to be about 30 percent higher across the board than in the rest of the public sector.

8. The criteria selected are (a) the transparency of the government, (b) the effectiveness of antitrust laws, (c) the security of property and person, (d) the fairness in the administration of justice, (e) the extent of improper practices in the public sector, and (f) the extent to which lobbying influences government decisionmaking. The rankings for each criterion are based on responses of business executives stationed in each of the economies in the survey to questions pertaining to the criterion. A Borda score was computed for each country by summing up its rankings for each of the criteria. The overall rank score for a group of economies is the average of their Borda scores.

9. Industrial associations have been important participants in the consultative process. In many cases, these associations are empowered by law to represent their sectors. Thus, the business community has strong representation in a council.

10. Though the channels of communication are still operational, the democratization of the polity has led to some chilling of relations. The country is currently undergoing rapid political change that has affected the business-government interface. There is a recognition in many quarters, including business, for the need to reestablish good relations but under a new form of collaboration. That form is likely to reflect a more even balance between the two sectors.

11. It is also widely known that the relatively few large private businesses have close links to the party.

12. In fact, interviews revealed that even some midsize firms have established relations of this type.

13. Johnson (1982) gives an interesting example: "The city of Musashino in the suburbs of Tokyo issued a policy statement saying that housing contractors who built large projects had to cooperate in providing or helping to buy land on which to build elementary schools. When a contractor ignored these guidelines, the city capped the water and sewage lines he had built for the project with concrete. The contractor took the city to court, but the court upheld the city" (p. 266).

CHAPTER 5

Strategies for Rapid Accumulation

A CCUMULATION OF PRODUCTIVE ASSETS IS THE foundation of economic growth. It is therefore not surprising that, as shown in chapter 1, the high-performing Asian economies (HPAEs) accumulated both physical and human capital much more rapidly and consistently than other economies and that accumulation accounts for a large portion of their superior performance. More interesting is the question of how the HPAEs were able to achieve these rapid rates of accumulation and, in particular, to what extent policies were responsible. This chapter examines the HPAEs' superior performance in three accumulation-related areas: human capital accumulation, financial savings, and investment. For each area, explanations fall into three broad categories:

- Conditions that were not the direct result of accumulation policy
- Policy fundamentals: areas in which nearly all governments intervene, but in which HPAE governments acted more effectively
- Activist policies: selective interventions undertaken in some HPAEs to increase accumulation.

Rapid economic growth and the attendant changes in economic structure not directly related to accumulation policies were important factors in increasing all three forms of accumulation. For example, the HPAEs' rapid shift from high birth rates to low birth rates increased the resources per child potentially available for education at home and in the classroom. At the same time, the rapid deceleration of population growth increased household savings, in turn creating resources for investment.

In addition, the HPAEs performed well in selecting and implementing fundamental economic policies related to accumulation. Every government spends on education, but the HPAEs spent their money more wisely, emphasizing universal primary and, later, secondary education. Similarly, every government tries to control inflation and secure property rights, and most regulate banking institutions to protect savers against default, all of which encourage savings and investment. The HPAEs did these things better than the rest. Moreover, as the HPAEs developed, their governments strengthened the legal and regulatory frameworks for bond and security markets to facilitate investment.

Besides fostering favorable general conditions and getting policy fundamentals right, some HPAEs have deliberately intervened in markets to solve specific coordination problems related to accumulation. These interventions aimed at boosting savings and investment rates are the most controversial of the HPAEs' accumulation policies. Generally, interventions have been more common and more successful in the three northern HPAEs—Japan, the Republic of Korea, and Taiwan, China—all of which have strong governmental institutions. With some notable exceptions, attempts to replicate such efforts among Southeast Asian newly industrializing economies have not been successful.

At the outset, we must acknowledge a fundamental methodological difficulty. Since we know the HPAEs had rapid accumulation (and to some extent were chosen as a group on that basis), we also know, even before examining their policies, that they were not inconsistent with rapid accumulation. The challenge is to separate policies that were neutral or perhaps negative but not sufficiently negative to hinder accumulation significantly from those policies that actually facilitated rapid accumulation. We do this, noting that our findings are based on analytic and empirical judgments rather than derived from statistical models.

Explaining East Asia's High Human Capital Formation

EXCEPT FOR IN THAILAND, THE QUANTITY OF BASIC EDUCATION provided to boys and girls of school age has been consistently higher in the HPAEs than in economies with similar levels of income. After having achieved universal primary schooling, thereby eliminating the gap between boys and girls at the primary level a decade or more earlier than most, the HPAEs rapidly expanded secondary education and were particularly effective in reducing gender gaps at that level.

What accounts for this extraordinary performance? We focus first on three enabling factors: high income growth, early demographic transitions, and more equal income distributions. Each of these greatly increased the resources available for education. We then shift focus to two policy variables: the overall budgetary commitment to education and the distribution of the education budget. We seek to show that the allocation of public resources to primary and secondary education was the major determining factor in East Asia's successful educational strategies.

Rapid Economic Growth

Rapid economic growth is the first factor that accounts for East Asia's extraordinary quantity of education. For example, during the decade 1965–75, GDP growth averaged 6.7 percent in Malaysia and 4.1 percent in Argentina. This implies that over the decade a constant share of GDP allocated to education would have doubled the resources available for education in Malaysia, while in Argentina they would have increased by less than half. Rapid growth also creates jobs, increases real wages, and raises the rate of return on labor force skills, thereby increasing the demand for education (King, Anderson, and Wang 1993). Thus, rapid growth operates on both the supply side of the market for educational services, by increasing the potential resources available for education, and on the demand side.

The rising real wages that are a product of rapid growth could have a dampening effect on educational opportunities, if the relative wages of teachers rise. Fortunately, rapid accumulation of human capital facilitates subsequent educational expansion by increasing the potential supply of teachers, thereby reducing the premium teachers command.[1] The wages of educated workers, including teachers, tend to rise at a slower rate than average wages. Therefore, the impact of rising wages on the cost of education and hence on enrollments is weakened.[2] For example, per pupil operating costs at the primary level average roughly 13 percent of per capita GNP in Indonesia and Malaysia but more than double that, 29 percent, in Sub-Saharan Africa.[3] In Indonesia and Malaysia the annual earnings of primary teachers are roughly 2.4 times per capita GNP. In Sub-Saharan Africa, however, where human capital is relatively scarce, that ratio is much higher.[4] The pattern is similar at the secondary level.

Declining Population Growth

East Asia preceded other developing regions in moving through the demographic transition, and the education sector was a major beneficiary. One important outcome of a deceleration of the rate of population growth is a decline in the rate of growth of the school-age population. During the 1980s, the growth rate of the population age 6–11 years was very low in East Asia—so low that the absolute number of schoolchildren in Korea, Singapore, and Thailand actually declined—but was phenomenally high in Sub-Saharan Africa. As a result, from 1965 to 1989 the share of the population up to 14 years old in Singapore fell from 44 to 24 percent, while in Kenya it rose from 47 to 51 percent. Similar contrasts are evident between other HPAEs and Sub-Saharan African economies (see table 5.1).

When the school-age population is growing rapidly, as in Kenya or Pakistan, rising expenditures on basic education are needed just to keep enrollment rates constant. With declining or slowly growing school-age populations, however, similar increases in expenditures can go for more schooling or better quality. Alternatively, expenditures as a proportion of GDP can be cut while current standards are maintained (see table A5.1, in appendix A5.1).

Table 5.1 Size and Growth of School-Age Population

Economy/region	School-age (0–14) population as percentage of total population		Growth rate of primary school-age (6–11) population (percent)	
	1965	1989	1965–75	1980–85
HPAEs				
Hong Kong	40	22	-1.1	0.3
Korea, Rep. of	43	26	0.7	-0.3
Malaysia	46	37	1.9	0.2
Singapore	44	24	-1.2	-2.2
Thailand	46	34	2.9	-0.1
Other selected economies				
Bangladesh	43	44	3.3	2.9
Brazil	44	35	2.0	1.7
Colombia	47	35	2.3	0.9
Kenya	47	51	3.8	4.7
Nigeria	46	48	3.8	3.4
Pakistan	46	45	2.9	1.8

Sources: 0–14 population figures, World Bank data; 6–11 population figures, Lockheed and Verspoor (1991).

Accordingly, declining, stagnant, or slowly growing school-age populations have allowed substantial increases in per pupil expenditure in all of the HPAEs. Table 5.2 shows the magnitude of the savings on expenditure on basic education in East Asia due to the decline in the proportion of the population of school age.[5] Consider the most striking example: if the share of the school-age population in 1988 were as large in Korea as in Kenya, the Korean government would have had to spend 5.6 percent

Table 5.2 Percentage of GNP Allocated to Education Saved Due to Lower Fertility Rates

Economy	Expenditure on basic education as a percentage of GNP	Percentage of GNP saved due to growth rates of school-age population that were lower than:		
		Kenya	Mexico	Pakistan
Hong Kong				
1975	2.0	1.2	1.0	1.0
1980–81	1.7	1.5	1.7	1.2
Japan				
1975	4.2	4.0	3.8	3.8
1988–89	2.8	4.8	2.8	3.9
Korea, Rep. of				
1975	1.9	0.6	0.4	0.4
1988–89	2.8	2.8	1.4	2.0
Malaysia				
1980–81	4.4	1.3	0.4	0.4
1988–89	4.0	1.6	0.4	0.8
Singapore				
1975	2.1	1.1	0.8	2.0
1980–81	2.2	2.0	1.3	1.3
Thailand				
1975	2.8	0.6	0.0	0.0
1988–89	2.6	1.3	0.3	0.8

Note: Method of calculation: [(Expenditure on basic education as a percentage of GNP) x (percent difference between East Asian and other economies in school-age population)] + (expenditure on basic education as a percentage of GNP) = an estimate of the additional share of GNP that would have been required, had population growth been more rapid. This is an indicator of the savings reaped in the education sector as a result of lower population growth.

Sources: For expenditure on basic education, UNESCO (various years); for data on school-age population, United Nations (various years, a).

of GNP on education instead of the 2.8 percent actually spent to achieve Korea's high enrollment rates. This suggests that lower fertility rates saved Korea 2.8 percent of GNP. Conversely, had Pakistan's school-age population grown at the relatively low Korean rate, the government of Pakistan could have increased enrollment rates by as much as 50 percent.

Equality in Distribution of Income

The more equal an economy's distribution of income, the higher primary and secondary enrollments tend to be. In a cross-section of more than eighty economies, there is a strong and statistically significant negative correlation between basic education enrollment rates and the level of income inequality, as measured by the Gini coefficient (Clarke 1992). As we discuss below, educational expansion can have an equalizing impact, so the causality in this relationship could run from enrollment rates to the distribution of income. However, there are a variety of reasons why low income inequality, which we document in chapter 1, might have been a third factor contributing to high enrollment rates in East Asia.

Due to greater income equality, the income of the poorest 20 percent of the population in East Asian economies is higher than in economies with the same average income but greater inequality (see table A5.4, at the end of the chapter). Because of budgetary constraints (and capital market imperfections that preclude their borrowing to invest in education), very poor households are unable to invest in their children even when the returns are high: the pressing need to subsist crowds out high-return investments. This is less likely to occur in East Asia because the incomes of the poor tend to be further above subsistence level.

Measures of the income elasticity of the enrollment ratio derived from cross-economy education expenditure equations are 0.31 and 0.43 at the primary and secondary levels (Schultz 1988). This implies that in East Asia the positive effect on school enrollments of lower inequality can be quite large. For example, given an income elasticity of basic education enrollments of 0.40, if the distribution of income was as equal in Brazil as in Malaysia, enrollments among poor Brazilian children would be roughly 33 percent higher. Moreover, the income elasticity of demand for basic schooling among poor families is likely to be substantially higher than average and may exceed 1.0. In this case, enrollments among poor Brazilian children would be 80 percent higher.

Coordination Problems that Hinder
Human Capital Formation

Numerous studies show that a person's earnings are higher the higher their human capital, as measured by their education and health status. As shown in chapter 1, the same is true for nations; we know that investments in education contribute significantly to economic growth. But neither of these points necessarily justifies public provision of education. Indeed, if the private returns are as high as social returns on these investments, individuals and households are likely to make adequate (from an economywide point of view) investments in human capital on their own. However, two kinds of problems generate a gap between private and social returns, which—if not countered by government action—will result in families investing less in their children's education than is in society's interest. First, there may be failures in the capital market and in information, discussed above, that reduce parents' ability or interest in investing. Second, educational investments have positive externalities, which imply that families that invest in education are not the sole beneficiaries.[6]

The difficulty of borrowing to send children to school affects the poor especially. Creditors cannot easily stake a future claim on embodied human capital (as they can for other types of collateral). Even poor families who might be willing to borrow, because schooling has high private returns, usually cannot. The poor are also likely to be less aware of future returns on education—and therefore invest less in their children's schooling than would make sense even from a strictly private point of view.[7] These market failures in principle suggest making loans available and improving information about future returns. A simpler, and more common, alternative is for government to reduce the direct costs of schooling by making public schooling available and free.

The second class of market failure—externalities—has more immediate implications for what type and level of schooling the government should subsidize and for what groups. There are several sources of externalities. An educated person may increase not only her household's income but also the income of other households, because her ideas and innovations spill over to others. Similarly, education may have social benefits not directly compensated monetarily, for example, a reduction in the spread of contagious diseases. In these and other cases, coordination problems exist, and governments acting on society's behalf have reason to choose a higher level of education than families acting alone.

Figure 5.1 Returns on Investment in Education by Level (Latest Year)

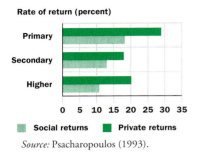

Rate of return (percent)

■ Social returns ■ Private returns

Source: Psacharopoulos (1993).

Table 5.3 Public Expenditure on Education as a Percentage of GNP

Economy/ region	1960	1989
HPAEs		
Hong Kong	—	2.8
Korea, Rep. of	2.0	3.6
Singapore	2.8	3.4
Malaysia	2.9	5.6
Thailand	2.3	3.2
Indonesia[a]	2.5	0.9
Average[b]	2.5	3.7
Other		
Brazil	1.9	3.7
Pakistan	1.1	2.6
Less developed economies[c]	1.3	3.1
Sub-Saharan Africa	2.4	4.1

— Not available.

a. Alternative sources of data indicate that expenditure on public education as a percentage of GDP was 3.0 percent in Indonesia in 1989.

b. Average does not include Indonesia.

c. Low- and middle-income economies.

Source: UNDP (1991).

Policy responses generally consist of making schooling available and free and in some economies compulsory. The difference between social and private returns from education is probably higher at the primary and secondary levels than at the university level (see figure 5.1). Many positive spillovers come from literacy acquired at lower levels of schooling, while the returns from training at the university level are almost fully captured by the higher income of university graduates. Vocational training may also have high social payoffs, if it improves worker productivity not only for the trainee but also for her co-workers. More importantly, evidence suggests that vocational training is most cost-effective if trainees have a solid base of primary and secondary education. All of this argues for universal primary and broadly based secondary education as a means to improve economic efficiency and income distribution.

Policies that Promoted Human Capital Formation

Higher shares of national income devoted to education cannot fully explain the larger accumulation of human capital in the HPAEs. In both 1960 and 1989, public expenditure on education as a percentage of GNP was not much higher in East Asia than elsewhere (see table 5.3). In 1960 the share was 2.2 percent for all developing economies, 2.4 percent for Sub-Saharan Africa, and 2.5 percent for East Asia. During the three decades that followed, the governments of East Asia markedly increased the share of national output they invested in formal education, but so did governments in other developing regions. In 1989 the share in Sub-Saharan Africa, 4.1 percent, was higher than the East Asian share, 3.7 percent, which barely exceeded the average share for all developing economies, 3.6 percent.[8]

Nor were initial conditions, for example the colonial legacy, decisive. While Korea did have much higher enrollment rates in 1950 than most developing economies, subsequent increases in primary and secondary enrollment rates account for Korea's present wide lead in enrollments over other middle-income economies. A comparison of Indonesia, a success story, and Pakistan, a laggard, is also illustrative. In 1987 Indonesia had achieved universal primary enrollment and a 48 percent secondary enrollment rate. By contrast, Pakistan's enrollment rates were 52 percent at the primary level and 19 percent at the secondary level. What proportion of these gaps is due to initial conditions? At the primary level, Indonesia increased its enrollment rate by nearly 80 percentage points since 1950, while Pakistan managed an increase of only 34 percentage points, implying that most of the current gap is explained by the pace of increase rather than initial conditions. For secondary schooling, Pakistan's enrollment rate in 1950 was actually higher than Indonesia's; all of the current gap is explained by the rates of increase during the past thirty-seven years.

Primary and Secondary Education. The allocation of public expenditure between basic and higher education is the major public policy factor that accounts for East Asia's extraordinary performance with regard to the quantity of basic education provided. The share of public expenditure on education allocated to basic education has been consistently higher in East Asia than elsewhere. Korea and Venezuela provide an extreme example that nicely illustrates the point. Table 5.4 indicates that in 1985 Venezuela allocated 43 percent of its education budget to higher education; by contrast, in the same year Korea allocated only 10 percent of its budget to higher education. Public expenditure on education as a percentage of GNP was actually higher in Venezuela (4.3) than

Table 5.4 Allocation of Education Budgets, 1985

Economy	Public expenditure on education as a percentage of GNP	Public expenditure on basic education as a percentage of GNP	Percentage of education budget allocated to higher education	Percentage of education budget allocated to basic education
Hong Kong	2.8	1.9	25.1	69.3
Indonesia[a]	2.3	2.0	9.0	89.0
Korea, Rep. of	3.0	2.5	10.3	83.9
Malaysia	7.9	5.9	14.6	74.9
Singapore	5.0	3.2	30.7	64.6
Thailand	3.2	2.6	12.0	81.3
Venezuela	4.3	1.3	43.4	31.0

a. Alternative sources of data indicate that in Indonesia public expenditure on education as a percentage of GDP was 3.3 in 1984–85 and 4.3 in 1985–86, and that the percentage of the education budget allocated to basic education was 81 in 1984–85 and 80 in 1985–86.

Row percentages do not add up to 100 since three of the categories into which educational funding is channeled—pre-primary, other types, and not distributed—have not been included in this table.

Sources: Column 1, UNDP (1990); columns 2 and 3, UNESCO (1989).

in Korea (3.0). After subtracting the share going to higher education, however, public expenditure available for basic education as a percentage of GNP was considerably higher in Korea (2.5) than in Venezuela (1.3). Box 5.1 shows how Indonesia's emphasis on primary education, contrasted with Bolivia's relative neglect of primary schooling, is reflected in rural educational opportunities.

The share of public funds allocated to tertiary education in East Asia has tended to be low, averaging roughly 15 percent during the past three decades.[9] In Latin America the share has been roughly 24 percent.[10] In South Asia, the share is close to the Latin American level. This had been the case in Sub-Saharan Africa as well, but in recent years the share has declined to East Asian levels.

By giving priority to expanding the primary and secondary bases of the educational pyramid, East Asian governments have stimulated the demand for higher education, while relying to a large extent on the private sector to satisfy that demand. In all developing regions the probability of going to university is markedly higher for secondary school graduates from high- than from low-income families. Typically, in low- and middle-income economies government subsidies of university education are not related to need, implying that they benefit families with relatively high incomes that could afford to pay fees closer to the actual cost of schooling.

At the same time, in many economies, Brazil and Kenya being notable examples, low public funding of secondary education results in poorly qualified children from low-income backgrounds being forced into the private sector or entirely out of the education system. Because of the higher concentration on basic education in East Asia, public funds for education are more likely to benefit children of low-income families who might otherwise have difficulty remaining in school.

Vocational Training. Human resources and the training to upgrade them have been important to the HPAEs' successful export drives, despite the high degree of labor intensity in their manufactured exports. High-level skills are essential for such manufacturing-related activities as management and entrepreneurship, information technology, finance, marketing, accounting, and law. Moreover, adaptive innovations on the shop floor, which are responsible for a major share of productivity in manufacturing, demand both higher- and lower-level skills. But while vocational training is widely recognized as important, such training is rarely cost-efficient when provided in the school systems. Firms prefer to do their own training, partly because many skills are firm-specific.

Box 5.1 Spending on the Kids: Primary Education in Bolivia and Indonesia

THE IMPACT OF DIFFERING SPENDING PRIORITIES WITHIN EDU-cation budgets is starkly evident in a comparison of primary schools in Bolivia and Indonesia. Both economies are at roughly similar levels of development, and both have predominantly rural populations, national illiteracy rates of about 20 percent, and social and cultural factors that hinder the education of girls. Moreover, the proportion of national resources devoted to education at all levels is roughly similar. Bolivia has an annual per capita GNP of about $650; Indonesia, $610. Both spend 2.3 percent of their GDP on education. But while Bolivia devotes only 41 percent of its education budget to primary schools, Indonesia spends nearly 90 percent on basic education.

The resulting differences are striking. In Bolivia, the education system officially covers only 60 percent of children. But even that low figure overstates educational attainment. Only 45 percent of rural schools provide education through the fifth grade; the remainder, mostly in remote areas, offer only three years of instruction. Repetition and dropout rates are high, especially for girls, and only one in ten children has a textbook. Partly because of inadequate resources, teacher training is poor, and administrative corruption is widespread.

Indonesia, by contrast, has deliberately focused resources on primary education, to good effect. Beginning in 1974 with a massive school construction drive, and continuing in 1978 with the abolition of primary school fees, the government endeavored to make primary education available to all children. By 1987, 91 percent of children in rural areas were enrolled in primary school, only slightly less than the 92 percent enrolled nationwide. With near universal education, the gender gap in enrollments has disappeared. While dropout and repetition rates are higher in the countryside than in the cities, and large regional gaps in enrollment ratios and illiteracy rates persist, the focus on primary education has been an effective way to make the most of limited education resources.

Like other developing economies, Indonesia must balance the desire to fund more intermediate and advanced education against the reality that stretching education budgets means less for the lower grades. In 1987, the government expanded free education, which had previously covered up to the sixth grade, to include up to the ninth grade. Educational quality declined, however, and the government has since identified improvement of primary schooling as a key educational objective.

Sources: World Bank (1990a; internal World Bank reports).

Few studies have been made of training in the HPAEs or other developing economies, in part because of the difficulty of defining training. One large survey of 48,000 manufacturing firms in Taiwan, China, concluded that firm-level training raised productivity by encouraging the efficient use of technology (Aw and Tan 1993). The study also found that returns from training were higher in industries with well-educated workers in an environment of rapid technological change. Another Taiwan, China, study with a smaller survey sample and stricter definition of training found that only 24 percent of firms provided training and only 7 percent of technicians received it. As would be expected, training was positively affected by the level of technology and negatively affected by labor turnover and high opportunity costs of training (San 1990).

Other studies in the HPAEs have reached similar conclusions. Enterprise and preemployment training have produced social rates of return of 20 percent in Malaysia. In-plant training for welders in Korean shipbuilding had a social rate of return of 28 percent, higher than in nonfirm training institutions (Middleton and others, forthcoming). On-the-job training was "an extremely systematic and powerful ingredient in the rapid growth of Japanese companies" (Konishi 1989).

In some instances, government efforts to promote training have gone awry. According to one study, Korea's 1974 Special Law for Vocational Training, which required firms to provide six months' training in approved schemes, discouraged firm-level training; firms considered the period too long and opted to pay a fine instead (Kim 1987; van Adams 1989). More narrow government efforts to forecast occupation demand or provide trained workers to fill anticipated jobs have also generally not been successful.

One exception is Singapore's use of training to promote the information technology sector. Singapore has achieved world leadership in information-related services through a concerted program that involved educational institutions (specializing in business and engineering software training), training subsidies to schools and office workers, computerization of the civil service, and establishment of TradeNet, an international information network (Hon 1992). This success illustrates the importance of a government's ability to foresee a major trend and coordinate complementary private investments. At the same time, businesses must stand ready to take advantage of the comprehensive support that the government provides. Other East Asian economies have had similar, if less spectacular, successes in telecommunications (Mody and others 1992).

Has training been more effective or widespread among the HPAEs than other developing economies? The evidence is too limited for a clear conclusion. However, it is clear that returns from training are augmented by economic growth and consequent job creation and are therefore higher in the HPAEs. Moreover, the HPAEs' extensive participation in international markets aided the success of their training programs. International competition encourages firms to train workers and increases the number of skill-intensive jobs, thereby ensuring that new skills do not erode. Training, then, appears to function like many other aspects of development in East Asia. It contributes to rapid, sustained growth but does not, in itself, make such growth possible.

Why East Asia's Educational Policies Worked

In most of the economies of East Asia, public investments in education were not only larger than elsewhere in absolute terms—they were also better. They responded more appropriately to coordination failures in the market for education. Emphasis on universal, high-quality primary education had important payoffs both for economic efficiency and for equity. The excess demand for secondary and tertiary education, generated by rapid attainment of universal primary education, was met largely by a combination of expansion of a public secondary system with meritocratic entrance requirements and a self-financed private system. This stands in stark contrast to many other low- and middle-income economies, which have stressed public subsidies to university education.

Explaining East Asia's High Savings Rates

As is the case with East Asia's rapid human capital formation, the region's high savings rates are in part an outcome of rapid growth and rapid demographic transitions. Government policy also encouraged (and sometimes compelled) increased savings through a variety of means. The most basic of these was the maintenance of macroeconomic stability. In addition, the HPAEs have addressed savings-related coordination problems with numerous measures designed specifically to boost savings rates. These range from policy fundamentals (such as regulatory supervision of banks, which address an absence of deposit insurance markets), to targeted interventions (such as restrictions on consumer credit and forced savings plans).

Growth and Demographics: The Effect on Savings

Many popular efforts to explain the East Asian miracle have invoked cultural factors to explain high savings rates and used those high savings rates to explain high rates of investment and growth. Neither element of such explanations has received much empirical support. Indeed, studies of the income-savings relationship in a broad cross section of economies indicate that while income and savings growth are highly correlated, incomes often have risen before savings rates rather than after, suggesting that growth drives savings rather than the other way around. Recent econometric studies support the idea that rapid income growth boosts savings rates as households acquire resources faster than they increase consumption (Carroll, Weil, and Summers 1993). According to this view, East Asia's high savings rates since the 1960s are partially an outcome of high growth rates rather than a cause.

We have attempted our own tests of the savings-growth relationship for the HPAEs (described in greater detail in appendix 5.1 and its corresponding table A5.2). Income growth has been a remarkably good predictor of increased savings rates in Indonesia, Japan, Korea, Thailand, and Taiwan, China, but savings has not been a good predictor of growth. Results are mixed for Hong Kong and Malaysia, and causation might run either way. In Singapore income changes were not a significant factor in the spectacular rise in savings rates in the 1970s and 1980s, consistent with the view that demographic factors and, to a lesser extent, the policies of the Central Provident Fund, a forced savings program, determined the rise (Monetary Authority of Singapore 1991).

Rapid changes in the size and age composition of households may have contributed to rising savings rates for many of the same reasons that rapid demographic transitions fostered human capital formation: as birth rates fell, the dependency ratio—that is, the ratio of non-working-age people to working-age people—decreased. Theories of savings based on the life cycle of increasing then decreasing income relative to consumption predict that societies with a high proportion of prime-age workers will save more than those with higher proportions of young or old people (Ando and Modigliani 1963; Modigliani 1970). Of course, the benefit of falling birth rates eventually will be reversed as the population ages and the old age dependency ratio rises, an effect seen in studies of European economies and Japan (see Blumenthal 1970; Horioka 1990).

For the HPAEs other than Japan, there is little evidence of the relationship between demographic changes and household savings. The Singapore study mentioned above showed that most of the increased savings rate from 19 to 46 percent between 1970 to 1989 was attributable to declining dependency ratios (Monetary Authority of Singapore 1991). In Taiwan, China, where household savings rates are generally very high, households headed by prime-age workers tend to save more, possibly reflecting in part preparation for old age. (But savings in older households are also remarkably high and stable, contrary to the view of the life cycle savings hypothesis [Deaton and Paxson 1992].) Demographic factors may also interact with corporate behavior to increase savings. In Japan the tradition of employees working beyond retirement age at reduced wages appears to contribute significantly to higher savings rates (Horioka 1990).

Policy Fundamentals and High Savings Rates

In addition to benefiting from higher growth and demographic shifts conducive to savings, East Asian governments selected, often through trial and error, a broad spectrum of policies that encouraged savings. Two fundamentals that facilitated high levels of savings were the management of macroeconomic policy and the making of budgetary choices.

The Role of Real Interest Rates. Foremost among macroeconomic fundamentals was the effort to control inflation discussed in chapter 3. Because high inflation rates also tend to be volatile, real interest rates are often negative and unpredictable, discouraging domestic financial savings. Moreover, since unanticipated high inflation erodes the real value of financial assets, volatility of inflation increases the risk associated with holding them. Conversely, low to moderate inflation, particularly at stable rates, encourages financial savings. Thus the HPAEs' generally superior record at avoiding long-term fiscal deficits and restraining inflation gave people the confidence to save (Neal 1990).

Table 5.5 documents average real interest rates in the HPAEs compared with other low- and middle-income economies. Real interest rates on deposits in the HPAEs were either positive or mildly negative. In con-

Table 5.5 Average Real Interest Rates on Deposits, Selected Economies

Region/economy	Period	Real interest rates: average (percent)	Real interest rates: standard deviation (percent)
HPAEs			
Hong Kong	1973–91	-1.81	3.16
Indonesia	1970–90	0.26	11.33
Japan	1953–91	-1.12	3.89
Korea, Rep. of	1971–90	1.88	5.86
Malaysia	1976–91	2.77	2.47
Singapore	1977–91	2.48	1.71
Taiwan, China	1974–91	3.86	7.92
Thailand	1977–90	4.41	5.32
Average		1.59	3.47
Other Asia			
Bangladesh	1976–92	0.96	3.59
Nepal	1976–89	-3.69	5.00
Philippines	1976–91	0.45	9.97
Sri Lanka	1978–92	2.38	6.01
Average		0.03	6.14
Latin America and Caribbean			
Bolivia	1979–91	44.33	81.46
Chile[a]	1965–91	31.84	96.49
Ecuador	1983–91	-6.57	18.76
Jamaica	1976–91	-3.95	11.33
Mexico	1977–92	11.42	17.97
Uruguay	1976–92	-1.89	15.62
Average		16.67	40.27
Europe and Middle East			
Egypt	1976–90	-6.32	3.52
Greece	1976–92	-3.07	4.64
Portugal	1976–92	-0.24	5.38
Tunisia	1977–88	-3.30	3.05
Turkey	1976–91	-15.60	28.32
Average		-5.71	8.94
Sub-Saharan Africa			
Ghana	1978–88	-28.31	36.62
Kenya	1967–90	-2.33	5.91
Nigeria	1970–91	-9.62	10.35
South Africa	1977–92	-1.58	4.64
Zambia	1978–90	-28.03	31.50
Zimbabwe	1978–90	-4.73	4.94
Average		-11.13	13.86
OECD economies			
France	1970–91	-1.83	3.32
Germany	1978–91	2.42	1.05
Sweden	1962–91	0.69	2.53
Switzerland	1981–91	-1.69	1.62
United Kingdom	1963–91	-0.80	5.33
United States	1965–91	2.22	2.38
Average		0.16	2.78

Note: Real interest rates = nominal interest rates adjusted for inflation, using the CPI.
a. If 1974 and 1975 are omitted from the calculation, then the average for Chile is -13.3 and the standard deviation is 65.38.
Source: International Monetary Fund data.

trast, other regions show many economies with large negative rates—on average rates were -11 percent in Mexico, -15 percent in Turkey, and -28 percent in Zambia. Real interest rates were also more volatile (as measured by the standard deviation) in other low- and middle-income economies than in the HPAEs. While the standard deviation was 3.5 in the HPAEs, close to the OECD economies at 2.8, on average it was 40 in Latin America, 14 in Sub-Saharan Africa, and 6 in South Asia. Malaysia and Singapore have maintained the most consistently positive and stable real interest rates on deposits, paralleling interest rate trends in the United States. Japan maintained negative, but highly stable, real interest rates on deposits until 1983 and has had very low but stable positive real interest rates since that time. Korea, especially Indonesia, and Taiwan, China, have had much greater volatility of real interest rates than the other HPAEs but still substantially less than in many other low- and middle-income economies.

Several studies have documented the positive association between real interest rates and the growth of savings deposits and broad money aggregates (Fry 1988; Lanyi and Saracoglu 1983; Gelb 1989). This is especially evident for changes from highly negative to positive real rates of interest. For example, when Taiwan, China, raised real interest rates on bank deposits from a negative 300 percent in 1949 to about 8.5 percent in 1953, the ratio of time and savings deposits to money stock rose from 2 to 34 percent in three years (Chiu 1992). Indonesia and Korea achieved similarly dramatic increases in financial savings after stabilizing inflation and shifting from negative to positive real interest rates. More recently, Argentina, Chile, Mexico, and Pakistan have done the same.

The Role of Public Savings. One direct way that any government can address the concern that aggregate savings are too low is to generate public sector savings through a combination of tax and expenditure policies. Although in theory forward-looking private savers should increase consumption (and reduce savings) to match any increase in public savings (because their future obligations are reduced), in practice households are faced with liquidity constraints and are not able to act on expectations. Thus total savings may rise with an increase in public savings (Summers 1985). Empirical evidence shows that government savings does not fully crowd out private savings. Furthermore, the method of raising public savings matters: on average, increasing public savings via reduced expenditures is more effective than raising taxation. For a sample of thirteen developing economies, a transitory increase of a dollar in public savings, made through a cut in expenditures, reduces private savings by only 16–50 cents. If the dollar increase in public savings is achieved through a current period tax increase, private savings declines by 48–65 cents (Corbo and Schmidt-Hebbel 1991).

Most HPAEs have maintained high public savings compared with other low- and middle-income economies through a combination of tax policy and expenditure restraint. The extent to which HPAE governments have restrained current expenditures relative to other developing and industrial economies is shown in figure 5.2, which gives average public consumption as a percentage of GDP between 1970 and 1988 for a sample of 111 economies. Indonesia, Japan, Korea, Singapore, and Thailand are in the bottom third of the distribution of all economies in terms of the share of public consumption, with public consumption shares below 15 percent of GDP. Malaysia and Taiwan, China, are exceptions, falling in the middle of the distribution. In Malaysia the high levels of public consumption reflected the explicit redistributional objectives of the New Economic Policy. As a group, the average share of public consumption in the HPAEs is below both the OECD economies and all other regional groupings of low- and middle-income economies.

In contrast to the situation in most developing economies, in the HPAEs, rates of public and private savings have been high and growing. For example, Singapore's public savings rose from 5.5 percent of GDP in 1974–80 to 18.5 percent in 1981–90, and private savings rose from 22.6 to 24 percent. Malaysia's public savings increased from an average 3.2 percent of GDP in 1961–80 to 10.3 percent in 1981–90, while its private savings increased slightly. Thailand's public savings was high in the 1980s (8–15 percent of GDP), but declined as a proportion of GDP in the mid-1980s, when the private savings rate rose dramatically (see table 5.6).

While in some other economies (for example, Pakistan, Zimbabwe, and Venezuela) public savings was relatively high and accounted for a major part of national savings, generally public savings in low- and middle-income economies was substantially lower than in the HPAEs and had declined. For example, public savings in the Philippines declined from an average of 10.4 percent of GDP in 1980–83 to 1.4 percent in 1984–87, leading to much lower national savings rates. Both public and private savings declined in the mid-1980s in Argentina and Chile. Brazil's public savings dropped from 8.3 percent of GDP in 1980 to 3.2 percent for the period 1983–85.[11] Some Sub-Saharan African economies (for example, Ghana) had negative public savings in the 1980s, offsetting increases in private savings.

Figure 5.2 Average Public Consumption as a Percentage of GDP

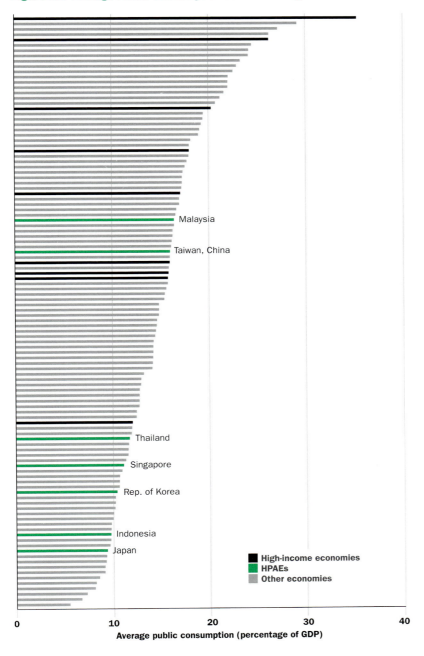

Average public consumption (percentage of GDP)

Legend:
- ■ High-income economies
- ■ HPAEs
- ■ Other economies

Source: World Bank data.

Table 5.6 Public and Private Savings of HPAEs and Other Selected Developing Economies

(percentage of GDP)

Economy/year	Public savings	Private savings
HPAEs		
Indonesia, 1981–88	7.7	14.0
Japan		
1945–54	5.3	12.0
1955–70	6.2	17.2
1971–80	4.6	20.1
1981–88	5.1	15.8
Malaysia		
1961–80	3.2	18.7
1981–90	10.3	19.1
Singapore		
1974–80	5.5	22.6
1981–90	18.5	24.0
Thailand		
1980–85	14.3	4.7
1986–87	8.6	14.6
Other developing economies		
Argentina		
1980–85	1.9	11.0
1986–87	4.2	1.2
Brazil		
1980–85	5.1	10.5
1986–87	6.9	12.5
Chile		
1980–84	3.9	2.3
1985–87	7.9	0.6
Colombia		
1980–84	2.6	13.6
1985–87	7.2	14.0
Costa Rica, 1980–87	7.3	7.7
Ghana		
1980–86	1.2	2.1
1985–87	-1.1	6.1
Mexico, 1980–87	4.3	17.5
Pakistan, 1980–87	16.9	-9.7
Philippines		
1980–83	10.4	11.5
1984–87	1.4	14.1
Venezuela, 1980–87	16.0	5.6
Zimbabwe, 1980–87	16.8	-1.7

Sources: Corbo and Schmidt-Hebbel (1991); Singapore (various years); Yan (1991); World Bank (1989a); Japanese Economic Planning Agency (various years).

Coordination Problems that Hinder Savings

Savings are affected by several types of coordination problems induced by features of financial markets. Below, we briefly describe each of these coordination problems and the policy responses of HPAE governments. The range of the HPAEs' policy responses to these actual or incipient market failures range from standard remedies that the HPAEs may have implemented better, such as the prudential regulation of banks, to more activist interventions, such as limiting competition or regulating interest rate spreads.

Absence of Deposit Insurance. People will only deposit funds with a bank or other financial institution if they are reasonably confident that the institution will return the funds as promised. In theory, private firms or even the banks themselves could sell insurance to depositors; in practice, they do not. (These points are discussed at greater length in Stiglitz 1993a.) The reasons are straightforward. Assuming a private firm did offer deposit insurance, depositors have no more reason to trust an insurer than they do the bank: either or both could fail. Indeed, a firm that insured several banks would risk nearly simultaneous losses during a general economic downturn or a bank run. The risk of such losses makes a private insurer's promise to deliver even more suspect than the bank's. Thus, without government efforts to guarantee that banks will be able to honor their liabilities, potential depositors would tend to save less and keep a higher proportion of their savings in nonfinancial assets.

Governments have a second motivation for insuring deposits. Financial failures of banks have a strong negative externality; when some banks fail, depositors lose confidence even in sound financial institutions, as the history of bank runs attests. Governments therefore try to prevent overt bank failures, frequently acting explicitly or implicitly as the insurer of last resort through the central bank.

High Transaction Costs. Private banks seek large deposits and those that are relatively inexpensive to service; they therefore compete for the deposits of corporations and affluent urban dwellers and make little or no effort to attract the savings of workers, poor people, and residents of small towns and the countryside. In addition, banks may refuse such marginally unprofitable deposits by setting minimum deposit levels. These practices raise the transactions costs for small savers and discourage them from making financial savings.

Isolation and Insufficient Savings. Some economists have also suggested that individuals acting on their own and their family's behalf may save less than would be desirable from the point of view of society as a whole. This is because they fail to consider the impact of their savings decisions on others. If savings decisions could be coordinated, each individual would save more and aggregate savings would rise (Dasgupta, Marglin, and Sen 1972). In such circumstances social returns on savings exceed private returns, and there may be a role for government efforts to increase savings.

Policies that Promoted Savings

Government responses to these coordination problems are varied. All governments take steps to alleviate the lack of deposit insurance markets and to promote stable financial institutions. These generally include prudential regulation of savings institutions and protection of depositors from bank defaults. In general, the developing HPAEs have performed these fundamentals better than many other developing economies. East Asian governments have attached great importance to maintaining savers' confidence in financial institutions. Often their policies have gone beyond prudential regulations to include protecting banks from competition to increase the financial strength of banking institutions.[12] Sometimes this has been done at the expense of long-run efficiency.

When necessary, all HPAE governments have bailed out troubled financial institutions through financial and management assistance or mergers with stronger banks (see table A5.5, at the end of the chapter). This is not to say that the HPAEs have not experienced banking crises. Indeed, some financial instability is probably unavoidable in economies that are expanding as rapidly as those in East Asia. Nonetheless, the crises that have occurred, for example, in the wake of the 1980s' real estate speculation boom in Hong Kong, Japan, Korea, Malaysia, and Thailand, have generally been brief and modest, particularly in comparison with the protracted and disruptive banking crises in Bolivia, Chile, Ghana, the Philippines, and Turkey during the same period.

Regulations to Promote Bank Solvency. Central banks and departments of finance in the HPAEs appear to have been generally more successful in supervising commercial banks, which have reported a relatively low proportion of nonperforming loans in their portfolios. There are some major exceptions: Indonesia in the late 1980s, Korea in the early 1980s, and Malaysia's Bank Bumiputera in the 1970s. Generally, however, non-performing loans have been less of a problem in the HPAEs than in many developing economies. For example, one study of twelve Latin American economies found that nonperforming loans accounted for nearly 14 percent of total loans in 1987, while the proportion of bad loans surpassed 20 percent in Argentina, Honduras, Uruguay, and Venezuela (Morris and others 1990). In Pakistan, required provisions for bad debts constituted 14 percent of total portfolios in 1989 (an internal World Bank report). In Sub-Saharan Africa, many banks have failed, and 25–40 percent of bank portfolios have had to be written off. While macroeconomic instability and low growth are partly responsible for this poor performance, inadequate prudential regulation also contributed.

The more effective prudential regulation of East Asian banks is apparent in the ease with which most of them adopted the international capital adequacy requirements set by the Bank for International Settlements (BIS) to ensure that banks do not take on inappropriate levels of risks. Hong Kong, Japan, and Singapore began to strengthen prudential regulation in the 1970s, and Malaysia, Thailand, and Taiwan, China, followed suit in the 1980s. All HPAEs have since adopted the BIS capital adequacy requirements. Indonesia, the last to do so, has had some difficulty achieving BIS capital requirement levels because it introduced proper prudential regulations rather late.[13]

By contrast, in Latin America only Ecuador adhered to BIS standards, while Colombia was in the process of adopting the standards (Morris and others 1990). Moreover, some Latin American economies have not established minimum capital requirements for new banks. In Sub-Saharan Africa, the net worth positions of banking systems sharply deteriorated in the 1980s, and adopting BIS standards would entail substantial recapitalization.

Most East Asian economies continue to rely on close contact between supervisors and banks to encourage prudence. This routine, often daily interaction enables regulators personally to assess the riskiness of a bank's portfolio. This pragmatic approach is evident in their attitude toward collateral requirements. To reduce the risk of borrower defaults, regulators encouraged banks to require substantial collateral. But because the collateral was usually real estate, banks became increasingly exposed in the 1980s to the risk of asset price declines.[14] Faced with potential insolvencies due to heavy real estate lending, regulators in Hong Kong, Japan, Thailand, and Taiwan, China, have limited the use of real estate as collateral and sought to reduce loan concentration by limiting lending to related parties. Enforcement has been difficult, however, because companies are closely held and disclosure rules are generally weak. Moreover, in several economies, notably Indonesia, Japan, and Thailand, banks and firms tend to have interlinking ownership.

Many East Asian financial systems appear to be moving toward a mixed system of enforcement, in which the highly structured exposure rules that characterize international supervision are backed by traditional moral suasion in which bank regulators use their control of branch licensing, rediscounts, and other regulations as leverage to ensure cooperation. The Bank of Japan, for example, has used constant interaction between city banks and the supervisory authorities, coupled with its tight control of branch licensing, to encourage prudent behavior. Malaysia's bank supervisors operate in a similar fashion.

Coping with Distressed Financial Institutions. In spite of generally good prudential regulation, there have been financial crises in East Asia brought about by a mix of macroeconomic shocks, insufficient prudential regulation, and speculative lending (see table A5.5, at the end of the chapter). However, governments' rapid and effective response has been able to maintain confidence by acting as implicit insurer without excessive fiscal costs. Rapid growth and spiraling real estate prices have often tempted financial institutions into property and sometimes stock speculation. This has happened repeatedly in Hong Kong (in 1965, 1982, and 1986), but it has also been a problem in Malaysia, Thailand, and, most recently, Japan. By the late 1980s, financial institutions in each of these economies were facing difficulties, as nonperforming loans rose due to the economic downturn.

Korea encountered similar difficulties but for somewhat different reasons, among them the heavy indebtedness of firms that had been beneficiaries of government-directed credit. When external demand fell in the 1980s, many firms had large excess capacity and poor debt service capability. Among them were government priority projects in shipping, overseas construction, textiles, and machinery. Because the firms were highly leveraged, they were financially vulnerable to changes in demand and interest rates.

When financial distress has occurred, HPAE governments have come to the rescue. Table A5.5 describes the origins of and responses to some of the significant banking crises in the HPAEs. While only Korea and Taiwan, China, have established explicit deposit insurance (both in the early 1980s), they and other HPAEs have for decades implicitly insured deposits by stepping in whenever necessary to prevent bank failures.

In some cases, especially in Japan, stronger banks were pressed to take over banks in financial trouble. When mergers have been impractical, East Asian governments have served as lender of last resort. Only Hong Kong and Thailand have liquidated insolvent financial institutions. Yet because of tougher prudential supervision and better economic growth, the costs of bank rescues in East Asia have been lower than in many other economies. During the 1980s the estimated fiscal cost of bailouts in the HPAEs was 0.5–1 percent of GDP, compared with 2.3 percent in the United States, 2.5 percent in Turkey, 3 percent in the Philippines, and 26 percent in Chile.

Protection of Banks from Competition. Nearly all governments regulate the creation of new financial institutions and the entry of foreign financial institutions to try to ensure that newcomers are solvent and will remain so. But many East Asian governments have gone further, limiting competition and protecting existing banks both from foreign banks and from new domestic competitors. With the notable exceptions of Hong Kong, Indonesia, and Singapore, which welcome the opening of new financial institutions provided they meet capitalization and other regulatory requirements, most HPAEs have had rigid restrictions on entry. When expansion has been permitted, it has mostly been through the licensing of new branches of existing banks. Despite limits on entry, the banking sectors in the HPAEs are no more concentrated than in other developing economies or OECD economies (see table A5.6, at the end of the chapter). This means that banking systems differ little in structure among economies, although the origins of their relatively high international degree of concentration may differ, as we shall discuss below.

Why were entry restrictions used rather than high net worth standards to encourage prudent behavior? Entry restrictions give governments a more discretionary tool to influence the behavior of banks than net worth requirements. Governments may exercise discretion in deciding which banks should expand (through more branches) and when. Banks have an incentive to respond to governments' actions lest they forgo the additional profits from asset growth. Net worth requirements do not provide governments this avenue of influence.

Have these restrictions on competition contributed to increased financial savings? The answer is ambiguous. Larger, more profitable banks have more to lose and so a greater incentive to maintain their reputations by prudent lending. Moreover, restricting competition increases profits, and higher profits increase the financial strength of the banking system (provided banks do not distribute profits to shareholders). These effects would raise saver confidence and hence increase savings. Yet, in most economies regulators have argued that the financial sector's tendency toward concentration is so great that governments must intervene to maintain competition within the banking sector, preventing monopolistic practices that squeeze clients, reduce efficiency and innovation, and hence, lower savings.[15]

Therefore, whether controlling competition results in favorable or unfavorable outcomes for savings depends on whether the increased solvency comes at the expense of efficiency. The evidence among developed economies supports the view that financial systems with fewer, larger banks outperform systems with many smaller banks (Vittas 1991). But in many developing economies financial markets are dominated by a few large, very inefficient banks whose size is based less on economies of scale than on restrictions of bank licenses and other limits on competition.

The impact of limited competition on banking efficiency varies across economies in East Asia. Japanese commercial banks, for example, are regarded as efficient, despite entry restrictions, because of the pressure of competition among existing banks (Sakakibara and others 1982). There is no dominant commercial bank in Japan. The top five banks are roughly equal in size, and they account for about 40 percent of total commercial bank assets (see table A5.6). In comparison to large German banks, Japanese banks tend to have lower lending margins (spreads), although small German banks have lower spreads than small Japanese banks. The Japanese banks also have lower lending margins than equivalent banks in the United States but approximately equal rates of return on equity (Ueda 1992). Gross interest margins as well as net operating costs (as a percentage of total assets) of banks in Korea, Malaysia, and Thailand were in line with OECD economies and substantially lower than other developing economies, notably Liberia, Sri Lanka, and Turkey, and selected economies in Latin America (Hanson and Rocha 1986). Conversely, studies of the banking system in Indonesia and Korea find that protection has led to less innovative practices (internal World Bank reports).

Thus the evidence does not conclusively support the efficacy of policies to limit entry. Where tendencies toward large financial institutions are strong, government efforts to limit entry will mainly reduce efficiency and lower innovation. This is especially true of restrictions in some economies on foreign banks, which tend to be the leaders in innovation.

Regulating Spreads. Except for Hong Kong and Singapore, all HPAEs have at times simultaneously regulated deposit and lending rates and consequently the spreads of financial institutions. If spreads are controlled, banks will earn limited rents despite protection from competition. In general, lending spreads of the HPAEs have been comparable to many OECD economies and lower than most other developing economies, indicating that controls on intermediation margins were generally effective. Figure 5.3 shows that average interest spread of the HPAEs (about 3 percent) is lower than average spreads in other developing regions, which range from 4.0 to nearly 10 percent. Margins in Indonesia, Thailand, and Taiwan, China, were about 3–4 percent in the 1980s. These margins are comparable to those in the United States (2 percent) and Japan (3 percent). In Korea and Malaysia they were generally higher at about 4.5 percent (see table A5.7, at the end of the chapter). Thus, while restricting competition generated some rents for banks, a combination of competition among incumbents, regulation of spreads, and eventual liberalization of entry re-

Figure 5.3 Spreads in Financial Intermediation, 1979–89

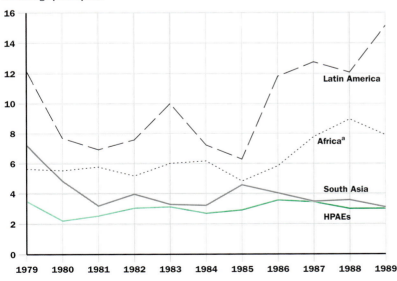

Percentage point spread

a. Includes countries in Sub-Saharan Africa and North Africa.
Source: International Monetary Fund data.

strictions made banks in East Asia relatively efficient compared with those in other low- and middle-income economies.

Regulated spreads are not always binding, however, because banks can circumvent them by charging fees or requiring compensating balances. Banks in Japan and Korea, for example, charged compensating balances. There is some evidence that these practices were sufficient to circumvent the regulations in Japan (Ueda 1992). Intermediation income of commercial banks in Korea has been higher than the simple difference between lending and deposit rates. In contrast, regulations on deposit and lending rates have been binding in the state-owned commercial banks of Indonesia and Taiwan, China. In Thailand, commercial bank lending rates tended to bunch around the ceiling rate, and interest rate spreads increased slightly after the mid-1980s due to a drop in deposit rates and the relatively unchanged lending rate ceilings (an internal World Bank report).

Creating Postal Savings Institutions. In addition to effective prudential supervision and regulation of entry and spreads, all of which encouraged savings by ensuring stable banks, Japan, Korea, Malaysia, Singapore, and Taiwan, China, established government-run postal savings systems to attract small savers. Postal savings systems offered small savers greater security and lower transaction costs than the private sector and were therefore particularly effective in attracting to the formal financial sector the savings of low-income and rural households.

Japan established the region's first postal savings program in 1875, with the explicit goal of fostering savings of rural dwellers and people with low to moderate incomes in the cities and towns. Until then, such people were effectively excluded from the financial system, which lacked rural networks and discouraged small depositors by requiring high minimum balances or paying very low interest rates on small deposits. The Japanese government heavily promoted postal savings among low-income households and made the interest income on small postal savings deposits tax free.

Similar institutions with the same savings mobilization goals were established in Korea, Malaysia, Singapore, and Taiwan, China. Like Japan, both Korea and Taiwan, China, have granted tax-exempt status to the interest income from postal savings during long periods. In Taiwan, China, postal savings offices account for about a third of all financial institution offices, and the postal savings service has longer business hours than other financial institutions (Shea, forthcoming). In Malaysia and Singapore, where postal savings have also accounted for a large proportion of domestic deposits, the governments separated management of the savings system from the post office in the early 1970s, when the proportion of postal savings in total savings declined, evidently because postal employees were not enthusiastic promoters of savings. Even so, the savings system continued to utilize the post offices as a deposit-taking branch network.

Postal savings systems can be an effective way of mobilizing household savings, provided that governments take care that the cost of administering the systems does not outstrip the benefits. Generally postal savings systems piggyback on the mail-delivery infrastructure, thus minimizing overhead and fixed costs. In the early years in Japan, the system often operated out of the houses of wealthy landowners that were already serving as postal branches. As postal savings expanded and the administrative burden rose, postal officials demanded wage increases. Overall, however, the postal system's cost of accepting deposits has been much less than that of the private banks (Mukai 1981).

Forced Savings. Besides the above measures, some HPAEs have tried to compel savings through several measures, including mandatory pension schemes and restrictions on consumption and borrowing for consumption. Because these measures constitute more active interventions in markets, their efficacy, even in East Asia, is open to question. Restrictions on consumer choices, including the basic consumption-savings decision, have welfare costs. Moreover, similar efforts in other economies have been spectacular failures. Examples include the widespread deprivation and massive waste associated with forced savings in the now-defunct command economies.

Three economies in East Asia, Japan, Malaysia and Singapore, have well-developed, mandatory pension plans. The impact of these plans on aggregate savings depends on the degree to which they substitute for voluntary savings. Evidence of the impact of pension funds in Japan and Singapore, the only two economies where the issue has been studied, is inconclusive. One study of savings in Japan found pension funds had no significant impact on total savings, although they did channel household savings into financial assets, thereby contributing to financial deepening (Dekle 1988). Another found a small negative effect (Noguchi 1985). This suggests that the Japanese pension fund squeezed out a portion of voluntary savings. Conversely, there is evidence that Singapore's Central Provident Fund boosted aggregate savings by about 4 percent of GDP during the 1970s and 1980s (Monetary Authority of Singapore 1991).

The lack of consumer credit to purchase housing, consumer durables, and other consumer items may have induced increased household savings in some East Asian economies. Bank regulators in Japan, Korea, and Taiwan, China, restricted credit available for consumer durables purchases. Maki (1993) offers evidence that the rapid increase in savings in Japan after World War II was driven by the need to acquire consumer durables, and he shows the same pattern existed in Korea and Taiwan, China. As household incomes and the demand for consumer durables increased, savings as a proportion of income rose rapidly. Once the excess demand for consumer durables was met, savings rates stabilized and even declined.

Have Policies Increased Savings?

How effective were policies in the HPAEs aimed at increasing savings? Favorable growth conditions and good policy fundamentals account for most of East Asia's superior savings performance. Macroeconomic stability combined with solid prudential regulation of financial institutions created an environment in which savings were secure and retained their value. Limits to competition among banks and the willingness of governments to rescue financial institutions in trouble had costs—reduced efficiency in the former case and fiscal costs in the latter—but these were moderate and may have been compensated for by the increase in savings engendered by public confidence in banks. Postal savings had the virtue of being both secure and accessible instruments for small savers. Governments in Japan, Korea, and Taiwan, China, as well as Malaysia and Singapore, operated these institutions efficiently, tapping a nontraditional source of financial savings at relatively low administrative costs.

Have measures that required consumers to save more than they would have voluntarily increased economic welfare? The answer is ambiguous. Restrictions on consumer credit raised savings rates temporarily in Japan but at a cost in terms of consumer welfare. Forced savings through pension schemes have not been a major factor in increasing savings rates in East Asia, except perhaps in Singapore, but public savings are an important and complementary source of high aggregate savings. To justify intervening in households' savings decisions, social returns on the increased savings must exceed the private opportunity costs determined by the rate of return on investment. This would be the case, for example, if total factor productivity growth were positive and a significant component of overall growth, either as a consequence of dynamic scale economies or of externalities associated with investment. The social return also must exceed the private return to justify intervening in households' savings decisions. In Japan (during its rapid growth period), Korea, and Taiwan, China, there is evidence that economywide productivity growth has been positive and rates of return to capital have been good. In Singapore, however, evidence suggests that aggregate total factor productivity growth is negative and rates of return to capital are low (Young 1992). Singapore may have compelled its consumers to save too much.

Explaining East Asia's High Investment Rates

ONE OF THE MOST REMARKABLE ASPECTS OF THE HPAEs IS their unusually high rates of private investment. Private investment in the HPAEs averaged about 7 percentage points of GDP higher than other low- and middle-income economies (see chapter 1). As with East Asia's high rates of human capital formation and savings, investment has been fostered by macroeconomic stability and rapid economic growth. Growth, savings, and investment interacted in a virtuous circle as high investment initially spurred growth, which resulted in increased savings to support continued high rates of investment. In addition, two general conditions have been particularly important to investment. These—secure property rights and complementary public investment in infrastructure—are key elements of the market-friendly institutional environment discussed in chapter 4.

Security of property rights is so obvious that it might easily be overlooked. Where foreign or domestic private investors fear complete or partial expropriation of their investments, private investment initiative is naturally reduced. Thus secure property rights embodied in the legal framework were a key to high investment rates. In addition, formal and informal mechanisms leading to enforcement of contracts were an important contributing factor.

Data also suggest that the developing HPAE governments have done a better job providing infrastructure themselves and, at times, creating the conditions for the private sector to provide it. Limited econometric evidence suggests that these investments, at least in the cases of Korea and Taiwan, China, generate very high rates of return (an internal World Bank report). Easterly and Rebelo (1993) present cross-economy estimates that infrastructure investment has a high payoff for economic growth. These investments have been highly complementary to private investment, especially in export-oriented manufacturing activities.

Table 5.7 shows some indication of infrastructural development for the developing HPAEs and selected low- and middle-income economies. Even if we set aside urbanized Hong Kong and Singapore, the HPAEs' per capita electricity generating capacity is equal to or exceeds that of economies at similar levels of per capita income. Similarly, from 1975 to 1985 the five developing HPAEs with nontrivial rural sectors increased telephone service much faster than other economies with roughly the same population per phone in 1975. For example, in Malaysia the number of telephones per person roughly quadrupled, while Brazil, Mauri-

Table 5.7 Direct Provision of Infrastructure, Selected Years

Economy	Percentage of roads paved		Electricity-generating capacity, per capita		Population per telephone	
	1971	1986	1965	1990	1975	1985
HPAEs						
Hong Kong	100	100	160.6	1,438.3	—	—
Indonesia	25	62.2	7.7	64.4	435	205
Korea, Rep. of	14.2	54.2	33.2	562.1	25	5
Malaysia	85	80	—	28.1	42	12
Singapore	—	95.8	182.3	1,133.3	—	—
Thailand	67	39.6	18.2	174.2	133	68
Other developing economies						
Bolivia	—	—	42.4	102.1	—	—
Brazil	4.5	7.1	87.9	351.7	35	12
Chile	11.6	12.4	169.5	309.0	24	16
Côte d'Ivoire	0.04	7.9	21.3	98.6	—	—
Ghana	—	—	52.4	79.7	—	—
India	34.9	48.0	20.9	89.5	352	203
Kenya	7.0	—	10.3	29.9	113	72
Mauritius	0.8	92.0	—	—	35	16
Mexico	60.0	33.3	117.0	339.6	21	11
Philippines	—	12.5	—	111.7	—	—
Sri Lanka	69.6	—	19.7	75.8	—	—

— Not available.

Sources: For population per phone, World Bank data; for percentage of paved roads, International Road Federation (various years); for electricity-generating capacity, United Nations (various years, b; 1976).

tius, and Peru had smaller gains.[16] Although increases in infrastructure are clearly correlated with income growth, recent econometric evidence suggests causality may run from infrastructure spending to growth (Easterly and Rebelo 1993; Canning and Fay 1993).

Coordination Problems that Hinder Investment

Beyond establishing favorable general conditions for investment, most HPAE governments have employed a variety of policies designed specifically to address coordination problems that may hinder investment. These problems are derived from shortcomings in markets for information and in markets for sharing risk; both types of problems exist in all economies, but the problems and the consequences tend to be worse in developing economies. For example, such developing-economy information problems as poor accounting standards and a dearth of merchant banks and other institutions to monitor corporate performance mean that bond and equity markets are often weak or entirely absent.[17] Similarly, while market mechanisms for sharing risk are limited in all economies—firms in developing and industrial economies often cannot buy insurance for the most serious risks they face—the consequences are more severe in developing economies in which lower wealth levels make households and firms more vulnerable. Furthermore, the transformations inherent in development, such as the creation of new firms and new industries and the absorption of new technologies, heighten uncertainty.

Policies to Promote Investment. HPAE responses to these problems can be grouped into three broad categories. First, as these economies have matured, policymakers have gradually increased their attention to the creation and improvement of bond and equity markets. However, while these markets are playing an increasingly important role, they were not generally a key factor in mobilizing investment during the HPAEs' economic takeoffs. Second, many HPAEs created development banks to ease constraints in long-term capital markets, as well as specialized institutions to provide financing to agriculture and small- and medium-size enterprises. These efforts appear, on balance, to have been more successful in the HPAEs than in other developing economies, for reasons we shall explore. Finally, HPAE governments have encouraged investment with a wide array of other mechanisms designed to increase the attractiveness of private investment.

The remainder of this chapter describes specific policies in each of these three categories—support for bond and equity markets, establishment of development banks, and mechanisms to increase the attractiveness of private investment—and attempts to evaluate whether each was effective in increasing investment. We devote particular attention to the third category, which includes several policies that involve a high degree of intervention in markets. At the simplest level, many HPAEs boosted corporations' retained earnings by adopting low corporate taxes. Some also reduced the cost of investment by adjusting tax, tariff, and exchange rate policies to hold down the relative price of capital goods. Several governments, particularly Japan, Korea, and Taiwan, China, tried to reduce risk for investors by shouldering some of it themselves or spreading it across other firms. The northern-tier HPAEs also stand out for their efforts to increase domestic investment by restricting capital flows. Finally, several HPAEs, again particularly the northern tier but also Malaysia, subsidized investment financing by slightly suppressing the interest rates on savings deposits and corporate borrowing. This last mechanism, which we term mild financial repression, plays a key role in capital allocation, the subject of the next chapter.

Bond and Equity Markets Developed after the Takeoff. Despite the phenomenal growth of Asian corporations, bond and equity markets have played a relatively small role in Asian finance. As table 5.8 shows, bonds on average between 1970 and 1990 accounted for less than 10 percent of the net financing of corporations for the five HPAEs for which data exist. This is higher than the share of bond financing in the OECD economies, however.

Ironically, policies that contributed to some of the HPAEs' success in developing other financial market institutions may have been inimical to the early development of a corporate bond market. In Japan, for example, the long-term credit banks' government-protected monopoly on the issue of long-term debentures discouraged the development of bond markets.[18] The Thai government created the same monopoly for its private long-term credit banks. In addition, the lack of government securities in most HPAEs, a direct outgrowth of their success at minimizing fiscal deficits, has deprived embryonic bond markets of the most widely utilized risk-free benchmark rate. This has impeded corporate bond issues, since markets find it difficult to determine simultaneously the risk-free rate and the risk premium associated with a specific corporate bond. In response, Hong Kong has issued bonds, even though the government did not need the financing, to establish a risk-free benchmark for the corporate bond market. Malaysia and Singapore are now considering following suit.

Table 5.8 Net Financing Sources of Nonfinancial Corporations in East Asia and Selected Other Developing Economies

Economy/year	Internal sources	External[a] sources			Other sources[b]
		Loans	Bonds	Equity	
East Asia					
Japan					
1956–65	41.9	47.4	2.6	8.1	—
1966–75	45.2	49.5	2.0	3.3	—
1976–83	54.6	40.3	1.7	3.4	—
Korea, Rep. of					
1970–79	27.6	52.5	4.8	14.8	—
1980–89	38.3	32.4	13.6	15.6	—
Malaysia, 1986–91	58.8	36.8	—	1.8	—
Taiwan, China					
1965–80	37.7	42.9	1.7	24.1[c]	-6.2
1981–90	29.9	33.6	6.2	28.6[c]	1.8
Thailand					
1970–76	51.4	30.2	12.6	9.3	-3.4
1977–83	51.8	28.9	11.9	10.8	-3.4
Other developing economies					
Brazil (top 62 private firms)					
1978–83	73.0	25.0	—	14.0	-12.0
Colombia (top 94 firms)					
1971–83	41.5	—	51.3[e]	7.7	—
1984–85	86.0	—	13.0[e]	1.0	—
Philippines, 1980–83	32.1	51.7	—	12.3[d]	7.1
India, 1970–85	23.3	47.8	—	13.2[d]	1.1
Turkey (top 175 firms)					
1979–81	36.0	—	53.0[e]	11.0	—
Selected OECD economies					
France, 1970–85	66.3	50.8	0.7	-0.4	-17.4
Germany, 1970–89	80.6	9.1	-0.6	0.9	10.0
United Kingdom					
1970–89	98.0	18.2	2.0	-8.0	-10.2
United States,					
1970–89	91.3	12.9	17.1	-8.8	-12.5

— Not available.
a. Includes trade credit.
b. Other may include sale of assets, capital and other transfers, and in the case of Thailand, the OECD economies, and Taiwan, China, statistical discrepancy.
c. Taiwan, China, equity is not exclusively new issues. The major portion are stockholders' equity and are equivalent to internal financing.
d. Combines bonds and equity.
e. Combines loans and bonds.
Sources: Brazil: Lees and others (1990). Colombia: World Bank (1991a). India: Reserve Bank of India Bulletins, 1980, 1988, 1991. Japan: Teranishi (1986); Shoven (1988). Korea: Bank of Korea, financial system in Korea, various years. Malaysia: Annual surveys of private investment in Malaysia, 1986–90, Bank Negara, Malaysia. OECD economies: Stiglitz (1993), citing Mayer and Jenkinson. Philippines: Central Bank of the Philippines, flow of funds of the Philippines, 1980–83. Taiwan, China, flow of funds in Taiwan District (ROC), 1991. Thailand: Flow of funds accounts of Thailand, 1983 and 1986. Turkey: World Bank (1983).

While bond markets have historically been small, this appears to be changing as the Asian economies mature. Asian corporations with their headquarters in Japan, Korea, Taiwan, China, and other HPAEs are increasingly issuing corporate bonds, drawing on the strength of their worldwide reputations and access to international financial markets.[19] Recognizing the value of a healthy bond market, Japan has eased laws that discriminated against corporate bonds. Similarly Thailand, and recently Indonesia, have strengthened rating and regulatory agencies, while Hong Kong has reformed its regulatory structures. Malaysia has introduced a corporate bond rating agency. Thus, while corporate bonds have not been important in Asia's takeoff, they are likely to play an increasing role in its financial future.

The story for equity markets is broadly similar to that for bonds: development has tended to follow rather than lead the HPAEs' economic takeoff. In this, the HPAEs are similar to other economies. Indeed, recent evidence shows that equity markets do not play a dominant role in capital formation in either developing or industrial economies (Stiglitz 1993a). Even so, as the East Asian economies have matured, governments have moved with varying degrees of success to promote their growth by streamlining listing procedures and strengthening safeguards against fraud. In Hong Kong, for example, the government pushed the 1986 merger of four competing exchanges into the unified Hong Kong Stock Exchange, and it has since gradually strengthened disclosure requirements and antifraud safeguards. Korea has prodded firms toward the equity market by limiting bank lending. Since 1987, Indonesia has liberalized restrictions on share issues and allowed foreign-owned joint ventures to operate securities firms.

Even so, before the remarkable bull market of the late 1980s, Asian stock markets played a relatively minor role in the mobilization of capital—except in Korea and Taiwan, China, where issues of shares accounted for more than 10 percent of net financing. Since 1985, new share issues have increased, and the proportion of external financing from equity has risen steeply.

Recent policies to support the development of equity and bond markets have been largely successful. The growth of stock market capitalization in the HPAEs was very rapid in the 1980s, although the volatility of stock prices in response to speculative pressures and capital inflows may have reduced their value in signaling efficient investments.[20] However, the Asian stockmarket boom is a relatively recent phenomenon, and its timing—beginning long after most HPAEs' economic takeoffs were well under way—suggests that it is a result rather than a cause of East Asia's rapid growth.

Development Banks. East Asian governments created a wide range of financial institutions to fill perceived gaps in the types of credit provided by private entities (see table A5.8, at the end of the chapter). They addressed the need for long-term credit for industry by creating development banks. Most have also created specialized institutions that provide credit to agriculture and small firms.

Industrial development banks have been substantial long-term lenders in Indonesia, Japan, Korea, and Taiwan, China, but not in the other HPAEs. In Japan, the development banks—the public Japan De-

velopment Bank (JDB) and the private Industrial Bank of Japan—
accounted for about two-thirds of loans outstanding for equipment investment in the 1950s and about half in the early 1960s. Their share in
total lending to industry was small, however, and has declined. At its
peak in 1953, the JDB accounted for 18 percent of new funds lent. Starting in the mid-1950s, job lending fell to 1–6 percent of new lending;
the rest was accounted for by private banks (Kawaura 1991).[21] The
Korean Development Bank made an average of a third of all loans and
guarantees in the 1970s, and the development bank of Taiwan, China,
the Bank of Communications, holds about half of the assets of the banking system. Conversely, Malaysia's development financial institutions
accounted for 2.9 percent of the assets of the financial system in 1980s.
Thailand's industrial development bank has only 1 percent of the assets
of the financial system. Hong Kong has no development bank.

Many other developing economies have also attempted to remedy
the perceived failure in long-term capital markets. Nearly all have been
unsuccessful in creating development banks. Development banks in
South Asia, Latin America, and Sub-Saharan Africa are beset with low
repayment rates; a representative sample of eighteen industrial development banks in developing economies had on average nearly 50 percent
of the value of their loans in arrears (World Bank 1989c). The most
commonly cited causes of development bank failures have been political
pressure to finance bad projects and the poor incentives for and capability of financial institutions to screen and monitor projects.

Development banks have performed much better in the HPAEs, especially those banks in the northern tier economies concentrating on industrial finance.[22] Financial performance has been adequate to good,
and the capacity to evaluate and monitor projects has at least in Japan
created spillovers for the rest of the formal financial system (JDB/JERI
1993).[23] Successful development banks in East Asia have applied commercial criteria in selecting and monitoring projects and firms, even
within the constraints set by government priority activities. Development banks in Japan and Singapore, for example, must select projects
that will repay, since the banks are expected to repay with interest the
funds they obtain from the government. Taiwan, China, introduced another mechanism when in the early 1960s it required borrowers receiving funds from the U.S. Agency for International Development to put
up matching funds and made lending to a nonperformer a criminal of-
fense, imposed on the loan officer.

Most East Asian governments have devised means to contain willful political interference in development banks. Japan, Korea, and Taiwan, China, have appointed senior officials from ministries of finance as chairmen, so they may withstand pressure from other parts of government. Others have controlled the types of lending. Thailand simply disallowed its development bank from lending to state enterprises. The high professionalism and institutional identification of staff, which is characteristic of successful development banks, is a positive factor as well.

Policies to Increase the Attractiveness of Investment

Besides fostering a climate conducive to investment, encouraging bond and equity markets and, in some instances, establishing development banks, each of the HPAEs responded to coordination problems that hinder investment with a variety of mechanisms to make private investment more attractive. Like most other governments that have tried to increase private investment, the HPAEs embodied many of these pro-investment policies in their tax codes. These codes varied across economies and over time, both in their specific intent and in the degree of success, but have nearly always aimed broadly to encourage investment. Because tax codes are often central to the quality of the investment climate, this section begins with a brief survey of tax policy in each of the HPAEs. We conclude the section, and the chapter, with a discussion of four highly specific mechanisms used in some of the HPAEs to encourage investment: low relative prices for capital goods, risk sharing, controls on capital outflows, and mild financial repression.

Tax Policies to Encourage Investment. The HPAEs have employed a wide variety of tax policies to increase investment by raising the retained earnings of companies. On one extreme, Korea and Taiwan, China, used complex tax codes not only to favor investment but also to direct the pattern of their industrial development. On the other extreme, Hong Kong has maintained a simple and largely neutral tax structure with low corporate tax rates. Other tax policy regimes fall in between. Singapore uses taxes to promote industrialization and to attain social objectives. Indonesia and Malaysia have relied heavily on oil revenues and so until recently have paid little attention to other aspects of tax policy. Like Korea and Taiwan, China, Thailand has tried to use tax policy to provide investment incentives; however, weak administrative capabilities mean such efforts have been distortionary rather than helpful. Box 5.2 further explores these issues for Korea, Malaysia, and Thailand.

Below we review briefly the investment-related aspects of the tax structure in each of the developing HPAEs.

■ In Taiwan, China, income taxes generate only a small share of revenue because of extensive exemptions. Income from dividends and interest were tax-exempt until 1981, as were capital gains until 1989. Corporate tax incentives have also been extensive. Research and development expenditures are excluded from the tax base. New industries receive a five-year tax holiday, and industry generally is offered accelerated depreciation of investments. Industries that the government deems strategic receive additional special tax credits (Tanzi and Shome 1992).

■ Korea was the first HPAE to establish a value-added tax (VAT). The VAT in Korea provided revenue to support incentives for investors in industry, particularly exporters. Tax incentives included credits, accelerated depreciation, and special exemptions. In contrast with the other HPAEs, Korea has continuously fine-tuned its tax policy to promote industrial development. From 1953 to 1986, there have been nine major tax reforms.

■ The most distinctive feature of Hong Kong's tax policy is its low rate structure and the low level of revenue it generates. The maximum personal income tax rate is about 15 percent, while corporate income taxes are 17.5 percent. Hong Kong uses low taxes to attract investments in contrast to the mix of high tax rates and high tax incentives offered in Korea and Taiwan, China.

■ Singapore's tax regime is as interventionist as those in Korea and Taiwan, China, but focuses special incentives on foreign investors and on promoting savings. (Contributions to the Central Provident Fund are tax-exempt for both employers and employees.) Malaysia has the highest level of taxation. Its tax-GDP ratio averaged 21.45 percent in 1979–88 but fell steadily during the period because oil revenues declined without compensating increases in non-oil revenues, and the government continued to expand tax incentives to sustain its industrialization drive. The resulting high deficit and emerging constraints on spending have focused attention on the need for systematic tax reforms.

■ Since the 1970s Indonesia has relied heavily on revenue from petroleum and gas, and did not until the early 1980s use tax policy for specific incentive objectives. In 1985 in response to dwindling oil revenues, it embarked on a comprehensive reform that unified personal and corporate income taxes, introduced value-added and urban real estate taxes,

Box 5.2 Why Tax Incentives for Investment Often Fail

DEVELOPING ECONOMIES TEND TO HAVE HIGHER corporate tax rates and make greater use of tax incentives than industrial economies. This has been particularly true in East Asia, where governments have tried to attract desirable investments with a wide variety of incentives, including reduced income tax rates, tax holidays, investment credits, accelerated depreciation allowances, and generous tax deductions.

How successful are such incentives? While well-designed tax incentives do work, poorly designed incentives may actually deter investment. For example, if losses incurred during a tax holiday cannot be carried over to the post-holiday period, then the holiday offers no advantage to new ventures that have yet to become profitable. While the HPAEs' high investment rates imply that their incentive regimes have worked better—or at least have been less distorting—than those in less successful economies, even in these generally well-run economies investment incentives have often gone awry. The difficulties of designing an effective incentives regime can be seen in the following examples.

Malaysia

Although the tax system has a major impact on the profitability of investments, the tangled incentives it embodies have often shown scant relationship to the export growth and increased equality among ethnic groups that the government intends to promote. Tax incentives vary widely across sectors, types of investment, and means of financing and have changed frequently over time. In 1983 buying machinery with retained earnings was much more advantageous tax-wise in the construction and tin sectors than in manufacturing. Between 1983 and 1987 the tax code consistently favored bond financing of machinery over bond financing of buildings, but the opposite was true for financing through retained earnings. Moreover, the supposed beneficiaries of tax holidays—infant industries and Malay firms—often were not profitable enough to reap the intended benefits. While investment has nonetheless flourished in Malaysia, the government concluded in 1989 that high corporate tax rates and highly variable incentives were doing more harm

and eliminated tax-based incentives. The reform has been modestly successful in reducing distortions and increasing tax revenues.

■ Thailand has one of the most complex tax systems among the HPAEs. Business and income taxes include a bewildering array of rates, mostly high. On top of this, the government adopted a complex system of tax incentives to direct investments into strategic sectors. The system's complexity and lack of bureaucratic capacity have resulted in poor implementation. In contrast with Korea and Taiwan, China, where tax incentives have generally worked as intended, incentives in Thailand appear to have done more harm than good. The government has begun to try to remedy the situation: in 1989 the personal income tax structure was partly simplified; a 10 percent VAT has been proposed to replace complex business taxes.

than good and began simplifying the tax system accordingly.

Thailand

Since 1960, the Board of Investment has granted investors fiscal incentives (such as tax and import duty reductions) and nonfiscal concessions (eased restrictions on foreign investment and employment of foreigners) on the basis of the contribution of proposed projects to the balance of payments, employment, development of poorer provinces, and other economic and social criteria. But one study found that 70 percent of all board-sponsored projects would have proceeded even without incentives. A detailed analysis of seven projects found that three with very high private returns actually had negative social returns. Studies also show that Thailand's tax holidays have been inefficient in promoting investment in terms of forgone revenue.

Korea

The Korean government has constantly tinkered with its tax system, employing at various times nearly every possible fiscal instrument to promote investment. These initiatives fall into three phases: first, tax rebates to encourage exports (1961–72); then, investment credits and tax holidays to promote heavy and chemical industries (1973–79); and finally, a value-added tax and more neutral overall tax regime to support adjustment and liberalization (1980–89). Throughout, GDP grew steadily and strongly, an indication that the shifting tax regime probably facilitated rather than fueled growth. One study using a general equilibrium model concluded that tax policies contributed only about 6 percent of Korea's total GDP growth from 1962 to 1982 and a mere 3 percent of manufactured export growth.

Such disappointing results in generally well-run economies suggest that other developing economies should consider them carefully before devoting scarce bureaucratic resources to devising and administering an investment incentives regime. While incentives are probably necessary to attract investment to an economy with high corporate taxes, the Hong Kong alternative—few incentives and a low, universal corporate tax—would appear to be a simpler and more dependable way to achieve the same results.

Source: Shah (1992).

Did the HPAEs' investment-friendly tax policies spur growth? Tax policies involve fiscal sacrifice, a transfer of income from taxpayers in general to investors. The assessment of whether these policies were successful depends on similar considerations to those applying to public or forced savings. If the increased investments were absorbed efficiently, as it appears they were in most of the HPAEs with activist tax policies, it is likely that they raised aggregate welfare. But the administrative burden associated with a complicated tax incentive structure such as Korea's or Singapore's has high social costs itself. The success of other economies in East Asia, such as Hong Kong, with very low but uniform taxes on corporate incomes, suggests that the major gains accrue from leaving retained earnings with corporations and promoting investment in equipment, rather than from attempting to fine-tune incentive structures to private investors through the tax system.

Low Relative Prices for Capital Goods. Unlike most other low- and middle-income economies, the HPAEs were able to hold down the relative prices of investment goods, especially equipment, during the 1980s (Bhattacharya and Page 1993). Figure 5.4 shows the relative price of investment of goods (ratio of the investment deflator to the GDP deflator) for forty economies for which consistent real private investment data are available. For the group as a whole, the price of investment goods increased about 15 percent faster than all other goods during the 1980s, in part because devaluations increased the domestic price of imported and import-intensive investment goods.

The HPAEs are different in several ways. First, the relative price of investment goods remained lower than in other developing economies throughout the global economic expansion of the 1970s and the adjustment period in the 1980s. Second, the relative price of investment goods declined during the early stages of adjustment from 1980 to 1984—a period when they were rising in most other developing economies—and only began to rise in 1985, when the HPAE economies were well on the way to recovery. By 1989, relative prices between HPAEs and other economies were again aligned. Thus in these economies de-

Figure 5.4 Investment Deflator/GDP Deflator

Index: 1970 = 100

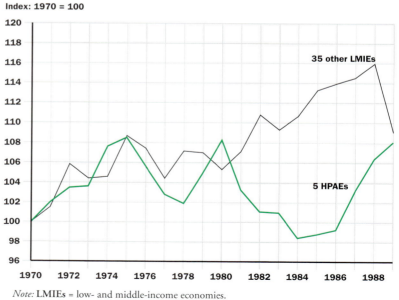

Note: LMIEs = low- and middle-income economies.
Source: Pfeffermann and Madarassay (1992).

clining real prices of investment goods smoothed the impact of adjust-ment on investment.[24]

Rising investment goods prices affect the relationship between in-vestment effort and investment outcomes. As the relative price of invest-ment goods rises (over time or across economies), more nominal investment expenditure is needed to achieve the same volume of physi-cal investment. For the HPAEs and the economies of the non-HPAE sam-ple, investment effort and outcomes coincided quite closely during the 1970s when the relative price of investment goods was essentially simi-lar. During the 1980s, the rising relative price of investment goods in non-HPAEs was reflected in an increasing divergence between investment effort and outcomes. By 1989 the difference was nearly 3 percentage points of GDP. By contrast, in the HPAEs, investment outcomes exceeded investment effort (for both public and private investment) for the entire period 1970–89.[25]

Tax, tariff, and exchange rate policies that kept the relative price of in-vestment goods in the HPAEs below that for other low- and middle-income economies undoubtedly contributed to growth. Since the same volume of nominal investment bought more real capital goods in these economies, output was increased and returns on nominal investments were higher.

Bounding Risks to Private Investors. Some HPAE governments, primarily in the northern tier, have attempted to increase investment by lowering the uncertainty associated with real investment, implicitly or explicitly shar-ing risks with the private sector. Risk-sharing mechanisms have come in many forms—recession cartels in Japan, firm and bank workouts in Korea, financial repression to recapitalize firms in Malaysia, signaling priorities and policy intentions through the directed-credit systems of Japan, Korea, and Taiwan, China, and credit guarantees to small and medium-size enterprises in Korea and Taiwan, China. Those that were effective all exhibited a common feature: firms benefiting from shared risk were monitored for performance. In this way governments miti-gated the problem that has plagued many public sector attempts to share risks with the private sector in other low- and middle-income economies: reducing the risk of failure to the private sector reduces the incentive to avoid failure. This can lead to a political dynamic in which gains are private but losses are socialized.

An important feature of Japanese industrial policy was the creation of recession cartels and the use of other forms of adjustment assistance in declining industries. Japanese antimonopoly law has been consistently lenient in allowing the organization of cartels under the administrative guidance of MITI to ease the exit of firms from declining industries. These cartels were especially common during the rapid growth period when they were used to ease the adjustment problems of declining industries. The cartel allows firms to share losses. They may also be eligible for subsidized loans to upgrade technology or restructure operations. In this way, bankruptcy or massive layoffs by one enterprise may be avoided (Ito 1992).

Japanese adjustment assistance has been especially prominent in mining, textiles, shipbuilding, and aluminum. In general it has succeeded in avoiding the abrupt dislocations that often characterize firm failures in market economies, but this orderly decline has been purchased at the cost of increased prices to consumers and lower returns to investors in firms that would have survived. Moreover, the cartels provide an incentive for firms to overinvest in capacity during good times, since they will be protected during downturns and their adjustment assistance will be related to their existing capacity.

Performance criteria play an important role, even in declining industries. Interaction among firms and between firms and MITI are a means to prevent free riding and to monitor performance. Thus the organization of an industrial adjustment assistance program in Japan conforms to the model of contests presented in chapter 2 and suggests that economies without similarly well-developed institutional capacity may wish to avoid the commitments to orderly exit policies.

In some HPAEs, most frequently in Japan and Korea, troubled priority projects have been bailed out by the government. Often, the financial cost of the bailout was large. In Japan the government took over some losses associated with financing declining industries, such as in coal mining. When government-supported heavy and chemical industry projects in Korea experienced severe excess capacity and financial difficulties in the 1980s, the government provided seventy-eight distressed firms with new, subsidized loans (totaling about 16 percent of commercial bank loans) and rescheduled outstanding ones. The government also provided banks, whose nonperforming loans rose substantially and whose profits declined (partly because lending rates were cut), with subsidized credit from the Central Bank and allowed them entry into attractive areas of financial services. In Indonesia, the government bought 35 percent of the equity of a large cement plant when it became financially troubled while operating only at 50 percent capacity (Kunio 1988).

Development bank lending may also confer implicit insurance. It frequently signals areas of government commitment, providing an additional measure of comfort to private investors and banks (JDB/JERI 1993). These commitments may extend to efforts to ease adjustment problems in promoted sectors. With government inducement, the Industrial Bank of Japan has led syndications for firms in distress and forced their restructuring, substituting for liquidation or external takeovers. In the 1980s Korea extended cheap development bank loans to firms that were not meeting their debt obligations.

Has bounding risk contributed to growth? Bounding risk by the private sector was apparently successful or at least not a failure in Japan, Korea, and Taiwan, China, but this is almost unique compared with the experience of other economies, developing or industrial. Risk sharing generates moral hazard problems, which Japan, Korea, and Taiwan, China, attempted to contain through fostering institutions to monitor priority projects. One consequence of shared risks was shared monitoring by the private and public sectors. Several institutions, including development banks, private financial institutions, firms, and various ministries in the government, often had stakes in the implementation of the project. The government's role as monitor of firms was important. For example, Korea's financial policies promoted high leverage, which made firms vulnerable to loan roll over decisions of financial institutions. Since the government was able to influence which loans were rolled over, it was able to use them as a lever for eliciting compliance from firms (Sakong 1993). Similar monitoring was rarely present in the Southeast Asian HPAEs, with the consequence that attempts to bound risk there were not successful.

Controls on Capital Outflows. Restricting capital outflows is one of the more controversial mechanisms employed by the HPAEs to increase domestic investment. Japan, Korea, and Taiwan, China, all employed such restrictions during the formative periods of their rapid growth. In each case the rationale was straightforward: if people were prohibited from sending capital abroad, they would save and invest at home. In addition the capital controls made repressing interest rates on deposits possible, since savers were denied higher-yielding assets abroad. Although all three economies have since liberalized controls on capital flows to varying degrees, the existence of restrictions at a time when these economies were achieving high and rising savings rates challenges the premise that free and open financial markets are always best for growth.

What impact, then, do capital export restrictions have on accumulation? The obvious failure of such restrictions in economies prone to capital flight suggests that capital is too fluid to be retained when domestic conditions are inimical to savings and investment. Therefore the simplest explanation for the seeming success of these restrictions in Northeast Asia is that the economies offered returns adequate to retain capital even without restrictions. Conversely, for reasons we discussed in chapter 4, these particular governments have been unusually successful in eliciting the cooperation of economic elites, the very groups and individuals who might otherwise ship capital offshore.

Thus, for certain periods in these three economies, government restrictions on outward capital flows may have contributed marginally to domestic accumulation, if only by raising the risk and therefore the cost of sending capital abroad. If so, such restrictions, which have the potential disadvantage of driving otherwise legitimate economic activity underground or even provoking capital flight, would rank among the comparatively risky interventions that are likely to prove successful only in economies that have able bureaucracies and have already established the fundamentals of growth. Moreover, as the trend toward capital account liberalization in Japan, Korea, and Taiwan, China, suggests, restrictions are probably useful only for a limited time: as economies grow, becoming more sophisticated and more closely linked to international markets, restrictions on capital exports inhibit efficiency and must be dismantled.

In any event, the success of the more open HPAEs undermines any suggestion that capital flow restrictions are somehow necessary for savings and growth. Hong Kong, Malaysia, and Singapore have all achieved high and rising savings rates while permitting and—in the case of the regional financial hubs, Hong Kong and Singapore—even encouraging free flows of capital. Indonesia attempted to control its capital account from independence until the early 1970s but due to the very open nature of its capital market chose to shift to a gradual policy of liberalization. Finally, Thailand has retained formal restrictions on capital movements, but the economy in practice exhibits a high degree of openness (an internal World Bank report). Thus, although capital account restrictions may have played a positive role in the early growth of some HPAEs, economies that have never imposed them or have since liberalized appear to have little to gain by imposing them.

East Asia's lesson about capital account restrictions may in fact be how to get rid of them rather than how to impose them. Both Japan and

Taiwan, China, were successful in liberalizing their capital accounts very gradually throughout the 1970s and 1980s, adjusting the pace as necessary to maintain macroeconomic stability and minimize interest rate and exchange rate volatility. Indonesia's capital market liberalization is described in box 5.3. But while gradual deregulation may be best for economies in which bureaucrats can craft economic policy with relatively little interference, sudden deregulation may be the only deregulation possible in economies where governments are less insulated and there is strong resistance to reform. In such cases policymakers must weigh the dangers of sudden liberalization against the risk that gradual reform may be derailed altogether.

Moderate Repression of Interest Rates. The final mechanism we discuss—the repression of interest rates on corporate borrowing—is perhaps the most controversial. Financial repression is often used to describe the situation when interest rates are at negative real levels. A more precise definition, the one we use here, is government intervention to hold interest rates below market-clearing levels. Of course, in many developing economies with capital account restrictions, managed exchange rates, and undeveloped capital and money markets, it is difficult to determine a market-clearing interest rate. In the absence of such rates, HPAE governments tended to use international interest rates, such as the London interbank offered rate, as guides for the opportunity cost of domestic savings. Given closed capital accounts or high transactions costs in moving funds abroad, they have sometimes had the latitude to maintain deposit rates below market-clearing levels without provoking capital flight or significant disintermediation into the informal markets, where higher real rates prevail.

Economic theory and empirical evidence agree that if a government holds real interest rates on deposits too low for too long people will have little or no incentive to accumulate financial assets, financial savings will fall, and economic growth will be adversely affected. Financial repression usually occurs when inflation runs ahead of adjustments in government-regulated nominal interest rates. This type of financial repression has often resulted in severely negative real interest rates, for example, in Argentina between 1972 and 1985, in Indonesia between 1973 and 1980, and in the Philippines between 1970 and 1985. Cross-economy regression analyses support a positive association between real interest rates and the rate of growth of economic output; that is, large negative real interest rates result in lower growth (Gelb 1989).

Box 5.3 Indonesia Moves Ahead by Putting the Cart before the Horse

CONVENTIONAL WISDOM HAS IT THAT GOVERN-ments should deregulate the real sector before the financial sector so that private banks will not become saddled with the nonperforming loans made to protected enterprises that subsequently founder when in a deregulated environment. Full liberalization of the capital account usually comes last, as a final stage in liberalization of the financial sector.

Indonesia has done things in reverse: first opening its capital account in the early 1970s, then rapidly deregulating the remainder of the financial sector in the late 1980s and early 1990s. Real sector reform, conversely, has proceeded slowly; several important sectors remain under the sway of monopolies and cartels. While an overall assessment of this unusual reform sequence is not yet possible, anecdotal evidence suggests the open financial system is speeding deregulation of the real sector by making credit available to new enterprises.

Indonesia established an open capital account in the early 1970s by lifting foreign exchange controls in the wake of political instability that had provoked ex-tensive capital flight. The open capital account was maintained throughout subsequent policy adjustments, and it helped to restore confidence by reassuring investors they could withdraw assets from Indonesia at any time. Even so, the financial system was highly regulated and became more so throughout the decade. To dampen inflation during the 1970s oil boom, the government imposed credit ceilings on individual banks, with subceilings differentiated by loan category. In addition, the government imposed interest rate ceilings on state bank loans and deposits. This resulted in government-subsidized negative real interest rates in the state banks, which held the vast majority of financial assets.

The end of the oil boom and the resulting drop in government revenue prodded the government into drastic reform of the financial sector. In 1983, as part of a comprehensive stabilization effort, the government sought to attract resources to the financial system by abolishing credit ceilings and interest rate controls. The reforms resulted in rapid growth of the banking system, but they also exposed the economy to shocks

The HPAEs have not used financial repression as a consistent and deliberate policy over time to secure resources to finance the budget or transfer resources to selected economic sectors. However, financial repression has been used in selected periods, usually after an external shock, to transfer resources to aid either ailing industrial borrowers or the banking system (see box 5.4). Most HPAE governments have at one time or another held interest rates below market-clearing levels while nonetheless achieving high and growing rates of aggregate and financial savings and output growth. This apparent anomaly raises a question similar to that for the HPAEs' evidently successful use of development banks and imposition of forced savings: did the Asian economies grow despite financial repression, or did financial repression actually contribute to the Asian miracle?

A policy of moderate financial repression at positive interest rates may actually have boosted aggregate investment and growth in the HPAEs by transferring income from depositors, primarily households, to borrowers, from sudden drops in foreign exchange reserves and bouts of speculation about further devaluation.

In 1988 the government began another round of reforms, encouraging competition to enhance financial sector efficiency. Officials reduced entry barriers to new domestic and joint-venture banks, relaxed branch requirements, lowered reserve requirements, and adopted measures to encourage nonbank capital markets. To ensure bank stability in the more open environment, officials strengthened prudential regulation in 1989, prohibiting banks from investing in stocks and replacing foreign borrowing ceilings with net open position ceilings of 25 percent of equity. The next year, the government slashed directed credit, reducing the number of eligible sectors from thirty-seven to four and adjusting interest rates for the remaining sectors much closer to market rates.

The reforms were immensely successful. From 1983 to 1991 the number of banks nearly doubled to 119, while foreign banks operating in Indonesia increased from 11 to 29. Private domestic bank branches rose from 559 in 1988 to 2,639 in 1991. As new products and services multiplied, private bank assets and the credit they extended increased dramatically. Between 1982 and 1991, private financial institutions increased their share of a rapidly growing financial assets pie from just 20 percent to 50 percent and their share of total credit from only 15 percent to 46 percent. While credit had been readily available only to producers and traditional services, it now became available to a wide range of borrowers, including consumers and investors in the real estate and stock markets.

Such rapid expansion has not been trouble free. When the government tightened liquidity requirements in 1990, banks scrambling to cover their positions pushed real deposit rates from 3.8 percent to 15.2 percent and real lending rates from 7.0 percent to 17.6 percent. Several banks have had trouble recovering loans, a problem foreseen in the conventional wisdom.

Sources: Bhattacharya and Page (1992); Bhattacharya and Pangestu (1993); Cho and Khatkhate (1989); Vittas (1992); an internal World Bank report.

primarily firms. Provided that the interest rate elasticity of household savings is sufficiently low and the corporate sector has a higher marginal propensity to invest than the household sector, the transfer may increase aggregate investment. Furthermore, the effective interest rate subsidy from households to firms increases the corporate profitability of investment by reducing borrowing costs. Reinvested, these higher profits boost the equity of firms, enabling them to invest in riskier projects and borrow more to finance these projects. This may have partly offset the weakness of the equity markets during the HPAEs' economic takeoff periods by providing firms an alternative to equity financing (Stiglitz 1993a).

Financial repression in the HPAEs has differed from that in most other economies in three important ways. First, the degree of repression was relatively moderate and, with a few short-lived exceptions, did not result in persistently negative real interest rates (see table 5.5). Second, as we have shown in chapter 3, repression was undertaken in an environment of macroeconomic stability and was not the unintended consequence of

Box 5.4 Setting Interest Rates in Closed and Open Economies: Financial Repression in Korea and Malaysia

THE INTERNATIONAL RECESSION OF 1980–81 CAME at a bad time for Korea. Highly leveraged and heavily committed to the U.S. market, Korean firms were squeezed simultaneously by high interest rates and sluggish sales. As firms faltered, Korean banks, too, showed signs of instability. The Korean government averted crisis by sharply lowering real interest rates on deposits and loans—thus engineering a massive transfer of wealth from savers (mostly households) to borrowers (mostly firms). With real deposit rates as low as a negative 9.2 percent in 1980, the wealth transfer that year was equivalent to about 2.1 percent of GNP. Such forceful financial repression worked only because unusually effective foreign exchange controls were in place. Households, unable to exchange their savings for foreign currency, temporarily accepted negative real interest rates. Moreover, intervention was relatively brief: real interest rates became positive in 1982 and have generally remained positive since.

Could short-term financial repression also work in an economy with a liberal capital account? The experience in Malaysia in the mid-1980s shows that it can, although the scope for intervention is narrower. In 1985, falling commodity prices and government spending cuts caused a sudden slowdown in the Malaysian economy. Unusually high real interest rates, coupled with heavy losses in real estate and share speculation, caused widespread failures in

deposit-taking cooperatives and large losses in some licensed banks and finance companies.

Alarmed, central bank officials moved in 1987 to bring down real interest rates. Officials reckoned that despite Malaysia's open capital account and the ease of moving deposits to Singapore, the higher intermediation costs of holding savings abroad would persuade most households to keep their savings in Malaysian banks, so long as real domestic interest rates on deposits were no more than about 2 percentage points below international rates. As it turned out, although domestic deposit rates were marginally positive in 1987–88, they were actually about 3.4 percentage points below the comparable London interbank offered rate.

Mild financial repression worked as intended: it helped to stem the spate of corporate failures and assisted in the recapitalization of the banks. Although deposit-lending spreads were strictly regulated, banks were permitted to retain part of the financial repression windfall: their profits rose to M$794 million in 1988, from losses of M$337 million in 1986. As in Korea, the period of financial repression was relatively brief. Because international interest rates declined during the next several years, the degree of repression and the incentive for capital flight gradually diminished. By 1990 Malaysian real interest rates were broadly in line with international rates.

rapid inflation. And third, bank regulators squeezed the deposit rate-lending rate spread, ensuring that the low rates paid to depositors (households) were passed on to borrowers (corporations).

Nonetheless, assuming that low interest rates are passed on to borrowers, financial repression will generate excess demand for credit. Several studies have argued that the rationing that results is inefficient and has negative consequences for growth (World Bank 1989c; Fry 1988). While this may be true in instances of strong financial repression, particularly those resulting in negative real interest rates, the negative effects of moderate financial repression with positive real interest rates may be weak.

Even without financial repression, banks do not allocate loans to the highest bidders. Since bidders for credit offer promises rather than payment, banks must evaluate the bidders and decide which promises are most likely to be kept. Since rationing already takes place in financial systems, the additional impact of moderate financial repression can be relatively small. Indeed, credit rationing may actually be good for growth, if the mechanism used to select borrowers generates incentives to perform. For example, Japan, Korea, and Taiwan, China, allocated subsidized credit on the basis of past performance, usually with exports as the criterion of success. Since the value of subsidized capital was high, firms perceived high marginal returns from greater effort and competed accordingly. We explore this function of credit allocation in detail in chapter 6.

Did moderate financial repression hinder growth? We address this question by examining the relationships between income growth, real interest rates, and inflation using two statistical methods and two data sets: a sample of nineteen economies that includes a subset with positive real interest rates, and time-series data for Korea and Taiwan, China. (Details are in appendix 5.2). In the nineteen-economies sample, inflation rates are far more important in explaining growth than real interest rates. In the subset of economies with positive real interest rates, the interest rate is statistically insignificant and actually has a negative effect on growth when inflation is included.

Similar tests can be made using time-series data for Korea and Taiwan, China. We use the difference between the curb rate and the institutional interest rate as a measure of financial repression. Its coefficient is statistically insignificant. In Korea, inflation and the curb market rate (our proxy for the equilibrium interest rate) significantly explain income growth. In Taiwan, China, none of the variables is significantly related to the growth rate. While these tests are not conclusive, they support the view that moderate financial repression did not necessarily hinder growth in Korea and Taiwan, China.

■ ■ ■

Which were the factors that contributed most to the HPAEs' extraordinary record of accumulation over the past thirty years? Judgments are difficult, given our incomplete understanding of the costs and benefits of all the policies used. But on balance the common elements across the eight economies tend to favor the importance of doing the fundamentals well—encouraging stable and predictable macroeconomic environments, universal primary (and later secondary) education, sound and solvent financial institutions, secure property rights and complementary public investments in infrastructure, and low relative prices of investment goods. Efforts to improve the institutional framework for capital market development came later in the process and were not responsible for takeoff. In some cases well-functioning development banks were a positive but not a determining factor.

More selective interventions—forced savings, tax policies to promote (sometimes very specific) investments, sharing risk, restricting capital outflow, and repressing interest rates also appear to have succeeded in some HPAEs, especially Japan, Korea, Singapore, and Taiwan, China. But the potential costs of these more selective interventions if misapplied can be very high in terms of consumer welfare, and strong institutional capability is necessary. They would not have succeeded without the important monitoring and disciplinary roles performed by the banks and public institutions of these economies. Where other East Asian economies have lacked this capability—in Indonesia, Malaysia, and Thailand—efforts at selective interventions to promote rapid accumulation have been generally unsuccessful.

Appendix 5.1: Granger Causality Tests for Savings Rates and Growth Rates

THE EXISTENCE OF A RELATIONSHIP BETWEEN VARIABLES proves neither the existence of causality nor the direction of influence. Granger-type tests are often used to test for causality between two variables, in this case the growth rate of real GDP per capita (g) and the gross savings rate (s). Tests were done for regression results for the eight East Asian economies and the United States. Vector autoregressions were performed on equations 5.1 and 5.2:

(5.1)
$$g_t = \sum_{k-1}^{r} g_{t-1} + \sum_{k-1}^{r} s_{t-k}$$

(5.2)
$$s_t = \sum_{k-1}^{r} s_{t-k} + \sum_{k-1}^{r} g_{t-k}$$

Then *F*-tests were performed to see whether the lagged savings rates are jointly significant (equation 5.1) and whether the lagged growth rates are jointly significant (equation 5.2). Up to five years of lagged rates are included. The results show a causal relationship from GDP growth rates to savings rates for most East Asian economies (see table A5.1).

The Granger definition exploits time-series relationships to identify causality. By this definition, *g* causes *s* if the prediction of the current value of *s* (s_t) *is strengthened by using past values of* g_t. Thus, *g* causes *s* if $\sigma^2(s_t | \bar{A}_t) < \sigma^2 (s_t | \bar{A}_t - \bar{g}_t)$ where $\bar{A}_t = \{A_k | k < t - 1\}$ denotes the information set that includes A_k for all past *k* up to and including *t*-1, and $\sigma^2 (s_t | \bar{A}_t)$ is the variance of s_t about the best predictor by $\bar{A}_t$.

To define causality in a time-series model involving two variables, we make two simplifying assumptions. First, that the set A_t includes s_t and g_t only, and not a third variable. Second, that transformations T_s and T_g exist, such that $S_t = T_s s_t$ and $G_t = T g_t$ are a pair of linear, covariance-stationary time series, and that S_t and G_t preserve the causality relationship of s_t and g_t. Ordinary or seasonal differencing is an example of such transformations.

Causality can be defined by using several representations of the time-series model for the independent and dependent variables. The autore-

Table A5.1 Public Expenditure per Student on Primary and Secondary Education
(U.S. dollars)

Economy	1965 Primary	1965 Secondary	1975 Primary	1975 Secondary	1985 Primary	1985 Secondary	1989 Primary	1989 Secondary
HPAEs								
Hong Kong			192.3	180.5	558.1	810.2		
Korea, Rep. of	9.0	14.7	51.2	32.9	389.8	352.5	609.6	449.9
Malaysia					351.2	572.5		
Singapore			193.3	314.7	834.0			
Thailand	17.6	67.7	49.0	74.8	133.0		188.1	229.5
Other selected economies								
Brazil			76.9	179.1	155.4	225.2		
Ghana	22.3	122.0			27.9	62.3	36.3	78.0
India	5.3	71.3	17.5	30.9	38.1			
Kenya	28.9	336.7			50.3	149.7	62.2	290.4
Mexico	23.8	56.6	110.2	315.2	101.9	287.5	93.8	300.2
Pakistan	5.9	7.1	15.9	33.4	21.1	122.6		

Note: Cells are empty where data are unavailable.
Source: Computed from UNESCO and World Bank data.

Table A5.2 Tests of Bivariate Granger Causality between the Real Per Capita GDP Growth Rate and the Gross Savings Rate

Economy, years	Years of lags	Lagged right-hand-side variable savings	Growth
Hong Kong, 1960–88	1	Sig	Sig
	2	Sig	Sig
	3	Sig	Sig
	4	Sig	Sig
	5	Sig	Sig
Indonesia, 1965	1	Sig	Sig
	2	NS	Sig
	3	NS	Sig
	4	NS	Sig
	5	NS	Sig
Japan, 1950–88	1	NS	Sig
	2	NS	Sig
	3	NS	Sig
	4	NS	Sig
	5	NS	Sig
Korea, Rep. of, 1955–88	1	Sig	Sig
	2	NS	Sig
	3	NS	Sig
	4	NS	Sig
	5	NS	Sig
Malaysia, 1955–88	1	Sig	Sig
	2	Sig	Sig
	3	NS	NS
	4	NS	NS
	5	NS	Sig
Philippines, 1950–88	1	NS	Sig
	2	NS	Sig
	3	NS	Sig
	4	NS	Sig
	5	NS	Sig
Singapore, 1960–84	1	NS	NS
	2	NS	NS
	3	NS	NS
	4	Sig	NS
	5	Sig	NS
Taiwan, China, 1950–88	1	Sig	Sig
	2	NS	Sig
	3	NS	Sig
	4	NS	Sig
	5	NS	Sig
Thailand, 1950–88	1	NS	Sig
	2	NS	Sig
	3	NS	Sig
	4	NS	Sig
	5	NS	Sig
United States, 1950–88	1	Sig	Sig
	2	Sig	Sig
	3	Sig	Sig
	4	NS	Sig
	5	NS	Sig

Sig: Significant.
NS: Not significant.
Note: Growth is real per capita GDP growth at 1985 international prices (RGDPL in Summers and Heston 1991).
Source: Summers and Heston (1991).

gressive representation was selected for this study. In this representation and by Granger's definition, if g_t does not cause s_t, lagged values of g cannot add to the predictive accuracy of s_t, given past values of s. Using the autoregressive representations, s_t can be regressed on its own past values and on past values of g to test whether g_t causes s_t by testing whether the coefficients of the lagged values of g are significantly different from zero (Granger 1969). The results indicate that past values of g are a very good predictor of s, but that the reverse is not true (see table A5.2).

Appendix 5.2: Technical Note on the Relationship between Interest Rates and Growth

PREVIOUS STUDIES, NOTABLY BY FRY (1984, 1988) AND GELB (1989), have tested the relationship between real interest rates *(R)* and the rate of GDP growth *(G)* using the following equation:

(5.3) $$G = \text{constant} + \beta_1 R + u.$$

Gelb's equations also include a shift variable to account for structural changes in growth rates following the breakdown of the Bretton Woods monetary system in 1973. Both Fry and Gelb apply ordinary least squares (OLS) estimation to pooled cross-economy time-series data. Both studies show a consistently positive and statistically significant relationship between economic growth and the real rate of interest.

But equation 5.3 has major shortcomings. First, it fails to distinguish between small and large degrees of financial system repression (the difference between the equilibrium rate of interest and the controlled or institutional rate). High negative real interest rates have severe negative effects on the economy and may have driven the results of equation 5.3, whereas moderate financial repression may have benign or positive effects that are not captured by the equation. These differences can be explored by splitting the sample in two according to degree of financial system repression, putting economies with negative real rates of interest in one group and those with positive real rates in another.

Second, financial regression is not the only reason for high negative interest rates. Other economic problems can affect interest rates as well. Many of the economies in the sample with high negative interest rates also had high and often volatile inflation rates (Murdock and Stiglitz 1993). Introducing inflation to the equation, this corrects for the rate of inflation in analyzing whether financial repression has a negative effect on growth:

$$(5.4) \qquad G = \text{constant} + \beta_1 R + \beta_2 \text{INF} + \epsilon.$$

Third, investment opportunities also affect real interest rates. A fall in the real institutional rate of interest does not mean a change in financial repression if the equilibrium rate falls equivalently because of lack of investment opportunities. This study, therefore, introduces better proxies for the degree of financial repression in the single economy regressions: the difference between the curb market rates and the banking system's interest rates. (These are available for Korea and Taiwan, China, but not for the other high-performing Asian economies.)

Fourth, OLS estimates could be biased when the regressors are correlated with the error term, as in equation 5.3. If an economy experiences a sudden increase in productivity, for example, the demand for credit will rise, and inflation is likely to turn out to be lower than expected. Both effects will result in a higher-than-expected real interest rate. Thus, two-stage least squares estimation (2SLS) is used in this study. (In the event, the results for OLS and 2SLS suggest that the conclusions in this study would not have been substantially changed had OLS estimates been used.)

Using pooled time-series data for twenty economies, this study estimated equation 5.3 applying a two-stage least squares estimation to both the complete sample and to the subsample of economies with positive average rates of interest. Average GNP growth rates were used as proxies for the growth rate, and real lending rates (from the International Financial Statistics' database) as proxies for real interest rates. The 2SLS estimation included the previous year's interest rate as the instrumental variable for the real interest rate, a year variable to account for any sectoral trend, and two measures of an index of relative income because standard growth models predict that poorer economies have higher equilibrium growth rates. All regressions include dummy variables for each economy.

Table A5.3 reports the results for the impact of the real interest rate and the inflation rate on the GNP growth rate. For the sample of twenty economies the real interest rate has a statistically significant and positive impact on growth (equation 5.3). But when inflation is included (equation 5.4), the coefficient of the real interest rate is no longer statistically significant, while the negative coefficient on the rate of inflation is. For

Table A5.3 Parameter Estimates for Interest Rates and Growth

Dependent variable growth rate	Real interest rate	Inflation rate	Real curb interest rate
Whole sample (2SLS):			
N = 292			
Equation 1	0.148**		
Equation 2	-0.001	-0.277*	
Subsamples of economies with positive real interest rates (2SLS): N = 89			
Equation 1	-1.220		
Equation 2	-0.858***	-0.551**	
Korea, Rep. of (time series, OLS), N =14			
Equation 1	0.391***		
Equation 2	0.059		0.363***
Equation 3	-0.389	-0.289	0.438***

*   Significant at the 10 percent level.
** Significant at the 5 percent level.
***Significant at the 1 percent level.
Note: Two-stage least square regressions were estimated on the whole sample of twenty countries and on the subsample of countries; OLS was used on the time-series analysis on Korea.
Source: World Bank data.

the subsample of economies with positive real interest rates, the coefficient of the real interest rate is not statistically significant except when inflation is included. Then the coefficient of the real interest rate is *significant* and *negative,* suggesting that lower real interest rates may have had a positive impact on growth. The coefficient on inflation remains negative and significant.

Table A5.3 also reports estimates of a time-series analysis of the relationship of interest rates, inflation, and growth in Korea. A third equation includes the real curb rate as a proxy for the equilibrium interest rate. For equation 5.3, the coefficient of the real interest rate is positive, large, and statistically highly significant. When the real curb rate is included, the real interest rate is no longer significant, but the real curb rate is. When the inflation variable is added, the real curb rate remains highly significant, but the real interest rate and the inflation rate do not.

When the same tests are performed on time-series information for Taiwan, China (not reported in table A5.3), the estimated coefficients have the same sign and similar magnitudes as those for Korea, but the standard errors are much larger and none of the coefficients is statistically significant.

Table A5.4 Income Distribution

Economy/region	GNP per capita growth (per year), 1965–90	Year	Income share of bottom 20 percent of households	Income share of top 20 percent of households	Ratio of top to bottom 20 percent of households
HPAEs					
Hong Kong	6.2	1980	5.4	47.0	8.7
Indonesia	4.5	1976	6.6	49.4	7.4
Japan	4.1	1969	7.9	41.0	5.2
		1979	8.7	37.5	4.31
Korea, Rep. of	7.1	1976	5.7	45.3	7.95
Malaysia	4.0	1973	3.5	56.1	16.03
		1987[a]	4.6	51.2	11.1
Singapore	6.5	1982–83	5.1	48.9	9.6
Taiwan, China		1976	9.5	35.0	3.68
Thailand	4.4	1975–76	5.6	49.8	8.89
Other Asia					
Philippines	1.3	1970–71	3.7	53.9	14.6
		1985[b]	5.5	48.0	8.7
Latin America					
Brazil	3.3	1972	2.0	66.6	33.3
		1983	2.4	62.6	26.0
Costa Rica	1.4	1971	3.3	54.8	16.61
		1986[c]	3.3	54.5	16.5
Mexico	2.8	1977	2.9	57.7	19.9
Peru	-0.2	1972	1.9	61.0	32.11
		1985–86[a]	4.4	51.9	11.79
Venezuela	-1.0	1970	3.0	54.0	18.0
		1987[c]	4.7	50.6	10.8
Sub-Saharan Africa					
Botswana		1985–86	2.5	59.0	20.0
Côte d'Ivoire	0.5	1986–87[c]	5.0	52.7	10.5
Ghana	-1.4	1988–89[c]	7.1	43.7	6.2
Kenya	1.9	1976	2.6	60.4	23.2
South Asia					
India	1.9	1964–65	6.7	48.9	7.2
		1975–76	7.0	49.4	7.0
		1983[c]	8.1	41.4	5.1
Pakistan	2.5	1984–85[b]	7.8	45.6	5.9

a. Data refer to per capita income.
b. Data refer to household expenditure.
c. Data refer to per capita expenditure.
Source: World Bank data.

Table A5.5 Nature, Causes, and Resolution of Banking System Crises

Economy	Nature of financial distress	Causes	Nature of bailout or rescue
Hong Kong, 1982–83	Nine deposit-taking companies (DTC) failed.	(a) Large exposure to real estate lending, fraud and mismanagement, and weak prudential regulation. (b) High international interest rates.	The government revamped regulatory and auditing system and liquidated troubled DTCs.
Hong Kong, 1983–86	Eight banks, including a major international bank, were in financial difficulties.	Large exposure to real estate lending and spillover effects from 1983 crisis since these banks owned DTCs as subsidiaries.	The government took over the larger banks and introduced new management, including top executives seconded from the largest commercial bank. Those not taken over by the government received credit from other commercial banks.
Japan, 1991	A Central Bank report has estimated the size of problem loans of the top 21 banks to be between 3.5–4.8 percent of banking system assets. Informal estimates of amount to be written off is about 1–1.5 percent of banking system assets.	(a) Excessive exposure to real estate lending, comprising about 90 percent of the bad loans, and a steep decline in real estate prices. (b) Inadequate prudential supervision. Banks were able to increase their exposure through loans to their nonbank affiliates.	Encouraged mergers of weaker banks with healthier ones. Groups of banks provided emergency loans to weaker banks. Nonperforming loans to be transferred to a separate financial institution, and the cost of the write-offs to be shared among commercial banks.
Malaysia, 1985–88	Failure of one deposit-taking cooperative in 1986 caused runs in 32 (out of 35) others. In addition, 4 (of 38) banks and 4 (of 47) finance companies were also in financial distress. Overall, 10.4 percent of total deposits of the banking system were affected.	(a) Predominant cause was fraud and speculation in real estate and stocks. (b) Deterioration in terms of trade.	The government rescued 24 insolvent cooperatives and consolidated and merged weak finance companies. The Central Bank injected fresh equity capital and replaced management of some banks.
Singapore, 1982	Domestic commercial banks' nonperforming loans rose to about $200 million or 0.63 percent of GDP.	Macroeconomic reasons.	The government worked out a two-year write-off period (using tax breaks).
Taiwan, China, 1983–84	Four trust companies and 11 cooperatives failed.	Cooperatives were arbitraging from an artificially steep yield curve.	Healthier banks took over the management or bought the shares of failed banks.

(Table continues on the following page.)

Table A5.5 *(continued)*

Economy	Nature of financial distress	Causes	Nature of bailout or rescue
Thailand, 1983–87	The government's cost of bail-out of 50 finance companies was estimated at US$190 million or 0.48 percent of GNP. Five commercial banks accounting for 24 percent of commercial bank assets were in financial difficulties in 1986–87.	(a) Fraud and speculation on real estate and exchange rate transactions. (b) High concentration of unsecured insider loans. (c) High international interest rates.	The government liquidated 24 finance companies and merged another 9, and the Central Bank took over the other 17 and sold them to new investors (including other banks). It bought some shares of troubled banks. It also created a "lifeboat fund" to provide emergency loans to troubled banks. The fund would be financed by contributions from commercial banks.
Chile, 1976	Entire mortgage banking system was insolvent.	Maturity mismatches of assets and liabilities as interest rates rose and inadequate capital requirements.	Troubled mortgage banks were liquidated.
Chile, 1981–83	Several financial institutions (or about 60 percent of the financial system's loan portfolio) were insolvent. In 1988, central bank holdings of bad commercial bank loans was nearly 19 percent of GDP. The bailout cost was estimated at US$6 billion, or 26.2 percent of GDP.	(a) Severe recession in 1981, drastic increase in interest rates, and decline in terms of trade due to the collapse of the price of copper. (b) Weak prudential regulation and supervision and rampant insider and speculative lending.	In 1981, the government liquidated 8 institutions. In 1983, it took over 8 (liquidating 3 and recapitalizing 5). The Central Bank also required banks to raise new equity and provided preferential exchange rate schemes to meet foreign liabilities and interest rate subsidies on debt-equity swaps to recapitalize banks.
Ghana, 1988	The net worth of the banking system was negative. Estimated cost of restructuring was US-$300 million or nearly 6 percent of GNP.	Huge foreign exchange losses and a high proportion of nonperforming loans.	
Norway, 1987–88	Thrift and banking systems had heavy losses.	(a) Collapse in the price of oil. (b) Imprudent lending.	Government forced banks to write off bad loans, restructure operations, and raise new capital. Encouraged mergers and also replaced the management and board of a leading bank.

Economy	Nature of financial distress	Causes	Nature of bailout or rescue
Philippines, 1981–87	Among smaller financial institutions, comprising 7.6 percent of deposit money bank assets, 182 failed. In addition, the government intervened in the two largest public banks and five private banks, accounting for more than two thirds of the assets of deposit money banks. By 1986, central bank assistance to financial institutions amounted to 19.1 billion pesos or 3 percent of GDP.	(a) Increases in oil prices and international interest rates, coupled with deterioration in the terms of trade. (b) High concentration of lending to related parties and inadequate prudential regulation and supervision.	Insolvent institutions were liquidated and depositors paid off by the deposit insurance corporation. The 2 public banks were restructured in 1986, and their bad portfolios were put under a separate agency under government management. Five private banks remained under direct central bank supervision.
Turkey, 1982–85	A financial crisis erupted with the collapse of several brokers, and five banks were rescued at a cost of 2.5 percent of GNP. Since 1985, 2 large banks were restructured.	Inadequate prudential supervision.	The government recapitalized the banks and insisted on their operational restructuring. The government tightened up on its prudential regulations.
United States, 1982–87	Of approximately 14,500 banks, 1,575 were reported in trouble in 1987. Between 1982 and 1988, about 424 banks failed.	(a) Predominant cause was speculative real estate loans. (b) Fraud and mismanagement.	Similar approach to that of the S&Ls. Federal Deposit Insurance Corporation liquidated banks (and compensated depositors), provided emergency loans, and acquired banks for resale.
United States, 1979–89	Between 1980 and 1988, about 1,506 (of 3,147) S&Ls were merged and 175 liquidated. In 1989 over 600 (one-fifth of all S&Ls) were insolvent. Total losses from crisis estimated at US-$130 billion, or 2.3 percent of GDP.	(a) Interest rate shock of 1981 reduced the value of banks' assets and increased interest to be paid to depositors. (b) Deregulation of S&Ls, without adequate prudential supervision, led S&Ls to lend to expand lending, and led to heavy exposure to poor-quality commercial loans and speculative real estate financing.	Federal Savings and Loan Insurance Corporation assisted in mergers (under new management) or liquidations of insolvent S&Ls. FSLIC also acquired problem assets for resale to new investors. Because of the large costs of restructuring, FSLIC received additional government funds in 1989.

Sources: *Far Eastern Economic Review* (various issues); Kaufman (1992); Remolona and Lamberte (1986); Sheng (1989, 1990); Sundavarej and Trairatvorakul (1989); World Bank (1989c); internal World Bank reports; interviews.

Table A5.6 Comparison of Banking System Concentration Ratios (Total Assets)

Economy	Year	3Bank	4Bank	5Bank	Herfindahl index[a]
East Asia					
Hong Kong[b]	1985	75	77	78	0.429
Indonesia	1988–89	48	59	69	0.100
Japan	1989	23	30	37	0.044[a]
Korea, Rep. of	1989	41	50	58	0.098[a]
Malaysia	1989	42	56	61	0.102[a]
Singapore	1989	60	69	71	0.132[a]
Taiwan, China	1989	32	41	50	0.079[a]
Thailand	1988	56	66	72	0.138
Other Asia					
Bangladesh	1986–88	–	74	–	0.200
Pakistan	1986–88[c]	–	–	84	0.260
Philippines	1986–88	–	40	–	0.060
Sub-Saharan Africa					
Algeria	1986–88	–	100	–	0.290
Botswana	1986–88	–	100	–	0.450
Cameroon	1986–88	–	82	–	0.180
Côte d'Ivoire	1986–88	–	67	–	0.140
Morocco	1986–88	–	70	–	0.180
Nigeria	1986–88	–	52	–	0.090
Senegal	1986–88	–	78	–	0.160
Tunisia	1986–88	–	80	–	0.190
Other					
Chile	1986–88	–	54	88	0.090
Turkey	1986–88	–	52	76	0.040
				81	
OECD economies				70	
Australia	1989	67	82	61	0.185[a]
Belgium	1989	50	63	41	0.088[a]
Canada	1989	54	69	43	0.140[a]
France	1989	49	49	89	0.119[a]
Germany	1983	43	–	75	–
Italy	1983	28	–	37	–
Spain	1983	28	–	–	–
Sweden	1983	76	–	0.4	–
Switzerland	1983	71	–	29	–
United Kingdom	1989	29	34		0.036[a]

– Not available.

a. The Herfindahl index is a measure of concentration derived by summing the squares of the shares of firms. A high Herfindahl indicates high concentration. The Herfindahl is underestimated for the following economies as it is derived from truncated samples: Australia (9 largest banks); Belgium (11 largest banks); Canada (8 largest banks); France (15 largest banks); Japan (20 largest banks); Korea (19 largest banks); Malaysia (6 largest banks); Singapore (5 largest banks); Taiwan, China (19 largest banks); United Kingdom (15 largest banks).

b. The data for Hong Kon g include commercial banks only, not other deposit-taking institutions.

c. The 5Bank concentration ratio for Pakistan is for 1991.

Sources: The Banker (1990); Revel (1987); internal World Bank report.

Table A5.7 Interest Rate Spreads of Commercial Banks, Selected HPAEs

Economy/year	Interest rate spreads
Indonesia	
1982	3.6
1986	2.2
Japan	
1972	3.6
1980	3.1
1980	3.2
1990	3.1
Korea, Rep. of	
1980	7.0
1985	5.6
1987	2.8
1988	3.8
1989	4.6
1990	4.5
Malaysia	
1980	4.0
1984	4.8
1987	6.1
1990	4.5
Singapore	
1980	4.0
1984	2.0
1987	3.2
1990	2.7
Taiwan, China	
1982	5.0
1989	2.5
Thailand	
1980	3.5
1985	3.0
1987	3.9
1990	3.2

Note: For Japan and Singapore, the difference between the lending interest rate and deposit interest rates are as reported in the IMF, International Financial Statistics; for Taiwan, China, the difference between weighted average loan rates and the weighted average deposit rates of locally incorporated banks; for Korea, the difference between average lending interest rates and deposit interest rates; for Malaysia, the difference between average lending interest rates and average cost of funds; for Thailand, the difference between average interest repaid on funding liabilities and average interest paid on all interest earning assets; and for Indonesia, the difference between interest earned and interest expense of public and private commercial banks.

Sources: Japan and Singapore, International Monetary Fund data; Taiwan, China, Chiu (1992); Republic of Korea, internal World Bank report; Malaysia, Yusof and others (1992); Thailand, internal World Bank report; Indonesia, Chant and Pangestu (1992).

Table A5.8 Outlines of Major Policy Implementation Financing Institutions

Name of institution	Total assets	Market share (ownership)	Sources of funds	Use of funds
Indonesia				
State Development Banks (BAPINDO)	4,903 billion rupiah (US$2,673 million) (1989)	7.5 percent (Government)	Borrowing from the central bank, corporate bonds	Finance for priority fields consistent with development plans' terms: Maximum 15 years; amounts: more than 2.5 rupiah
Regional Development Banks	7,767 billion rupiah (US$4,322 million) (1989)	(27 states)	Mainly deposits	Finance for regional development
Private Development Banks			Deposits, medium- and long-term securities	
Development-type finance companies	479 billion rupiah (US$290 million) (187.8)	N.A.	Partially financed by the government and central bank	
Korea, Rep. of				
Korea Development Bank	17,687 billion won (US$26 billion)	5.9 percent (Government)	Industrial finance debenture, borrowing from the government	Loans to manufacturing for equipment and working funds
Export-Import Bank of Korea	2,214 billion won (US$3 billion) (1989)	0.7 percent (Government)	Borrowing	Medium- to long-term export and import financing
Korea Long-Term Credit Bank	3,961 billion won (US$6 billion) (1989)	1.3 percent	Corporate bonds, long-term borrowing	Medium- to long-term finance for private enterprises
Industrial Bank of Korea	8,841 billion won (US$13 billion)(1989)	2.9 percent	Deposits, borrowing	Loans and discounts to small and medium-size enterprises
Malaysia				
Malaysia Industrial Development Finance Corporation (MIDF)	553 million ringgit (US$204 million) (1988)	(Half government, half private)	Borrowing from the government and central bank	Finance for industry, in particular small and medium-size enterprises in the food, metals, lumber, and rubber industries
Development Bank of Malaysia	821 million ringgit (US$329 million) (1987)	2.6 percent (Government, 98 percent)	Borrowing from the government	Medium- to long-term finance and guarantees for Bumiputera enterprises; terms: 1 to 5 years for working capital
Industrial Bank of Malaysia	241 million ringgit (US$97 million) (1987)	(Government)	Borrowing from the government and central bank	Finance for shipbuilding and shipping industry
Sabah Development Bank	1,069 million ringgit (US$49 million) (1987)	(Government)	Government subscription, foreign bonds	Medium- to long-term finance for agriculture, industry, electric power, and real estate
Agricultural Bank of Malaysia	1,725 million ringgit (US$663 million) (1987)	(Government)	Government subscription, borrowing from government institutions	Finance for the promotion of commerce and industry in Sabah and Sarawak

Name of institution	Total assets	Market share (ownership)	Sources of funds	Use of funds
Philippines				
Development Bank of the Philippines (DBP)	13.7 billion pesos (US$611 million) (1989)	2.1 percent (Government)	Deposits, long-term borrowing	Finance for small and medium-size industry. Terms: maximum 12 years for equipment funds. Finance for agriculture terms: maximum 4 years for working capital, maximum 13 years for medium- to long-term funds Housing finance terms: max 25 years for housing construction
The Land Bank of the Philippines (LBP) Philippine Amana Bank (PAB)		(Government)		Finance for promotion of the agrarian reform. Finance to support social and economic development for Moslem
Taiwan, China				
Export-Import Bank of China		(Government)	Borrowing from the central bank	Medium- to long-term export and import financing terms: 10 years or shorter
Bank of Communications		(Government)	Borrowing from the government, postal savings	Medium- to long-term export and import financing terms: 10 years or shorter
Thailand				
Industrial Finance Corporation of Thailand	29,598 million baht (US$1,152 million) (1989)	(Half government, half private)	Overseas borrowing bonds, borrowing from government and central bank	Medium- to long-term finance for the steel, nonferrous metal, and chemical industries Terms: 5 to 8 years normal, 15 years maximum
Bank for Agriculture (BAAC)	45,004 million baht (US$1,752 million) (1989)	5.2 percent (Government)	Deposits	Finance for farmers and agricultural cooperatives
Government Housing Bank (GHB)	27,811 million baht (US$1,088 million) (1989)	(Government)	Deposits, overseas borrowing	Housing loans, finance for housing development project

Note: Share is the proportion of total assets to financial institutions at the end of 1989; in the case of Indonesia, the figure is for before the end of March 1989.
Sources: Foundation for Advanced Information Research (1991). Korea, Central bank reports, Export-Import Bank of Japan business handbook. Taiwan, China, Export-Import Bank of Japan business handbook, reports from the Dai-ichi Kangyo Bank, Ltd. Malaysia, Central bank reports. Thailand, Bank of Thailand Annual Reports 1989. The Philippines, Central bank report, Export Import Bank of Japan business handbook. Indonesia, Japan Center for International Finance reports, reports from the Daiwa Bank Ltd.

Notes

1. See chapter 6 below for a more detailed discussion of the relationship between educational expansion, the growth of labor demand, and the educational structure of wages.

2. From cross-economy school expenditure equations estimated by Schultz (1988), the elasticity of enrollments with respect to the relative price of teachers is -0.80 and -0.70 at the primary and secondary levels.

3. Of course GNP per capita is much higher in East Asia than in Sub-Saharan Africa. Because of the bias that results from using exchange rates rather than measures of purchasing power parity, we do not attempt to weigh the effect on costs of higher GNP per capita against the effect of lower teachers' wages relative to GNP per capita.

4. The relationship between the abundance of human capital and teacher pay is not firm. In Korea, where

human capital is most abundant, the earnings of primary teachers are roughly 5 times per capita GNP. However, because pupil-teacher ratios are higher in Korea, operating costs as a percentage of per capita GNP are, at 16.5 percent, not much higher than in Indonesia and Malaysia, suggesting an important role for policy both in determining teachers' wages and in controlling costs. See Tan and Mingat (1992), pp. 28–34.

5. Implicit in the calculations is the assumption that expenditure per pupil would remain the same even if the growth of the school-age population was faster.

6. There may also be problems on the supply side—inadequate capital markets or entrepreneurial deficiencies—that limit the private provision of educational services. Psacharopoulos, Jimenez, and Tan (1986) present estimates of private and social returns from education. See Psacharopoulos (1993) for more recent estimates. Behrman (1993) cites the many criticisms of these estimates, including their failure to account for ability and for quality of education. Neither he nor others, however, question the existence of some gap between private and social returns.

7. In fact, it is difficult to distinguish empirically between the effects of not being able to borrow and the effects of poor information on the demand for schooling.

8. Government expenditure on education, expressed as a percentage of GNP, was used as an explanatory variable in a cross-economy regression in which expected years of schooling of the school-age cohort (essentially an aggregate of enrollment rates) is the independent variable. For a sample of fifteen Asian and Latin American economies, the expenditure variable was insignificant. See Tan and Mingat (1992).

9. In Korea and Taiwan, China, the share of public expenditure on education allocated to higher education has increased during the last decade or so for two reasons. On the one hand, universal and near universal enrollment rates have been achieved at the primary and secondary levels, respectively. On the other hand, the increase has been consistent with the shift in the structure of production and exports to more technologically sophisticated and skill-intensive products, and the consequent increase in the demand for engineers and other skilled workers.

10. Given the smaller size of the basic education age cohort in East Asia than in Latin America (see below in the text), this difference underestimates the gap between the two regions in the strength of the public sector's commitment to basic education.

11. However, since the mid-1980s, public savings in Argentina, Brazil, Chile, Colombia, Costa Rica (since 1983), and Mexico (in 1987) have increased in response to fiscal adjustments, leading national savings to rise (an internal World Bank report).

12. In Japan, by managing excess competition, industrial policy may have also assisted in the stability of financial institutions. Japan's recession cartels, for example, may have avoided large and systematic bankruptcies, which surely helped the solvency of financial institutions.

13. The danger of easing interest rates and entry controls without simultaneously strengthening prudential regulations and capital adequacy requirements has been evident in Indonesia, where low capital requirements for entry and poor enforcement of prudential regulations led to mounting concern about insolvent banks.

14. In several economies, the risk was aggravated by the banks' tendency to speculate in securities. Table A5.4 shows that the major source of financial disruptions in Hong Kong, Malaysia, Thailand, and, recently, Japan was real estate and securities speculation.

15. Stiglitz (1993a) notes that in economies in which governments do not take an active pro-competitive stance, there are a limited number of firms in the banking sector. Furthermore, even when there are a large number of banks, effective competition (if viewed from the perspective of the receiver of the financial service) is likely to be limited. This is because information pertinent to a single borrower is specialized, and each of the major categories of loans represents a different product market. There are differences in the kind of information that is needed across product categories and few economies of scope across the categories. Patterns of specialization among financial institutions confirm this view.

16. Data on quality are extremely limited, but available measurements suggest that infrastructure in the

HPAEs may be of better quality than in other developing economies. Table 5.7 shows the percentage of roads that are paved in a large selection of low- and middle-income economies.

17. There is a large literature not only documenting the relative unimportance of equity markets as a source of finance but also explaining why this is so, both in terms of the evidence concerning the negative effect of share issues on share price and in theoretical terms. See Stiglitz (1993a).

18. Long-term credit banks, but not city banks, issued coupon debentures of a maturity of five years, and this has been central to the segmentation of short- and long-term finance (Packer 1992).

19. Korea's bond market has been expanding more than other East Asian economies, except for Japan. But most of these bonds are government guaranteed. Firms have begun to issue bonds, because government has begun to control the debt-equity ratios of large corporations (an internal World Bank report). Many of the corporate bond issues may be simply a form of bank financing that carries a government guarantee.

20. This is known as the price discovery function of stock markets.

21. More substantial long-term lending to industry has been carried out by other development banks (for example, Eximbank, the Small Business Finance Corporation, and private long-term credit banks).

22. While the experience of East Asian economies with development banks has been generally positive, there also have been failed development banks. In Japan (Reconstruction Finance Bank in 1952) and Thailand (Industrial Bank in 1959), insolvent development banks were closed. Development banks lending to small and medium-size

enterprises in Indonesia and Malaysia have reported difficulties because of a growing volume of arrears.

23. For example, in the 1950s and 1960s, the ratio of write-offs and bad loans to total assets of JDB was lower than private commercial banks (JDB/JERI 1993). The Development Bank of Singapore has evolved into Singapore's largest private commercial bank, largely on the basis of its excellent financial performance (Gordon 1983). Yaron (1992) suggests that traditional financial indicators may not be the best indicator of performance of development banks, since they have been established with development objectives. He measures instead the degree of dependence of development banks on subsidies from the government. With some exceptions (for example, Malaysia's Bank Bumiputera, Indonesia's Bapindo), the HPAEs' development banks are self-reliant.

24. There is remarkable uniformity in the pattern of investment outcomes exceeding investment efforts among the five HPAEs in the sample. Malaysia is perhaps the least representative in the sense that during the 1970s (and up to 1982) the nominal investment share exceeded the real investment share. All five economies, however, had real investment shares that exceeded the nominal share between 1982 and 1985. Korea continued to show a declining relative price of investment goods throughout the 1980s, while Thailand had a major increase in relative capital goods prices in 1988–89.

25. De Long and Summers (1991) obtain a similar result for the relative price of equipment (to the GDP deflator). They predict the real equipment price for the sample of sixty-two economies as a function of relative 1980 GDP per worker. Of the six HPAEs in their sample (Singapore and Taiwan, China, are excluded), Indonesia and Malaysia lie close to but above their predicted values; Hong Kong, Japan, Korea, and Thailand are all significantly below their predicted values. Real equipment prices are unusually low in these economies.

CHAPTER 6

Using Resources Efficiently: Relying on Markets and Exports

IT IS APPARENT THAT THE HIGH-PERFORMING ASIAN economies were unusually successful in strategies to achieve rapid accumulation. But high levels of physical and human capital formation are not a guarantee of economic success, as the modern economic history of the former Soviet Union and Eastern Europe sadly attests. Resources, once accumulated, need to be allocated to high-yielding activities. This chapter first considers the strategies, explicit and implicit, that the HPAEs used to achieve efficient allocation in three areas: the labor market, the capital market, and international trade. It then turns to industrial policy—deliberate, government-sponsored interventions to alter industrial structure—which was an important feature of public policy in some HPAEs, and asks whether these efforts have resulted in superior economic performance. Finally, the chapter considers the role of manufactured exports in promoting the demand for skilled labor and the acquisition and mastery of best-practice technology.

Explaining East Asia's Efficient Resource Use

THE HIGH-PERFORMING ASIAN ECONOMIES HAVE EFFICIENTLY absorbed unprecedented rates of growth of physical and human capital for thirty years. As we showed in chapter 1, all of the HPAEs had total factor productivity growth that exceeded that of more than 70 percent of developing economies between 1960 and 1989, and some—Japan, the Republic of Korea, Hong Kong, Malaysia, and Taiwan, China—had among the highest rates of TFP growth in the world.

This means that factors, once accumulated in the HPAEs, contributed much more to output growth than would be predicted on the basis of the average performance of a broad sample of economies, both developing and industrial.

How have the East Asian economies succeeded in using resources efficiently? Good fundamentals again tell much of the story. Price distortions, while present, were limited, and markets were allowed to work. HPAE governments have relied primarily on market mechanisms to guide allocative decisions in both labor and capital markets. Labor markets in the HPAEs have been remarkably free of the interventions that restrict labor mobility and create small, high-wage elites in other developing regions. While capital markets have been frequently controlled, restrictions on deposit and lending rates have generally distorted markets less than in most other low- and middle-income economies (as we demonstrated in chapter 5). Government efforts to direct credit have generally been undertaken within the framework of moderate interest rate subsidies, and financial institutions have been given the final decision on the creditworthiness of investment projects. This has meant that loans supplied through directed credit have been monitored and generally have been repaid. The relative prices of capital and labor have broadly reflected their relative scarcities.

The HPAEs have also used the international economy more effectively than many other low- and middle-income economies. Each of the HPAEs, except Hong Kong, went through an early phase of protection of import-substituting industries. But these policies were later modified by reductions in import controls and tariffs, combined with strong incentives to export (see chapter 3). This opened up much of the modern economy to international competition and introduced world prices as performance standards, not only for exports but also for the intermediate and capital goods used in export production. As a result, domestic prices for traded goods in the HPAEs are more closely aligned with international prices than in many other developing economies.

Apart from these fundamentals, however, most HPAEs selectively intervened in financial markets and used a combination of policies to promote the development of specific industries. Most HPAEs have directed credit to priority sectors and sometimes to specific firms. Where these programs have been effective in allocating resources to high-yielding investments—for example, automatic credit for exporters—it was because allocation rules were performance-based, and borrowers were actively monitored; in short, effective contests were created. These conditions have been more common in the three northern HPAEs that have strong governmental institutions.

Indonesia, Japan, Korea, Malaysia, Singapore, and Taiwan, China, have tried to use targeted industrial policy to promote the development of specific knowledge- and capital-intensive industries. We test the relationship between industrial policy and productivity-based catching up and conclude that industrial policy has generally not been successful in changing industrial structure or raising productivity. What, then, has contributed to the HPAEs' apparently superior performance in adopting and mastering international best-practice technologies? We argue that the combination of competitive discipline and well-functioning factor markets with a pro-export orientation—the export-push strategy—employed by all eight of these economies was responsible for their superior productivity performance.

Manufactured exports accelerated the acquisition and mastery of international best-practice technologies in highly imperfect international technology markets. High and rising levels of human capital in the HPAEs, especially the superior educational attainment and cognitive skills of the industrial labor force, helped to ensure that these new processes and equipment were used and adapted effectively. Thus export orientation and high human capital formed a virtuous circle; exports raised the returns from education, and education raised the returns from exporting.

Using the Market: Labor Markets in East Asia

WHILE HUMAN CAPITAL ACCUMULATION MAY BE A NECESsary condition for sustained rapid growth of output and wages, it certainly is not a sufficient condition. The Philippines, the republics of the former Soviet Union, and Sri Lanka are prominent examples of economies that have had high school-enrollment rates but low rates of growth of per capita income and of wages. Utilizing human capital in activities that yield high returns on the prior investment in education and training is as important to growth as the accumulation of human capital.

We have frequently looked to coordination failures in markets to understand why public policy might be used to help markets function better. In the case of labor markets, however, coordination failures are limited, and information, although not perfectly symmetric between workers and employers, is better than in capital markets.[1] Externalities, as we showed in the previous chapter, primarily affect investment decisions in human capital, not interactions in the labor market. Thus, there is a presumption that, if left to themselves, labor markets would perform their coordinating (allocative) role quite well.

Two conditions must be fulfilled for a growing supply of educated labor to be utilized in high-return activities. First, there must be rapid growth of labor demand relative to supply and, in particular, of demand for skilled labor. Second, the labor market must perform well. It must be efficient, flexible, and responsive to changing conditions so as to ensure that workers are employed in jobs in which their skills are most productively utilized. If these two conditions are not fulfilled, there is a risk that rapid educational expansion may result in labor market problems that erode the benefits of human capital accumulation and have a seriously adverse impact on the growth of output and wages.

In our assessment of why human capital in East Asia appears to have been efficiently utilized and why changes in labor market outcomes have been so favorable, we focus on two factors: the dynamics of labor supply and demand and labor market performance. We also examine the interactions between these two factors. Then we consider whether there are any common denominators in the policies of East Asian governments that have contributed to the efficient utilization of human capital.

Labor Supply and Demand in the HPAEs

Shifts in the aggregate supply and demand for labor in East Asia compared with other developing regions have led to more rapidly rising real wages (see figure 6.1). East Asia's more rapid rate of increase of wages, following an initial period during which wages did not increase, is the result of slower growth of supply and more rapid growth of demand for labor.[2] For a given rate of growth of labor demand, the slower the rate of increase of labor supply, the bigger the increase in wages likely to result from competitive pressures in the labor market. One measure of the dampening influence of labor force growth on the rate of increase of real wages was obtained for a cross section of twenty-two economies in the 1970s; a 1 percent increase in labor force growth resulted in a 1 percent decline in real wage growth (Gregory and Lal 1977).

Figure 6.1 Increase in Real Earnings

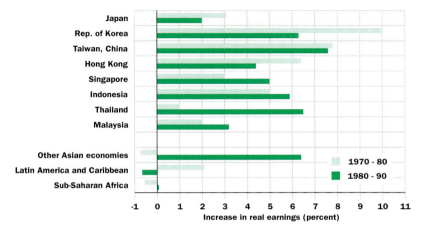

Note: Index for Taiwan, China: 1979 = 100. Other Asian economies are Bangladesh, India, Pakistan, and the Philippines.
Sources: World Bank data; Taiwan, China, National Statistics.

Labor Force Growth. During their period of industrialization in the nineteenth century, the populations of the currently high-income economies grew, on average, at an annual rate of only 0.8 percent.[3] Today, the population of Sub-Saharan Africa is growing at roughly four times that rate; the populations of Latin America and South Asia are growing at roughly three times that rate. Only in East Asia have population growth rates, and the share of the population less than fourteen years old, declined to levels approaching those that prevailed in the high-income economies.[4]

We have already seen how the early demographic transition in East Asia markedly reduced the rate of growth of the school-age population to levels well below those in other developing regions, thereby easing the financial burden of maintaining education enrollment rates. The early demographic transition also reduced, with a lag, the rate of growth of new entrants into the East Asian labor force. The annual rate of labor force growth during the 1980s was 2.6 percent in Sub-Saharan Africa and Latin America and 2.2 percent in South Asia. In East Asia the rate was 1.8 percent (see table 6.1). The labor force growth rate in Singapore is only 0.8 percent, about the same as that experienced by the high-income economies in the nineteenth century. In Sub-Saharan Africa the rate of labor force growth continues to increase. In East Asia, despite increases in the participation rates of women, labor force growth rates have been declining much faster than in Latin America or South Asia.

Table 6.1 Labor Force Growth Rates

Economy/region	1980–85	1985–2000
HPAEs	2.5	1.8
Indonesia	2.4	2.2
Korea, Rep. of	2.7	1.9
Malaysia	2.9	2.6
Singapore	1.9	0.8
Thailand	2.5	1.7
South Asia	2.2	2.2
Latin America and Caribbean	2.8	2.6
Sub-Saharan Africa	2.3	2.6

Source: World Bank (1987b).

Growth of Labor Demand. Not only has the growth of labor supply been slower in East Asia than in other developing regions, but the growth of labor demand has been faster. For the period 1960–90, the rates of growth of wage employment in manufacturing, construction, and services have tended to be substantially higher in East Asia than in Sub-Saharan Africa, Latin America, or South Asia. This is not because growth of employment has been unusually slow elsewhere. With the exception of the 1980s, during which output and employment stagnated because of the macroeconomic adjustments made necessary by debt-service problems, the pace of industrial sector employment growth in Sub-Saharan Africa, Latin America, and South Asia was more than double the pace in the currently high-income economies during the period 1880–1900 (see table A6.4, at the end of the chapter). Rather, the interregional difference reflects the unusually rapid growth of employment in East Asia.

Even as it has been growing rapidly, labor demand in East Asia has become increasingly skill-intensive. As a share of wage employment, white collar and technical employment increased steadily during the 1970s and the 1980s; in Korea, for example, it rose from 29 percent in 1980 to 36 percent in 1990, and in Taiwan, China, from 32 to 40 percent during the same period (see table 6.2). The pace of change in the occupational structure of employment is lower in other developing regions. The change in the occupational composition of labor demand in the HPAEs reflected increases in the abundance of educated labor, and consequent declines in its relative price, as well as changes in compara-

Table 6.2 Professional and Technical, Administrative and Managerial, Clerical, and Sales Occupations as a Percentage of Total Employment

Year	Hong Kong[a]	Korea, Rep. of	Singapore	Taiwan, China
1980	29.0	—	42.9	31.8
1981	29.2	30.8	42.8	32.7
1982	30.6	—	44.2	33.1
1983	32.1	—	45.6	33.1
1984	32.9	—	46.5	33.7
1985	34.3	—	46.5	34.2
1986	34.3	37.9	46.2	34.3
1987	34.1	—	47.0	35.1
1988	34.6	—	46.1	37.2
1989	35.4	—	46.8	38.5
1990	36.2	—	60.0[b]	39.8

— Not available.

a. Total employment for Hong Kong includes unemployed who have previously held jobs.

b. Includes service workers.

Source: Fields (1993).

tive advantage. East Asian exporters shifted into more technologically sophisticated, skill-intensive goods as rapidly rising wages of unskilled labor eroded international competitiveness in labor-intensive manufactured goods.

What accounts for the extraordinary pace at which labor demand, and in particular the demand for skilled labor, has expanded in East Asia? Since the demand for labor is derived from the demand for output, the explanation must be sought, in the first instance, in those factors that contributed to East Asia's rapid output growth: high rates of savings and investment and high rates of return on investment. But it is also important to consider the extent to which the path of growth of output has been more labor demanding in East Asia than in other developing regions. As we shall see, the dynamism of agriculture and export-push strategies contributed to rapid increases in the demand for labor and to rising skill-intensity of labor demand.

Letting Markets Work: Public Policy in the Labor Market

The term "labor market" generally refers to the complex of interactions between employees and employers. The labor market thus bears the responsibility for melding the changing needs of the economy's productive apparatus with the changing skills and preferences of labor force participants (Berry and Sabot 1981). In the course of economic development, workers—most of whom are following educational, training, and vocational paths different from preceding generations—tend to shift toward more dynamic sectors, from self-employment to wage-employment, and toward higher-skilled occupations.[5] An efficient, flexible, and responsive labor market allows rapid matching of skills to needs, improving resource allocation across firms and industries and thereby contributing to growth.[6] While in most developing economies, labor markets have tended to function rather well, where they have not, the costs have at times been high.[7]

In East Asia, more than elsewhere, governments resisted the temptation to intervene in the labor market to counter outcomes unpalatable in the short run or to particular groups (for example, wages below where workers believed they ought to be, educated unemployment, or the employment of educated workers in lower-level occupations). A relatively high level of efficiency in the allocation of labor was achieved by allowing wages and employment to be determined largely by the interaction of those supplying and those demanding labor services, rather than by government legislation, public sector leadership, or union pressure.

How Well Did East Asian Labor Markets Perform?

In East Asia, wages were pulled up by increases in the demand for labor, whereas elsewhere there was a greater tendency for wages to be pushed up artificially. Earnings growth was determined more by the growth of the economy as a whole than by growth in any particular sector (Fields 1992). In economies with highly segmented labor markets, the opposite is the case.

East Asia's Flexible Labor Markets. By not allowing the price of labor in some sectors to rise well above what workers could earn elsewhere in the economy, most HPAEs avoided the creation of a high-wage labor elite. For example, there is evidence for Taiwan, China, of a remarkably integrated labor market; there is no significant correlation between the growth rate of earnings and the growth of output within sectors. Manufacturing wages for unskilled labor are only 20 percent higher than agricultural wages. By contrast, in Colombia and Jamaica, where labor markets are highly segmented, workers with the same level of skill earn nonagricultural wages that exceed agricultural wages by 150 percent

(Fields 1992). Still larger intersectoral wage gaps have been observed in East Sub-Saharan Africa (Ranis 1992). Another notable feature of the structure of wages in East Asia, as illustrated by Korea and Taiwan, China, is the modest size of the gap between skilled and unskilled wages in the nonagricultural sector (see figure 6.2; also see Ranis 1992). The small gap did not result from minimum wage legislation pushing up unskilled wages. Rather the growth of demand for unskilled labor, in combination with marked increases in the abundance of educated workers, compressed the occupational structure of wages.

One benefit of the compressed wage structure in the HPAEs was that it reduced the incentive for educated workers to conduct a lengthy search for a relatively high-wage job, and thereby remain unemployed, rather than fill a job slot at a lower occupational level. Conversely, a segmented labor market may provide an incentive to workers in low-income employment, and to the unemployed, to lobby the government to provide more high-wage jobs than justified by the derived demand for labor.[8] Thus, the share of the public sector in the increase in total wage employment in recent decades is a crude indicator of the magnitude of public sector surplus labor, and hence labor market segmentation.[9] As table 6.3 shows, in all the Sub-Saharan African, Latin American, and South Asian economies for which data were available, employment in the public sector grew more rapidly than wage employment in the private sector. The median share of the public sector in the increase in total employment was between 71 and 87 percent.[10]

With the exception of Malaysia, the experience of the East Asian economies is markedly different. Omitting Malaysia, the share of the public sector in the increase in total wage employment in those East Asian economies for which data were available was less than half the median share for other developing economies. The limited growth of public employment in these East Asian economies is evidence that public surplus employment has been kept in check and stronger evidence that the scope for lobbying for make-work jobs has been limited. The need to maintain international competitiveness helped to limit growth of public employment because importers who purchased intermediate inputs from public enterprises lobbied for low prices. Moreover, governments striving for macroeconomic stability strictly limited the size of the public enterprise deficits that they would finance.

In Malaysia the share of the public sector in the increase in total wage employment is as high as in other developing regions. The increase in

Figure 6.2 Industrial Wage Gaps

Wage gap, Taiwan, China

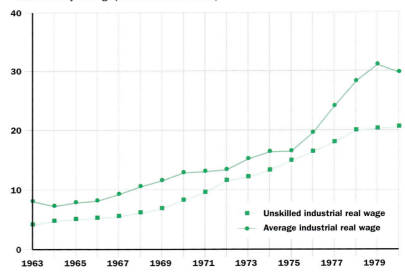

Wage gap, Rep. of Korea

Sources: Kuo (1983); Taiwan, China (various years, 1988); Korea (1978); Kim (1990).

Table 6.3 Growth of Wage Employment in the Public and Private Sectors, Selected Developing Economies

Economy/region	Period	Average growth (percent per year)			Percentage share of public sector in increase of total wage employment
		Public	Private	Total	
Latin America and Caribbean					
Brazil	1973–83	1.4	0.0	0.3	92
Costa Rica	1973–83	7.6	2.8	3.5	34
Panama	1963–82	7.3	1.8	2.7	45
Peru	1970–84	6.1	–0.6	1.1	140
Trinidad	1970–84	4.7	1.2	1.9	51
Venezuela	1967–82	5.1	3.4	3.7	27
Middle East and North Africa					
Egypt	1966–76	2.3	–0.5	2.2	103
Sub-Saharan Africa					
Ghana	1960–78	3.4	–5.9	–0.6	—
Kenya	1963–81	6.4	2.0	3.7	67
Tanzania	1962–76	6.1	–3.8	1.6	190
Zambia	1966–80	7.2	–6.2	0.9	418
South Asia					
India	1960–80	4.2	2.1	3.2	71
Sri Lanka	1971–83	8.0	0.9	3.9	87
HPAEs					
Taiwan, China	1965–85	2.3	6.5	5.0	10
Thailand	1963–83	6.3	5.5	5.7	33
Unweighted mean		5.2	0.6	2.6	

Sources: Knight and Sabot (1991); Taiwan, China (various years).

public employment was not a response to lobbying induced by labor market segmentation. Rather, public employment was used to increase employment opportunities for the historically disadvantaged ethnic Malay majority. The Bumiputera program can be seen as an aggressive affirmative action policy that resulted in considerable public surplus labor (Freeman 1992). In contrast to many governments in similar circumstances, however, when the macroeconomic costs of public employment began to mount, the Malaysian government, manifesting the adaptability that served governments so well throughout the region, changed direction.

Why Were East Asian Labor Markets More Flexible? Rapid growth was a key factor in making wages more flexible in the HPAEs. Workers are generally more willing to accept flexibility of wages around a rapidly rising trend because downward adjustment implies a slower rate of increase rather than an absolute decline in real earnings (Shah and Mathur 1992). This is manifested in wage-setting practices that tie compensation to enterprise performance, another example of how the extraordinary labor market dynamics in East Asia contributed to superior labor market performance.

But some HPAE governments also intervened in labor markets, primarily for political reasons, to suppress the activities of industry- or economywide unions and to ensure that wage bargains were set at the enterprise level. We have suggested that the rapid growth of wages contributed to the explanation of why, in contrast to other regions, wages were not maintained above market-clearing levels in East Asia. An alternative, or perhaps complementary, explanation is that governments, in collaboration with employers repressed labor markets.

Wage-setting practices. One manifestation of the link between rapid growth and wage flexibility is the apparent willingness of workers, especially in the northeastern economies of Asia, to accept wage structures that include a substantial element of performance-based bonuses. This practice links compensation to enterprise, rather than wholly individual performance. It is common for current cash compensation to have two components—a base wage and a bonus (Shah and Mathur 1992). To the extent that "special cash payments" are more responsive to changing economic circumstances than are base wages, this arrangement could help account for the greater flexibility of wages in East Asia than elsewhere. During the period 1958–83 in Japan, econometric evidence shows that the ratio of bonus payments to base wages varies positively and significantly with such indicators of aggregate economic conditions as corporate profits. By contrast, there was no significant relationship between base pay and corporate profits (Freeman and Weitzman 1987).

Nevertheless, the impact of changes in bonuses on total compensation appears to be marginal. While bonus payments as a proportion of total current compensation (15 percent or more in Japan and Korea) or of corporate profits (40 percent or more) tend to be large, the elasticity of bonus payments with respect to profits is small. In Korea, most bonus payments have become contractually linked to the base wage, and in Japan the implicit link of bonuses to base wages appears to be strong (Shah and Mathur 1992).

How repressed were HPAE labor markets? Repression in the labor market can take two forms: direct restraint on wage levels or growth (wage repression) or restraint on organized labor (labor repression) with indirect restraint on wages. Wage repression was clearly not a necessary ingredient in the East Asian recipe for economic success. The governments of Hong Kong, Japan, Korea, and Taiwan, China, did not repress wages, and yet in these economies output, exports, and ultimately wages all increased at rates well above the international norm. These economies were adept at adjusting to changing comparative advantage as labor abundance gave way to labor scarcity. At the other extreme, the government of Singapore repressed wages, at times quite severely, and the consequent costs of labor shortages appear to have been high, leading the government to abandon the policy (Fields 1992; Freeman 1992). Several HPAE governments have repressed labor organizations. Korea, Singapore, and Taiwan, China, suppressed independent unions.[11] Malaysia has independent unions but highly restrictive labor laws. Hong Kong and Japan do not intervene in labor relations. However, in Japan most unions are company based.

In Korea and Taiwan, China, real wages increased at roughly the same pace as real GDP. Nevertheless labor relations in Korea have been deteriorating in the 1990s, so that labor relations problems serious enough to threaten economic growth have arisen, partly in reaction to repression of unions (Freeman 1992). In Singapore during 1972–79, real wages increased at less than one-quarter the rate of increase of real GDP. This divergence was the consequence of the government's aggressive, and quite open, intervention on the side of wage repression in the market for labor.[12] The minister of labor was quoted in the press as saying, "It is clear that an essential element in our new strategy must be a tighter grip on wage increases. . . . If we do not quickly and willingly change to low gear on the wages front, we shall further discourage investment and aggravate the unemployment problem" (reprinted in Fields 1992).

If wages fall well below market-clearing levels and employers are prevented by the government from using wage competition to bid up the price of labor, chronic shortages of labor are likely to be the result. This is what occurred in Singapore, with the result that the rate of growth of output, as well as the rate of improvement of living standards, declined. In 1979 the government recognized the costliness of this constraint and changed course: a policy of "wage correction" was adopted with the explicit aim of alleviating labor shortages and shifting the economy away from labor-intensive and toward capital- and skill-intensive industries. Although the high wage policy was abandoned in 1981, in the 1980s the growth rate of wages accelerated and matched the growth rate of GDP (Fields 1992).

Hong Kong represses neither wages nor unions. With respect to the labor market, the government of Hong Kong is among the least interventionist in the world. Despite labor laws that are favorable to union formation and action, union membership in private sector firms is low; unions engage in relatively little collective bargaining and are generally considered to be "weak." Perhaps because wages were rising rapidly in Hong Kong, workers did not feel the need for collective action. Hong Kong demonstrates that East Asian economies need not aggressively repress unions to have a weak union movement, suggesting, for example, that in Korea there may have been few benefits to offset the political and economic costs imposed by labor repression (Freeman 1992).

Japan's experience with labor unions is another counterexample to the belief that East Asian success required government repression of labor. The Japanese example may be the more telling of the two because in Japan, in contrast to Hong Kong, union membership is high and unions are, at least potentially, quite strong. Yet unions did not extract economic benefits for their members at the expense of economic growth (Freeman 1992).

How Did Efficient Labor Markets Contribute to Growth?

The benefits of maintaining wages at or marginally below, rather than well above, market-clearing levels were numerous and substantial.[13] First, because inflated wages were avoided, the profits of firms and, most likely, aggregate savings rates were higher. As a consequence, retained earnings accounted for a higher proportion of investment finance than otherwise would have been the case, reducing reliance on underdeveloped capital markets. The probable net effects, therefore, were higher levels of investment, greater competitiveness in international markets, and faster rates of growth of output, employment, and ultimately earnings.[14]

Superior labor market performance in East Asia thus contributed to sustaining the extraordinary dynamics of labor demand we documented above. Moreover, by not allowing the price of labor to become inflated relative to the price of capital, wage restraint encouraged the use of more labor-intensive technology. As a means of avoiding excessive capital intensity, this was particularly important, given that government interventions tended to lower the price of capital.

Efficient use of skilled labor also contributed to the high levels of public sector savings in most of the HPAEs. If the government capitulates to demands for make-work jobs, the subsidies required to finance the resulting gap between the wage and the marginal product of labor are likely to divert scarce savings from productive investments, lowering the rate of capital accumulation and steadily eroding the growth potential of the economy.[15] For a time, Malaysia was an East Asian illustration of this point, but there are many more examples outside the region where governments have been slower to take corrective action.

If the government provides make-work jobs, squandering the productive potential of human capital may be another consequence. In the worst case, which unfortunately is quite common, workers in whom a substantial educational investment has been made are paid the prevailing (relatively) high public sector wage to do jobs in which their marginal productivity is zero or even negative.[16] In this way creation of make-work jobs impedes the process of human capital deepening that is central to education's contribution to economic growth. Had the labor market been allowed to function without intervention, these same workers would have entered lower-paying occupations, and the consequent increase in the educational level in those occupations would have contributed to an increase in labor productivity.

Because wages were responsive to changes in the demand for labor, adjustment to external macroeconomic shocks, such as those induced by the oil crises of the 1970s, was often quicker and less painful in the HPAEs (Mazumdar, forthcoming). If the price of labor does not adjust quickly and smoothly to macroeconomic shocks or to secular changes in the macroeconomic environment, then either the quantity of labor must adjust or the rates of output growth or inflation are likely to. In relation to fluctuations in aggregate demand, employment stability tends to be much greater in East Asia than in other regions, so that East Asian economies generally adjust to downturns without laying off workers (Shah and Mathur 1992).

Assisting the Market: Financial Markets and Allocation

CAPITAL MARKETS PERFORM THEIR ALLOCATIVE FUNCTION IN three ways: they aggregate savings, allocate funds to competing investments, and monitor performance. Without financial intermediation, firms would have to rely on retained earnings to finance investment, so marginal returns to investment would diverge markedly, especially in the short run. Thus the policies described in chapter 5 that contributed to the deepening of financial sectors also contributed to better capital allocation. In addition to private capital markets, governments in East Asia, like governments in many developing economies, have attempted to allocate credit directly to high-priority activities. Elsewhere, directed-credit programs have been catastrophic failures. In some HPAEs—particularly Japan, Korea, and Taiwan, China—these programs have caused less damage to capital allocation and may have been beneficial.

Our examination of capital market performance begins by documenting the high rate of financial deepening in the HPAEs. We then describe the nature and magnitude of directed-credit programs and assess their performance. We show that, where these programs appear to have had the most beneficial results, they supplemented fundamentally sound capital market policies with improved selection and monitoring. Interest rate subsidies were small, loans were repaid, and strict performance criteria were used to ration funds. These preconditions for effective directed credit were present in only a few of the HPAEs. Where they were absent, directed-credit programs largely failed.

East Asia's Record of Growing Financial Depth

The growth of financial assets in East Asia has been very rapid—faster than the growth in aggregate savings—leading to substantial growth in the financial depth of East Asian economies. Figure 6.3 compares East Asia's ratio of M2 (time plus demand deposits) to GDP, which is often used to measure the depth of the financial sector, with the M2/GDP ratio for a group of low- and middle-income economies and the OECD economies. The relatively greater financial depth in East Asia far surpasses most developing economies and compares well even with the OECD economies. A broader measure of financial depth, the ratio of financial liabilities (M3) to GDP, shows a similar trend.

Korea is unusual in that its ratio of M2 to GDP is low compared with many developing economies at similar levels of per capita income, and these ratios have increased more slowly than Korea's income growth would predict. The largest incremental change was evident after the interest rate adjustments in 1965. However, M2 fails to capture the presence of a vast nonbank financial sector. The rapid growth of income in Korea since the 1970s has been accompanied by large in-

Figure 6.3 Financial Depth in HPAEs, Other Developing Economies, and Selected OECD Economies

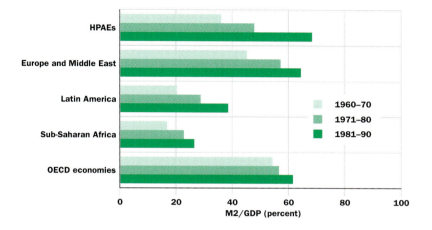

Note: Latin America includes Argentina, Barbados, Bolivia, Brazil, Chile, Columbia, Costa Rica, Ecuador, El Salvador, Guatemala, Jamaica, Panama, Trinidad and Tobago, Uruguay, and Venezuela. Europe and Middle East includes Algeria, Egypt, Greece, Morocco, Portugal, Syria, Tunisia, and Yugoslavia. Sub-Saharan Africa includes Cameroon, Congo, Côte d'Ivoire, the Gambia, Ghana, Kenya, Madagascar, Mauritania, Nigeria, Senegal, Sudan, Tanzania, Togo, Uganda, and Zimbabwe. OECD economies include Austria, Belgium, Canada, Denmark, Finland, Germany, Ireland, Netherlands, Norway, Spain, Sweden and Switzerland.

Note: M2/GDP = [currency + demand deposits + time deposits + savings deposits (except large certificates of deposit)] as a percentage of gross domestic product.

Source: International Monetary Fund data.

creases in the assets of nonbank financial institutions (King and Levine 1993).

Financial assets in industrial and developing economies, including East Asian economies, are held largely in deposits with banks and other financial institutions and to a very limited extent in government or private securities (World Bank 1989c). The public policies described in chapter 5 that have emphasized the development of banks and other savings institutions may partly explain this composition, but there also are market explanations. Equity and bond markets develop slowly, especially in emerging markets. In East Asia, the combination of rapid growth of financial assets in the banking system and rising savings during the past two decades has meant that banks have played an increasingly important role in capital allocation.

Financial Markets, Coordination Failures, and the Role of Government

The lack of perfect information that characterizes all markets is most serious in capital markets, where acquiring information to facilitate better selection and monitoring of projects is a key function. Imperfect information has several consequences for allocative efficiency. As we noted in chapter 5, bond and equity markets are slow to develop. This places increased emphasis on the role of banks in selecting borrowers and monitoring their performance. But credit markets are not like auction markets or markets for ordinary commodities. Because banks cannot discern perfectly the probability of default, they cannot simply allocate credit to the highest bidders—those who promise to pay the highest interest rates. Rather, they must choose among agents willing to pay the going rate those that seem most likely to repay the loan. This allocative process is, in effect, a form of rationing. Moreover, it gives banks some control over entrepreneurs, who must maintain their good credit standing in order to renew loans.

Financial institutions evolve in response to these market limitations. For example, bank-client arrangements respond to incomplete information through relationship banking. Loan contracts are characterized by more than just interest rates. The nature and amount of collateral become key. Yet despite efficiency-enhancing market responses, capital markets remain imperfect. Market power by banks may raise intermediation margins, resulting in monopoly rents for the banking sector. Banks also face incentives to misallocate resources; underfunded banks tend to finance excessively risky projects. Social returns on investment may differ markedly from the private returns to investors, and social perceptions of the riskiness of investments may differ substantially from private assessments.

For the above reasons, most governments are reluctant to rely entirely on private markets to allocate capital. Two types of government involvement are therefore common: first, efforts to reduce misallocation of resources by financial institutions; and second, efforts to control banking spreads to limit monopoly rents. While these measures are by no means unique to East Asia, the HPAEs have been unusually active in exercising them. In addition, most HPAEs have gone a step further and attempted to direct credit to specific sectors, industries, and even firms. We discuss this more complex and controversial topic in a separate section below.

Reducing Bad Investment Choices. Portfolio requirements, either to avoid excessive lending in some areas or to increase lending in others, directly influence the allocation of credit by banks. In chapter 5 we argued that East Asian governments have emphasized the safety of banks through both regulations that monitor and enhance the solvency of banks and measures that avoid financial disruptions. These have positive effects on resource allocation. Solvent banks have fewer incentives than under-funded ones to take excessive risks in lending. Solvent banks can also lend more.

Portfolio requirements to enhance prudent lending—such as limits on lending to real estate projects—also may guide credit away from some activities to others with higher-perceived social returns. In general, restrictions on lending have favored producers. For example, East Asian governments have often restricted lending to real estate and other spec-ulative activities. These governments are concerned not only that such lending increases the riskiness of banks' portfolios but also that it diverts lending away from manufacturing. Thailand, for example, does not specify how much of their portfolio banks should lend to industry, but it provides lending guidelines that favor lending to industry and agri-culture and limit lending to other activities, including real estate and securities.

Most HPAEs were assisted in their efforts to influence lending deci-sions because they directly held a high proportion of savings deposits. Table 6.4 shows that in Indonesia, Korea, until recently, and Taiwan, China, very large shares of total deposits of the financial system were held in publicly owned commercial banks. In addition the governments of Japan, Malaysia, Singapore, and Taiwan, China, have discretion over a large (and growing) proportion of total deposits in postal savings and/or provident and insurance funds. Some governments have also been able to complement those resources with budgetary allocations or borrowing from abroad.

Japan and Singapore have the most well-defined programs for allo-cating savings held by public financial institutions. The financial insti-tutions created under the Fiscal Investment and Loan Program (FILP) of Japan allocate funds originating from the government's postal savings, national welfare deposits, and national pension deposits. The FILP ab-sorbed 20–40 percent of household savings during the rapid growth pe-riod. The Development Fund of Singapore, whose resources originate primarily from the provident funds, lends directly to the government's

Table 6.4 Proportion of Total Deposits with Government Financial Institutions in East Asia
(percentage of total deposits)

Economy/year	With government or postal savings institutions	With pension/ provident insurance funds	With public commercial and specialized banks	Total
Indonesia				
1971–76	N.A.	N.A.	—	—
1976–80	N.A.	N.A.	79.9a	79.9[a]
1981–85	N.A.	N.A.	71.7	71.7
1986–90	—	N.A.	61.3	61.3
Japan				
1960	10.8	4.3	N.A.	15.1
1970	14.3	8.0	N.A.	22.3
1980	25.3	12.2	N.A.	37.5
1990	20.9	12.2	N.A.	33.1
Korea, Rep. of				
1971–75	4.8	N.A.	80.7	85.5
1976–80	1.0	N.A.	80.0	81.0
1981–85	2.2	N.A.	57.9[b]	60.1
1986–90	1.1	N.A.	32.1	33.2
Malaysia				
1971–75	4.1	30.8	—	34.9
1976–80	3.6	24.7	—	28.3
1981–85	2.0	24.9	—	26.9
1986–89	1.5	30.4	—	31.9

statutory boards and government corporations. Indonesia, Korea, Malaysia, and Thailand have guided their state-owned commercial banks to finance priority projects.

Limiting Banking Spreads. As we pointed out in chapter 5, regulations intended to encourage prudent behavior and enhance solvency can reduce the level of competition among banks and increase the average spread between borrowing and lending rates. High spreads reduce the efficiency of resource allocation by reducing the volume of investment that can be supported by a given level of savings. Thus, there may be a tradeoff between efforts to mobilize financial savings by promoting the solvency of banks and the efficient use of savings.

Economy/year	With government or postal savings institutions	With pension/ provident insurance funds	With public commercial and specialized banks	Total
Singapore				
1971–75	2.1	21.6	—	23.7
1976–80	9.5	30.0	—	39.4
1981–85	11.0	34.6	—	45.6
1986–90	12.7	34.9	—	47.6
Taiwan, China				
1971–75	10.8	N.A.	67.9	78.7
1976–80	13.8	N.A.	63.6	77.4
1981–85	19.2	N.A.	53.5	72.7
1986–90	19.4	N.A.	52.4	71.8
Thailand				
1971–75	12.7	N.A.	1.1	13.8
1976–80	10.0	N.A.	3.7	13.7
1981–85	8.2	N.A.	1.6	9.8
1986–90	7.6	N.A.	2.2	9.8

— Not available.

N.A. Not applicable, since these particular types of financial institutions were nonexistent in the respective economies.

a. The figure reported is for 1978–80.

b. The commercial banks were privatized in 1983.

c. The figures for Taiwan, China, are based on the deposits of all commercial banks and are consequently overestimated because only 12 of the 16 commercial banks are government owned. Nevertheless, the government-owned banks account for the major share of commercial bank deposits.

Sources: Indonesia: *Indonesian Financial Statistics* (various issues). Japan: JDB/JERI (1993); *Economic Statistics Annual* (various years). Korea: *Economic Statistics Yearbook* (various years). Malaysia: *Quarterly Bulletin* (1990). Singapore: *Yearbook of Statistics* (1991); *Economic and Social Statistics* (1960–82, 1985). Taiwan, China: *Statistical Yearbook* (various years). Thailand: *Quarterly Bulletin* (various issues).

Except for Hong Kong and Singapore, all HPAEs at various times have simultaneously regulated deposit and lending rates and consequently the spreads of financial institutions. As a result, rents derived from imperfect competition have been modest. Our evidence led us to conclude in chapter 5 that, in comparison with other developing economies, banking system spreads were relatively low in East Asia and have declined as entry restrictions and interest rates have been liberalized (see table 5.7). Given the rapid growth of the financial systems in the HPAEs and their limited intermediation margins, we conclude that regulators have done a good job of balancing the need to limit competition in order to enhance bank solvency with the need to limit imperfect competition rents. HPAE regulators did not always get it right, however. It is notable that, in Indonesia and Thailand, regulated intermediation margins were substantially higher than those after liberalization of entry and interest rates.

Using Directed Credit

Like many governments, those in East Asia have gone beyond the indirect guidance described above to target credit directly at priority activities. The categories to which they directed credit have differed little from other developing economies. However, HPAEs, particularly Japan and Korea, have used unusual mechanisms that have helped to increase loan repayment rates and overall success of directed credit. They have limited the size of credit subsidies, and they have applied stringent standards to the selection and implementation of projects.

Criteria for Selecting Directed-Credit Targets. There are three broad types of directed-credit interventions. First, governments can direct credit to specific firms or industries. Second, they can direct credit on the basis of broad functional criteria, such as promotion of exports or small and medium-size enterprises. Third, they can direct credit to accomplish social objectives, such as mass housing or redistribution of assets among ethnic groups. HPAE governments have engaged in all three.

Targeting firms or industries. Japan during its postwar reconstruction and Korea during the 1970s directed substantial credit to specific sectors and firms, mostly in heavy and chemical industries (HCIs) (see table 6.5). Japan's FILP accounted for about a third of new equipment lending in the 1950s. Between 1973 and 1981, Korea's policy loans were about 60 percent of the total loans of its deposit money banks. Most of Japan's priority lending targets through the early 1960s were industries associated with large optimum scales and increasing returns to scale; so were Korea's during the HCI period. Indonesia and Malaysia, conversely, had disappointing experiences with credit interventions targeted to specific industries in the 1970s and early 1980s and abandoned the schemes in favor of more functionally directed credit. Hong Kong and Thailand have not been active in using credit instruments to push selected industries.

In contrast with many other developing economies, where directed credit often went to public and quasi-public enterprises, directed credit in the HPAEs has generally gone to the private sector. Consider the cases

Table 6.5 Proportion of Loans Accounted for by Government's Policy Loans, Japan and Republic of Korea

Year	Japan		Republic of Korea	
	Policy loans as a share of loans/discounts[a]	Policy loans as a share of new industrial equipment funds	Policy loans as a share of outstanding loans[b]	Foreign trade loans as a share of policy loans
1955	13.2	32.1	—	—
1960	11.0	22.8	—	—
1965	9.6	15.9	—	—
1970	9.8	13.8	47.41	11.71
1975	10.6	16.0	52.43	19.05
1980	14.1	17.6	59.78	19.24
1985	13.7	11.5	52.77	24.35
1990	11.8	8.1	—	—

— Not available.

a. Policy loans pertain to all loans made under Japan's Fiscal Investment and Loan Program (FILP). Outstanding loans are of all financial institutions.

b. Policy loans include loans under some kind of explicit preferential credit program, that is, loans extended preferentially in terms of interest rate and availability or supported by the Central Bank's automatic rediscounts. Outstanding loans are the value of all loans and discounts to the private sector made by the Bank of Korea, deposit money banks, and two development institutions. Foreign trade loans include all loans for foreign trade by deposit money banks and all loans by the Korean Export-Import Bank.

Sources: Japan: JDB/JERI (1993). Korea: Stern and others (1992).

of Turkey and Mexico. Loans by the banking system to public enterprises in Turkey in 1975 were 28 percent of bank assets, and to the public administration, 19 percent; those proportions rose to 24.9 and 35.9 percent, respectively, in 1980. In Mexico, the largest development bank provided about 75 percent of its industrial loans to four state-owned enterprises. Unfortunately, these public enterprises often did not perform well, economically or financially. In East Asia, Indonesia, Malaysia, and Singapore have directed credit to state enterprises, but the proportions of total credit were not persistently high, the parastatals tended to perform better financially, and the interest rate subsidies were not large (except in Indonesia).[17] Korea was an exception; its lending to the public steel plant, POSCO, was substantial but is widely considered a success story.

Targeting exporters and small and medium-size enterprises. The broadest functional targeting of credit in the HPAEs has been to exporters. All East Asian economies except Hong Kong and Singapore have subsidized export credits, often through the central bank rediscount system (see table 6.6). Exporters from all industries have had access. Small and medium-size firms, which often had to rely on curb markets, found export financing one of their few ready sources of formal finance. Box 6.1

(Text continues on page 284.)

Table 6.6 Characteristics of the Export Credit Schemes in East Asia

Hong Kong	Offers export credit insurance with a slight subsidy through the Hong Kong Export Credit Insurance Corporation (HKECIC).
Japan	Between 1946 and 1972, the Bank of Japan (BOJ) rediscounted export bills at low rates of interest (1 to 2 percentage points lower than that applicable to general trade bills). During this period, the BOJ directed 10 percent of its loans to export finance (which financed 50 percent of total export-related bank lending).
Korea, Rep. of	Offers concessional rediscounting of preshipment credit based on letters of credit (LCs). The differential between loan rates of this export credit and general loan rates was between 3 and 20 percentage points until 1982, when this difference was eliminated. In 1984 the differential was restored at 1.5 percentage points.
	The Korean Export-Import Bank provides longer-term postshipment finance.
	Provides export credit insurance, but this has been used sparingly (by about 3 percent of exports in 1980).
Malaysia	Since 1977, the Export Credit Refinancing (ECR) facility has rediscounted export bills for postshipment financing.
	Since 1979, the ECR refinances preshipment export credits at subsidized rates for eligible exports, based on letters of credit. A domestic letter of credit was also introduced to enable the financing of indirect exporters.
Singapore	In 1975 the government established a rediscount facility for exports and re-exports.
	The Export Credit Insurance Corporation provides insurance for exports by Singapore.
Taiwan, China	Offers firms short-term preshipment loans based on LCs. After products are shipped, firms are eligible for loans based on LCs, documents against acceptance of payment, and shipment documents. In addition, the Central Bank provides a special discount rate to designated domestic banks for export loans, usually at 1 percentage point lower than the usual discount rate. The export loan rate was about 3 to 5 percentage points below the minimum interest rate for secured loans between 1970 and 1980, and it dropped to 1 to 2 percentage points after 1980.
Thailand	The Bank of Thailand rediscounts at subsidized rates 50 percent of the value of lending to exports by commercial banks. Commercial banks lend on the basis of LCs.

**Table 6.7 Real Interest Rates on Directed Credit,
Selected HPAEs and Other Developing Economies**

(percent)

Economy	Directed credit	Nondirected credit
HPAEs		
Indonesia, 1981–83, liquidity credits	-1.7–4.0	—
Japan, 1951–60	0.5–3.0	3.1–4.6
Korea, Rep. of, 1970–80, industry	-2.7	2.9
exports	-6.7	2.9
Taiwan, China, 1980–89, industry	1.9–3.9	4.6
1984–85, exports	1.5	4.6
Other developing economies		
Brazil, 1987	-23.5	—
Colombia, 1981–87, industry	1.5	13.5
India, 1992	-2.5–4.0	7.0
Mexico, 1987–88	-24.0	6.0
Turkey, 1981, industry	-4.0–15.0	13.9
1980–89, exports	-14.0	13.0

— Not available.
Sources: JDB/JER (1993); World Bank data.

income economies. Directed-credit programs in the HPAEs had higher real interest rates than in other developing regions. Given capital's high international mobility, we conclude that interest rate subsidies in the HPAEs were lower than in other regions.[19]

The HPAEs generally have smaller shares of their credit systems subject to government direction than other developing economies. For example, in the early 1980s, roughly three-fourths of loans from Turkey's financial system were made at government directive. In Pakistan directed credit as a proportion of nongovernment credit was 54–68 percent in the late 1980s and 1990s (an internal World Bank report). In Brazil, about 80 percent of the total average stock of credit was directed in 1986–87. Colombia's directed credit to industry in 1984–87 was on average 56 percent of total credit. By contrast, in East Asia, Korea's policy loans in the HCI period were more than 50 percent of total credit, and Japan's never exceeded 15 percent of total credit. Indonesia briefly had 48 percent of its total loans in priority liquidity credits in 1982, but it reduced these rapidly following the liberalizations of 1983 and 1991.

Moreover, directed credit is becoming less important. While earlier efforts of governments in East Asia concentrated on developing the banking system and guiding its lending decisions, more recent policies have been directed at deregulating financial markets: Japan started in the 1970s and the others in the 1980s. The features of deregulation are similar: interest rates are gradually deregulated, directed credit is reduced, and entry restrictions are slowly eased (see table A6.5, at the end of the chapter). The majority of HPAEs deregulated their interest rates during the 1980s, jointly with efforts to liberalize their economies and their financial markets. The deregulation of entry has been much more limited, however, except in Indonesia. This process in the East Asian economies has been gradual and was meant to minimize disruption in the manufacturing sector.

Institutional Mechanisms for Selection and Monitoring. In contrast to most other economies that have tried but failed to use directed credit, Japan and Korea appear to have strong institutional capacity for project design, appraisal, and monitoring. Because of this, directed credit has generally gone to projects that are creditworthy and viable. More important—and in sharp contrast to many developing economies— funds have usually been utilized for the purpose for which they were allocated. The result has been a high level of loan repayments and a correspondingly low level of loan losses.

In Japan, officials working within government sectoral guidelines operated much like loan officers in private commercial banks, scrutinizing project proposals and the firms involved to ascertain their ability to repay. Once a loan was approved, close cooperation between development and commercial banks ensured continuous monitoring of the performance of the borrower and enabled development banks to take early action if loan repayment was in arrears. Coupled with Japan's overall economic success, effective pre-appraisal and monitoring resulted in very low loan losses. The Japan Development Bank, the main government lender, experienced write-offs of a mere 0.09 percent of average loans outstanding in 1951–55 and just 0.01 percent in 1956–65, lower than commercial and trust banks that focused on short-term lending and had a more diversified portfolio. The JDB's superior performance may be partly explained by its greater reliance on collateral security, particularly equipment purchased with the loans. Fear of losing collateralized equipment gave borrowers a strong incentive to repay their loans.

In Korea, the government, banks, and industrial firms worked together and shared responsibility for the success of directed-credit pro-

jects. Various institutional arrangements such as monthly export promotion meetings and monthly briefings on economic trends, discussed
in chapter 4, supported this close consultation (Cho and Hellmann
1993). Enforcement of government goals—primarily the imperative to
export—was achieved by rewarding successful firms with continued
credit support while reducing credit to less successful firms. Such con-
tinual and pragmatic review and adjustment of policy implementation
reduced, but did not always eliminate, the moral-hazard costs of government intervention.

Other HPAEs fall along a spectrum between Taiwan, China, which has
utilized mechanisms similar to Japan and Korea and has had similar success, and Indonesia, which was plagued by the problems discussed below
and has largely discontinued directed credit.

In contrast with Northeast Asia, credit allocation decisions in many
developing economies were often motivated by political and noneconomic considerations. Projects were designed with conflicting objectives and lacked proper evaluation. Moreover, the very large rents that
could be obtained from subsidized credit were a strong incentive to corrupt practices. In smaller economies, credit allocation to specific sectors
became credit to individual firms, because of the limited number of
companies involved. Consequently, projects were subject to govern-
ment-monopoly negotiations and were prone to poor appraisal and dis-
bursements without proper documentation. Credit allocation to large
and politically powerful firms or state-owned enterprises were characterized by weak monitoring and follow-up on debt recovery, producing
high loan losses and eventually large-scale failure of directed-credit
programs.

How Did Financial Market Policies Contribute to Growth?

Capital market policy fundamentals are undoubtedly the major factor explaining the contribution that capital markets have made to the efficient use of resources in the HPAEs. Rapid deepening of financial
markets, combined with prudent restrictions on lending by banks for
real estate and stock speculation, are probably the most important contributions of East Asia's financial policies to growth. Recent cross-
economy evidence shows that the average level of financial development
is strongly correlated with the average rate of per capita income growth,
both before and after controlling for initial conditions (King and Levine

1993). Moreover, the level of financial development importantly predicts economic growth.[20]

What about attempts by government to direct the allocation of credit? Here the record is mixed. We conclude that credit directed to exporters was a positive factor in accelerating growth. All East Asian economies provided automatic, generous access to credit (or credit guarantees) to exporters with varying degrees of subsidies. Japan, Korea, and Taiwan, China, went a step further: they used exports as a criterion to determine whether priority firms, regardless of the market for the actual priority investment, continued to receive credit.[21] Other more specific directed-credit programs had both positive and negative results. In general, the economies with strong civil services and highly professional public financial institutions—Japan, Korea, Singapore, and Taiwan, China—apparently had some success in implementing credit policies to promote priority industries and firms. Key to this success was the use of economic performance criteria and the monitoring of firms by banks and bureaucrats.

These traits were evident in an extensive study of Japan's policy-based lending in the immediate postwar period (JDB/JERI 1993). The study found that interest rate subsidies were no more than 2–3 percentage points and that effective monitoring kept loan losses very low. Moreover, directed credit was a minor aspect of the overall financial system, accounting for less than 10 percent of total loans. The study identified three characteristics of Japan's policy-based lending: reliance on the private sector; the close correspondence between national economic plans and directed credit; and respect for the managerial independence of the government financial institutions responsible for channeling funds to the targeted sectors by selecting individual firms according to purely economic criteria.

By comparison, Korea's use of directed credit during its economic takeoff in the 1960s and 1970s was more extensive, and interest rate subsidies were larger. As in Japan, the government in Korea consulted closely with businesses and banks, attempted to monitor performance closely, and relied on a competitive business environment to provide an objective measure of performance. Accordingly, policy-based lending probably contributed to the rapid expansion of Korean industry, particularly manufactured exports (Cho and Kim 1993). Most of the directed lending to priority industries in Korea translated into investments in equipment. Despite Korea's severe adjustment problems due to the HCI drive during the early 1980s, rapid growth resumed easily in the mid-1980s, in part because of increasing utilization of the HCI investments, which were in physical capital, as demand increased.

However, the cost of extensive and highly subsidized directed credits was substantial—and likely to increase as development proceeded. Directed credits burdened banks with nonperforming loans, interfered with the financial system's efficient operation, hindered the growth of financial savings, and sometimes threatened macroeconomic stability. Korea was able to weather these difficulties partly because its closed capital market at the time enabled the government to suppress interest rates on deposits, thereby funding the subsidies for loans to corporations. In addition, relatively easy credit in international capital markets and Korea's strong relationship with two key lenders, Japan and the United States, helped to ensure the availability of foreign capital, which was either funneled into directed credit or went to bail out troubled enterprises unable to repay subsidized loans. Today, both the greater openness of capital markets in most developing economies and the heightened competition in international capital markets suggest that financial repression and directed credits are now less viable options for developing economies.[22]

To argue that directed-credit programs in general reached their target groups and that loans were effectively monitored does not establish that they contributed positively to growth. To do this, microeconomic evidence is needed to establish two facts: government lending promoted investment and did not simply displace investment from other sources, and the social returns on the incremental investment exceeded private returns, justifying the targeting of specific sectors. Such evidence is rare—even for the northern-tier HPAEs—but two recent studies attempt to address these questions for a sample of firms in Japan.[23]

A careful microeconometric study of Japan's industrial credit programs in general machinery, electrical machinery, and precision instruments during the 1980s—sectors selected because of their high potential for externalities due to innovation and learning—reaches the following conclusions:

- Government lending had a large, positive, and statistically significant impact on both gross and net investment; the three-year cumulative effect of a one-dollar increase in debt financing from government sources was more than two dollars of additional gross investments in fixed capital assets.

- Government lenders withdrew credit once firms had earned access to private credit markets and, in turn, extended credit to new borrowers rather than preexisting borrowers, consistent with (though certainly not conclusively establishing) the claim that credit was being allocated according to objective lending standards, rather than on the basis of political considerations.
- The characteristics of firms receiving increasing government credit indicate that assistance was targeted toward firms most likely to grow, invest, and generate technological externalities; firms receiving credit had research and development investment shares in output approximately twice those of firms not receiving increasing government financing.

The authors conclude: "Possibly because of the institutional structure of these lending programs, it appears that economic logic rather than political capture motivates policy-based lending decisions. Government credit is withdrawn quickly from seasoned firms, is targeted toward growing, R&D intensive firms, and produces substantial increases in investment and access to private credit. The fact that these results are measured with data from the 1980s leads one to expect even larger effects for earlier periods" (Calomiris and Himmelberg 1993).

Limited evidence from the 1960s tends to confirm Calomiris and Himmelberg's conjecture. Horiuchi and Sui (1992) examine the role of the Japan Development Bank's directed credit in promoting private investment during the 1960s, when JDB was the major policy-based institution lending to medium-size and large firms. Their sample consisted of 477 medium-size firms listed on the Tokyo Stock Exchange in 1965. Among their results are:

- JDB lending resulted in a net increase in new investment.
- JDB loans were accompanied by incremental lending from private banks, suggesting that JDB's loans did not crowd out private bank lending.
- JDB's loans to firms preceded the firms' increased borrowing from private banks and improved the access to credit of firms that were not attached to private "main banks" (often firms affiliated with a *keiretsu* bank).

Thus, directed credit appears to have acted as a signaling and insurance mechanism. By selecting among borrowers, the JDB encouraged complementary lending from private financial institutions with a consequent net increase in investment. Moreover, policy-based lending was most successful when it was directed at nontraditional borrowers. The JDB's loans stimulated greater lending by private banks to firms not affiliated with main banks but did not have the same impact on firms affiliated with main banks.

Another study of credit programs in Japan and Korea based on an analysis of the objectives and outcomes of the programs adds an additional element, noting the positive role of coordination achieved through government lending programs. During the 1950s the bulk of directed credit in Japan was given to "basic industries"—electricity, iron and steel, and coal mining—that were characterized by increasing returns to scale and that produced basic inputs for other parts of the economy. Once these basic industries were developed, Japan subsequently promoted industries whose expected spillover effects on the economy were large, for example, machine tools (JDB/JERI 1993). During the 1970s, Korea channeled most of its directed credit for fixed investments in manufacturing to the HCI industries, among them such producer goods industries as steel and machinery. Using a framework not dissimilar to the contest framework outlined in chapter 2, the study reaches a similar conclusion: the coordinating role of government in Japan and Korea has diminished over time, and hence the effectiveness and desirability of using credit programs to improve coordination among private firms are diminishing as well (Cho and Hellmann 1993).

But many other directed-credit programs, even in the HPAEs, did not meet their objectives. In fact, the track record of most directed-credit programs in Indonesia, Malaysia, and Thailand was so poor that their governments, demonstrating the pragmatic flexibility that we have argued characterizes economic policymaking throughout the HPAEs, abandoned many of them. Limited differentials between directed credit and market interest rates and smaller volumes of directed credit relative to the size of the financial system meant that financial market distortions in the HPAEs, even from unsuccessful attempts to direct credit, were not generally large. In addition, the focus of HPAE governments on providing credit for the private sector meant that, in general, loss-making public enterprises were not priority lending targets, unlike in other developing economies.

Using the International Market: Trade and Industrial Policy

WHILE THE LINK BETWEEN INTERNATIONAL TRADE AND economic growth is widely accepted, the precise nature of the relationship is controversial. Early writing on trade policy and growth stressed the benefits of neutral incentives between production for the domestic market and production for export. With neutral incentives, it was argued, resources would flow to sectors in which the economy was most internationally competitive (Corden 1971), and gains in technical efficiency (or "X-efficiency") would result from a more competitive environment (Nishimizu and Page 1991). Studies in the late 1960s and early 1970s convincingly demonstrated the extreme bias in incentive structures against exports and agriculture in most developing economies and the resulting high costs of import-substituting industrialization.[24] Recent theoretical work has argued that, where market power, economies of scale, learning, or externalities are significant, departures from neutral incentive regimes (low and uniform tariffs) may improve economic performance (Krugman 1986). This literature, however, unlike the earlier carefully documented studies of the costs of protection, provides very little evidence concerning the importance of these factors or the potential benefits to growth of departures from trade neutrality.[25]

Proponents of trade neutrality and intervention both cite the records of the high-performing Asian economies as evidence supporting their views. As we noted in chapter 1, international trade is important in all the HPAEs and is the factor most consistently correlated with their success. Balassa (1991), Krueger (1993), Hughes (1992), and others argue that openness to international trade, based on largely neutral incentives, was the critical factor in East Asia's rapid growth. Conversely, advocates of trade interventions, while acknowledging the importance of trade, note that incentives deriving from quantitative restrictions on imports, tariffs, and subsidies were not neutral among sectors (or firms) during their periods of rapid growth. They argue that the HPAE governments successfully intervened to change comparative advantage (Amsden 1989; Wade 1990; Singh 1992).

Industrial policy interventions, which often use trade policy instruments, are motivated by the belief that shifting industrial structures toward newer and more modern sectors increases the opportunities for capturing dynamic scale economies that result from learning. During their heavy and chemical industries programs, Japan and Korea were the most active HPAEs in promoting individual industries and sectors. Singapore and Taiwan, China, have also actively provided incentives for technological upgrading. Malaysia had an HCI program reminiscent of Japan's and Korea's, while Indonesia has attempted to leapfrog from labor-intensive manufacturing to high-technology industries such as aircraft and electronics.

How have trade and industrial policies affected growth in East Asia? To answer this question we first examine those conditions that might justify government efforts to promote specific sectors. We then describe the trade and industrial policy regimes in the HPAEs and compare their domestic relative prices with international prices to determine the extent of interventions. Finally, we evaluate two approaches to increasing productivity. We find, on the one hand, that government efforts to promote specific industries generally did not increase economywide productivity. On the other hand, the evidence shows that broad government support for exports was a highly effective way of enhancing absorption of international best-practice technology, thus boosting productivity and output growth.

Market Failures, Trade, and Industrial Policies

Why should governments interfere with the level playing field created by the international market? Our discussion of coordination failures in chapter 2 touched on many of the reasons, but it may be useful to review some of the arguments specifically as they apply to trade and industrial policy.[26] Among the many reasons for discrepancies between social and private returns cited earlier, four stand out:

■ *Interdependent investments and economies of scale.* Increasing returns from scale and capital market imperfections may mean that investments that could be internationally competitive at optimal scales will not be undertaken. This is especially true with large, interdependent projects for which optimum scale depends on simultaneous investment in upstream and downstream industries. The larger the indivisibilities and returns from scale, the more likely that private initiatives will be absent.

■ *Strategic negotiations.* In negotiations with other economies and foreign companies, governments can alter the nature of the market environment by intervention. The outcome of any bargaining problem depends on the strength of competition on both sides. By coordinating the actions of buyers of technology and trying to increase competition among sellers, governments can appropriate more of the surplus associated with the transfer of technology than they otherwise could (Stiglitz 1993a).

■ *Pecuniary externalities.* Pecuniary external economies arise if, as the size of a competitive industry increases, the long-run supply curve falls (Marshallian real externalities). Such gains in productivity are attributable to economies of scope in the use of specialized equipment and greater specialization of individual skills. When economies are small, current prices may not convey adequate information about prospective lower costs of production through larger plant size (Scitovsky 1953; Chenery 1959).[27] Externalities can also arise from the interaction between suppliers and buyers about the design or production of a product leading to a better or cheaper good than is available internationally. In this case, the source of the externality is the nontradability of some types of inputs or knowledge—otherwise the improved method or product could be obtained from international suppliers.

■ *Learning.* Externalities related to learning have traditionally been identified as important sources of market failures in developing economies. When firms gain knowledge of production from other firms without incurring costs, real externalities are present.[28] Because of incomplete appropriability of knowledge, individual firms may spend less on obtaining production knowledge than is socially optimal.[29] Externalities due to learning may also be conferred on other firms by the first entrant. These include the demonstration that the sector is physically and economically feasible and the leakage of information on technology and marketing (Pack and Westphal 1986; Rob 1990).

Economists initially responded to these market failures with arguments supporting the protection of so-called infant industries. Protection was seen as necessary so that firms could gain the experience needed to lower costs and become viable.[30] Industrial policy advocates take the argument a step further. Because they associate learning with capital- and knowledge-intensive industries, they advocate a rapid shift in industrial structure toward these activities, even if they are not internationally competitive at present levels of scale, knowledge, and factor prices. In this view, the short-run allocative costs of establishing internationally uncompetitive industries will be outweighed by the long-run benefits of rapid productivity change in the promoted and linked sectors. But as the many infant industries that have never grown up amply demonstrate, protection does not ensure that the promised learning and economies of scale actually materialize.

Trade Policies in the HPAEs

Most HPAEs began industrialization with a protectionist orientation and have gradually moved toward increasingly free trade. Along the way (as we showed in chapter 3), they often tapped some of the efficiency-generating benefits of international competition through mixed trade regimes: they granted exporters duty-free imports of capital and intermediate goods while continuing to protect consumer goods. Export prices were set in the international market and were often substantially less than current marginal or average costs.[31] Losses on export production offset profits in the protected market, while competition in the international market ensured that the firm would not suffer from loss of cost discipline. More recently, all the HPAEs have reduced their protection of import-substituting industries.

Below we describe the evolving patterns of protection in the HPAEs, with the exceptions of Hong Kong and Singapore, which adopted essentially free trade stances early in their development.

Japan. Japan pursued an early import-substituting industrialization strategy, similar in many dimensions to those of Argentina, India, and other less successful economies. As late as 1968, effective rates of protection (ERPs) in Japan were still quite high and exhibited the cascaded pattern from raw materials (low) to consumer products (high) that is typical of most developing economies (see table 6.8). Unlike many import-substituting economies, however, there was surprisingly high protection of machinery (final producer goods), confirming other research indicating that the Japanese authorities engaged in an intensive effort to develop this sector. ERP levels in the machinery sector were reduced during the 1970s, only after it was evident from export performance that the sector had become internationally competitive (Itoh and Kiyono 1988). Quite high levels of protection were afforded sectors such as iron and steel and nonferrous metals as late as 1970. Protection in capital-intensive sectors such as pulp and paper and chemicals also remained high, to say nothing of the remarkably high levels in textiles.[32]

Korea. There is considerable evidence, summarized in Pack and Westphal (1986), that Korea selectively protected sectors that the gov-

Table 6.8 Effective Rates of Protection in Japan
(percent)

Type	By type of goods					
	1963		1968		ERP-NRP	
	NRP[a]	ERP[b]	NRP	ERP	1963	1968
Raw materials	3.1	0.8	3.9	0.9	-2.3	-3.0
Producer goods	13.7	29.6	15.2	22.3	15.9	7.1
Intermediate producer goods	12.3	28.0	14.1	21.7	15.7	7.6
Final producer goods	15.9	32.3	16.9	23.2	15.4	6.3
Consumer goods	21.6	44.6	23.6	35.8	23.0	12.2

Industry	By industry[c]		
	1963	1968	1972
Manufacturing	32.3	24.2	14.4
Textiles	54.3	28.2	18.6
Spinning	27.1	12.5	15.0
Weaving	44.6	30.5	15.5
Products	72.8	32.8	22.4
Wood products	14.0	25.6	16.1
Paper and pulp	9.7	18.0	11.0
Publishing	-16.7	1.0	-0.9
Leather and rubber products	30.9	21.8	12.3
Chemicals	33.4	17.7	8.8
Petroleum and coal products	19.5	14.5	7.1
Nonmetallic minerals	22.2	15.7	8.1
Iron and steel	30.1	30.0	17.1
Nonferrous metals	30.4	34.1	22.1
Metal products	13.8	19.9	9.9
Machinery	36.7	20.0	7.7
General machinery	23.0	14.5	8.7
Electrical machinery	30.9	16.5	5.4
Transport equipment	61.5	31.0	9.2
Precision instruments	34.9	22.9	10.4

a. NRP=Nominal Rate of Protection.
b. ERP=Effective Rate of Protection.
c. ERP based on simple averages of tariff rates.
Sources: For top panel, Itoh and Kiyono (1988); for bottom panel, Shouda (1982).

ernment hoped to promote. Protection consisted of both tariffs and nontariff barriers. Table 6.9 presents a summary measure that combines the effect of nominal tariffs and nontariff barriers.[33] The figures span the period 1966–85, and thus include the early efforts at industrial promotion, the HCI drive, and the subsequent liberalization. The 1966 figures show a relatively protectionist stance that becomes somewhat more

Table 6.9 Overall Degrees of Import Liberalization by Major Industry for the Republic of Korea, Selected Years (Consolidating Both QRs and Tariffs)

(percent)

Major industry	1966	1970	1975	1980	1983	1985
I. Primary Industry	42.0	56.5	55.1	58.8	65.3	71.2
II. Food, beverages, and tobacco	30.0	32.4	38.4	49.6	49.6	64.1
III. Textiles, clothing, and leather products	34.7	36.6	43.8	74.0	74.3	87.8
IV. Wood and its products	24.2	64.0	69.1	76.5	82.7	92.4
V. Paper, paper products, and printing and publishing	39.5	54.7	54.5	78.4	88.8	90.8
VI. Chemicals, petroleum, coal, rubber, and plastic products	47.9	57.1	58.4	65.9	75.2	80.0
VII. Nonmetallic mineral products	41.0	77.0	76.8	89.1	89.2	91.7
VIII. Basic metal products	44.7	73.3	74.8	86.2	90.1	92.0
IX. Metal products, machinery, and equipment	41.0	59.3	55.4	63.6	69.7	77.8
X. Other manufacturing	31.8	39.5	38.7	58.2	65.4	76.1
All manufacturing (II-X)	37.5	47.7	52.6	66.8	71.3	79.8
Light industry (II-VX)	33.7	38.2	43.7	62.3	63.8	76.8
Heavy and chemical industry (VI-IX)	44.5	62.5	61.2	70.5	76.5	81.7
All-industry average (I-X)	39.6	50.8	52.3	65.6	70.4	78.5

Note: This table gives the degrees of import liberalization by major industry; these are obtained by averaging sectoral data, weighted by the current price value of domestic production for respective years.

Source: Sakong (1993).

liberal by 1975. Nevertheless, even by 1983, when Korea's success had become an established fact, most sectors were still protected by some combination of tariffs and nontariff barriers. While Korea utilized a variety of instruments, especially export targets and rebates, to ensure that exporters faced international prices for their tradeable inputs, there was considerable protection of goods sold on the domestic market.

Taiwan, China. Wade (1990) provides a careful description of the extent of intervention by authorities of Taiwan, China, in product markets. The pattern of protection is not dissimilar from that of Korea. As late as 1972, a significant percentage of items were subject to nontariff barriers, and two-thirds of potential imports were subject to nominal tariffs in excess of 30 percent. As late as 1980, more than 40 percent of imports received nominal protection in excess of 31 percent.

Indonesia, Malaysia, and Thailand. As we described in chapter 3, Indonesia, Malaysia, and Thailand all had import-substitution regimes that while modest by international standards, nevertheless favored production of manufactured goods for the domestic market at the expense of agriculture and exports. Malaysia was notable for low, if variable, protection of import substitutes, while protection levels in Indonesia and Thailand were higher. All three economies began export-push trade strategies during their periods of protection of the domestic market. Tables 6.10, 6.11, and 6.12 provide recent data on the structure of effective protection for these three economies. Effective protection rates are declining but in Indonesia and Thailand they remain sufficiently high to result in some anti-export bias. The free trade regime for exporters in these economies partially offsets the structure of protection.

The Closeness of East Asian Domestic Prices to International Prices

Notwithstanding the protection that exists in all the HPAEs except Hong Kong and Singapore, domestic prices in these economies are closer to international prices than in other developing regions. Two bodies of evidence lead us to this conclusion. First, nominal tariff rates ad-

Table 6.10 Selected Effective Rates of Protection, Malaysia, Selected Years

(percent)

Sector	1969	1979	1987
Food products	83	88	—
Beverages	20	38	-22
Tobacco	125	—	-26
Textiles	—	58	15
Apparel	400	45	6
Wood products	33	38	82
Furniture	40	84	43
Paper and paper products	140	66	29
Printing and publishing	—	26	-9
Industrial chemicals	230	32	12
Petroleum refineries	—	22	5
Rubber products	60	129	14
Plastic products	265	312	163
Iron and steel	84	63	289
Fabricated metal products	40	26	30
Nonelectrical machinery	1,600	89	19
Electrical machinery	130	4	12
Transport equipment	185	59	65

— Not available.

Note: The effective rate of protection is the percentage by which value added at domestic prices exceeds value added at world prices.

Source: Salleh, Yeah, and Meyanathan (1993).

Table 6.11 Selected Effective Rates of Protection, Indonesia, Selected Years

(percent)

Sector	1975	1987	1990
Food, beverages, and tobacco	336.2	122	124
Textiles, cloth, and footwear	231.8	102	35
Wood products	-1.2	25	33
Paper and paper products	87.3	31	20
Printing and publishing	—	—	—
Industrial chemicals	28.4	14	13
Petroleum refineries	—	-1	-1
Rubber and plastic products	426	57	48
Iron and steel	18.2	13	10
Fabricated metal products	—	—	—
Nonelectrical machinery	—	—	—
Electrical machinery	—	—	—
Transport equipment	—	—	—
Non-oil	—	-1	1
Cement	63.6	60.2	53.6
Manufacturing total (excluding oil sector)	74.1	68	59

— Not available.

Note: The effective rate of protection is the percentage by which value added at domestic prices exceeds value added at world prices.

Source: Bhattacharya and Pangestu (1993).

justed for the presence of nontariff barriers are lower in the HPAEs than in most other developing economies. Second, comparisons of real GNP across a broad range of economies indicate that domestic relative prices for tradable goods in the HPAEs are closer to international prices than in other regions.

Table 6.13 presents one of the few systematic attempts to compare nominal tariff rates for a broad range of developing economies (Erzan and others 1989).[34] The authors have also attempted to adjust for the effect of quantitative restrictions on levels of protection. (We have added comparable data for Taiwan, China, and have computed the average nominal tariffs for Korea, Malaysia, Thailand, and Taiwan, China.[35]) Nominal tariffs in the HPAEs are lower than for any other grouping of developing economies except the island economies of the Caribbean and the oil states of West Asia. The difference between Latin America (albeit before its recent trade liberalizations) and the HPAEs is striking. Thus while these economies favored production of import substitutes, they did so less than most other developing economies.

Table 6.12 Selected Effective Rates of Protection, Thailand, Selected Years
(percent)

Sector	1971	1974	1978	Sept. 1981	March 1983	Oct. 1984	Nov. 1984	April 1985
Averages								
All sectors	87.2	18.6	70.2	—	—	—	—	—
Excluding food, beverages, and tobacco	44.2	45.9	90.3	—	—	—	—	—
Manufacturing	—	—	—	77.4	67.4	65.3	57.0	66.3
Textile products	—	—	—	248.5	144.4	127.8	108.0	118.4
Leather products	—	—	—	151.3	199.7	199.0	167.0	152.7
Wood products	—	—	—	60.7	53.7	55.0	49.7	62.0
Paper and pulp	—	—	—	39.5	43.0	43.0	39.0	53.5
Chemical products	—	—	—	54.3	52.9	51.9	46.6	44.5
Rubber products	—	—	—	48.7	46.0	46.0	39.3	42.0
Other nonmetal products	—	—	—	99.8	102.7	102.3	89.8	108.5
Metal products	—	—	—	63.3	62.0	61.9	53.9	70.9
Machinery	—	—	—	14.1	23.6	23.6	21.0	29.3
Consumer goods and motor vehicles	—	—	—	34.9	33.4	33.5	30.6	45.6

— Not available.

Note: The effective rate of protection is the percentage by which value added at domestic prices exceeds value added at world prices.
Source: Brimble (1993).

Table 6.13 Average Tariffs and Para-tariffs, by Region 1985

Tariff/ para-tariff	Caribbean	Central America	South America	North Africa	Sub-Saharan Africa	West Asia	Other Asia	Developing HPEAs[c,d]	All regions
Tariffs									
Economies unweighted[a]	16	23	34	29	32	7	36	19	26
Economies import-weighted[b]	17	24	38	30	35	4	22	17	24
Tariff plus para-tariffs									
Economies unweighted[a]	18	65	46	36	34	9	42	24	34
Economies import-weighted[b]	17	66	51	39	36	5	25	20	30

a. Simple averages across products and economies.
b. Simple averages across products; across countries, averages weighted by total imports.
c. Includes Korea, Malaysia, and Taiwan, China.
d. For Taiwan, China, 1981 data.
Source: Erzan and others (1989).

This is borne out by comparisons of international and domestic prices. Figure 6.4 shows an index of outward orientation based on international comparisons of price levels and price variability for the HPAEs compared with other regional groupings (Dollar 1990). The HPAEs as a group are more outward oriented than other regions; their relative prices are closer to and more consistently related to international prices. Of course, there is substantial variation among the HPAEs. As would be expected, Hong Kong, Malaysia, and Singapore rank in the top two deciles of the index, consistent with evidence on their structures of effective protection. Somewhat surprisingly, Thailand, with higher effective protection, also is ranked in the top decile, while Indonesia is in the top third. Japan, Korea, and Taiwan, China, rank in the fifth and sixth deciles, below such developing-economy comparators as Brazil, India, Mexico, Pakistan, and Venezuela. This is consistent with the evidence that the three northern HPAEs intervened far more frequently and systematically in their economies than the southeastern HPAEs (Dollar 1992). While any large, multi-economy effort at real price comparisons is subject to methodological and empirical criticism, the results are broadly indicative and consistent with other evidence: East Asia's relative prices of traded goods were closer on average to international prices than other developing areas.

Openness to Foreign Technology

An important factor in East Asia's successful productivity-based catching up was openness to foreign ideas and technology. Governments encouraged improvements in technological performance by keeping

Figure 6.4 Index of Outward Orientation

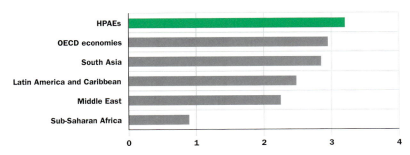

Source: Dollar (1990).

several channels of international technology transfer open at all times, even though some, such as direct foreign investment (DFI), were restricted or closed for varying periods. In contrast to most economies with import-substituting industrialization strategies, even when protection was practiced with respect to the domestic market, the search for and absorption of foreign technology was encouraged. While Japan and Korea set obstacles to DFI, they were hospitable to licensing, though even here the Japanese attempted to ensure that they did not incur excess costs. Singapore was exceptionally welcoming to direct foreign investment, and a major task of the economic planning agency was to locate appropriate foreign investors. Malaysia has aggressively sought export-oriented DFI, particularly from Japan (see box 6.2). None of the HPAEs was hostile to the establishment of local buying offices by international purchasers, an important source of production and marketing knowledge. This selectively permissive attitude toward the acquisition

Box 6.2 Foreign Investment Brings Export Technology to Malaysia

IN THE 1970S AND EARLY 1980S, DIRECT FOREIGN investment was welcome in Malaysia. Government policy encouraged foreign investors, yet the effect was inhibited by the conflicting goal of increasing local participation in corporate ownership. Then, the recession of 1985–86, large fiscal and trade deficits, and declining investment brought an all-out push for DFI, especially for export. New policies offered greater tax incentives and relaxed domestic equity participation requirements for potential investors, bringing technology and export and employment opportunities.

The new flexibility had a dramatic effect on foreign investment. DFI approvals in Malaysia, which averaged US$300 million a year in 1983–85, jumped to US$2 billion by 1988. The investments became more dynamic. In 1988 a quarter of the DFI originated from Japan, followed by Taiwan, China, and the United States—in contrast to the previous ten years, when the greatest source of DFI had been Singapore, naturally attracted by historical ties and physical proximity. New investments were directed

toward electrical and electronic products, chemical products, rubber products, basic metal products, and petroleum. More of the investments were dedicated to exports than ever before.

The benefits to Malaysia of DFI have been substantial, particularly in generating foreign exchange and employment. However, some critics argue that linkages with the local economy have not been strong—at least, not as strong as in neighboring recipients of DFI. Two important reasons for that are the young age of many of the investments in Malaysia and the relative scarcity of management capacity, skilled labor, and high-quality suppliers, a result of Malaysia's late start as an HPAE. But the foreign investment projects themselves have contributed to building know-how in the economy. In 1985 the thirteen American semiconductor manufacturers in Malaysia spent more than $100 million in training Malaysian workers, mostly engineers and technicians. Local value added has been rising as established firms upgrade their technology to keep up with world markets, and firms have added testing of of knowledge of international best practice was a reflection of the view that the world market for goods and services provided an opportunity, not a threat.

In contrast, many other developing economies that tended to emphasize the dangers of opening to world markets were equally suspicious of open policies with respect to knowledge acquisition. Suspicion of external trade was often reflected in a mistrust of DFI and licensing. The absence of exports reinforced the suspicion. Even where DFI was permitted in inward-oriented economies, it was not viewed as providing access to international best practice but rather as a source of additional domestic production. Thus some economies in Latin America that were hostile to licensing nevertheless allowed DFI in production for the domestic market. The basic difference between these economies and Singapore, which was much more heavily dependent on DFI, is that the multinational corporations locating in the latter could only do so to export,

---

semiconductors to their assembly activities. There is also no doubt that DFI has created a lot of employment—often for poor rural Malay women—to the tune of 85,000 in electronics alone in the late 1980s.

Malaysia has found that, as investments mature and local and regional linkages are fortified, multinationals that are often thought of as "footloose" stay, and the positive spillovers created by successful ventures encourage more investment. For example:

■ Since the 1970s, DFI has made Malaysia the world's third largest producer of semiconductors, garnering almost US$3 billion in net exports in 1986. In the late 1980s, Siemens built in Malaysia its fourth plant in the world to manufacture megachips (the other three were in Germany, Japan, and the United States). But foreign companies have not kept to semiconductors—investments in electronics have spread both backward and forward. National Semiconductor recently built Malaysia's first wafer fabrication plant to supply its local semiconductor plants; Motorola and Hitachi have followed suit. Seagate has expanded production of disk drives from Singapore

to Malaysia. The expertise Malaysia has built up in electronics is considerable. Nixdorf Computer AG, which recently established a US$3 million software center to create applications for UNIX-based workstations, was attracted to Malaysia by the fact that its software engineers cost one-fifth of Germany's. Intel called in its Malaysian experts to help set up a chip assembly line in Arizona.

■ Malaysian plants produce a range of products, from color TVs, radio cassette players, and toasters to computer peripherals. Many companies that started small in Malaysia have stayed and expanded. Sharp has become involved in several joint ventures in Malaysia, where it assembles color televisions and computer monitors. Sony began to manufacture in-house some of the components for its new color TV plant in Malaysia in the late 1980s. Matsushita's Malaysian operations, which grew in the mid-1980s as expenses rose in Japan, have come to supply 10–15 percent of the world market for room air conditioners.

Source: Lim and Fong (1991).

given the small internal market. Korea and Taiwan, China, with larger domestic markets, created a similar situation by encouraging DFI in production for export and in those sectors where substantial technology transfer could be anticipated. In contrast, the large import substitution economies, such as Argentina, Brazil, and Mexico lured investment of foreign firms by offering access to protected domestic markets.

Industrial Policies

We define industrial policies, as distinct from trade policies, as government efforts to alter industrial structure to promote productivity-based growth. Productivity-based growth may derive from learning, technological innovation, or catching up to international best practices. All the HPAEs, except Hong Kong, have employed industrial policies as defined above. Japan and Korea had the most systematic set of policies to alter industrial structure. Efforts in Taiwan, China, were less systematic but were nonetheless widespread. Industrial policy in Singapore was more functionally directed at the rapid upgrading of technology by direct foreign investors, regardless of type of output. Indonesia, Malaysia, and Thailand have all used industrial policies but much less systematically than the northeastern HPAEs.

Industrial Growth and Productivity Change. HPAE industrial growth patterns differ from the patterns in most other low- and middle-income economies in the relative size and growth rates of two important industrial subsectors: metal products, electronics, and machinery; and textiles and garments. Table 6.14 shows the share of value added in nine International Standard Industrial Classification (ISIC) subsectors as a percentage of the total value added of manufacturing. Among the HPAEs, metal products, electronics, and machinery (ISIC subsector 38, or MPM) have grown unusually fast. The sector's share of manufacturing value added doubled in Japan and Singapore, nearly tripled in Indonesia and Korea, and quadrupled in Malaysia. More surprising than the importance of growth in MPM, which provides vital inputs to numerous other manufacturing subsectors, is the continued importance of textiles and garments even as the rapidly developing Asian economies shifted from labor- to capital-intensive production.

Appendix 6.1 describes our method for determining the projected relative importance of specific industrial subsectors in cross-economy comparisons. As can be seen in table 6.15, both capital-intensive sectors

Table 6.14 Current Price Value Added as a Share of Manufacturing Value Added

Economy/ region	Food, beverages, and tobacco	Textiles and clothing	Wood and wood products	Paper and printing	Chemicals and rubber	Non- metallic minerals	Basic metals	Metal products and machinery	Other	Total manu- facturing
HPAEs										
Hong Kong										
1973	0.05	0.48	0.02	0.05	0.12	0.01	0.01	0.23	0.03	1.00
1988	0.06	0.38	0.01	0.08	0.10	0.01	0.01	0.33	0.04	1.02
Indonesia										
1973	0.59	0.14	0.01	0.01	0.16	0.03	0.00	0.05	0.01	1.00
1988	0.26	0.15	0.11	0.03	0.15	0.05	0.09	0.14	0.01	0.99
Japan										
1953	0.09	0.16	0.04	0.10	0.16	0.05	0.12	0.24	0.02	0.98
1989	0.09	0.05	0.03	0.08	0.16	0.04	0.07	0.46	0.01	0.99
Korea, Rep. of										
1986	0.23	0.19	0.05	0.06	0.21	0.06	0.04	0.13	0.02	1.00
1988	0.11	0.15	0.02	0.05	0.18	0.04	0.07	0.36	0.02	1.00
Malaysia										
1969	0.16	0.05	0.07	0.11	0.27	0.01	0.06	0.06	0.23	1.02
1988	0.18	0.07	0.07	0.04	0.27	0.06	0.03	0.27	0.01	1.00
Singapore										
1969	0.14	0.05	0.07	0.06	0.30	0.03	0.03	0.29	0.02	0.99
1989	0.05	0.04	0.01	0.05	0.20	0.01	0.01	0.61	0.01	0.99
Thailand										
1968	0.26	0.17	0.13	0.04	0.09	0.16	0.02	0.12	0.01	1.00
1986	0.42	0.22	0.03	0.03	0.09	0.08	0.02	0.11	0.01	1.01
South Asia										
India										
1970	0.12	0.21	0.01	0.05	0.18	0.04	0.12	0.25	0.01	0.99
1986	0.12	0.15	0.01	0.04	0.24	0.05	0.10	0.29	0.01	1.01
Pakistan										
1970	0.24	0.34	0.00	0.03	0.20	0.04	0.02	0.08	0.04	0.99
1986	0.30	0.21	0.00	0.02	0.26	0.07	0.04	0.09	0.00	0.99
Latin America										
Brazil										
1970	0.17	0.13	0.05	0.06	0.19	0.06	0.12	0.20	0.02	1.00
1985	0.14	0.12	0.03	0.05	0.24	0.04	0.08	0.27	0.03	1.00
Chile										
1970	0.17	0.12	0.02	0.02	0.10	0.03	0.34	0.16	0.00	0.96
1986	0.25	0.08	0.03	0.10	0.16	0.04	0.28	0.07	0.00	1.01
Colombia										
1970	0.34	0.19	0.02	0.06	0.17	0.04	0.03	0.14	0.01	1.00
1988	0.30	0.15	0.01	0.07	0.19	0.06	0.06	0.15	0.01	1.00
Mexico										
1970	0.31	0.08	0.01	0.07	0.15	0.06	0.24	0.09	0.00	1.01
1984	0.28	0.05	0.00	0.05	0.17	0.11	0.19	0.15	0.00	1.00

Source: Pack (1993b).

(MPM) and labor-intensive sectors (textiles) play a greater-than-predicted role in manufacturing in most of the HPAEs (except Indonesia and Malaysia). Besides the unexpected prominence of textiles and garments, the analysis yields another surprise. Chemicals and nonmetallic minerals, two sectors often associated with industrial modernization, are not large in the HPAEs by international standards.

Detailed sectoral growth rates of total factor productivity are available for Japan, Korea, and Taiwan, China. There are now sufficiently long time-series data to conclude that in these economies, TFP growth has accounted for a substantial fraction of the growth of constant price value added in manufacturing. Table 6.16 shows a variety of estimates of long-term TFP growth rates. Given the length of time of the observations, it seems unlikely that the measured growth rates of TFP could be attributable to cyclical phenomena or growing capacity utilization of initial large investments.[36]

Strategies of Selective Promotion. Here we describe the strategies of selective promotion that have evolved in the HPAEs as they developed their industrial policies.

Japan. Early Japanese industrial policy aimed to encourage sectors that faced income-elastic demands in the international market and exhibited economies of scale, large fixed costs, and the potential to learn from experience. This purely economic rationale was supplemented by a sense that some sectors were critical to national morale and the

Table 6.15 Actual/Predicted Share of GDP Originating in Manufacturing Sectors

Economy/ region	Food, beverages, and tobacco	Textiles and clothing	Wood and wood products	Paper and printing	Chemicals and rubber	Non-metallic minerals	Basic metals	Metal products and machinery	Other	Total manu-facturing
HPAEs										
Hong Kong										
1973	0.21	10.31	0.89	0.53	0.78	0.14	0.37	2.86	0.35	1.25
1988	0.43	118.95	0.36	0.65	0.67	0.14	0.17	1.96	0.38	1.26
Indonesia										
1973	1.63	0.75	0.30	0.18	0.40	0.20	0.00	0.44	0.06	0.62
1986	0.75[a]	0.25[a]	1.42	0.06	0.54	0.95	0.62	0.11	0.01	0.57
Japan										
1963	0.75	2.98	2.42	1.36	0.73	0.63	1.00	2.41	0.67	1.23
1989	0.98	13.52	0.88	0.66	0.69	0.52	0.71	1.69	0.14	0.97
Korea, Rep. of										
1968	0.99	1.75	2.03	1.04	0.94	0.73	0.52	2.07	0.20	1.04
1988	0.85	2.74	0.71	0.64	0.99	0.62	1.13	2.76	0.32	1.26
Malaysia										
1969	0.35	0.25	1.55	0.89	0.80	0.05	0.69	1.03	1.43	0.64
1981	0.94	0.68	3.28	0.57	0.89	0.70	0.57	2.44	0.07	0.97
Singapore										
1973	0.31	2.14	2.40	0.49	2.09	0.75	1.53	12.56	0.13	1.41
1989	0.26	11.32	0.51	0.47	1.72	0.27	0.61	5.10	0.14	1.38
Thailand										
1968	0.90	1.21	4.89	0.70	0.36	1.69	0.22	3.16	0.09	0.95
1986	0.34	3.33	1.85	0.71	0.65	1.39	0.33	1.82	0.22	1.68
South Asia										
India										
1963	0.50	6.00	0.54	2.33	0.33	0.37	0.80	3.74	0.32	1.10
1986	0.56	2.39	0.18	1.02	0.89	0.35	0.68	2.51	0.09	0.92
Latin America										
Brazil										
1963	0.91	1.80	1.84	1.03	0.69	0.51	1.31	2.28	0.00	1.02
1985	0.94	1.70	1.21	0.78	1.12	0.48	0.91	1.92	0.36	1.09
Chile										
1963	1.12	3.04	1.21	1.07	0.79	0.73	1.63	2.65	0.24	1.21
1980	1.18	1.06	1.25	0.94	0.67	0.48	4.36	0.88	0.03	1.01
Mexico										
1965	1.37	0.49	0.41	1.08	0.76	0.84	2.37	0.64	0.00	0.95
1984	1.57	0.64	0.15	0.60	0.70	1.05	1.94	0.82	0.00	0.92

a. Predicted value was negative; calculated here as positive.
Source: Pack (1993b).

Table 6.16 Long-Term TFP Growth Rates by Sector

Sector	TFP growth rate		
	Korea	Japan, 1960–79	Taiwan, China, 1966–86
Food	7.30	-1.76	2.0[a]
Beverages	7.90	0.0	—
Tobacco	13.40	—	—
Apparel	—	1.98	10.5
Textiles	10.70	0.47	7.6
Leather	12.60	1.03	—
Shoes	—	1.03	—
Wood	9.40	2.81	0.3[b]
Furniture	12.10	1.74	—
Paper	8.20	1.44	2.3[c]
Printing	10.70	-0.18	—
Chemicals	13.10	3.36	3.3
Petroleum	-0.30	-3.55[d]	0.0[b]
Rubber	11.40	1.02	6.3[b]
Nonmetallic minerals	2.80	—	2.4
Basic metals	—	—	7.2
Iron and steel	3.70	1.34	—
Metal products	7.60	3.41	4.4
Nonelectrical machinery	8.00	2.30	6.7[e]
Electrical machinery	10.70	5.37	—
Electrical equipment	—	—	7.1
Transport equipment	11.20	4.32	2.7
Precision instruments	—	—	11.0
Plastic products	—	0.92[f]	0.0
Other manufacturing	7.50	-1.76	—
Average	8.8	1.2	4.6

—Not available.
a. Food and beverages.
b. Rubber, petroleum, and wood products.
c. Paper and paper products.
d. petroluem ref. and coal.
e. All machinery.
f. Plastic.
Source: Pack (1993b).

achievement of international respect.[37] In later years, industrial policy had a narrower technological focus, for example, promoting establishment of the technological base for very large-scale integrated circuits (Borrus, Tyson, and Zysman 1986). Among the sectors carefully nurtured were steel, automobiles, textiles, shipbuilding, and aluminum refining in the earlier years and then electronics and semiconductors in later years.[38] (Effective rates of protection in these industries can be seen in table 6.8.)

Japanese industrial policy until the early 1970s had several strands (Yamamura 1986; Yamamura and Yasuba 1985). The government directed credit to large firms and protected the domestic market to help the firms realize static and dynamic economies of scale. MITI allocated foreign exchange to favored large firms and tried to ensure that technology payments to foreign firms were neither excessive nor duplicated, often forcing licensees to share their information with other Japanese firms. Relatively high levels of protection were used as part of a strategy to help firms to export successfully. As late as 1978, the average of effective rates of protection across the manufacturing sector was 22 percent.[39] Such rates may have been responsible for the very low level of manufactured imports, an issue widely discussed in the scholarly literature (Balassa and Noland 1988).

Korea. Korea's policies were similar to Japan's with respect to selected credit, protection, and limitation of entry into specific sectors (Pack and Westphal 1986). However, the Korean government promoted individual firms more often to rectify perceived entrepreneurial and skill deficiencies, using export performance to determine whether firms deserved continued promotion. Other policies to encourage industrial growth and exports included making direct and indirect inputs to exports available at world prices. In Korea, the selectively promoted sectors were the heavy and chemical industries: iron and steel, metal products, machinery, electronics, and industrial chemicals. The motivation for these appears to have been both strategic—to increase defense capability—and economic—to shift to capital- and technology-intensive sectors in anticipation of a loss of competitive advantage in labor-intensive sectors.[40] The costs of the HCI drive are still not fully known, but they were high (see box 6.3). Although there are no recent estimates of Korean rates of effective protection, there is considerable anecdotal information suggesting that the government afforded these sectors relatively high protection.

Taiwan, China. The intervention of Taiwan, China, in manufacturing has been similar to Japan's and Korea's, though less important quantitatively. Wade (1990) has documented tariffs, quantitative restrictions, and selective credit policies, maintaining that the success of Taiwan, China, was at least partly attributable to an intensive government effort to direct the economy's sectoral evolution. This conflicts with the standard neoclassical view that its development was primarily attributable to low protection, the availability of inputs to exporters at international prices, a conservative macroeconomic policy reflected in low inflation, and competitive factor markets (Little 1979).

Unlike the situation in Japan and Korea, in Taiwan, China, it is difficult to discern a pattern of economic incentives. Wade (1990) notes that a guiding principle in the 1960s may have been the existence of

---

Box 6.3 The HCI Drive: Costs of Intervention

THE KOREAN GOVERNMENT'S INTERVENTION policy, most notably the HCI promotion, has often been evaluated from the perspective of the success or failure of industrial policy. Another important approach in evaluating intervention policy, however, would be to estimate the fiscal/financial cost associated with intervention. Government intervention incurred direct costs in the form of subsidies to strategic sectors through policy loans and tax exemptions, especially during the 1973–79 period of HCI promotion. Intervention also incurred indirect costs in the form of accumulated nonperforming loans and the resulting portfolio difficulties of commercial banks.

The promotion of the HCI sector was supported by a broad range of fiscal and financial instruments. Government funds devoted to the HCI sector amounted to 5 percent of the total budget during the promotion period. In addition, profit tax exemptions of up to 100 percent for the first three years and 50 percent for the next two years provided effective tax rates about two-thirds lower for strategic industries; at the height of the HCI drive in 1977 alone, about 82 billion won in tax revenues (3 percent of total taxes collected) was lost. The predominant source of financial support for HCI was preferential policy loans directed to key industries. In 1977, for example, 45 percent of the total domestic credit of the banking system was engineered in direct support of the HCI sector. Implicit interest subsidies to the HCI sector in 1977 alone were an estimated 75 billion won, or 0.4 percent of GNP (calculated by applying an interest differential of 3–4 percent vis-à-vis the interest rates for general bank loans). This estimate should be con-

sidered the lower bound, however. Those industries whose credit was squeezed were forced to borrow at curb market rates. The real effective subsidies for HCI borrowers were therefore as high as 3 percent of GNP.

As the Korean government opted to bail out the struggling heavy machinery, shipbuilding, overseas construction, and shipping industries in the mid-1980s, nonperforming loans of commercial banks accumulated rapidly, and accordingly bank profitability seriously deteriorated. During 1986–87, for example, the share of nonperforming loans in total assets reached almost 10 percent. Between 1985 and 1988, 78 corporations were "rationalized." During this process, write-offs of principal alone amounted to 1 trillion won, or about 1 percent of GNP in 1985. Far more damaging was the further issuance of subsidized funds to rationalized firms and the preferential access to Central Bank discounts, which has hurt the balance sheet.

As the Korean government abandoned HCI preferences during the traumatic economic adjustments of 1979–81, the direct costs of interest subsidies all but disappeared. In contrast, it has taken more than a decade to begin to deal with the indirect costs in the form of accumulated nonperforming loans and squeezed bank profitability. Not until 1993 did the Korean government announce a medium-term plan to transfer policy loans—which still account for more than 40 percent of total domestic credit—to separate accounts and to handle their financing through the budget at yet to be determined costs.

Sources: World Bank (1987); Leipziger and Petri (1993); Nam (1991); Kim (1990).

gaps in the domestic input-output table that revealed potential areas of import substitution. The autobiography of a major architect of the island's development supports this view (Li 1989). Although anecdotal evidence summarized by Wade demonstrates considerable intervention in many sectors, there are no studies of effective rates of protection or subsidy after the early 1970s. The more recent intentions of the government may be discerned directly from two infrastructural efforts, namely, the Hsinchu Science Park and the Industrial Technology Research Institute. Both were major investments undertaken by the government to provide the basis for a rapid shift toward higher-technology sectors.

Malaysia. In the 1980s Malaysia experimented with a heavy and chemical industries drive similar in focus to those of Japan and Korea but dependent on public investment. The Look East policy adopted in 1981 was, apart from its sociocultural aspects, an explicit attempt to emulate the heavy industrialization efforts of Japan and Korea, which were regarded as successes. The government created the Heavy Industries Corporation of Malaysia (HICOM) to be the vehicle for the heavy industrialization push. HICOM targeted a number of large-scale, capital-intensive projects for development including iron and steel, nonferrous metals, machinery and equipment, paper and paper products, and petrochemicals. While public investments were intended to be catalytic in each of these activities, the government actively promoted joint ventures with private (usually foreign) investors. By 1988 HICOM had set up nine companies, employing a total of 4,350 workers, involved in steel, cement, motor vehicle, and motorcycle engine manufacturing. The highest profile of these investments was the PROTON car project, a joint venture with Mitsubishi designed to produce 100,000 units per year.

The ambitious targets of the HICOM program ran into the macroeconomic constraints described in chapter 3—declining terms of trade and a deteriorating fiscal position. Prompt responses to the deteriorating macroeconomic situation included reductions in public investment in the HICOM program. Poor management and low profitability also forced the treasury to bail out loss-making enterprises, a practice it could not sustain under the fiscal austerity of the adjustment program. With the shift to policies of privatization of public enterprises and private sector development in the late 1980s, the HICOM period had ended (see box 6.4).

Indonesia and Thailand. Neither Indonesia nor Thailand has made the systematic efforts to change industrial structure characteristic of

Box 6.4 Recognizing a Mistake, Malaysia Privatizes

THE PUBLIC SECTOR IN MALAYSIA WAS RELATIVE-ly small until the late 1970s, when the government rapidly expanded the number of state firms, partly to give Malays opportunities and partly out of a conviction that the government could speed development. Much of the growth in the early 1980s was due to HICOM, the Heavy and Industrial Corporation of Malaysia, which established nine subsidiaries in such areas as steel, automobiles, cement, and paper.

State firms, especially in HICOM, performed less well than expected, and in 1984 the deficit of the public enterprises reached 3.7 percent of GNP. As rising fiscal deficits and declining terms of trade threatened macroeconomic stability, the government began to privatize in 1983. Of more than 800 state firms existing in the mid 1980s, about a hundred had been sold by 1990. Many were small commercial and manufacturing operations, but some were quite big, including an airline, a shipping company, and a telecommunications firm.

There have been glitches. For instance, the public offerings have been heavily oversubscribed, suggesting that the government underpriced its shares, perhaps losing as much as US$150 million in the sale of four big companies. Also, more attention to promoting competition in monopolistic situations would benefit consumers, whether firms are privatized or not. Finally, privatization has proceeded very slowly; while it continues to this day, the Malaysian public sector remains formidable.

In any case, privatization in Malaysia has meant more than outright sales. It has included a host of schemes that have reduced the control of the state over productive activities even where the public sector has retained a controlling interest, as with PRO-TON, the automobile company in HICOM. Even when firms have not literally been privatized, the firms have experienced a change in regime: managers increased their control over decisionmaking and responded more to the market. The result was that many so-called privatized firms became more productive and innovative. Nor can the macroeconomic benefits be overlooked: in the end, the federal government anticipates that at least 15 percent of its outstanding debt will have been transferred to privatized firms.

Malaysia's slow but steady divestiture and the benefits it realized by adapting flexibly to the circumstances of each case provide an example for many other developing economies, where privatization is an official goal, yet much less has been achieved. A detailed analysis of the companies that were privatized shows consistent gains in social welfare. As two cases below illustrate, changes in incentives and a broader role for private sector interests have frequently been more important than the change in ownership per se.

Malaysian Air Systems Berhad (MAS). When 48 percent of MAS was sold to the public in 1985, there was no change in management or de jure authority. Even so, management gained de facto control over investment decisions and eventually won permission to raise domestic fares. While the fare increase hurt consumers, less rationing of tickets raised consumer welfare. Moreover, while MAS had about broken even in the early 1980s, it became a profitable tax-paying corporation.

Kelang Container Terminal (KCT). In 1985, 90 percent of KCT was sold to decentralized public enterprises and 10 percent to the private sector. Although the public sector retained control, the state firms that took over, many representing Bumiputera interests, had a direct incentive to earn profits. KCT was a lucrative company before the sale, monopolizing container traffic in and out of the capital region, and remained so afterward; but the quality of its services was substantially improved, worker productivity increased, and its market share rose.

Sources: Jones and Abbas (1992); Lim (1992); Salleh (1991); World Bank (1988).

Japan, Korea, Malaysia, and Taiwan, China. Thailand's Board of Investment (BOI) has attempted to promote various activities viewed as having the potential for technological learning, but, as we pointed out in chapter 3, it is difficult to discern any systematic effort to change industrial structure from the pattern of promotion of the BOI. Indonesia has used public investment in an effort to move toward high technology industries. Indonesia's technology development efforts represent an extreme case of state-supported technological upgrading, but the public sector research facilities and strategic industries have few links with the private industrial sector. One experiment with leapfrogging into high technology industries—Indonesia's attempt to create an aircraft industry—is described in box 6.5.

Did Industrial Policy Increase Productivity?

Have attempts to alter industrial structure helped accelerate productivity change? We attempt to answer this question by addressing two related issues in appendix 6.1:

- First, did industrial policy alter the sectoral configuration of industries in ways that we would not predict based on factor intensities and changing relative factor prices? If changes in the sectoral composition of output are largely market-conforming, industrial policies must have failed in at least one of their objectives: to guide industrial development along paths that it would not take if it were guided by market forces.
- Second, what were the rates of productivity change in industry in the HPAEs, and what were their sectoral patterns? If rates of productivity change in industry are low overall or in promoted sectors, prima facie, industrial policy did not meet its productivity-enhancing objective.

In both cases, our answers lead us to conclude that industrial policies were largely ineffective.

Industrial Policy Only Marginally Altered Industrial Structure. The cross-economy comparisons of industrial structure raise questions about the efficacy of government efforts to promote or discourage specific sectors. In Korea, for example, despite the government's extensive efforts to speed the private sector's shift from labor-intensive to capital- and technology-intensive industries, the relatively labor-intensive textiles and garments sector was nearly three times bigger than international norms predicted in 1988, a substantial increase relative to international norms from 1968. During the same period, Korea merely maintained the international norm in chemicals, a heavily promoted sector; while other heavily promoted sectors, basic metals and metal products and machinery, achieved only modest improvements. Similar surprises are evident in Singapore, which, like Korea, has a government that aggressively inter-

Box 6.5 Indonesia's Turbulent Leap into High Technology

SECTORAL TARGETING TO ACHIEVE RAPID PRODUCTIVITY change is a risky business—particularly when publicly funded firms are permitted to rely on protected domestic markets rather than being subjected to international competition. The dangers of such a course are evident in the difficulties encountered by Indonesian aircraft producer P.T. Industri Pesawat Terbang Nusantara (IPTN), which has absorbed $1 billion in government funds since its establishment in 1979 but has yet to become internationally competitive or genuinely profitable.

In theory, IPTN is expected to use the domestic market as a springboard to international sales. The strategy is to shift from producing aircraft under license, to co-design and co-production, to sole design and production. In practice, IPTN's captive domestic market is too small to generate the economies of scale necessary for efficient aircraft production. Moreover, the company has had little exposure to the world market. Of the 230 aircraft (130 helicopters, 100 fixed-wing) that IPTN has manufactured since its inception, about 90 percent have been sold to Indonesian airlines, the military, the police, and the state-run oil industry.

Foreign sales are unlikely to improve. While other aircraft manufacturers have been busy forging technological alliances to shrink the time from design completion to production, IPTN is increasingly trying to go it alone. Its major product for this decade, an independently designed fifty-seat turboprop, is not scheduled for delivery until 1995, five years after design completion. By then, the world market for similar aircraft, already crowded, will have several other entrants, all pricing their aircraft aggressively. IPTN can ill afford a price war. Company results through 1985, the most recent available, indicate that IPTN was not profitable when capital costs are taken into account. Nothing in the company's performance since then indicates that the situation has improved.

vened through a variety of mechanisms to promote capital- and technology-intensive industries. Here, the importance of textiles relative to the predicted norm has increased even more sharply. The textile sector went from double its predicted size in 1973 to eleven times in 1989. Over the same period, metal products and machinery declined from twelve to five times its predicted size.

Appendix 6.1 describes a simple test of the impact of industrial policy on the basis of the factor proportions theory of comparative advantage (Hecksher-Ohlin-Samuelson). We assume that given the relative labor abundance in all of the HPAEs early in their industrialization, the share of labor-intensive manufactures in total manufacturing should rise as they begin exporting. We compare statistically the pattern of growth of the industrial sector in each economy with its pattern of factor intensities. We argue that if industrial structure is determined primarily by market forces, low wages and low capital intensity at the beginning of the period of active industrial policy will predict the pattern of industrial growth. If industrial policy to promote capital- and knowledge-intensive sectors was important in determining the sectoral pattern of growth, however, this should not be the case. Indeed, the opposite should be true; high wages (a measure of human capital intensity) and high capital intensity at the end of the promotion period should predict changes in industrial structure.

We have performed these tests on each of the Four Tigers plus Japan for periods relevant to their industrial promotion efforts, using two-digit ISIC classifications of industrial sectors (see table A6.2 in appendix 6.1). Our effort to differentiate between a comparative-advantage-based evolution of industrial structure versus one characterized by significant intervention is notable mainly for a number of negative results. In particular, in Korea—the economy for which significant intervention is best documented—during 1973–80 the most rapid growth in sectoral shares of value added occurred in lower-wage or lower value-added per worker sectors. In Korea at the two-digit level, sectoral growth was broadly market conforming in terms of traditional factor intensities. The results for Japan are inconclusive. In Hong Kong there is no relationship between our explanatory variables and patterns of production. In Singapore, for the period 1980–89, output grew more rapidly in more capital- and knowledge-intensive sectors, supporting the view that the Singaporean authorities successfully intervened to encourage increasingly capital-intensive development. But, given the rapid growth in the capital-labor ratio in Singapore, this result also conforms to factor proportions theory predictions.

These findings do not imply that governments were not attempting to influence industrial structure. They undoubtedly were. But they suggest that, despite government intentions, the manufacturing sector seems to have evolved roughly in accord with neoclassical expectations; industrial growth was largely market conforming.

Rates and Patterns of Productivity Change in Industry. There is both good news and bad news for advocates of industrial policy in the productivity performance of East Asian industry. The good news is that, on average, rates of productivity change in industry in Japan (before 1973), Korea, and Taiwan, China, which are the only economies for which we have detailed sectoral estimates of TFP growth, were high by international standards; productivity-based catching up was taking place (Page 1991). The bad news is that, in general, productivity change has not been higher in promoted sectors. Japan may be an exception. Between 1960 and 1979 chemicals and the metalworking machinery complex have unusually good TFP performance (Jorgenson, Kuroda, and Nishimizu 1987). Japan's industrial structure differs from international norms in these sectors and exhibits quite high values of the share of value added in total manufacturing. These industries are those that observers usually point to as having received significant government support, including efforts to stimulate productivity growth.

A number of calculations of TFP have been carried out for Korea for a variety of periods (Dollar and Sokoloff 1990; Lim 1991). From these studies a number of patterns can be identified that are broadly consistent with one another. Most striking are the high values of TFP change in most sectors by international standards (Nishimizu and Page 1991). Although the Korean government selectively promoted chemicals and iron and steel (included in basic metals), the large growth in the share of iron and steel was accompanied by quite low TFP performance between 1966 and 1985; textiles and clothing, conversely, had very high rates of TFP growth. The promoted chemical sector, whose relative size was decreasing, was characterized by considerably higher-than-average TFP growth during this same period.

The government in Taiwan, China, did not attempt to influence sectoral evolution as strongly as the government of Korea. Nevertheless, there was more than a small effort devoted to encouraging specific sectors, particularly those viewed as either capital- or technology-intensive.

The three sectors that exhibited the greatest expansion in the share of value added—apparel, electrical equipment, and metal products—are all characterized by below-average wages, capital-labor ratios, and labor product. Moreover, there is no statistical relationship between wage or capital intensity and productivity change at the sectoral level. In fact, the highest sectoral rates of TFP change are recorded in textiles and apparel.

Recent sectoral TFP growth rates for industry in Malaysia from 1973 to 1989 show a similar pattern of great variability in the TFP growth rates in promoted sectors, from high in nonelectrical machinery and paper and paper products to low in iron and steel and transport equipment. Textiles and apparel, a nonpromoted sector, are among the TFP leaders (Maisom 1992). In short, there is no apparent relationship between the sectors promoted under the HICOM drive and rapid productivity growth.

Overall, the evidence that industrial policy systematically promoted sectors with high productivity change is weak. In Japan there is some support for the assertion that TFP growth was higher in selected sectors, while in Korea and Taiwan, China, activities that were not promoted (for example, textiles) had TFP performance as impressive as those that were. Moreover, attempts to determine whether high rates of TFP growth combined with rapid growth of promoted sectors can plausibly explain the very high overall rates of TFP change in manufacturing yield mostly negative results (see appendix 6.1). The main reasons for manufacturing's success in Japan, Korea, and Taiwan, China, lay in the high general rates of TFP growth, including those in labor-intensive, nonpromoted sectors.

How Manufactured Exports Increased Productivity

DOES THIS MEAN THAT PUBLIC POLICY HAD NO ROLE IN THE rapid rates of TFP change found for many of the HPAEs? We believe not. In chapter 1 we described how rapid TFP change in developing economies can be a result of the ability to move quickly closer to international best practices. We termed this "productivity-based catching up." We believe that rapid growth of exports, a result of the export-push policies of the HPAEs, combined with the superior performance of these economies in creating and allocating human capital, provided the means by which they attained high rates of productivity-based catching up and TFP growth.

How did the unusually high rates of growth of exports and human capital contribute to the productivity performance of the East Asian economies? Most explanations of the link between TFP growth and exports emphasize such static factors as economies of scale and capacity utilization. While these may account for an initial surge of productivity soon after the start of an export push, they are insufficient to explain continuing high TFP growth rates. Rather, the relationship between exports and productivity growth may arise from exports' role in helping economies adopt and master international best-practice technologies. High levels of labor force cognitive skills permit better firm-level adoption, adaptation, and mastery of technology. Thus, exports and human capital interact to provide a particularly rapid phase of productivity-based catching up.

Of course, it is possible that the move to a higher production function occurred before the growth in exports—that TFP growth caused export growth rather than the reverse.[41] But even if exports began on the basis of productivity change due to such domestic efforts as plant reorganization, the cumulative magnitude of productivity growth over many years is most unlikely to have been a result of purely domestic efforts.[42] It stretches credibility to suggest that the large cumulative effects of TFP growth in Japan, Korea, and Taiwan, China, could have been achieved by the plant floor innovations proposed as important sources of productivity growth at lower TFP growth rates (Pack and Page 1993). Were that the case, it would be difficult to explain why these gains far outstrip productivity increases in the industrial economies during their own rapid-growth periods, when TFP growth was attributable largely to domestic factors. Clearly, then, an increased ability to tap world technology has been an important benefit of exports.[43]

Exports' Role in Imperfect Knowledge Markets

Why do exports facilitate the move toward international best-practice technologies? The knowledge that permits this shift is available only in quite imperfect markets. Often the markets do not exist—some knowledge is simply not sold, because its owners fear that licensing or direct foreign investment will eventually leak the knowledge to future competitors. Even where markets exist, they are likely to be characterized by bilateral monopoly, so that a variety of difficulties confront firms trying to purchase such knowledge (Arrow 1969).

In markets with imperfect knowledge, mechanisms that help an economy or firm obtain technology can confer an externality—a pecuniary one if knowledge is obtained at a lower cost, a real externality if the knowledge transfer is more efficient. For example, the transfer may be more beneficial if knowledge is obtained as a result of the self-interest of purchasers of exports in the OECD economies, rather than through arm's-length purchase.

Exporting helps to overcome some imperfections in the market for knowledge and permits its acquisition through a variety of mechanisms. These include:

■ *Purchase of new equipment.* The purchase of new equipment is a straightforward method of obtaining new technology insofar as it is embedded in equipment. The two main impacts of exports in this case are in providing the competitive pressure for firms to make such purchases (if the equipment is used to produce exports), and, more generally, in earning the foreign exchange to finance the purchase of machinery.

■ *Direct foreign investment.* The firms that generate much of the world's new technology are reluctant to part with it. They perceive that the best use of their new knowledge with respect to developing economies often is through exports of products to them. In East Asia, however, most of the incoming DFI has been intended for production of exports rather than as a strategy for domestic sales. An economy's recent export performance frequently signals whether it is a desirable location for export-oriented DFI. Economies with rapid export growth are preferred in part because such growth often reflects good macroeconomic management. Moreover, economies with significant export growth have generally provided more infrastructure useful to exporters than internally oriented economies.[44] DFI makes crucial production and marketing knowledge available to developing economies. It permits them to begin manufacturing along the world's best-practice production function by substituting foreign physical and human capital for absent local factors.[45] As local labor learns from the presence of best-practice knowledge and equipment, knowledge tends to become diffused through labor mobility and informal contacts among managers. Even when the investing firm attempts to hinder such diffusion, significant knowledge transfers are inevitable.[46]

■ *Technology licensing.* Licensing existing technologies, both rights to proprietary equipment and details about production processes, offers developing economies substantial opportunities for improving their levels of best practice. During the 1950s and 1960s, Japan benefited considerably from licensing (see, for example, Nagaoka 1989). The net gains were large, as the licenses were obtained at relatively low cost compared with the domestic research expenses avoided. However, there is some evidence, and a growing subjective sense, that arm's-length licensing is decreasing as an option for closing technology gaps. Technology developers, the licensors in the OECD economies, have become wary of helping potential competitors, even if contracts preclude exports to other economies for the duration of the license. Particularly in R&D-intensive sectors such as chemicals, machinery, and electronics, firms are increasingly unwilling to license technology; they believe royalties provide an inadequate return for actions that may impair their own long-term competitiveness. This creates an imperfect or nonexistent market for critical technology transfers.

Exporting economies have an advantage in coping with this situation. Licensing firms prefer cross-licensing agreements in which they obtain access to the licensee's own technology or to its manufacturing skills. Given asymmetries in knowledge, the best test of the potential partner's abilities is its performance in export markets. Moreover, the fact that a firm has exports and the requisite technical and commercial skills to produce them improves the bargaining position of the licensee. Sales of licenses contain a significant element of rent (Pack 1993c), so the cost of licenses will be lower where the seller perceives the strengths of the purchaser as signaled by exports. Finally, where a market does exist for technology licenses, the foreign exchange to pay for fees is more likely to be available in economies experiencing rapid growth in exports.

■ *Transfer of nonproprietary technology.* The free or inexpensive transfer of nonproprietary knowledge is easier if an economy begins its industrialization effort in labor-intensive sectors using relatively old machine designs and production technology. When exports are based on comparative advantage, precisely these conditions are met. Hong Kong, Korea, Singapore, and Taiwan, China, all began rapid industrialization in labor-intensive and low-technology manufacturing. The equipment was readily purchased, and the production knowledge was available at low cost from engineering publications, trade literature, and independent consultants.[47] The simpler equipment was conducive to local productivity-enhancing improvements, often on the part of blue collar workers (Ranis 1973). Moreover, in labor-intensive industries it was easier to acquire and absorb information from customers without a large stable of educated engineers.

■ *Information from customers.* In the presence of imperfectly traded information, knowledge provided by purchasers of an economy's exports can be quite important. This has been shown by Westphal, Rhee, and Pursell (1985) in Korea and independently corroborated in Taiwan, China, by a number of researchers (see, for example, Gee 1989). Buyers want low-cost, better-quality products from major suppliers. To obtain this, they transmit tacit and occasionally proprietary knowledge from their other, often OECD-economy, suppliers. Such knowledge transfers are more common in simple production sectors such as clothing and footwear and with older technologies that are either in the public domain or are not closely guarded.

■ *Knowledge from returning nationals.* Drawn partly by the high wages made possible by exports, many residents of Korea and Taiwan, China, trained abroad, particularly in new sectors such as electronics and computing, have returned home to work. Many returning nationals have received education in OECD economies and then worked for OECD-economy firms.[48] Their return has provided significant transfer of best-practice methods. For example, foreign-educated nationals account for *all* the postgraduates employed in the industry of Taiwan, China (Pack 1993a). This source of knowledge of international best practices becomes more important as changing factor prices dictate a shift to more capital- and technology-intensive sectors in which higher-level skills are needed to unlock knowledge that may be embodied in patents, licenses, or the use of specialized nontraded equipment.

■ *Domestic research.* In both Korea and Taiwan, China, a considerable proportion of R&D has been devoted to improving exports and reducing production costs. There is no evidence that the gap between R&D and commercial needs frequently seen in the import-substituting economies has been a problem.

How Exports and Human Capital Increase Productivity

Access to international best-practice technology and rapid formation of human capital supplement and reinforce one another. It is doubtful that the HPAEs could have made as productive use of foreign knowledge and imported capital without highly skilled domestic engineers and workers. Conversely, without foreign knowledge it is very unlikely that total factor productivity growth would have been as large. Intensive efforts by highly skilled managers and technicians in individual plants in inward-oriented Latin American economies to improve the productivity of existing capital stock with internal innovations did not generate high- productivity growth.[49]

The HPAEs' rapid export growth has often generated positive interaction between human capital, physical capital, and knowledge. The externalities generated by manufactured exports in the high-performing Asian economies in the form of cheaper and more effective knowledge transfers would have undoubtedly been less productive had there been fewer skilled workers to facilitate their absorption, while the HPAEs' rapid increase in education levels reflected in part rising private rewards for greater education made possible by exports and export income.[50] Thus labor force skills, flexible markets for labor, low domestic distortions, and export incentives all interacted to promote high rates of technological upgrading and productivity change.

We can use the cross-economy regression framework developed in chapter 1 to look at the impact of trade and industrial policies on growth (see table 6.17). We introduce two variables into the basic cross-economy regression: the index of openness (as described above, the degree to which domestic prices conform to international prices) and measures of export performance.[51] Openness to the world economy captures not only efficiency gains induced by the need to remain globally competitive but also the likely allocative benefits of having relative prices close to international prices.

Introducing these two trade-related variables substantially increases the explanatory power of the cross-economy regression. The effect of openness is positive. Economies with limited relative price distortions grew more rapidly.[52] We choose as our measure of export performance two indicators—the average share of manufactured exports in total exports and the share of manufactured exports in GDP.[53] Manufactured export performance is strongly correlated (at the 1 percent level) with high rates of per capita income growth. When the share of manufactured exports in total exports is introduced together with the openness index, only the latter is significant. Conversely, when the share of manufactured exports in GDP is used, the openness index remains positive and significant. One possible interpretation of these results is that a high concentration of manufactured exports relative to total exports, rather than openness, contributes relatively more to productivity change in a cross-economy framework, which would be consistent with our reasoning concerning export externalities.[54]

Estimates of the sources of total factor productivity growth (described in appendix 6.2) confirm the results of the cross-economy regressions and add some insights into possible interactions between exports

Table 6.17 Output, Growth, and Investment
(dependent variable: rate of growth of real GDP per capita, 1960–85)

Number of observations:	92	86	69	97	79
Intercept	-0.4237 *	-0.0124	-0.2324	-0.0055	-0.3943 *
	(0.1650)	(0.0083)	(0.1550)	(0.0085)	(0.1748)
GDP relative to U.S., 1960	-0.1033 **	-0.0459 **	-0.0837 **	-0.0381 **	-0.0892 **
	(0.0268)	(0.0108)	(0.0256)	(0.0123)	(0.0280)
Primary enrollment, 1960	0.0259 **	0.0210 **	0.0216 **	0.0221 **	0.0239 **
	(0.0081)	(0.0064)	(0.0079)	(0.0069)	(0.0085)
Secondary enrollment, 1960	0.0317	0.0211	0.0218	0.0206	0.0156
	(0.0203)	(0.0134)	(0.0210)	(0.0148)	(0.0210)
Growth of population, 1960–85	0.1322	0.2693	0.2054	0.1856	0.1222
	(0.2699)	(0.2346)	(0.2806)	(0.2376)	(0.2870)
Average investment/GDP, 1960–85	0.0568 *	0.0659 **	0.0625 *	0.0444	0.0436
	(0.0259)	(0.0232)	(0.0291)	(0.0242)	(0.0276)
Dollar openness index	0.0042 *		0.0023		0.0040
	(0.0017)		(0.0016)		(0.0018)
Average manufactured exports/total exports, 1960–85		0.0002 **	0.0003 **		
		(0.0001)	(0.0001)		
Average manufactured exports/GDP, 1965–85				0.0011 **	0.0011 **
				(0.0003)	(0.0004)
Adjusted R^2	0.3947	0.4912	0.5217	0.3530	0.3938
RMSE	0.0159	0.0124	0.0132	0.0147	0.0155

** Statistically significant at the 0.01 level.
 * Statistically significant at the 0.05 level.
Note: Coefficient is top number. Standard error is bottom number in parentheses.
Source: World Bank staff estimates.

and human capital. We attempt to explain variations across economies in TFP growth rates in terms of relative income, educational attainment (as measured by the average stock of education per person), openness, and our measures of manufactured export performance (see table 6.18). The education stock variable, while positive, does not explain variations in TFP growth among economies. This is appropriate, since we have measured TFP growth net of human capital's contribution. Openness is consistently associated with superior TFP performance, controlling for other variables. Both indicators of export performance are also consistently and positively correlated with higher rates of TFP growth.

We also find some evidence of a positive interaction between the share of manufactured exports in total exports and in national income and the stock of education. The coefficient of the interaction term between these two variables is positive but not significant at conventional levels, and the export share variable becomes insignificant. When we consider the contribution of the variables taken together to explaining the variation in TFP growth rates, however, it is statistically positive. We conclude that export

Table 6.18 Determinants of Total Factor Productivity Growth, 1960–89
(dependent variable: rate of growth of real GDP per capita, 1960–89)

Number of observations:	67	67	51	51
Intercept	-64.9123 **	-71.1186 **	-72.0692 **	-70.8604 **
	(14.0585)	(14.8657)	(15.6104)	(15.4608)
GDP relative to U.S., 1960	-4.8047 *	-5.5757 **	-2.3509	-2.1562
	(1.9771)	(2.0637)	(2.3225)	(2.3008)
Educational attainment, 1960	0.1471	0.0680	0.1574	0.0738
	(0.0874)	(0.1082)	(0.1064)	(0.1207)
Dollar openness index	0.6493 **	0.7154 **	0.7225 **	0.7134 **
	(0.1417)	(0.1508)	(0.1574)	(0.1558)
Average manufactured exports/total exports, 1960–85	0.0314 **	0.0159		
	(0.0066)	(0.0142)		
Interaction term: Educational attainment 1960 times manufactured exports/total exports, 1960–85		0.0032		
		(0.0026)		
Average manufactured exports/GDP, 1965–85				-0.0686
				(0.0966)
Interaction term: Educational attainment 1960 times manufactured exports/GDP, 1965–85			0.0625 *	0.0284
			(0.0269)	(0.0201)
Adjusted R^2	0.6333	0.6376	0.4507	0.4628

** Statistically significant at the 0.01 level.
 * Statistically significant at the 0.05 level.
Note: Coefficient is top number. Standard error is bottom number in parentheses.
Source: World Bank staff estimates.

performance and education interact positively; higher levels of education raise the contribution of manufactured export concentration to TFP growth.[55] This is consistent with our hypotheses that manufactured export orientation and high labor force skills interact to facilitate the acquisition and mastery of technology with attendant spillovers.

The evidence from our cross-economy estimates is supported by a number of recent microeconomic studies that attempt to test the link between exports and productivity growth. Pack and Page (1993) present evidence from Korea and Taiwan, China, that at the sectoral level rapid export growth is correlated with the pattern of productivity change; exporting sectors have higher sectoral rates of TFP growth. Wei (1993) uses city data from China and finds a statistically significant relationship between export growth and productivity growth. Perhaps most compelling, Aw and Hwang (1993), using firm microeconomic data from Taiwan, China, find a statistically significant relationship between productivity differences among manufacturing firms and export orientation.

How Have Trade and Industrial Policies Contributed to Growth?

The early admirers of HPAE trade policy clearly overstated the neutrality of incentives between domestic and foreign sales and understated the variation across sectors. But the revisionists who see in the HPAEs' success evidence that highly targeted industrial policy worked overlook the fact that the calculations on which both relied were static, that firms based their decisions not only on current levels of protection and factor prices but on the certain knowledge that they would need to compete in the future. Effective rates of protection may shape short-term tactics but the long-term strategies of currently protected firms are more likely to reflect their expectations of the future.

Thus, the emphasis on exports was decisive for the entire manufacturing sector; promotion of individual sectors was less important, since all but the very dull knew that their turn to export would come sooner than they would have preferred. Given the widespread national understanding established by government statements and actions in Japan, Korea, and Taiwan, China, that exporting was the standard by which all economic activity would be judged, even firms benefiting from higher-than-average rates of protection in the domestic market understood that in the near future they would be forced to compete in world markets. Sustained reduction in import protection sent a similar message to producers in the Southeast Asian newly industrializing economies. Governments were credibly committed to export competition. Exports were important because they ensured that, given the HPAEs' high human capital base, productivity growth would be facilitated by the improved ability to tap international knowledge.

■ ■ ■

What are the main factors that contributed to the HPAEs' superior allocation of physical and human capital to high-yielding investments and their ability to catch up technologically? Mainly, the answers lie in fundamentally sound, market-oriented policies. Labor markets were allowed to work. Financial markets, although subject to more selective interventions to allocate credit, generally had low distortions and limited subsidies compared with other developing economies. Import substitution, although an early objective of public policy in all the HPAEs except Hong Kong, was quickly accompanied by the promotion of exports and duty-free admission of imports for exporters. The result was limited differences between international relative prices and domestic relative prices in the HPAEs. Market forces and competitive pressures guided resources into activities that were consistent with comparative advantage and, in the case of labor-intensive exports, laid the foundation for learning international best practice and subsequent industrial upgrading.

Does this mean that selective interventions played no role in East Asia's superior growth? Our conclusion is that selective interventions were neither as important as their advocates suggest nor as irrelevant as their critics contend. All eight economies succeeded in establishing automatic access to credit for exporters; this simple contest was an important component of their export-push strategies. Other directed-credit programs were less successful. Where they appear to have resulted in allocation of credit to high-yielding activities, mainly in Japan, Korea, and Taiwan, China, it was because of careful screening and monitoring of projects and an orientation toward the private sector. Where they failed, governments limited the damage by offering more limited subsidies than the credit programs in other developing economies. Finally, we have concluded that industrial policy, with the possible exception of Japan, did not alter industrial structure or patterns of productivity change. The most successful selective intervention in the HPAEs—the commitment to manufactured exports—was also the most general.

Flexible markets, low price distortions, high levels of human capital, and industrial and trade policies that tilted incentives in favor of exports—all combined to allow rapid growth of manufactured exports and, through it, rapid technological catching up.

Appendix 6.1: Testing the Impact of Industrial Policy on Productivity Change

GOVERNMENT POLICIES THAT CORRECT MARKET FAILURES should give rise to growing total factor productivity in the entire industrial sector, though the resulting pattern of TFP growth across subsectors is not easily predictable. Knowledge-based imperfections are likely to yield TFP gains, primarily in the subsectors in which the intervention occurs. Subsidization of knowledge acquisition in textile production will mainly benefit other textile firms as knowledge seeps out to them or trained engineers go to other textile firms. Some knowledge in textiles may benefit closely related sectors such as clothing through production of fabrics that are better suited to local conditions, that is, are not obtainable on the world market.

The sectoral locus of gains is important for several reasons. First, empirical efforts to relate government intervention to productivity growth are desirable as a weak test of the effects of intervention. Productivity gains in the entire industrial sector or the entire economy attributable to other factors might mistakenly be ascribed to the intervention, even if it had actually reduced productivity growth. Undoubtedly, the productivity gains from correcting various market failures may diffuse to many sectors, but most should have a major impact in the initial sector of intervention.

Empirically, many of the intersectoral interactions will be measured as intrasectoral at the two-digit level. Improved production engineering in spinning may improve TFP in weaving. Both, however, are included in the two-digit ISIC textiles branch. Equal diffusion to all sectors seems implausible. While there are individual examples in economic history (Rosenberg 1976), there is no evidence that this is the general prototype. Moreover, recent research on the pattern of spillovers of R&D in industrial economies demonstrates that the major beneficiaries are closely related sectors, often sectors that would be identical within a two-digit classification (Jaffe 1986). The nonsubstantiated claim that the spread of externalities is both large and diffuse provides an all too easy refuge for those who argue for the benefits of selective intervention and then offer as evidence effects that are plausibly attributable to the efforts of market agents.

How We Compared the Relative Importance of Industrial Subsectors

To compare the transformation of the sectoral structure of manufacturing in Asia with the transformation projected from international norms, we utilized the following equation:

$$\log(VA_i/\text{GDP})_j = b_0 + b_1\log(\text{GDP}/\text{POP})_j + b_2(\text{POP})_j$$

where VA_i is value added originating in sector i in economy j, GDP is gross domestic product, and POP is total population (Chenery 1960). The equation attempts to capture the influence of demand elasticities and the evolution of supply. POP factors in scale economies, although in a world of free trade this may not matter.[56] The equation is purely descriptive and has no normative content. Indeed, a given pattern might indicate that all economies follow some initial leader and undertake policies to emulate its sectoral evolution. Despite its flaws, the equation provides benchmarks to determine whether the relative importance of industrial subsectors in the HPAEs differed significantly from the weightings observed in other economies.

For purposes of comparison, we utilized equations estimated by Syrquin and Chenery (1989) to derive the predicted sectoral shares of value added in GDP. Table 6.15 presents the results for eight branches of manufacturing, showing the ratio of actual, v^A, to predicted, v^P, shares of gross domestic product for various sectors. Thus a value of 1 represents conformance to the international norm, values less than 1 indicate that the sector is smaller than predicted, and values greater than 1 indicate that the sector is larger than predicted.

In general, the results conform to our expectations of these economies. Three economies known as manufacturing powerhouses have larger overall manufacturing sectors than international norms based on the international norms for economies with similar incomes would predict: Hong Kong (1.26), Korea (1.26), and Singapore (1.38). But there are also several surprises; these are the focus of our narrative. Given the rough nature of the cross-economy analysis, we have not attempted to test the statistical significance of deviations from the norm.

Effects of Industrial Policy on Aggregate Productivity Growth

Aggregate TFP in any period can be decomposed by weighting each sector's level of total factor productivity, $A_{i,t}$, by the sector's share in value added, $v_{i,t}$. The growth of TFP will then depend on changes in $A_{i,t}$ and changes in $v_{i,t}$. Algebraically, this relation can be written as:

$$(6.1) \qquad \Delta \text{Log } A = \Sigma_i v_{it} \log A_{i,t} - v_{i,t-1} \log A_{i,t-1}$$

Equation 6.1 gives the growth in A due to the increase in productivity of existing sectors, $\log A_{i,t} > \log A_{i,t-1}$, or the growth in the value-added share of these sectors, $v_{i,t} > v_{i,t-1}$ whose productivity is growing.[57] As will be seen below in table A6.1, small differences in the rate of growth of sectoral TFP, $A^{*}_{i,t}$, lead to large cumulative differences in $A_{i,t}$.

As the text of chapter 6 points out that on the basis of international comparisons two sectors were generally overrepresented in the industrial sectors of the HPAEs: metal products and machinery, and textiles and apparel. Only the former sector was promoted in HPAEs that used industrial policy. We define two types of sectors, those favored by government policy, f, and those subject to benign neglect, b. The implicit model of those who believe that industrial policy has had an important effect is that changes in the deployment of resources were not based on conventional competitive advantage but that the government created competitiveness in new sectors. Sectoral growth was stimulated in capital- or technology-intensive sectors rather than unskilled labor-intensive sectors that were more "natural" for economies such as Korea or Taiwan, China, in the 1960s. Moreover, it is implicitly assumed but not empha-

Table A6.1 Effect of Sectoral Composition on Manufacturing-Wide Growth of TFP

Economy	TFP growth, actual value-added weights	TFP growth, adjusted weights
Korea, Rep. of, 1966–85	6.7	6.1
Japan, 1960–79	2.3	1.9

Note: Weighted by value-added shares that would have prevailed if the metal products and machinery sector had conformed to that predicted by the equations estimated by Chenery and Syrquin (1989).

Sources: Pack (1993b). Based on Kuroda, Jorgenson, and Nishimizu (1985) for TFP estimates for Japan.

sized that TFP growth was greater in the selectively promoted sectors as a result of static and dynamic scale economies.[58]

If industrial policy was important in determining the rate of industrial productivity growth in the HPAEs, it should be the case that:

a. Sectors were begun or grew more rapidly in terms of factor commitment than would have occurred without intervention. In terms of equation 6.1, $v_{f,t}$ increases more than would have been "normal" from its initial level, $v_{f,t-1}$. Thus, it is necessary to demonstrate that the sectors to which resources flowed were not those that would have grown on a simple comparative advantage basis. If, however, the sectors that grew, $v_i > v_{i-1}$, are characterized by low wages, or low capital intensity as measured by capital-labor ratios, this is consistent with growth according to comparative advantage.

b. Favored sectors had higher levels of TFP, $A_{f,t} > A_{f,t-1}$. Even if (a) can be demonstrated, it is necessary to show that the government correctly forecast future growth of TFP in sectors or that it created differential rates of TFP growth resulting in $A^*_{f,t} > A^*_{b,t}$.

c. There was a quantitatively important introduction of new, modern sectors, v_m, which exhibited higher levels of TFP than existing ones. In terms of (a), the sectoral structure of output is radically changed by the growth of modern sectors that are introduced at high levels of TFP, and this raises average manufacturing-wide productivity.

Because the HPAEs were such successful exporters, predicting the impact of selective interventions on the sectoral pattern of production depends to a considerable extent on one's preferred theory of international trade—Ricardian, Hecksher-Ohlin-Samuelson, neotechnology, and so on. To demonstrate the impact of selective intervention, it is necessary to posit a counterfactual model. This is obviously exceptionally difficult, and to be rigorous requires a general equilibrium model that in turn has difficulties of its own, such as correctly specifying sectoral production functions and learning patterns. Again, the "natural" evolution of an economy also depends on one's preferred theory of international trade. Nevertheless, a weaker test can be applied. If the evolution of the sectoral structure of industry in the HPAEs can be attributed to comparative advantage, it is difficult to support the view ex post of a strong impact of industrial policy.

Implicit here is that the "natural" evolution among industrial sectors can be predicted by the factor endowments theory of comparative advantage, or Hecksher-Ohlin-Samuelson (HOS). Although large numbers of additional explanations of the patterns of trade have been put forward in the last two decades, many of them are attempts to explain intrasector trade and specialization among products that broadly require the same factor proportions. HOS theory yields predictions about the factor content of exports and imports, not directly about the structure of total production. However, given the extraordinary growth of exports in the Four Tigers and their size in the GDP, the changing structure of production in these economies was decisively affected by trade patterns. This is less true of the larger economies, Indonesia, Japan, Malaysia, and Thailand.

Predicting the Pattern of Sectoral Growth

The newer literature setting out the merits of intervention has not tested whether the sectoral evolution of successful Asian economies has differed from what would have occurred had there been neutral policies. Nevertheless, showing that many instruments were selectively employed is not the same as proving that they had a significant quantitative impact on the sectoral structure of production. Even where effective rates of protection differ among sectors, the impact on sectoral structure is not easily predictable. In general equilibrium, the movement of resources has no monotonic relation with ERPs (Black and Taylor 1974; Bhagwati and Srinivasan 1979).

For each economy, four simple regressions are run of the form:

$$(6.2) \qquad v^*_i = f(x_i)$$

where v^*_i is the change in the current price share of value added in sector i, relative to value added in all manufacturing. The independent variables, x_i, are the wage per worker at the beginning, w_b, or end of the period, w_e, or value added per worker at the beginning or end of the period, va_b or va_e. In competitive labor markets, the wage per worker should measure the skill intensity of workers in each sector. Value added per worker should reflect both skill and capital intensity and is a proxy for technological complexity. Although value added per worker and the wage rate are likely to be correlated, both are used, as there is a possibility of divergence. Governments also may have employed one or the other as indicators in targeting sectors. Wage per worker may be translated as "good jobs," while value added per worker is a natural measure of "high productivity."

Consider the movement from inward orientation to more neutral incentives. The static Hecksher-Ohlin model predicts that for low-income economies sectors that exhibit low physical and human capital-labor ratios by international standards are the natural candidates for growth. Hence, the prediction is that dv_{1*}/dw_b and $dv_{1*}/dva_b < 0$. While many newer theories of trade, including neotechnology and those emphasizing increasing returns subordinate differences in factor endowments, they are more likely to describe intra-industry patterns of trade among industrial economies than the evolution of the sectoral structure of production of developing economies whose production structure is likely to reflect differences in factor proportions.

If intervention has been of great importance in promoting the expansion of capital- or knowledge-intensive sectors and, eventually, affecting trade patterns, the data should show $dv_i/dw_b > 0$ and/or that $dv_i/dva_b > 0$. An alternate test of the impact of selective promotion is to test whether the sectors that expanded exhibited high capital intensity or wages at the end of the period. A result favoring the interventionist view would be dv^*_i/dw_e or $dv^*_i/dva_e > 0$; the sectors that grew most exhibited a high capital or high-wage intensity at the end of the period.

We have performed these tests on each of the Four Tigers plus Japan, using two-digit ISIC classifications of industrial sectors. Table A6.2 shows the sign of the regression coefficient and its significance for each period for each economy. The years chosen reflect a distillation of the existing literature for each economy on significant intervals during which intervention was practiced. It is not possible in all cases to utilize the ideal interval. In Japan, for example, data from before 1953 vary considerably in definition from those after 1953.

These are clearly very simple tests of the determinants of structural changes in production but capture the spirit of the opposing views. The statistical results must be employed carefully. Even if it is shown that there was a significant negative correlation between v^*_i and w_b, supporting the HOS view, some of the individual sectors that grew most may still have been high-wage sectors. Thus, we will examine some individual sectors as well as report the statistical results.

Korea. For most periods, the signs of the wage and value-added variables in Korea are negative. For the period 1973–80, the one characterized by promotion of the heavy and chemical industries, the negative coefficients of w and va for the beginning of the period are significant. The same pattern occurs in 1980–88 as well as the entire 1973–88

Table A6.2 Signs of Regressions Explaining Change in Value-Added Share of Sectors

Economy	Period	W_B	W_E	V_B	V_E
Hong Kong	1973–80	–	+	–	+
	1980–88	+	+	+	+
	1973–88	–	+	–	+
Japan	1953–63	–	–	–	–
	1963–73	+	+	+	+
	1973–80	–	+	–	+
	1980–89	+	+	+	+
Korea, Rep. of	1968–73	–	–	–	+
	1973–80	–**	–	–***	–*
	1980–88	–	–	–**	–
	1973–88	–	–	–***	–**
Singapore	1969–73	–	–	–	+
	1980–89	+	+**	+	+*
	1973–89	+	+	+	+*
Taiwan, China	1966–86	–	–	–	–

+ and - signs are sign of coefficient.
* Significant at the 0.10 level.
** Significant at the 0.05 level.
*** Significant at the 0.01 level.

Note: $W_{B(E)}$ = Wage per employee at the beginning (end) of the period. $V_{B(E)}$ = Value added per worker at the beginning (end) of the period.

Source: Pack (1993b).

period. This implies that at the two-digit level the relative size of more labor-intensive sectors increased during each period. On the face of it this result is surprising. Quite apart from policies of selective promotion, this was a period in which both labor skills and the capital stock were growing. One would have expected, according to the Rybcyznski theorem, that the labor-intensive sectors would have declined in importance.

Part of the explanation for the relative growth of labor-intensive sectors despite the promotion of ostensibly capital-intensive subsectors is that the major branches that grew most rapidly in these years, and indeed over the entire period 1968–88, were machinery, electrical machinery, and metals—all sectors exhibiting somewhat less-than-average labor productivity at both the beginning and end of the period. Conversely, some of the declining sectors including iron and steel, industrial chemicals, and paper and paper products, were sectors with greater-than-average va_b and va_b. A more complete explanation of the continuing growth of labor-intensive sectors is that they experienced more rapid growth in TFP, and the cost-reducing effect of productivity change stimulated expansion of output by more than the output growth induced in capital-intensive sectors by the decreasing relative cost of capital and skills due to accumulation and subsidies.

In sum, the regressions for Korea indicate that: (a) the more labor-intensive sectors maintained their relative position or grew; (b) many of the promoted sectors themselves were not capital intensive at the two-digit level; and (c) subsidies to the cost of capital may not have been sufficient to overcome the ongoing differentials in TFP growth among sectors. Moving away from the anecdotes about individual chaebol, the quantitative importance of government intervention to alter the structure of production is not confirmed at the sectoral level.

Japan. The regression results shown for Japan in table A6.2 have no significant coefficients. At least a simple version of HOS does not work, probably not surprisingly as Japan by the earliest year considered in the table, 1953, was sufficiently advanced so that intra-industry rather than interindustry trade would have become an important determinant of the sectoral production structure. Scale economies or a neotechnology explanation of production and trade patterns are more useful at this stage of development. Going back to 1945, which the data do not permit, would not change this picture much insofar as this earlier period was one of reconstruction, in some cases of fairly advanced sectors that had been quite important before and during World War II. A simple HOS story would be interesting to test for the period from the Meiji restoration onwards. Once an economy is in a world of technology- and scale-economy-based development, the requisite conditions exist to allow almost any assertion to be made about the determinants of the sectoral evolution of production.

Hong Kong and Singapore. The two island economies reveal different patterns of development. In Hong Kong there is no relationship between our explanatory variables and patterns of production. In this sense it is similar to Japan but derived from different causes. The slow growth of capital stock per worker in Hong Kong, partly reflecting large immigration, militated in favor of a slower change in industrial structure. There is simply very little variance to be explained in the value-added shares in Hong Kong.

In Singapore for the period 1980–89, output grew more rapidly in those sectors that at the beginning and end of the period exhibited greater value added per worker, supporting the view that the Singaporean authorities intervened to encourage increasingly capital-intensive development. Given the rapid growth in the capital-labor ratio in Singapore, this result also conforms to the Rybcynski predictions.

Taiwan, China. Like the results for Korea, the signs of the wage and value-added variables for Taiwan, China, are negative, although insignificant. Again, this implies that the relative size of more labor-intensive sectors increased during each period, albeit weakly, at the two-digit level. Growth was market conforming; government intervention did little to alter the structure of production at the sectoral level.

The Evolution of Sectors: Market Conforming or Not?

The preceding effort to differentiate between a comparative-advantage-based evolution of industrial structure versus one resulting from intervention is notable mainly for a number of negative results. In particular for Korea, during 1973–80, the years of greatest intervention, the most rapid growth in sectoral shares of value-added occurred in lower wage or lower value-added per worker sectors. Despite government intentions, the manufacturing sector may have evolved roughly in accord with neoclassical expectations. It is also possible that the government undertook measures such as the provision of social overhead capital and technical services such as the Korean Institute for Science and Technology, which facilitated the "neoclassical" transformation.

Singapore, in contrast to Korea, confirms the casual empiricism of many observers, as well as numerous accounts of the goals of government policy that industrial growth emphasized capital- and knowledge-intensive sectors. The sectors that grew most exhibited higher wages and labor productivity than the laggards. There is no evidence of a factor-proportions-based expansion. In contrast, the evolution of sectors in Japan and Hong Kong does not permit a simple view of its determinants. This is not surprising for Japan given that HOS is designed to predict the determinants of trade patterns rather than production, and trade constitutes a relatively small share of Japanese GDP. In the postwar period, certainly after 1953 when our data begin, Japanese trade patterns are more likely to have been dominated by technological development and scale economies. The failure of Hong Kong to conform to neoclassical comparative advantage is at first glance surprising, given the enormous importance of its trade. There was, however, relatively little variation in the dependent variable, the change in the sectoral shares of value added.

Patterns of Sectoral Productivity Growth

This section considers two issues, namely, the pattern of sectoral productivity growth and the impact of the changing composition of production on the manufacturing-wide rate of growth of productivity. The issue here is whether given the observed values of sectoral TFP growth, A^*_i, the unusual evolution of the sectoral pattern of production in some of the economies had a significant quantitative impact on overall TFP growth.

Going back to equation 6.1, the analysis focuses on whether the changing structure of v_i, given the pattern of A^*_i, contributed to more rapid growth. The value of A^*_i is taken to be exogenous. Of the economies considered here, detailed sectoral growth rates of TFP are only available for Japan and Korea (surprisingly, sectoral TFP growth rates are not available for Hong Kong or Singapore), but these are two of the three economies in which activist industrial policies were employed most consistently to achieve productivity-based catching up.

Korea. Calculations of A^*_i have been carried out for a variety of periods by Dollar and Sokoloff (1990) and Lim (1991). What is most striking is the high absolute values of A^*_i in most sectors. From these studies a number of patterns can be identified that are broadly consistent with one another. There is no simple correlation between promoted sectors and TFP growth. Was selective promotion important in the sense that resources were shifted toward sectors in which TFP growth was (exogenously) high, increasing A^* for the entire industrial sector? To answer this we first calculate the manufacturing-wide growth of A^* using the observed value-added shares at the end of the period 1966 to 1985, utilizing the A^*_i values calculated by Lin. We then recalculate the value-added weights assuming that the sectors in ISIC 38 had been at their predicted value, v^P, on the basis of international norms as a share of sectorwide value-added and reassigning the residual value added to all other sectors equally. Thus, instead of accounting for 38 percent of manufacturing value added, sector 38 accounts for 14 percent in this calculation.[59]

The result is shown in row 1 in table A6.1. The actual sectorwide growth rate, A^* was 6.7 percent, the recalculated one 6.1 during a period in which the growth rate of manufacturing value added was 17.5 percent per annum. Even if the "excess" growth of the MPM sector may have been attributable to selective intervention, its rate of TFP growth was not sufficiently above that of other sectors to make a large contribution to overall sectoral TFP growth. The major reason for Korea's manufacturing success lay in high individual values of A_{i^*} for most sectors in most periods.

Japan. As in the case of Korea, a considerable literature argues that Japan's selective industrial policy was critical for its industrial success. Nevertheless, many Japanese analysts are skeptical of its effects, as are many analysts from other economies.[60] The existing literature indicates that many of the critical acts of the Japanese government with respect to industrial policy occurred in the ten years following World War II. Indeed, a very good case can be made that many of the major policies occurred in the period from 1868 to 1920, but these are more difficult to analyze with systematic quantitative evidence rather than anecdotally.[61] Chemicals and the metalworking machinery complex have unusually good performance. These industries are those that observers usually point to as having received significant government support, including efforts to stimulate productivity growth.

A calculation, similar to that for Korea, to determine the impact on A^* for the entire manufacturing sector of the unusual size of sector 38 can be done for Japan. Table A6.1 shows the actual growth of A^* for 1960–79 and the estimated growth, had the sectors constituting 38 been at the international norm, 24 percent of manufacturing value added rather than 41 percent in 1979. The value of A^* would have declined from 2.3 to 1.9, a relatively small decrease given the growth rate of manufacturing value added of 8.7 percent per annum. If selective promotion is interpreted to mean that only a few sectors rather than all are aided, Japan's growth rate would have been only slightly slower without an industrial policy. It is possible that industrial policy significantly increased the values of A^*_i in sectors other than those promoted due to one or more externalities. While this may be the case, it is likely that most externalities occur within individual sectors or in closely related ones. Given the many branches constituting the metal products and machinery sector, the externalities should have been revealed in its own TFP value.

Appendix 6.2: Tests of the Relationship between TFP Change and Trade Policies

THE ECONOMY-SPECIFIC TFP GROWTH RATES CALCULATED IN chapter 1 allow us to make an alternative test of the relationship between trade and industrial policy and growth. We specify a regression of the following form:

(6.3)   TFPG = f(RGDP, PRIM, SEC, OPEN, EXPTS)

where TFPG is the estimated rate of total factor productivity growth with physical capital, human capital, and labor as inputs; RGDP is GDP relative to the United States in 1960; PRIM and SEC are the primary and secondary school enrollment rates; OPEN is the index of relative price conformity; and EXPT is our measure of manufactured export performance.

Table A6.3 summarizes our attempts to test the relationship between these variables and rates of TFP change derived from our production function estimates. The regressions control for other sources of variation in TFP by introducing a variable that has been shown in previous work to be significantly correlated with TFP growth—relative income level—

Table A6.3 Regression of TFP Growth, 1960–89

(dependent variable: total factor productivity growth, 1960–89)

Number of observations	67	67	51	51	69	69	53	53
Intercept	-1.6419 **	-1.6354 **	-50.4684 **	-48.5615 **	-1.6376 **	-1.5849 **	-56.1891 **	-53.0556 **
	(0.3647)	(0.3571)	(13.0955)	(13.5162)	(0.4387)	(0.4304)	(14.1887)	(14.8046)
GDP relative to U.S., 1960	-3.7120 **	-2.9925 **	-5.8388 **	-5.3838 *	-3.3238 **	-2.4679 *	-5.0403 *	-4.4383
	(0.9148)	(0.9709)	(1.9294)	(2.0687)	(1.0219)	(1.0935)	(2.1467)	(2.2899)
Primary enrollment, 1960	2.5605 **	2.3853 **	2.1281 **	2.0941 **	2.6731 **	2.4607 **	1.6685 *	1.6382
	(0.5736)	(0.5690)	(0.6721)	(0.6787)	(0.6646)	(0.6599)	(0.8181)	(0.8225)
Secondary enrollment, 1960	1.3899	1.1991	1.0627	0.8992	3.0430 **	2.6034 *	3.8069 *	3.4443 *
	(1.0633)	(1.0457)	(1.5588)	(1.5899)	(1.1417)	(1.1406)	(1.5790)	(1.6525)
Dollar openness index			0.4943 **	0.4750 **			0.5543 **	0.5227 **
			(0.1328)	(0.1371)			(0.1441)	(0.1502)
Average manufactured exports/total exports, 1960–85	0.0284 **	0.0250 **	0.0288 **	0.0275 **	0.0641 *	0.0354	0.0486	0.0356
	(0.0057)	(0.0059)	(0.0070)	(0.0073)	(0.0246)	(0.0283)	(0.0255)	(0.0305)
HPAEs		0.8176		0.2895		1.0957		0.4817
		(0.4261)		(0.4531)		(0.5648)		(0.6810)
Adjusted R²	0.5879	0.6050	0.6904	0.6863	0.4457	0.4687	0.5710	0.5673

** Statistically significant at the 0.01 level.
 * Statistically significant at the 0.05 level.
Note: Coefficient is top number. Standard error is bottom number in parentheses.
Source: World Bank staff estimates.

as a control (De Long and Summers 1991; Mankiw, Romer, and Weil 1992; Pack and Page 1993). The coefficient on relative income (RGDP60) is generally interpreted as summarizing the productivity (TFP) gains realized as a consequence of moving from lower to higher technological levels. This catching up is the component of TFP change made possible by the difference between average practices and best practices. As we noted in discussing the cross-economy regressions, in time-series analyses of aggregate total factor productivity growth, estimates of TFP consist of two components—intrasectoral TFP growth and the impact of factor reallocation among sectors. Thus, the shift variable RGDP60 may capture the reallocation effect of structural change on TFP in addition to productivity-based catching up.

The use of school enrollment rates is an attempt to test for externalities in human capital formation. In our growth-accounting framework, the contribution of human capital to output should be reflected in the elasticity of output with respect to human capital. We have argued that primary education in particular can have growth-enhancing externalities through the better ability to use and master technology. These externalities may not be captured by the human capital variable and would then be included in the estimates of TFP change. We attempt a similar test for secondary education.

Openness to the world economy is another important candidate for explaining rapid TFP growth. The theoretical case for this view rests not only on allocative efficiency but also on externalities associated with trading activities and on "X-efficiency" gains from creating a more competitive environment for domestic industry. Several previous studies have found such effects, including Harrison (1991), Dollar (1991), and Thomas and Wang (1992). We test one definition of openness, Dollar's (1990) measure of the correspondence between domestic and international relative prices.

Table A6.3 presents our tests of the relationship between exports and productivity change. We choose as our measure of export performance two indicators—the average share of manufactured exports in total exports and the share of manufactured exports in GDP.[62] When the share of manufactured exports to total exports is introduced into the basic specification, it is positive and highly significant (at the 0.01 level). The share of manufactured exports to GDP is significant at the 0.05 level in the basic specification; however, when the degree of openness or the HPAE dummy is introduced, manufactured exports drop out.

Table A6.4 Average Annual Rates of Growth of the Labor Force by Sector

Group and period	Agriculture	Industry	Services	Total
Industrial economies[a]				
1880–1990	0.4	2.1	2.1	1.2
Developing economies[b]				
1960–70	1.1	3.8	3.9	2.0

a. Developing economies include the countries of Africa with the exception of South Africa; Latin America; Asia with the exception of China, the Democratic Republic of Korea, Japan; Mongolia, and Viet Nam; and Oceania with the exception of Australia and New Zealand.

b. Industrial economies include Australia, Canada, Japan, New Zealand, South Africa, the United States, and countries in Western Europe.

Source: Squire (1981).

Table A6.5 Financial Liberalization in the East Asian Economies

Economy	I Deregulation of interest rates	II Stimulation of competition	III Development of financial markets	IV Reform of regulatory and supervisory systems
Hong Kong	*1964:* To stop interest rate wars under free markets, deposit rates set under the direction of the Exchange Banks Association (EBA) by joint agreement between all banks. No lending rate restrictions. Best Lending Rate quoted by the two note-issuing banks used as implicit floor. *1981:* With very limited exceptions deposit rates are set by the Hong Kong Association of Banks (HKAB). HKAB was created in 1980 as a statutory body whose rules were binding on all its members. It replaced the EBA which was a voluntary trade association with only persuasive powers over its members. These interest rate agreements were binding only for banks.	Traditionally liberal "laissez faire" environment allows for free entry. Very significant international banking presence. All domestic banking institutions are privately owned. *1981:* To avoid excessive competition the government classified all banking institutions into three categories (Licensed Banks, Licensed Deposit-Taking Companies (DTCs), and Registered Deposit-Taking Companies) by strictly differentiating their deposit-taking operations. *1990:* Revised classification of institutions to a system comprising of Licensed Banks, Restricted License Banks, and DTCs. At that time there were over 168 licensed banks from over 25 different countries.	*1969–71:* Three more stock exchanges established. *1973:* Abolished foreign exchange controls to promote Hong Kong as an international financial center. Eliminated capital gains and income gains taxes. *1982–83:* Abolished withholding taxes on interest payments on all deposits. *1986:* Unified the four stock exchanges into the Hong Kong Stock Exchange to enhance efficiency. Established the Stock Index Futures Market. *1990:* Created an Interest Rate Futures market.	*1967:* Doubled minimum net worth requirements for licensing banks from HK$5m to HK$10m. Enforced stricter auditing and accounting standards. *1976–82:* Revised DTC ordinance to require registration with the Commissioner of Banking. DTCs were required to submit detailed monthly returns of assets and liabilities and have their accounts audited and published annually. *1986:* New banking ordinance strengthened supervision by unifying banking and DTC supervisory organizations. It maintained single-borrower lending limits and real estate investments at 25 percent of paid-up capital for banks and DTCs, and introduced a new framework to measure capita assets to risk ratios. *1989:* Established the Securities and Futures Commission to supervise security market operations. Council of the Exchange created to guide operations. Legal revisions were made on information disclosure obligations and to prevent insider trading.
Indonesia	*1983:* Interest rate restrictions on most deposit categories of state banks eliminated. Interest rates of private banks were deregulated earlier. Credit ceilings abolished. Central bank discount window policies were revised. Some priority lending maintained. *1990:* Drastically reduced central bank refinance facilities and revised interest rates under the program to approach market rates.	*1986–88:* Eased restrictions on scope of financial institutions' activities. Banks were allowed to own multiservice financial companies (leasing, venture capital, consumer finance). *1988:* Relaxed licensing/ branching restrictions and lifted bans on entry of new private domestic and foreign banks. NBFIs allowed to issue certificates of deposit (CDs).	*1984:* Central bank certificates issued through auctions to stimulate money markets. *1985:* Security houses established to serve as market makers in money market instruments. Bankers' acceptances (BAs) introduced. *1988:* Established over-the-counter (OTC) market to encourage firms to go public. Licensed new private stock exchanges. Equalized tax treatment of time deposits, CDs, and equity. Permitted Banks and NBFIs to raise capital from the securities market.	*1977:* Introduced a quantitative bank rating system. *1988:* Set lending limits for single borrowers/ companies. Reorganized supervisory and monitoring system, hired more staff, implemented an off-site monitoring program. Supervision of rural banks shifted to central bank. *1991–92:* Instituted strict loan loss provisioning guidelines and Bank for International Settlements (BIS) minimum capital adequacy standards. Required publication of bank financial statements. Increased powers of Bank of Indonesia with regard to seeking more documentation, undertaking examinations, replacing management, as well as revoking a bank's license. Formed the Securities and Exchange Commission to monitor, regulate, and establish rules for operation of capital markets.

(Table continues on the following page.)

Table A6.5 *(continued)*

Economy	I Deregulation of interest rates	II Stimulation of competition	III Development of financial markets	IV Reform of regulatory and supervisory systems
Japan	Lending rates were controlled but flexible within the established minimum and maximum range. Deposit rates were precisely controlled. *1975–85:* Gradual and progressive elimination of regulations and liberalization of interest rates. Freed interest rates in the interbank call and bill markets (1978), authorized banks to issue large CDs at market rates (1979), Money market certificates (MMCs) offered at market rates (1985), frequently adjusted deposit rate ceilings. *1986:* Rates on money market instruments freed. Interest rate restrictions on smaller time deposits and deposits other than time deposits maintained.	*1980:* Allowed entry of foreign banks, which by 1981 were operating on an equal footing with domestic banks. *1984:* Sale and purchases of public bonds by banks permitted. Expanded euroyen activities allowed. *1985:* Trust banks owned by foreign banks opened. *1989:* Small and medium business banks (Sogo) converted to regional banks. *1991:* Bank licenses given to banking subsidiaries of foreign securities firms.	*1971–72:* Established the bill discount and Tokyo Dollar call markets. *1976:* Preexisting government bond repurchase (gensaki) market recognized. *1980:* Restrictions on international capital flows abolished. *1983:* Sale of public bonds initiated. *1985:* Government bond futures market and BA market started. *1986:* Treasury Bill Issues started. Foreign securities firms granted membership in the Tokyo Stock Exchange. Japan off-shore market started. *1987:* Domestic commercial paper (CP) market started. Stock futures trading at the Osaka Securities Exchange started. Banks, securities firms, and insurance companies allowed to participate in overseas financial futures markets. *1988:* Stock index futures trading started. *1989:* Tokyo financial futures market started.	The Ministry of Finance with its seven bureaus is the primary regulatory and supervisory authority. Under wide powers from the Banking Law, Securities and Exchange Law, Trade and Foreign Exchange Control Law, and other legislation, it examines financial institutions, supervises deposit insurance, defines permissible and non-permissible activities, and licenses and supervises financial institutions. *1971:* Established the Deposit Insurance Corporation to increase depositor protection. *1982:* New banking law enacted. *1986:* Investment management business law implemented. *1988:* Laws concerning financial futures and mortgage securities business enacted.
Korea, Rep. of	*1965:* Increased ceilings on institutionally administered interest rates. Reform measures were reversed in 1972. *1982:* Abolished credit ceilings and reduced scope of directed-credit activities. Most preferential interest rates abolished as well. *1984:* Minimum and maximum bank interest rate ranges introduced. Interest rate restrictions on interbank lending abolished. Banks allowed to issue CDs at rates higher than for time deposits. *1988:* Most bank and non-bank financial institution (NBFI) lending rates and long-term deposit rates liberalized. BOK still controls short-term deposit rates, total volume of credit, and minimum credit guidelines to small and medium firms and conglomerates.	*1972:* Established Investment and Finance Companies to increase competition. *1981–85:* Privatized state-owned commercial banks and allowed entry of new domestic and foreign banks. Removed discriminatory laws against foreign banks (number of foreign bank branches increased from 18 in 1979 to 64 in 1990). Banks permitted to diversify range of activities with credit cards, trust business, and repurchase agreements. Also eased barriers on entry and operations of NBFIs and reduced favorable regulatory advantages for NBFIs over banks. *1986:* Foreign banks allowed to issue CDs. Limits for issue of CDS further liberalized in 1990.	*1970s:* Preferential tax policies to induce firms to list. *1981:* Commercial paper market established. Set up open-ended investment trusts for foreign investors. *1987:* Set up an OTC market. *1989:* Unified the call money market, previously divided between the banking and non-bank sectors. *1990:* Passed legislation to convert investment finance companies into securities houses. *1991:* Restrictions on foreign-currency-denominated deposit holdings relaxed.	*1982:* Established deposit insurance scheme. *1983–1991:* Revised banking laws to strengthen supervision capabilities. Instituted detailed reporting requirements and authorized the Office of Banking Supervision and Examination (OBSE) to conduct two surprise visits annually. Capital adequacy standards revised to meet BIS standards by 1995. With limited exceptions, single-borrower lending limits set at 25 percent of banks' net worth in addition to limits on loans to subsidiaries. Ministry of Finance (MOF) supervises and imposes prudential guidelines on operations of NBFIs. Stipulates minimum-capital-adequacy requirements, imposes credit exposure limits, and prohibits finance companies from owning real estate except for their own operational purposes.

Economy	I Deregulation of interest rates	II Stimulation of competition	III Development of financial markets	IV Reform of regulatory and supervisory systems
Malaysia	*1971:* Interest rates for fixed deposits of more than four years, maturity freed. *1972:* Interest rates on all commercial bank deposits over one year maturity freed. *1973:* Interest rate restrictions on Finance Companies abolished. *1978:* All commercial bank lending and deposit rates liberalized as well. However, informal restrictions on prime lending rates and on rates for priority sectors were retained. *1983:* Central bank–administered Base Lending Rate introduced as floor. *1991:* Interest rate liberalization completed. Base lending rate freed from administrative control. Some priority sector lending guidelines still remain.	Maintains 1974 ban against foreign bank branches. However, domestic banks face increased competition as they have been encouraged to expand branching networks in smaller town and rural areas. *1974–76:* New financial instruments such as negotiable CDs and bankers' acceptances introduced.	*1976:* Kuala Lumpur Stock Exchange established. *1987:* Malaysian government securities with market-based coupon rates introduced. *1988:* Foreign securities houses permitted to hold up to a 49 percent stake (increased from 30 percent) in local securities houses. *1989–90:* Established an off-shore banking market. Central bank issued guidelines on the issue of private debt securities. *1991:* Established a corporate credit rating agency.	*1973:* Revised Banking Act—more explicitly defined guidelines for licensing, duties of banks, protection of depositors, ownership, management, and control of banks. *1983–86:* Operations of Islamic bank and DTCs brought under central bank supervision. *1988:* Issued a code of ethics with guidelines on minimum standards of conduct for bankers. Included specific guidelines for share trading activities also. *1989:* Banking and Financial Institutions Act—conjugated the Banking Act of 1973 and Finance Company Act of 1969. Stricter single-borrower lending guidelines and credit worthiness standards enforced. Instituted a standardized format of financial reporting to increase transparency.
Singapore	*1975:* Complete financial liberalization. Bank cartel system of determining interest rates abolished and banks left free to quote their own deposit and lending rates of interest. Relaxed exchange controls; completely dismantled by 1978.	*1970:* Accelerated internationalization of banking sector with a liberal policy toward admission of international financial institutions and development of the Asian Dollar, Asian Bond, and off-shore banking markets. First license in six years given to a foreign bank to operate in Singapore. *1971:* Only restricted banking licenses given to foreign banks to protect local banks from excessive competition.	*1968:* Asian Dollar Market established. *1973:* Singapore Stock Exchange created. *1983:* Established the Singapore International Monetary Exchange to supersede the Singapore Gold Exchange as part of a move toward 24-hour global trading in financial futures and other sophisticated financial instruments. *1986–87:* Four domestic banks permitted to take full equity positions in local brokerages. Foreign banks and brokerages, however, limited to no more than a 49 percent stake.	*1971:* Established Monetary Authority of Singapore. Along with central banking functions, supervises financial institutions through operational guidelines and reviews of statements that banks must submit to it. Banking Act set minimum capital requirements, minimum cash reserve ratios, liquidity ratios, single borrower limits, and restrictions on property loans and limits on property acquisition. *1985:* Stock Exchange oversight committee established and margin trading requirements strengthened. Increases in capital bases of brokerage houses instituted.
Taiwan, China	*1980:* Liberalized CD rates. *1984:* Flexible maximum and minimum lending rates introduced. *1985:* Commercial banks allowed to set prime rate within central bank–administered range. Revoked regulation prohibiting maximum deposit rates from exceeding minimum lending rate. *1986:* Consolidated thirteen categories of regulations on deposit rate ceilings into four. *1989:* Complete deregulation of interest rates.	*1989:* Amended banking laws to allow for establishment of new private banks and an expanded scale and scope of permitted activities without legislative approval. Also relaxed entry restrictions for foreign banks and allowed them to engage in trust, savings, and long-term lending businesses.	*1960–61:* Established Taiwan Stock Exchange. *1976:* Established open money market (CP, CDs, and BAs) with market-determined interest rates. *1984:* Created off-shore banking unit market. *1988:* Comprehensive securities companies and branch offices of foreign securities companies conditionally allowed. *1989–90:* Established a foreign exchange call market for the US$, DM, and yen.	*1960:* Set up Securities and Exchange Commission to regulate and supervise capital market operations. *1985:* Established a deposit insurance corporation. *1988–89:* Amended Securities Transaction Laws to require registration of firms rather than licensing. Revised banking laws to prohibit unlicensed institutions from taking deposits, and increased powers of regulators in dealing with unlicensed institutions. Strengthened minimum capital requirements and minimum staff requirements for each type of financial business.
Thailand	*1980:* Interest rate ceilings for financial institutions freed from 15 percent limit imposed by usury law. *1984:* General credit restrictions abolished but restrictions on bank lending rates reimposed. Ceilings for loans to priority sectors lowered. *1989:* Abolished deposit rate ceilings on commercial bank time deposits greater than one year. *1990:* Abolished deposit rate ceilings on commercial bank time deposits greater than one year. Also reduced overdraft ceilings from 50 million baht to 30 million baht.	Ceilings on lending rates still regulated. *1988:* Revoked 1962 banking law that prohibited new domestic or foreign bank branches. *1989:* Introduced new financial products like long term loans with a three-, five-, or seven-year maturity.	*1962:* Bangkok stock exchange started but closed in 1970s due to poor listings. *1974:* Established the Securities Exchange of Thailand. *1979:* Security Repurchase Market established. *1984:* Established the transferable CDs market. *1985:* Introduced Bangkok Interbank Offered Rate.	*1972:* Tightened restrictions and implemented a licensing system to prevent fraud and mismanagement by Finance Companies. *1978:* Increased supervisory powers to control insider trading and stock price manipulations. *1979:* Revised banking laws and finance company laws. Restrictions on family ownership and insider lending tightened. *1985:* Additional supervisory enhancements instituted—on-site monitoring and off-site surveillance, regular periodic submission of income and expense accounts, balance sheets, etc. Introduced punitive measures and sanctions for illegal activities, defined minimum-capital-adequacy standards, single-borrower exposure limits, and an asset portfolio classification system. *1989:* Securities and Exchange Commission created with responsibilities to supervise and regulate the securities industry.

Sources: Kaufman (1992); Hendrie (1986); Cheng (1986); Skully and Viksnins (1987); World Bank (1989a); internal World Bank reports; Viner (1988); Suzuki (1987); Federation of Bankers Association of Japan (1991); Foundation for Advanced Information Research (1991); Ghose (1987).

Notes

1. See Greenwald and Stiglitz (1988) on the effect of coordination failures in labor markets.

2. Alternatively, constant real wages could be due to a reduction in surplus labor (Lewis 1954; Ranis and Fei 1961).

3. A population will double in 87 years when it is growing at an annual rate of 0.8 percent; when it is growing at 3.2 percent a population doubles in only 22.5 years. See Squire (1981) for a historical comparison of population and labor force growth in developing countries in the currently high-income countries in the nineteenth century.

4. For the period 1989–2000 population is estimated to grow at an annual rate of 0.8 percent in Hong Kong, 0.3 in Japan, 0.9 in Korea, 1.2 in Singapore, and 1.4 in Thailand. Indonesia and Malaysia are forecast to grow at higher rates of 1.6 and 2.3 percent, respectively. The share of the population less than fourteen years old was 31 percent, circa 1900, in the currently high-income countries. In 1989 it was 30 percent in East Asia and 36 percent in Latin America; in 1986 it was 46 percent in Sub-Saharan Africa.

5. Increases in the technological complexity of non-agricultural production and in the size of establishments bring greater division of labor and, hence, increases in skill differentiation at the same time that greater availability of educational opportunities increases the supply of educated workers.

6. Labor market efficiency is assessed by comparing marginal productivities in losing and receiving activities. Evidence of changes in labor allocation suggests that individuals choose among alternative occupations, industries, and geographic areas as though they had a fine regard for marginal costs and benefits. Though behavior consistent with rational decisionmaking on the part of individuals is a necessary condition, it is not sufficient to ensure optimal allocation of labor. It is also necessary for workers to be price-takers and to be free to enter any industry or occupation for which they are qualified. Restrictions on freedom of entry arise from such sources as monopsony power, discrimination, government interventions, and workers' associations.

7. The costs do not derive solely from the misallocation of labor implied by gaps in marginal product among workers with the same human capital endowments. The costs of such static misallocations rarely exceed 1–2 percent of GNP. Dynamic costs can run much higher when, for example, employment in enterprises is excessive (implying a wedge between the wage and the marginal product of labor) and the subsidies required to keep firms afloat divert scarce savings from productive investments. See Gelb, Knight, and Sabot (1991).

8. A labor market is segmented when some workers receive higher wages than others with the same level of human capital simply by virtue of their sector of employment.

9. Clearly, a high share of the public sector in wage employment growth is not definitive evidence of a relatively high share of surplus labor in the "modern sector." The public sector could be finding productive jobs for all its employees.

10. In more than one-third of the economies, private sector employment actually decreased, implying that the public sector accounted for all the observed increase in total wage employment.

11. While there is no doubt about the role of government in suppressing unions in Korea and Singapore, in Taiwan, China, there is some question whether government action, for example, prohibiting the Chinese Federation of Labor from engaging in collective action, was decisive. Market forces, and in particular the size distribution of firms, also help explain why so few workers in Taiwan, China, are union members. See Fields (1992) and chapter 4.

12. See Fields (1992), who notes that until 1972 unions were free to bargain over wages, which were largely determined by market forces, and Freeman (1992), who, referring to the post-1972 labor market policy regime, has asserted, "Singapore is possibly the most interventionist government in the capitalist world." It is interesting to note that the same instrument—the National Wages Council, a deliberation council discussed in chapter 4—was used dur-

ing the period of wage repression, during the accelerated growth of real wages in the 1980s, and now to maintain real wage growth in line with productivity increases.

13. Looking beyond the group of East Asian economies on which we have focused, labor repression is not generally associated with economic growth. Freeman (1992) notes that "most dictatorships that suppress unions are incompetent in economic affairs—vide Burma in East Asia," though he recognizes that this generalization is not an adequate dismissal of the argument that in some economic circumstances, such as those prevailing in the "miracle" economies, repression might be good for development.

14. See Ranis (1993) for documentation for Korea and Taiwan, China.

15. Gelb, Knight, and Sabot (1991) show how in response to unemployment the creation of public sector jobs with zero marginal product can over little more than a decade reduce a moderately growing economy to economic stagnation while having little or no impact on the number unemployed.

16. The governments of Côte d'Ivoire, Egypt, Mali, and Sri Lanka all have at various times explicitly acted as "employer of last resort," particularly for university graduates. Guarantees of jobs to workers who cannot find "suitable" employment elsewhere generally resulted in the mushrooming of public sector payrolls. See Gelb, Knight, and Sabot (1991).

17. When Indonesia attempted to direct credit to industry in the late 1970s, it was immediately channeled almost wholly to two public enterprises. Indonesia withdrew this directed credit scheme in 1986.

18. Malaysia, for example, lent substantial fractions of credit to public enterprises between 1975 and 1989; the federal government lent directly to public financial and nonfinancial corporations. Its lending reached the equivalent of 22 percent of banking assets in 1975, declining to 16 percent in 1980 and 9.8 percent in 1989. These loans carried real interest rates, which were mildly negative to slightly positive, compared with the substantial negative real rates of many other economies (Caprio, Atiyas, and Hansen forthcoming).

19. Other evidence on the extent of subsidies can be obtained from the reduction in financial burdens to enterprises that borrow from subsidized lending programs. In Japan, the cost reductions have been large in sea transport (more than 20 percent); 5–10 percent in electrical power, transport machinery, and the coal mining industry; but very modest in other industries. Ogura and Yoshino (1988) estimate the financial benefits arising from the reduction in interest rates of Japan's directed-credit programs was less than 2 percent of total investments in manufacturing between 1961 and 1973. In Korea, some investment projects and exporters received substantial interest rate subsidies during the HCI drive of the 1970s, but these large subsidies have since declined.

20. King and Levine (1993) also show that high central bank shares in total credit are bad for growth. Hence, the macroeconomic restraint discussed in chapter 3 permitted rapid expansion of private credit.

21. When exports were not used as an explicit allocation criterion, Japan often used international prices as a standard of good performance. Its industrial rationalization programs used as criteria cost reductions that were based on the costs of international competitors. This was enforced through the threat of international competition as imports were gradually liberalized (for example, machine tools and steel).

22. The merits of well-managed and focused directed-credit programs have long been advocated by Japanese government officials. For example, a study by the Overseas Economic Cooperation Fund has argued that government involvement in directing credit is warranted when there is a significant discrepancy between private and social benefits, when the investment risk of particular projects is too high, and when information problems discourage lending to small and medium-size firms (OECF 1991). Use of policy-based lending rather than other forms of industrial assistance (for example, lower taxes, grants, and so on) is premised on the argument that the main constraint facing new or expanding enterprises is their access to external finance at reasonable terms and conditions. Directed-credit programs involving small subsidies overcome this constraint, but Japanese officials have stressed that to avoid the misuse of funds and abuse

of credit programs, strong emphasis must be placed on the maintenance of macroeconomic stability to minimize distortions in incentives and on effective monitoring to ensure the timely repayment of loans.

23. These studies are preliminary outputs of a World Bank research program on the Effectiveness of Credit Policies in East Asia, which is intended to provide empirical tests of the effectiveness of directed-credit programs.

24. Among the best known of these are Balassa and others (1971), Little, Scitovsky, and Scott (1970), and Krueger and Bhagwati (1973). *World Development Report 1991* provides a good summary of the arguments for the linkage between neutral incentives and growth.

25. For an interesting attempt to test one of these propositions—externalities accruing to exports—in a general equilibrium framework, see de Melo and Robinson (1992).

26. Among the earliest formal discussion of market failures in development are Scitovsky (1953) and Chenery (1959). A thorough survey of many of the issues is given by Corden (1974). More recent discussions include Pack and Westphal (1986) and Itoh and others (1988). World Bank (1992c) provides a recent survey of the issues and an application to the evaluation of World Bank industrial development projects.

27. Economic growth will eventually preclude the need for policies to capture the productivity gains from economies of either scope or scale.

28. For a review of many of these, see Stewart and Ghani (1992).

29. In general, real externalities provide a valid argument for trade policy interventions only if they allow goods to be produced at less than the imported c.i.f. (costs, insurance, and freight) price. This is not, however, sufficient to justify intervention. A socially successful intervention depends on whether the present discounted value (PDV) of future producer surplus exceeds the PDV of the cost of subsidies.

30. More recent discussions have discounted this argu-

ment, saying that if a firm really were to be profitable in the long run, it would pay for the firm to encounter losses today. But this counterargument runs into problems: it is based on the premise that capital markets are perfect.

31. Export prices can be set in the international (unprotected) markets at long-run marginal cost. It is possible to show, under certain simplifying assumptions (see Spence (1981), that optimal production of the firm entails setting the marginal value of output equal to the long-run marginal cost.

32. In the early and mid-1970s, nominal tariff rates and effective protection began to decline (Itoh and Kiyono 1988; Komiya 1990). Although there is disagreement over the extent of the reductions in effective protection, there is agreement that effective rates of protection were substantial before the early 1970s.

33. While effective rates of protection or subsidy calculations would provide a better measure of the quantitative impact of protection, the figures shown furnish a notional indicator, consistent over time, of the extent of reduction of nominal tariff rates and nontariff barriers.

34. It would be more desirable to compare effective rates of protection, since it is value-added prices that matter for resource allocation, but the most recent systematic cross-economy studies based on comparable definitions utilize evidence for only one year in the 1960s and early 1970s. There are few recent estimates to provide comparable figures.

35. Singapore has been excluded since its zero duty rates will bias the estimate downward.

36. Pack (1988) expressed doubt about the robustness of the evidence for Korea and Taiwan, China. When the paper was written in 1985, the TFP estimates for both economies were based on data that began in the mid- to late 1960s and ended in the late 1970s, a sufficiently short period so that increasing capacity utilization or one-time benefits from scale economies could have accounted for a substantial share of unexplained growth. One study of Korea (Kim and Kwon 1977) was indeed convincing in demonstrating that correct measures of capacity utilization eliminated the residual for much of the period in

question. Additional observations are now available, and improved estimates of the capital stock make it seem likely that the measured TFP accurately reflects unexplained growth.

37. On these issues, a particularly good discussion is given by Itoh and others (1991), part I.

38. For details, see the various chapters in Komiya, Okuno-Fujiwara, and Suzumura (1988).

39. Itoh and Kiyono (1988). These estimates are based on nominal tariff rates, not implicit price comparisons. Given the presence of quantitative restrictions, they are likely to be minimums.

40. For extensive discussions, see World Bank (1987a).

41. In Korea and Taiwan, China, the initial spurt in exports was in labor-intensive products as predicted by the static theory of comparative advantage. These, however, are also the sectors that Dollar and Sokoloff find exhibited greater TFP growth between 1963 and 1979 in Korea. Wang (1990) finds a similar pattern for Taiwan, China, for 1966–86. Exports may have resulted from this initial spurt in productivity. But analysis of Taiwan, China's, early export growth by Scott (1979) and the analysis of the Korean trade incentive system by Westphal (1978) suggest that factor proportions, supplemented by a small pro-export bias, plausibly account for the earliest export growth.

42. A recent study of TFP growth in Chile, for example, finds that following the 1970s' liberalization, accelerated TFP change due to organizational change and product quality upgrading lasted at most six years (Perry and Herrara, forthcoming).

43. Undoubtedly, domestic skills were important in allowing the technology obtained from abroad to be utilized productively.

44. On the role of infrastructure in Taiwan, China, see Ranis (1979).

45. DFI was not a major source of investment growth in Japan, Korea, or Taiwan, China, but it has been very important in other HPAEs. Even in Taiwan, China, DFI accounted for 15 percent of employment growth in 1975–84 and demonstrated the viability of new exports. Moreover, much of the investment was in relatively small firms in which employees were exposed to new equipment and the relevant production engineering. Since labor turnover in these foreign-invested firms was substantial, the total impact of DFI on effectively introducing new technology was quite high (Pack 1993b).

46. For efforts to assess the empirical importance of spillovers from DFI, see Blomstrom (1989) and Haddad and Harrison (forthcoming).

47. See Rhee and Westphal (1977) for evidence on the use of older technology to achieve exports of textiles in Korea during the 1960s and 1970s and Ranis (1979) for Taiwan, China.

48. On Taiwan, China, see, for example, *Wall Street Journal*, June 1, 1990, and Liu (1987). On Korea, see Westphal, Rhee, and Pursell (1981).

49. Katz, ed. (1987) report the results of these studies. The firms investigated made intense efforts to improve productivity despite the protection afforded by the import-substitution regime, an example of the too often forgotten point that protection has both income and substitution effects on the effort expended to reduce costs. In the firms considered, the substitution effect clearly outweighed the income effect. Nevertheless, calculations based on most of the studies suggest very low rates of growth of capital productivity, an exception being the results for one steel plant analyzed by Dahlman and Fonseca (1987). TFP estimates are not easily extracted from the data reported for most of the studies in Katz, ed.

50. The importance of interactions may explain the phenomenon noted by Behrman (1987) that between 1960 and 1981, the average level of schooling in all developing economies increased by two-thirds, yet in most economies this had little effect in stimulating growth. Education has a smaller effect where complementary changes do not occur; thus, high education may be necessary but is hardly sufficient.

51. Previous studies using this approach are De Long and Summers (1991), Mankiw, Romer, and Weil (1992), and Pack and Page (1993).

52. Several previous studies have found such effects, including Harrison (1991), Dollar (1992), and Thomas and Wang (1992). We use as the openness variable Dollar's measure of the correspondence between domestic and international relative prices (1990). This measure uses Summers and Heston's international comparisons of price levels to develop an index of "outward orientation" for ninety-five developing economies (1988).

53. Alternative specifications using the rate of growth of total exports were also employed with similar but less robust results. Data on the rate of growth of manufactured exports is not available for a large sample of economies.

54. This conclusion is reinforced by the arguments that low distortions relative to international prices can arise from having a significant share of the economy operating at export prices; in that case, the share of manufactured exports in GDP may be more strongly collinear with the openness index.

55. We ran two joint F-tests on the regressions including the interactive term. The F-tests were both consistent with a high degree of multicollinearity between the interaction term and the export term. The F-test rejects the null hypothesis that, taken jointly, the coefficients on the three variables (education, manufactured exports/total exports, and the interactive term) are not significantly different from zero (taken together, the three are significantly different from zero at the 0.01 level). Likewise, the F-test rejects the hypothesis that, taken jointly, the interactive term and the ex-

port variable are not significantly different from zero (taken together, the two are significantly different from zero at the 0.01 level). Where there is a high degree of multicollinearity between the variables, the coefficients on the interaction term and the export variable, despite being separately insignificant, should still be treated as best point estimates.

56. The discussion of scale economies has recently been revived by Murphy, Shleifer, and Vishny (1989).

57. An alternative to equation 6.1 is: $A^* = \Sigma v_i A_{*i}$, which assumes that sectoral shares are constant.

58. Another interpretation would be that there was an initial disequilibrium in marginal productivities among sectors and that industrial policy accelerated the movement of factors to higher marginal productivity sectors. With respect to labor, the issue is moot in the Four Tigers as they typically had relatively competitive labor markets.

59. Put differently, it has been shown earlier that Korea's v^P/v^A ratio for MPP was 2.76. If this had been 1, the actual share of value added would have been 13 rather than 36 percent; that is, the share would have been constant at the 1968 level. If factors had been allocated to all the remaining sectors equally, the sectorwide average value for A^* would have been 0.061 rather than 0.067.

60. See Itoh and others (1991), Komiya and others (1988), Saxonhouse (1983), and Trezise (1983).

61. For a very useful account of many of the measures in the earlier period, see Lockwood (1954).

62. See note 53 for an explanation.

CHAPTER 7

Policies and Pragmatism in a Changing World

T HIS BOOK HAS SHOWN THAT THERE IS NO SINGLE East Asian model. Rather, the eight high-performing Asian economies have used different and changing sets of policies to achieve rapid growth with equity. In this chapter, we evaluate six key policy fundamentals used by the HPAEs. We then examine institutions to promote growth and finally assess three policy interventions. We end by considering how the changing global economy is likely to constrain future use of the HPAEs' most successful intervention: the export-push strategy.

Foundations of Rapid Growth— Getting the Fundamentals Right

T HE STRESS ON POLICY FUNDAMENTALS IS A HALLMARK OF ALL eight HPAEs. These widely shared, market-friendly policies are the foundation of East Asia's economic success. In chapter 2 we identified several broad policy areas as fundamental, and in subsequent chapters we described their relevance to the strategic functions of accumulation, allocation, and productivity change. Here we briefly review some key aspects of these policies. Although implementing these fundamentals successfully is often difficult, the benefits are substantial, as demonstrated by their crucial role in the rapid growth of the HPAEs. Moreover, despite changes in the global economic environment, these policies remain viable options for developing economies today.

Ensuring Low Inflation and Competitive Exchange Rates

Macroeconomic stability and low inflation were necessary preconditions for rapid growth in all eight HPAEs. The key element was the management of the fiscal deficit. Fiscal policies have been generally conservative in avoiding inflationary financing of budget deficits, and some HPAEs, such as Singapore and Taiwan, China, have run sustained budget surpluses. While Indonesia, the Republic of Korea, and Malaysia acquired considerable foreign debt, their debt to export ratios were lower than other developing economies, so creditors never lost faith and they never faced a full-blown debt crisis requiring rescheduling. Moreover, budget rules and legislation requiring that sovereign debt be used for development expenditures helped to ensure that borrowing funded investment rather than consumption. The successful record of low inflation and sustained growth of the HPAEs reinforces the view that there is no substitute for fiscal discipline.

The HPAEs' success in export-driven growth was predicated on competitive real exchange rates. Prudent fiscal and monetary policies coupled with flexible exchange rate management were used to keep exchange rate movements aligned with changing structures of trade protection and inflation differentials with trading partners. The HPAEs avoided strategies of macroeconomic stabilization that stressed the role of the exchange rate in breaking inflationary expectations. Rather, exchange rate adjustments were supported by expenditure-reducing fiscal measures. While Indonesia, Korea, and Thailand have had periods of real appreciation, they did not try to maintain a fixed exchange rate regime in the face of inflation rates much greater than those of their trading partners.

The HPAEs responded to external shocks more quickly and effectively than other developing economies. East Asian policymakers have been more adept at managing fiscal contractions—cutting expenditures and increasing revenues in a growth-oriented framework—to attain viable deficit targets. In contrast, governments elsewhere committed to funding large entitlement programs—income transfers, untargeted subsidies, excessive public sector employment, and loss-making public enterprises—often lacked the flexibility to deal efficiently with budget contractions. Rather than cutting spending on entitlements, they have often resorted to cutting public investment.

In each HPAE, a technocratic elite insulated to a degree from excessive political pressure supervised macroeconomic management. The insulation mechanisms ranged from legislation, such as balanced budget laws in Indonesia, Singapore, and Thailand, to custom and practice in Japan and Korea. All protected essentially conservative macroeconomic policies by limiting the scope for politicians and interest groups to derail those policies.

Building Human Capital

We have shown that the broad base of human capital was critically important to rapid growth in the HPAEs. Because the HPAEs attained universal primary education early, literacy was high and cognitive skill levels were substantially above those in other developing economies. Firms therefore had an easier time upgrading the skills of their workers and mastering new technology. In addition, rapid human capital accumulation reduced income inequality by increasing the relative abundance of educated workers, thereby lowering the scarcity rents associated with cognitive skills. These benefits were particularly evident in the countryside.

Basic education in the HPAEs is highly oriented toward the acquisition of general academic skills, while post-secondary education tends to be oriented toward vocational skills. Some HPAEs have also been unusually large-scale importers of educational services, particularly in vocationally and technologically sophisticated disciplines. In addition, enterprise-level training, much of which was subsidized, accelerated technological acquisition.

The benefits of closing the gap between girls and boys in primary and secondary school enrollments have been substantial, even in economies in which female labor participation rates are low. Better educated mothers raise better educated children, complementing public investments in basic education. The rapid increase in the educational attainment of women contributed to the early decline in fertility, which in turn resulted in a less rapidly growing school-age population. As a result, more resources were available per child, in homes and in the classroom.

Creating Effective and Secure Financial Systems

Financial sector policies in the HPAEs were designed to facilitate two crucial functions. First, they encouraged financial savings. Second, they channeled savings into activities with high social returns. There was great variety in the policies and institutions used to accomplish these ends, but several fundamental approaches were important in all eight economies. These included generally positive real interest rates on deposits and the creation of secure bank-based financial systems.

Positive real interest rates on deposits were the most important factor in encouraging financial savings. All of the HPAEs had periods, usually early in their development, when real interest rates on deposits were negative. But in general real interest rates were more stable and more consistently positive in East Asia than in other developing regions, where high inflation has often meant that volatile and highly negative real interest rates prevailed.

HPAE governments also encouraged savings by fostering stable and secure banking systems through a combination of protection and regulation. Protection of established banks included government limits on the creation of new domestic banks, the entry of foreign banks, and the operation of competing non-bank financial institutions. Regulation included enforcement of prudent behavior, such as limiting speculative lending. Although the HPAEs had no explicit deposit insurance, they promoted confidence in the banking system by devising rescue programs as needed, sometimes, as in Japan and Korea, pressuring stronger banks to absorb weaker banks. In addition, many of the HPAEs encouraged savings by creating postal savings plans to lower transaction costs of savings for small savers.

Balancing the advantages of protection against the need for competition has been a major challenge for HPAE bank regulators. East Asia's banking sector structures, as well as some measures of bank efficiency (profitability and borrowing-lending margins), suggest that banks in the HPAEs have been at least as efficient as those in other developing regions. Even so, innovation and efficiency undoubtedly suffered from limits on competition. Partly in response, HPAEs gradually have opened their banking systems to increased domestic and foreign competition. Governments have also promoted bond and equity markets to increase the depth of maturing financial sectors.

Several HPAEs supplemented commercial banks—and met the need for long-term capital—by creating specialized development banks. These banks furthered the growth of the financial sector by establishing procedures for project financing and monitoring that commercial banks then copied. In contrast to development banks in many other developing economies, which tend to be subject to extensive government meddling, HPAE development banks controlled project selection and monitoring independently, albeit within broad government guidelines. As a result, their bad debts were usually associated with economic downturns rather than the willful default common in economies where government officials are closely involved in day-to-day management.

Limiting Price Distortions

Despite the HPAEs' many market interventions, relative price distortions were limited and indeed smaller than in most other developing economies. Flexible labor markets and capital markets with positive real interest rates meant that wages and interest rates reflected more closely true scarcities of labor and capital. Thus resources were generally drawn into labor-intensive production in early stages of development, shifting to capital- and knowledge-intensive activities as physical and human capital deepened.

A combination of competitive real exchange rates and moderate protection levels meant that domestic prices of traded goods were closer to international prices in the HPAEs than in other developing regions. The large weight of exports in total output, duty-free imports for exporters, and extensive domestic competition meant that all the HPAEs had higher proportions of their manufacturing sectors operating at or near international prices than the import-substituting economies of Latin America, South Asia, or Sub-Saharan Africa.

Absorbing Foreign Technology

While none of the HPAEs except Hong Kong and Singapore was entirely open to international trade, all were open to foreign technology. Japan, Korea, and to a lesser degree Taiwan, China, relied heavily on licensing, imports of machinery, and reverse engineering during their rapid growth periods. Hong Kong, Singapore, and the Southeast Asian HPAEs, in addition, welcomed direct foreign investment that came bundled with technical, managerial, and sometimes labor force skills. Licensing has become more and more problematical because owners of technology are reluctant to share it, even for a fee. However, the success of the Southeast Asian HPAEs with other forms of technological acquisition suggests this need not be a serious barrier to growth.

The alternative path of self-reliance has little to recommend it. Some developing economies, such as Argentina and India, have restricted capital goods imports to promote the growth of domestic machine-building industries. In these cases, however, domestic machinery generally falls short of international standards. Such machinery becomes yet another high-cost import substitute that inhibits exports.

Limiting the Bias against Agriculture

Agriculture has played a more central role in the HPAEs than in many other low- and middle-income economies. Wide adoption of Green Revolution technology, high investment in rural infrastructure, and limited direct and indirect taxation of agriculture meant that rural incomes and productivity rose more rapidly in East Asia than in other regions.

As in other economies, agricultural sectors in the HPAEs were a source of capital and labor for the manufacturing sector. But in East Asia these resources were generally pulled into manufacturing by rising wages and returns, rather than squeezed out of agriculture by high taxes and stagnant or declining relative incomes. As a result, rural-urban income differentials were smaller in the HPAEs than in most other developing economies.

Creating Institutions to Promote Growth

THE SUCCESS OF THE EAST ASIAN ECONOMIES STEMS PARTLY from the policies they have adopted and partly from the institutional mechanisms they created to implement them. All of the HPAEs created secure institutional environments for private investment that led to very high levels of private sector–led growth. HPAE civil services range from the highly meritocratic and insulated bureaucracies of Japan, Korea, Singapore, and Taiwan, China, to the less effective and less insulated public administrations of Indonesia and Thailand. Nevertheless, each of these economies has a core of technocratic managers. In Indonesia and Thailand, their scope is limited to management of the macroeconomy. In the other HPAEs, competent civil services administer a much wider range of policy instruments.

How did these economies create a reputable bureaucracy? First, pay mattered. The salaries of bureaucrats (except in Singapore) usually fell short of those for equivalent positions in the private sector, but they were sufficiently high to attract and retain good economic managers.

Second, in the HPAEs with high-quality bureaucracies, rules and procedures governing public sector employment were institutionalized and insulated from political interventions. In particular, recruitment and promotion were merit based. Third, public employment was accorded high status. These factors improved the quality of the bureaucracy, discouraged corruption, and created an esprit de corps among civil servants that helped insulate the bureaucracy from political pressures.

Each of the HPAE governments created institutions to improve communication with the private sector. Formal deliberation councils established in five of the economies—Hong Kong, Japan, Korea, Malaysia, and Singapore—included government officials, journalists, labor representatives, and academics. The economic and political benefits of these councils, and of the more informal mechanisms in the other HPAEs, are impossible to measure systematically. It is likely, however, that economically they improved coordination among firms and improved the flow of information between businesses and government. Politically they helped establish a commitment to shared growth and reduced rent-seeking. Information sharing made it more difficult for firms to curry special favors from the government and for government officials to grant special concessions. Thus the deliberation councils helped check opportunistic behavior. The deliberation councils in Japan, Korea, and Singapore also performed an important monitoring function, assessing performance at the industry or economy level and administering contests.

Consultative mechanisms in Indonesia and Thailand were less formal, and their role in facilitating business-government communication was much more limited. Malaysia's experiment with deliberation councils is quite recent but appears to hold some promise in the area of macroeconomic management.

Intervening in Markets

MOST OF THE HPAEs, ESPECIALLY THOSE IN NORTHEAST Asia, intervened in markets in an effort to hasten growth. All interventions carry with them costs, either in the form of direct fiscal costs of subsidies or forgone revenues, or in the form of implicit taxation of households and firms—for example, through the structure of protection or interest rates controls. One of the main characteristics of interventions in the HPAEs is that in general they have been carried out within well-defined bounds limiting the implicit or explicit costs. Thus, price distortions were present but not excessive; interest rate controls generally had as benchmarks international interest rates and were binding at positive real levels. Explicit subsidies were also kept within bounds. Given the overriding importance that each of the HPAEs ascribed to macroeconomic stability, interventions that threatened to undermine that policy fundamentally, were modified or abandoned—for example, the heavy and chemical industries drive in Korea or the heavy industrialization push in Malaysia. These limits to intervention stand in sharp contrast to many other developing economies, where interventions have not been consistent with macroeconomic discipline.

Whether these interventions contributed to the rapid growth made possible by good fundamentals or detracted from it is the most difficult question we have tried to answer. It is much easier to show that the HPAEs limited the costs and duration of inappropriately chosen interventions—itself an impressive achievement—than to demonstrate conclusively that those interventions that were maintained over a long period accelerated growth. In this book we have evaluated three sets of policy interventions: the promotion of specific industries or industrial subsectors, directed credit, and the export-push strategy. We conclude that promotion of specific industries generally did not work and therefore holds little promise for other developing economies. Directed credit has worked in certain situations but carries high risk. The export-push strategy has been by far the most successful of the three sets of policy intervention and holds the most promise for other developing economies.

Promoting Specific Industries Generally Did Not Work

Industrial policy narrowly defined—that is, attempts to achieve more rapid productivity growth by altering industrial structure—was generally not successful. In Japan, Korea, Singapore, and Taiwan, China, promotion of specific industries had little apparent impact. Industrial growth tended to be market-conforming, and productivity change was not significantly higher in promoted sectors. Although governments in these four economies were undoubtedly trying to alter industrial structure to achieve more rapid productivity growth, with the exception of Singapore their industrial structures evolved largely in a manner consistent with market forces and factor-intensity-based comparative advantage.

It is not altogether surprising that industrial policy in Japan, Korea, and Taiwan, China, tended to be market conforming. These economies, although selectively promoting capital- and knowledge-intensive industries, still aimed to create profitable, internationally competitive firms. Taiwan, China, placed great emphasis on price competitiveness in evaluating the performance of its large public investments in intermediate and capital goods. Moreover, in Japan especially, but also in Korea, institutional mechanisms that stressed cooperative relations and exchange of information between firms and government introduced a large amount of market information into the process of industrial policy formulation. And the yardstick used to evaluate industrial policies' success—mainly export performance—provided a market test of the success or failure of the policy instruments chosen. Thus the seeming success of industrial policy in these three economies probably rests not on picking winners—that is, on the adroit selection of which industrial subsector to promote—but on the setting of export targets for promoted industries and the use of export performance to assess policies.

Our tests may have failed to capture one important aspect of industrial policy in Japan and Korea: information exchange in a competitive framework—in short, contests—may have lessened investment coordination problems and resulted in earlier and better investments in what ultimately became market-conforming sectors. But among the HPAEs, only Japan and Korea had the institutional capacity to organize and referee the kind of contests used in formulating and implementing industrial policies.

Despite their potential benefits, collaborative arrangements, especially when combined with access to scarce resources such as foreign exchange and credit, have a high risk of capture by the participants. Capture was avoided—and resource allocation may have been improved—in Japan and Korea by the combination of repeated relationships between business and government and the use of exports, not domestic GDP growth, as the yardstick by which the success of the industrial strategy was measured. In other HPAEs, such elaborate contests were not used—for example, in Hong Kong, Singapore, or Taiwan, China—or were unsuccessful, as in the cases of the heavy industrialization drive in Malaysia or recent attempts at technological leapfrogging in Indonesia.

Repressing Interest Rates and Directing Credit Worked Sometimes

All HPAEs controlled interest rates on deposits and loans during much of their rapid growth. Low real interest rates on deposits and loans increased corporate equity by transferring resources from savers (mostly households) to borrowers (mostly firms). At the same time, by limiting the spread between deposit rates and loan rates, governments prevented banks from earning excessive rents. On the downside, such controls undoubtedly discouraged banks from taking on riskier, nontraditional clients.

Interest rate repression was key to the HPAEs' directed-credit programs. Low interest rates on loans resulted in excess demand for credit, which permitted governments to take an active role in credit rationing. This in turn gave governments strong leverage with which to influence the behavior of firms. In this section we discuss why directed credit was relatively successful in the HPAEs but often had large negative consequences elsewhere. We then consider whether such policies could be effectively adopted in the increasingly open capital markets of most developing economies.

Interest rate subsidies were smaller in the HPAEs than in other developing economies. In several HPAEs, government-directed credit served primarily to signal commercial banks and private investors which sectors enjoyed government support. Banks and private investors then selected projects within those sectors and offered them additional funding at commercial rates. Moreover, credit was frequently allocated according to export performance. Our evidence leads us to conclude that credit programs directed at exports yielded high social returns and, in the cases of Japan and Korea, other directed-credit programs also may have increased investment and generated important spillovers. Even within East Asia, however, when interest rate subsidies were large, or export performance criteria were not imposed, directed credit often went to inefficient ventures and those with low social returns.

The financial sector policies used by the HPAEs in the 1960s through the early 1980s took place in a world economy in which it was possible to close domestic capital markets. Since the early 1970s, developing economies have become ever more integrated with the global capital market. While this has reduced governments' already limited ability to restrict capital flight and speculative capital inflows, it has also given them access to less expensive capital and offered them better possibilities to hedge external shocks. At the same time, increased integration has constrained policymakers, who are finding it more and more difficult to maintain interest rates at variance with international markets.

The developing economies' growing integration with global financial markets can be seen in the evolution of their stock markets. Until the mid-1980s, foreign investors' access to domestic securities in developing economies was often restricted. Since then, fourteen of the twenty largest developing-economy stock markets have become substantially more open to foreign investment. The influence of international interest rates on domestic rates reflects a similar trend toward global integration. Indonesia, for example, began to open its capital accounts in 1971 and freed domestic interest rates in 1981. Since then, interest rates in Indonesia have followed international rates.

Although capital outflow restrictions are generally ineffective, they do hinder the movement of some institutional capital, for example, domestic pension funds. They may also hinder the flight of household and individual savings in instances when the transaction costs of sending capital abroad are greater than the incentive for doing so. Because these barriers do matter, developing economies continue to be less open financially than they are commercially. This can be seen in the ratio of gross capital flows to GDP compared with the ratio of exports-plus-imports to GDP. For the aggregate of all developing economies, the former is only 13 percent, while the latter is 45 percent.

Nonetheless, the limited impact of capital restrictions in deterring capital flight has persuaded a growing number of developing-economy governments to open to global financial markets. In some cases, for example, Chile and the Philippines, the removal of capital outflow regulations has had the paradoxical effect of stimulating a net inflow by assuring investors they can expatriate their money at will. Even where governments have not liberalized restrictions, the globalization of the economy, particularly increases in trade and advances in transport and telecommunications, is rapidly eroding the isolation of closed economies.

Under these conditions, the choice for developing-economy policymakers is not between financial integration with the global market and isolation. Rather, it is between two-way integration that permits outflows and thus facilitates inflows, on the one hand; and de facto one-way integration that consists primarily of unauthorized capital flight, on the other. The HPAEs have recognized this changing global environment; all are moving—albeit at different speeds—to liberalize their financial sectors and integrate them more closely into international financial markets.

Financial sector interventions—specifically repression of interest rates and contest-based direction of credit—may have contributed to rapid growth in such economies as Japan, Korea, and Taiwan, China. But each of these economies had competent and insulated bureaucracies and banks to select and monitor projects, and each applied export performance as the main yardstick for credit allocation. In addition, these governments were able during the early stages of rapid growth to close their financial markets to the outside world. Few developing economies today have the institutional resources to consistently impose performance-based criteria for credit allocation. Moreover, the capital markets of all economies are becoming more and more integrated. Thus, successful repression of interest rates and contest-based credit allocation may only be possible for the very few developing economies with strong institutions and then only to a very limited degree.

Export Push: A Successful Mix of Fundamentals and Interventions

The export-push strategy—the use of fundamentals and interventions to encourage rapid export growth—was the HPAEs' most broad based and successful application of selective interventions. Furthermore, of the many interventions tried in East Asia, those associated with their export push hold the most promise for other developing economies. While the changing trading environment will limit the use of highly targeted policies—similar to those of Japan and Korea during their early export growth—the broad pro-export stance characteristic of all eight HPAEs remains viable.

Trade policies in all the HPAEs (except Hong Kong) passed through an import-substitution phase with high and variable protection of domestic import substitutes. In all cases, however, policies that strongly favored the production of import substitutes to the detriment of exports were abandoned, and HPAE governments adopted strategic pro-export policies that established a free trade regime for exporters and offered a range of other incentives for exports. This export-push approach provided a mechanism by which industry moved rapidly toward international best practice, despite highly imperfect world markets for technology.

Export-push strategies were implemented in three very different ways in the HPAEs. Hong Kong and Singapore established free trade regimes, linking their domestic prices to international prices; the export push was an outcome of the very limited size of the domestic market coupled with neutral incentives between producing for the domestic or international market. Both economies made export credit available, although they did not subsidize it, and Singapore focused its efforts on attracting foreign investment in exporting firms.

In Japan, Korea, and Taiwan, China, incentives were essentially neutral *on average* between import substitutes and exports. But within the traded goods sector, export incentives coexisted with substantial remaining protection of the domestic market. Export incentives, moreover, were not neutral among industries or firms. There was an effort in Japan, Korea, Singapore, and Taiwan China, to promote specific exporting industries. Protection was combined with either compulsion or strong incentives to export. In Korea, firm-specific export targets were employed; in Japan and Taiwan, China, access to subsidized export credit and undervaluation of the currency acted as an offset to the protection of the local market.

In the HPAEs that intervened selectively to promote exports, contests based on performance in global markets played the allocative role that is normally ascribed to neutral exposure of both import-substituting and exporting industries to international competition. But these contest-based incentive structures required high government institutional capability. One of the keys to success of the export push in some of the HPAEs, especially Japan and Korea, was the government's ability to combine co-operation with competition. They were able to do this first, because their civil services and public institutions were largely staffed by competent and honest civil servants, and second, because firms and bureaucrats knew that there was a single yardstick for performance: exports.

Export targets provided a consistent yardstick to measure the success of market interventions. When protected sectors interfered with the exports of other sectors, exporters could successfully seek redress. For example, domestic content rules imposed on foreign direct investors in Taiwan, China were suspended when they interfered with exports. The emphasis on export competitiveness gave businesses and bureaucrats a transparent and objective system to gauge the desirability of specific actions. Interventions could not be made arbitrarily, as these could be appealed at a higher level of government if they interfered with exports.

The more recent export push-efforts of the Southeast Asian newly industrializing economies (NIEs) have relied less on highly specific incentives and more on gradual reductions in import protection, coupled with institutional support of exporters and a duty-free regime for inputs into exports. Recent strategies to attract direct foreign investment in Indonesia, Malaysia, and Thailand have also been explicitly export oriented. Direct foreign investment in many other developing economies is too often directed at serving a protected domestic market and hedged by restrictions on exports.

The Export-Push Strategy in a Changing Trading Environment

The early HPAE export drives—those of Hong Kong, Japan, Korea, Singapore, and Taiwan, China—took place amid the expanding world economy of the 1950s to the mid-1970s. Economic growth in the industrial economies was rapid, barriers to trade were declining, and global efforts to spur free trade under the General Agreement on Tariffs and Trade (GATT) were the order of the day. Times have changed. Economic growth has slackened in the mature economies that traditionally provided the main markets for developing-economy exports. Regional trade groupings are becoming more and more prominent. Industrial economies have begun to retaliate against allegedly unfair export practices by imposing quotas or countervailing duties. In such a trading environment, can today's developing economies successfully emulate the export-push strategies of the early HPAEs?

In the following section we break this question into two parts. First, will there be adequate, open markets for developing-economy manufactured exports? Second, will the need for market access constrain the developing economies' use of export-push strategies? We conclude that markets will be adequate and open and that an export push, therefore, remains possible. However, global realities will limit developing economies' ability to adopt the more interventionist instruments of export promotion. The experience of both the northern HPAEs, with their mixed export-push regimes in which protection of the domestic market coexisted with incentives or requirements to export, and the Southeast Asian NIEs, with their gradual trade liberalizations coupled with improvements in export institutions and availability of export credit, suggests that economies that are in the process of trade liberalization would benefit from providing specific incentives to manufactured exports. Modest subsidies to exports could be linked, for example, to the bias against exports in the domestic economy and bound by strict time limits linked to the pace of trade policy reform.

Moreover, if there are important externalities to exporting, a further tilt toward exports can be justified on welfare-economic grounds, even if the trade regime is neutral between import substitutes and exports. This might argue for functional export promotion measures such as guaranteeing access to export credit, providing tax incentives, or improving market access for small and medium exporters. But, these measures will need to follow internationally acceptable rules to assure market access in importing economies, and must be of limited duration. Fiscal discipline, moreover, will require that the costs of promotional programs be kept in check.

Why There Will Be Adequate Markets

The success of the southern-tier HPAEs' export drives in the late 1970s and 1980s, along with the continued rapid growth of exports from the northern HPAEs, indicates that export drives can succeed even when industrial-economy markets are not expanding rapidly. In contrast with the success of earlier export drives, which depended primarily on increased consumption in the industrial economies, the later drives have depended on consumers in industrial economies buying goods made in Asia instead of goods made elsewhere. If industrial-economy markets remain open, developing-economy exports can continue to expand in this manner.

Contrary to concerns in some high-income economies about a flood of exports from the developing world, these exports remain tiny relative to the size of the major, industrial economies. In 1980, developing-economy exports of manufactured goods accounted for just 2.4 percent of total manufactured goods consumption in the European Community (EC), North America, and Japan. By 1988, despite the success of Asian and other exporters, this had grown to just 3.1 percent. Even if exports from all developing economies had grown as fast as those from Korea during this period, their total share would still have amounted to only 3.7 percent of total consumption by 1988 (World Bank 1992b).

The scope for export expansion remains substantial. Indeed, individual developing economies, particularly smaller economies currently contemplating an export-led expansion, could safely assume that demand for their products is infinitely elastic. This is even true for Hong Kong's exports, which in 1990 accounted for a hefty 2.4 percent of world merchandise trade (Riedel 1988). Emerging exporters are unlikely to approach this level for many years to come. In 1989, for example, Sub-Saharan Africa's exports of manufactured goods amounted to just 0.43 percent of world exports (United Nations 1992).

Even if industrial economy markets gradually become less accessible, changes in the global trading environment are creating new opportunities for South-South trade. As recently as the mid-1980s, import-substitution strategies in most developing economies forced developing-economy exporters to rely heavily on industrial-economy markets. Since then, formerly closed economies in Asia, Sub-Saharan Africa, the Middle East, and Latin America have responded to debt problems, slow growth, and the need to raise fresh capital by becoming more and more outward oriented—and therefore more open to imports. They have assumed greater obligations under the GATT and through numerous regional trading arrangements.[1] Under these circumstances, the potential for South-South trade has increased considerably.

But while global markets are growing, they are also becoming more and more competitive. Each economy seeking to emulate the East Asian export-push model will encounter difficulties because many other economies are trying to do the same. For example, Collins and Rodrik (1991) estimate that Eastern Europe and the republics of the former Soviet Union will increase their share of world trade from 10 to 23 percent, relying initially on agricultural commodities and labor-intensive goods that compete directly with the products of other developing economies.

Despite this heightened competition, several trends suggest that expanding global markets will remain open to developing-economy manufactured exports. One of these is the continuing effort to open markets under the auspices of the GATT (see box 7.1). The other is the growing role of regional trading blocs, which present a major opportunity for increased global trade (see box 7.2). Who provides the market if all economies push exports? The dramatic growth of trade within Asia makes clear that export-oriented economies create markets for imports. To compete internationally, exporters must meet global standards of quality and price, for which they need access to technology, capital, and intermediate inputs at world prices. As a result, production in Asia has become more and more international, with capital goods coming from Japan, labor-intensive assembly being performed in low-

Box 7.1 Increased Access under the GATT

THE GATT HAS BEEN INSTRUMENTAL IN FACILITATING FREER trade. Since the end of World War II, tariff rates around the world have plummeted. Among the major industrial economies, weighted-average tariff levels have been lowered to below 5 percent. The current Uruguay Round of trade negotiations is addressing:

- Increasing market access, including more open trade in agriculture, textiles, and natural resources and the removal or reduction of remaining tariff and nontariff barriers
- Extending the GATT to new areas, principally trade in services, standards, and the enforcement of intellectual property rights, and trade-related investment requirements imposed by governments
- Strengthening GATT rules, especially those covering antidumping, subsidization, product standards, import licensing, "safeguards" (temporary import protection), and dispute settlement.

In short, the Uruguay Round is covering a broad, ambitious agenda. Even at this late date it is impossible to know how successful the round will be. Success could offer important opportunities for developing-economy exports, particularly in such areas as agriculture and tropical products. Progress in eliminating the Multifibre Arrangement would also bring major benefits, particularly to new entrants into textiles and apparel—although here some economies might lose existing rents. At the same time, however, a successful Uruguay Round may erode preferential treatment thus far accorded some developing economies. Developing-economy governments may be obliged to toughen their enforcement of intellectual property rights, while easing trade-related investment requirements. They could also face tougher rules of origin and anticircumvention measures concerning dumping allegations. On the whole, however, the Uruguay Round holds considerable promise for the developing economies.

Conversely, developing economies would lose important opportunities if the round fails. These would be particularly serious in agriculture because the global nature of agriculture markets makes regional solutions ineffective. Developing economies would also be adversely affected by the increased use of unilateral and bilateral restrictions in the event of a GATT failure.

Box 7.2 Regional Trading Blocs

PROGRESS TOWARD GLOBAL INTEGRATION COULD be reversed if the world economy splits into regional trading blocs, each centered on a major currency and closed to outsiders (Thurow 1992). Some observers worry that the emerging regional trading blocs will impose subtle and not-so-subtle protectionist measures. In both the European Community (EC) and the North American Free Trade Area (NAFTA), for example, firms are already lobbying for rules to limit the market access of extra-regional competitors. Typically these rules require that products entering one member economy contain a minimum regional content to qualify for entry to the markets of other members. (In the United States–Canada Free Trade Area, a 50 percent regional value-added content requirement was required for eligibility for regional access. In the NAFTA, there are special rules for automobiles and textiles. The textile provision is particularly protectionist—it requires triple transformation, such that finished clothing products have to be cut and sewn from fabric spun from North American fibers. This could result in considerable trade diversion.) Regional blocs may also tighten enforcement of rules against dumping as another means of protection.

But concerns about regional protectionist tendencies are easily overstated. Unlike their predecessors, the new blocs go beyond liberalization of trade to include liberalization of investment (Lawrence 1993). This in turn necessitates the liberalization of national production standards that would otherwise raise the cost of regionally integrated production. Moreover, in each instance where regional economic groups are emerging, the motivation has been at least partly to further access to global markets and international capital flows. Stronger regional integration need not be associated with higher external barriers. Indeed, regional blocs could have positive global effects, provided the blocs remain open to trade from outside. Deeper integration within Europe, for example, will facilitate trade with the rest of the world. A common set of standards makes it easier for *all* who wish to sell in Europe—not just insiders. Tough rules to prevent governments from subsidizing domestic firms aid all competitors, not only those located in the European Community.

Emerging regional arrangements may provide an incentive for some economies to open more rapidly than they would have otherwise. For example, the formation of the EC was an important impulse for the Kennedy Round (Lawrence 1993). As Mexico moved into the NAFTA negotiations, it simultaneously made overtures toward the Pacific and toward Central and South America. Mexico is now seeking to join the OECD, is negotiating to form a free trade area with Venezuela and Chile, and has signed agreements for freer trade with several Central American economies.

Developing economies will be affected differently by the emergence of regional blocs. Economies that currently enjoy preferential access to the U.S. and EC markets under schemes such as the generalized system of preferences, the Caribbean Basin Initiative, and the Lomé Convention are likely to see the value of these privileges erode. If, however, regional arrangements further multilateral liberalization, they will open new opportunities for trade, and if blocs succeed in stimulating the growth of their members, those outside the regions will find increased export opportunities.

wage economies such as Indonesia and Thailand, and more sophisticated operations such as design, marketing, and finance being provided from Hong Kong, Singapore, and Taiwan, China. Thus despite its reputation for protection, Asia has generated particularly rapid increases in trade.

How the Need for Market Access Will Constrain Interventions

Developing economies seeking to increase trade and attract investment will experience greater pressures to open their economies and bring their practices more closely in line with those in industrial economies. Those that attempt to use more interventionist versions of the export-push model will risk retaliation from industrial-economy markets or punishment under the GATT. For some policy options, such as financial repression, increasing integration with global markets will limit the scope for intervention.

Over the years, developing economies have claimed and received exemptions from GATT rules (Whalley 1990). By invoking Article XII, to safeguard their balance of payments, or Article XVIII, which allows promotion of infant industries, developing economies have been able to escape GATT disciplines more or less indefinitely. Thus developing economies have been free to implement trade policies of their choice at home while benefiting from the openness of industrial economies. But as GATT shifts from a narrow focus on tariffs to a broad approach that seeks agreements on rules, developing economies will find it more and more difficult to hang onto exemptions. Under Uruguay Round proposals, rules governing intellectual property, subsidies, countervailing duties, and trade-related investment would eventually be the same for industrial and developing economies. Although developing economies would have up to eight years to bring their practices into line, the trade obligations of developing economies clearly are increasing. Changing rules about dumping illustrate the case. Industrial economies are increasingly applying antidumping and countervailing duty measures to developing economy exports (Lawrence 1991). These measures will make it more difficult to follow the example of Japan and Korea, which protected domestic industry in order to subsidize exports.

Developing economies that seek access to the emerging regional trading blocs may find that it comes tied to increased obligations that could inhibit adoption of the interventionist policies. For example, interventionist versions of the export-push model could not be implemented within the EC with its stringent rules on state aid and its provisions allowing for the free movement of capital and for the community to implement competition policies. Moreover, no economy exposed to European competition could operate an effective infant industry strategy.

Does this imply the Asian export-push model is a historic relic? Clearly not. Indeed, an essential feature of the East Asian export push has been the ability to adapt to the global environment. The world market continues to present immense opportunities for those who export. New opportunities emerge as economies everywhere liberalize and the NIEs shift to the production of more advanced products. Moreover, Asian exporters have prospered during the past two decades despite a decline in global growth and a rise in protectionist actions.

Exports can be promoted by a variety of means that are consistent with developing economies' emerging obligations for market access and limited subsidies. Improved institutions—making customs services, duty drawbacks, and free trade status for exporters and their suppliers work well—are all consistent with agreements on international trade and are effective mechanisms for export promotion. Access to export credit, while more controversial, was an effective instrument in all of the HPAEs and remains feasible for other developing economies.

■ ■ ■

We began this book with the objective of understanding East Asia's success. We found that the diversity of experience, the variety of institutions, and the great variation in policies among the high-performing Asian economies means that there is no East Asian model of rapid growth with equity. Rather, each of the eight economies we studied used various combinations of policies at different times to perform the functions needed for rapid growth: rapid accumulation, efficient allocation, and high rates of productivity improvement. Most of the policies that the HPAEs used reflected sound economic fundamentals: they enhanced the working of markets, helped prices communicate information about relative economic costs, and fostered competitive discipline.

Some economies—notably Japan, Korea, and Taiwan, China—went beyond fundamentals and intervened in markets with industrial, trade, and financial sector policies. On balance, some of these interventions contributed to their extraordinary growth, but this was only possible because of highly unusual historical and institutional circumstances. The governments in these economies were more successful than most in combining the benefits of economic cooperation with the benefits of vigorous competition. They did this by creating contests with exports as the yardstick of success, with subsidized credit and other government-controlled favors as prizes and with government officials as competent and usually honest referees. In other economies, including some of the HPAEs, similar interventionist policies have failed, largely because governments offered incentives without a clear link to economic performance and strong institutional support. They offered prizes but lacked the rules and referees.

What can other developing economies learn from the East Asian miracle? While there is no recipe for success, there are some positive lessons: keep the macroeconomy stable; focus on early education; do not neglect agriculture; use banks to build a sound financial system; be open to foreign ideas and technology; and let relative prices reflect economic scarcities. And there are some negative ones: promoting specific industries or attempting to leap stages of technological development will generally fail; strongly negative real interest rates and large subsidies to borrowers debilitate the financial system; and directing credit without adequate monitoring and selection of borrowers distorts allocation. Finally, we found that a successful export push, whether it results from an open economy and strong economic fundamentals, or from a combination of strong fundamentals and prudently chosen interventions, offers high economic gains. Of all the interventions we surveyed, those to promote exports were the most readily compatible with a wide diversity of economic circumstances.

East Asia's own responses to changing domestic and international circumstances put these lessons in perspective. The HPAEs are themselves involved in a continuing process of reform, adapting policy instruments and institutions to achieve the objectives of continued growth with equity. In many cases these reforms involve reducing, modifying, or abandoning policy instruments that were judged to have succeeded in the past. Korea's financial sector reform, Indonesia's trade reforms, Thailand's promotion of foreign investment, and Malaysia's privatization programs are cases in point. The outcome of these initiatives will provide further valuable lessons on how successful policy instruments shift over time, as the relative roles of markets, the public administration, and the private sector change in response to economic and social development.

The experience of the HPAEs broadens our understanding of the range of policies that contribute to rapid growth. It also teaches us that willingness to experiment and to adapt policies to changing circumstances is a key element in economic success. What we have not discovered fully is why the governments of these economies have been more willing and better able than others to experiment and adapt; answers go beyond economics to include the study of institutions and the related fields of politics, history, and culture. Taking such large realities into account complicates rather than simplifies the task of development. The challenge for policymakers becomes twofold: to use policies compatible with existing institutions and to avoid policies that exceed the economy's institutional capacity, while at the same time improving institutions in order to make a wider range of policy options available.

Note

1. In the past, regional arrangements were motivated by the desire to pursue import-substitution policies on a larger scale and were therefore doomed to failure; the more recent initiatives are motivated by a desire to consolidate more outward-oriented strategies. Subregional arrangements are flourishing: In Latin America, for example, these include the North American Free Trade Area; Mercosur (Argentina, Brazil, Paraguay, and Uruguay), which aims at a common market for goods and services by 1994; the Andean Pact (Bolivia, Colombia, and Venezuela, with Ecuador and Peru slated to join); the Central American Common Market (Costa Rica, El Salvador, Guatemala, Honduras, Nicaragua, and Panama); Caricom; and a free trade area between Chile and Mexico that aims at reducing tariffs to zero by 1998. While progress toward formal arrangements within Asia have been less apparent (although the free trade area within the Association of Southeast Asian Nations is an exception), intra-Asian trade has increased rapidly.

Bibliographic Note

THIS REPORT HAS DRAWN ON A WIDE RANGE OF MA-
terials, including specifically commissioned background
studies, outputs of related World Bank–sponsored research, economic and sector work carried out by Bank
operational staff, and the extensive academic literature
on the East Asian economies. Citations in the text and
footnotes refer to specific sources used. The principal sources and specific
contributions to individual chapters are discussed below. Lists of background and other commissioned papers and references for works cited are
at the end of this note.

Many members of the World Bank Staff assisted in the design of the
research and made helpful comments on one or more drafts of the report.
They include: Yoshiake Abe, Ramgopal Agarwala, Harold Alderman,
Paul Armington, Ahmad Ahsan, Mark Baird, Gerard Caprio, Ajay
Chhibber, Yoon-Je Cho, Jaime de Melo, Shanta Devarajan, Ron Dun-
can, William Easterly, Gunnar Eskeland, Delfin Go, Jeffery Hammer,
James Hansen, Gregory Ingram, Paul Isenman, Estelle James, Emmanuel
Jimenez, Christine Jones, Koji Kashiwaya, Homi Kharas, Miguel Kiguel,
Elizabeth King, Michael Kline, Brian Levy, Samuel Lieberman, Will
Martin, Deepak Mazumdar, Saha Meyanathan, Vikram Nehru, Arvind
Panagariya, Martin Ravallion, D. C. Rao, Anandarup Ray, Setsuya Sato,
Andrew Sheng, Lyn Squire, Vinaya Swaroop, Shekhar Shah, Jee-Peng
Tan, Jacques Van der Gaag, Dominique van de Walle, Dimitri Vittas,
Andrew Warner, David Wheeler, Shahid Yusuf, and Heng-Fu Zou.

Those outside the World Bank who contributed with comments and
material include: Alice Amsden, New School for Social Research; Masahiko
Aoki, Stanford University; Jere Behrman, University of Pennsylvania;
Robert Cassen, Oxford University; Gary Fields, Cornell University; Richard

Freeman, Harvard University; Richard Hanushek, University of Rochester; Shigeru Ishikawa, Ayoama Gakuin University; Hirohisa Kohama, University of Shizuoka; Kazuo Koike, Hosei University; Lawrence J. Lau, Stanford University; David Lindauer, Vassar College; Kazushi Ohkawa, International Development Center of Japan; Kenichi Ohno, University of Tsukuba; Moises Naim, Carnegie Endowment for International Peace; Peter Petri, Brandeis University; Gustav Ranis, Yale University; Changyong Rhee, University of Rochester; Helmut Reisen, OECD; Hilton Root, Stanford University; Il Sakong, Institute for International Economics, Seoul; Herman van der Tak; Shujiro Urata, Waseda University; Robert Wade, Institute for Advanced Study, Princeton; and Toru Yanagihara, Hosei University.

Chapter 1

The data for this chapter are taken from the data base compiled for a research project, How Do National Policies Affect Long-Term Growth? directed by William Easterly and Ross Levine. It is an expanded version of the data contained in Summers and Heston (1991). A summary of the results of the research project are contained in a symposium issue of the *Journal of Monetary Economics* (forthcoming). Additional data are drawn from the World Bank Economic and Social Data Base (BESD) and from the *World Development Report* data base. The TFP estimates were made possible by access to preliminary estimates of constant price capital stock series developed by the Bank's International Economics Department, under the direction of Vikram Nehru (Nehru 1993). Stanley Fischer generously provided his country-specific estimates of TFP growth, which underlay the results reported in Fischer (1993).

Maurice Schiff (1993) provided calculations of agricultural incentives in East and South Asia, based on the methods developed in Schiff and Valdes (1992). The discussion of export performance is drawn primarily from Bhattacharya and Page (1992). Analysis of the demographic transition is drawn primarily from Birdsall and Sabot (1993). Ed Campos (1993) provided most of the background work on income distribution. The discussion of private investment draws heavily on Madarassay and Pfeffermann (1992). Box 1.1 draws on Birdsall and Sabot (1993). Box 1.2 draws on Pack (1993) and Pack and Page (1993).

Substantial research on the economic transition in China has been conducted by the Macroeconomics and Transitional Economies Division of the World Bank's Policy Research Department. This research effort which is led by I. J. Singh is summarized in Chen, Jefferson, and

Singh (1992). The Asian Miracle Research Project has also funded research by professor Shigeru Ishikawa and his associates on the rapid growth of China's coastal provinces. Preliminary outputs of that research will be available in the fall of 1993.

Chapter 2

This chapter draws primarily on Pack (1993), Page and Petri (1993), and Stiglitz (1993). The description of contests also draws on Leipziger and Kim (1993), Uy (1993), Okuno-Fujiwara (1993), and Ito (1993). *World Development Report 1991* provides the basis for the discussion of the market-friendly approach. Box 2.1 draws on *World Development Report 1991*. Box 2.2 draws on a paper prepared by Nancy Birdsall and John Page for the Colloquium on Lessons of East Asia, February 1993. Box 2.3 draws on material provided by Jaime de Melo. Helpful discussions with Vinod Thomas, Robert Wade, and participants in the Development Economics Study Group, Tokyo, and the Trade and Development Seminar at Stanford University contributed to the chapter.

Chapter 3

This chapter draws on Bhattarcharya and Pangestu (1993); Christensen, Dollar, Siamwalla, and Vichyanond (1993); Corden (1993); Dahlman and Sananikone (1993); Leipziger and Kim (1993); and Salleh, Yeah, and Meyanathan (1993). Many of the data on macroeconomic performance are drawn from a research project, How Do National Policies Affect Long-Term Growth? directed by William Easterly and Ross Levine. The concept of "export push" is due to Colin Bradford (1990). William Easterly, Lant Pritchett, and Michael Walton provided major inputs. Box 3.1 draws on Corden (1993). William Easterly prepared box 3.2. Box 3.3 is based on Ira C. Magaziner and Mark Patinkin, *The Silent War* (New York: Random House, 1988), by permission. Box 3.4 was prepared by Varuni Dayaratna.

Chapter 4

Chiah Siow Yue, Oh-Hyun Chang, Chaianan Samudavanija, Hadi Soesastro, and Bruce Tolentino provided information and analysis for their countries. Hilton Root and Mary Shirley made important contributions. Discussion of the role of small and medium-size enterprises has drawn heavily on the results of a research project, Support Systems for Small and Medium Enterprises in East Asia, directed by Brian Levy.

Chapter 5

Material on human capital accumulation is drawn primarily from Birdsall and Sabot (1993). Robert Cassen provided the material on vocational training. Data and analysis on savings and investment are drawn primarily from Uy (1993), Stiglitz (1993a, 1993b), and Stiglitz and Murdock (1993). Yoon Je Cho, Dimitri Vittas, and Andrew Sheng made important contributions to the analysis of financial repression, based on the results of a research project, Effectiveness of Credit Policies in East Asia. The section on tax policy draws on Shah (forthcoming) and on preliminary results of a research project, Tax Policy and Tax Administration in East Asia. Discussion of the relative price of investment goods is based on data drawn from Pfeffermann and Madarassay (1992). Lant Pritchett made important contributions to the chapter.

Box 5.1 was written by Myriam Quispe. Box 5.2 was prepared by Leora Friedberg. Andrew Sheng provided the material on which box 5.3 is based. Box 5.4 was written by Jennifer Keller.

Chapter 6

The discussion of labor market performance is based primarily on Birdsall and Sabot (1993) and draws on contributions by Fields (1993), Freeman (1993), and Ranis (1993). The discussion of the capital market draws primarily on Uy (1993), Stiglitz (1993a, 1993b), and on contributions by Andrew Sheng, Yoon-Je Cho, and Dimitri Vittas. The sections on industrial policy and exports are based on Pack (1993) and Pack and Page (1993). Data on export performance are drawn from the BESD and *World Development Report 1991* data bases. Discussion at the 1993 Carnegie-Rochester Conference on Public Policy were helpful in improving the sections on export externalities and growth.

Box 6.1 was written by Brian Levy. Box 6.2 was prepared by Leora Friedberg. Box 6.3 draws on a recently completed internal World Bank report on Indonesia's industrial sector. Box 6.4 was prepared by Leora Friedberg. Box 6.5 was prepared by Danny Leipziger.

Chapter 7

Discussions of the international trading environment and boxes 7.1 and 7.2 are drawn from Lawrence (1993). Discussion of the international capital market is largely based on *Global Economic Prospects and the Developing Countries* (World Bank 1993a). Vinod Thomas made a number of helpful comments.

Background Papers

Behrman, Jere R., and Ryan Schneider. "An International Perspective on Schooling Investment in the Last Quarter Century in Some Fast-Growing Eastern and Southeastern Countries."

Birdsall, Nancy, and Richard H. Sabot. "Virtuous Circles: Human Capital Growth and Equity in East Asia."

Campos, Ed. "The Institutional Foundations of High-Speed Growth in the High-Performing Asian Economies: Part I, Insulation Mechanisms and Public Sector–Private Sector Relations."

___. "The Institutional Foundations of High-Speed Growth in the High-Performing Asian Economies: Part II, The Bureaucracy as an Instrument of Development."

Chia, Siow Yue. "The Role of Institutions in Singapore's Economic Success."

Corden, W. Max. "Seven Asian Miracle Economies: Overview of Macroeconomic Policies."

Dekle, Robert. "Raising Saving Rates: Lessons from the Japanese Experience."

Fields, Gary S. "Changing Labor Market Conditions and Economic Development in Hong Kong, Korea, Singapore and Taiwan."

Freeman, Richard. "Does Suppression of Labor Contribute to Economic Success? Labor Relations and Markets in East Asia."

Kim, Chang-Shik. "Government-Business Relationship in Korea: Selective Case Studies."

___. "Trade Policy and Industrial Transformation in Korea."

Lawrence, Robert Z. "The Global Environment for the East Asian Model."

Murdock, K., and Joseph E. Stiglitz. "The Effect of Financial Repression in an Economy with Positive Real Rates."

Pack, Howard. "Industrial and Trade Policies in the High-Performing Asian Economies."

Pack, Howard, and John M. Page, Jr. "Accumulation, Exports and Growth in the High-Performing Asian Economies."

Page, John M., Jr., and Peter A. Petri. "Productivity Change and Strategic Growth Policy in the Asian Miracle."

Ranis, Gustav. "Labor Markets, Human Capital and Development Performance in East Asia."

Samudavanija, Chaianan. "High Speed Growth and High Performance in a Technocratic Polity: The Thai Case."

Shah, Shekhar, and Subodh C. Mathur. 1992. "Sources of Labor Market Flexibility in East Asia: A Review of Selected Issues."

Stiglitz, Joseph E. "Some Lessons from the Asian Miracle."

Uy, Marilou. "The Role of Capital Markets and the Role of Government."

Studies of the High-Performing Asian Economies

These papers will be published shortly as World Bank Country Studies under the series title The Lessons of East Asia.

Bhattacharya, Amar, and Mari Pangestu. "Indonesia: Development Transformation since 1965 and the Role of Public Policy."

Chau, Leung Chuen. "Hong Kong: A Unique Case of Development."

Christensen, Scott, David Dollar, Ammar Siamwalla, and Pakorn Vichyanond. "Thailand: The Institutional and Political Underpinnings of Growth."

Dahlman, Carl, and Ousa Sananikone. "Taiwan, China: Policies and Institutions for Rapid Growth."

Kim, Kiwan, and Danny Leipziger. "Korea: A Case of Government-Led Development."

Leipziger, Danny, and Vinod Thomas. "Country Lessons from East Asia."

Petri, Peter. "Government Policy and East Asia's Success."

Salleh, Ismael, Kim Leng Yeah, and Saha Dhevan Meyanathan. "Malaysia: Growth, Equity, and Structural Transformation."

Soon, Teck-Won, and C. Suan Tan. "Singapore: Public Policy and Economic Development."

Thomas, Vinod, and Yan Wang. "Government Policies and Productivity Growth: Is East Asia an Exception?"

Studies of Public Policy in Japan

These papers were presented at a Seminar on Public Policy during Japan's Rapid Growth, Tokyo, January 1993.

Horiuchi, Akiyoshi. "Government Control of Financial Mechanism in Postwar Japan: A Tentative Report."

Itoh, Motoshige. "Industrial Policy and Corporate Growth in the Automobile Industry: Japan's Postwar Experience."

Koike, Kazuo. "Human Resource Development Systems in Japan."

Kuroda, Masahiro, Takanobu Nakajima, and Kanji Yoshioka. "Industrial Policy and Economic Growth in Japan 1960–1985: Preliminary Report."

Kuroda, Masahiro, and Shoko Negishi. "Comparison of the Structural Changes in Asian Countries: Outline."

Maki, Atsushi. "The Relation between Household Saving Rate and Economic Growth: Consumer Stimulus to Purchase Durable Goods."

Ohno, Kenichi. "Dynamism of Japanese Manufacturing: Evidence from the Postwar Period."

Okuno-Fujiwara, Masahiro. "Government Business Relationship in Japan: A Comparative Institutional Analysis."

Shimomura, Yasutami. "Industrial Policy in the Rapid Growth Period: Evidence from Early Writings."

Teranishi, Juro. "Emergence and Establishment of the Financial System in Postwar Japan: Government Intervention, Indirect Financing and the Corporate Monitoring System."

Ueda, Kazuo. "The Industrial Bank of Japan and Public Financial Institutions."

Urata, Shujiro. "Technological Progress by Small and Medium Enterprises in Japan."

Yoshikawa, Hiroshi. "Demand-Led Growth and Income Distribution: The Postwar Japanese Experience."

Yoshino, Naoyuki. "The Low Interest Policy and Economic Growth of Japan."

References

Ahluwalia, Isher Judge. 1985. *Industrial Growth in India.* New Delhi: Oxford University Press.

Aigner, D., and P. Schmidt, eds. 1980. "Specification and Estimation of Frontier Production, Profit, and Cost Functions," a special issue of *Journal of Econometrics* 13: 1–138.

Amsden, Alice H. 1989. *Asia's Next Giant: South Korea and Late Industrialization.* New York: Oxford University Press.

Ando, Albert, and Franco Modigliani. 1963. "The Life Cycle Hypothesis of Savings: Aggregate Implications and Tests." *American Economic Review* 53(1).

Arrow, Kenneth J. 1969. "Classificatory Notes on the Production and Transmission of Technological Knowledge." *American Economic Review* 59(2): 29–35.

Asian Wall Street Journal. 1993. "Matsushita Builds Export Base in Malaysia." May 18.

Aw, Bee-Yan, and Amy R. Hwang. 1993. "Productivity and the Export Market: A Firm Level Analysis." Pennsylvania State University, State College, Pa.

Aw, Bee-Yan, and Hong W. Tan. 1993. "Training, Technological Capacity, and Firm Level Productivity." Working Paper. World Bank, Private Sector Development Department, Washington, D.C.

Balassa, Bela. 1982. *Development Strategies in Semi-Industrializing Economies.* Baltimore, Md.: Johns Hopkins University Press.

———. 1991. *Economic Policies in the Pacific Area Developing Countries.* New York: New York University Press.

Balassa, Bela, and Associates. 1971. *The Structure of Protection in Developing Countries.* Baltimore, Md.: Johns Hopkins University Press.

Balassa, Bela, and Marcus Noland. 1988. *Japan and the World Economy.* Washington, D.C.: Institute for International Economics.

The Banker. 1990 (July): 155–85.

Barro, Robert J. 1989. "A Cross-Country Study of Growth, Savings, and Government." NBER Working Paper 2855, Cambridge, Mass.

———. 1990. "Government Spending in a Simple Model of Endogenous Growth." *Journal of Political Economy* 98 (5, pt.2): S103–25.

———. 1991. "Economic Growth in a Cross Section of Countries." *Quarterly Journal of Economics* 105(2): 407–43.

Barro, Robert J., and Jong-Wha Lee. 1993. "International Comparisons of Educational Attainment." Paper presented at a conference on How Do National Policies Affect Long-Run Growth? World Bank, Washington, D.C. February.

Behrman, Jere R. 1987. "Schooling in Developing Countries: Which Countries Are the Under- and Over-Achievers and What Is the Schooling Impact?" *Economics of Education Review* 6(2): 111–28.

Behrman, Jere R., and Ryan Schneider. 1991. "How Do Pakistani Schooling Investments Compare with Those of Other Developing Countries?" Williams College, Williamstown, Mass.

———. 1992. "An International Perspective on Schooling Investment in the Last Quarter Century in Some Fast-Growing Eastern and Southeastern Countries." Background paper for *The East Asian Miracle.* World

Bank, Policy Research Department, Washington, D.C.

Bell, Clive, Peter Hazell, and Roger Slade. 1982. *Project Evaluation in Regional Perspective*. Baltimore, Md.: Johns Hopkins University Press.

Berry, R. Albert, and William Cline. 1979. *Agrarian Structure and Productivity in Developing Countries*. Baltimore, Md.: Johns Hopkins University Press.

Berry, R. Albert, and Brian Levy. 1993. "Indonesia's Small and Medium Industrial Exporters and Their Support Systems." Report prepared for the World Bank, Policy Research Department, Washington, D.C.

Berry, R. Albert, and Richard H. Sabot. 1981. "Labor Market Performance in Developing Countries: A Survey." In Paul Streeten and R. Jolly, eds., *Recent Issues in World Development*. Oxford: Pergamon Press.

Bhagwati, Jagdish N. 1978. *Anatomy and Consequences of Exchange Control Regimes*. Cambridge, Mass.: Ballinger Press, for the National Bureau of Economic Research.

Bhagwati, Jagdish N., and T. N. Srinivasan. 1979. "Trade Policy and Development." In Rudiger Dornbusch and Jacob A. Frankel, eds., *International Economic Policy*. Baltimore, Md.: Johns Hopkins University Press.

Bhattacharya, Amar, and John M. Page, Jr. 1992. "Adjustment, Investment, and Growth in High-Performing Asian Economies." Paper presented at a conference on the New Development Economics in Global Context, American University in Cairo, May 28–30.

Bhattacharya, Amar, and Mari Pangestu. 1993. *Indonesia: Development Transformation since 1965 and the Role of Public Policy*. World Bank Country Study, Washington, D.C.

Biggs, Tyler, and Brian Levy. 1988. "Strategic Intervention and the Political Economy of Industrial Policy in Developing Countries." In Dwight Perkins and Michael Romer, eds., *Reforming Economic Systems in Developing Countries*. Cambridge, Mass.: Harvard Institute for International Development.

Birdsall, Nancy, David Ross, and Richard H. Sabot. 1993. "Underinvestment in Education: How Much Growth Has Pakistan Forgone?" Paper presented at the Ninth Annual General Meeting of the Pakistan Society of Development Economists, Islamabad, Pakistan, January.

Birdsall, Nancy, and Richard H. Sabot, eds. 1993a. *Opportunity Forgone: Education, Growth, and Inequality in Brazil*. World Bank, Washington, D.C.

___. 1993b. "Virtuous Circles: Human Capital Growth and Equity in East Asia." Background paper for *The East Asian Miracle*. World Bank, Policy Research Department, Washington, D.C.

Black, Stephen L., and Lance Taylor. 1974. "Practical General Equilibrium Estimation of Resource Pulls under Trade Liberalization." *Journal of International Economics* 4(1): 37–58.

Blomstrom, Magnus. 1989. *Foreign Investments and Spillovers*. London: Routledge.

Blumenthal, T. 1970. "Savings in Postwar Japan." East Asian Research Center, Harvard University, Cambridge, Mass.

Boadway, Robin, Dale Chua, and Frank Flatters. Forthcoming. "Investment Incentives and the Corporate Tax System in Malaysia." In Anwar Shah, ed., *Fiscal Incentives for Investment in Developing Countries*. New York: Oxford University Press.

Bonelli, R. 1992. "Growth and Productivity in Brazilian Industries: Impacts of Trade Orientation." *Journal of Development Economics* 39(1): 85–111.

Borrus, Michael, Laura D'Andrea Tyson, and John Zysman. 1986. "Credit Policy and International Competition." In Paul R. Krugman, ed., *Strategic Trade Policy and the New International Economics*. Cambridge, Mass.: MIT Press.

Boskin, Michael J., and Laurence J. Lau. 1992. "International and Intertemporal Comparison of Productive Efficiency: An Application of the Meta-Production Function Approach to the Group of Five Countries." *Economic Studies Quarterly* 43(4): 298–312.

Bradford, Colin I., Jr. 1986. "East Asian Models: Myths and Lessons." In John P. Lewis and Valeriana Kallab, eds., *Development Strategies Reconsidered*. U.S. Third World Policy Perspectives 5. Washington, D.C.: Overseas Development Council.

___. 1990. "Policy Interventions and Markets: Development Strategy Typologies and Policy Options." In Gary Gereffi and Donald L. Wyman, eds., *Manufacturing Miracles: Paths of Industrialization in Latin America and East Asia*. Princeton, N.J.: Princeton University Press.

Brimble, Peter John. 1993. "Industrial Development and Productivity Change in Thailand." Ph.D. diss., Johns Hopkins University, Baltimore, Md.

Bruton, Henry J., G. Abeysekera, N. Sanderatne, and Z. A. Yusof. 1993. *The Political Economy of Poverty, Equity, and Growth: Sri Lanka and Malaysia*. New York: Oxford University Press.

Calomiris, Charles W., and Charles P. Himmelberg. 1993. "Directed Credit Programs for Agriculture and Industry: Arguments from Theory and Fact." Paper presented at the Annual Bank Conference on Development Economics, World Bank, Washington, D.C., May 3–4.

Canning, David, and Marianne Fay. 1993. "The Effect of Infrastructure Networks on Economic Growth." Columbia University, New York, January.

Caprio, Gerard, Jr., Izak Atiyas, and James Hanson, eds. Forthcoming. *Financial Reform: Theory and Experience.* Cambridge: Cambridge University Press.

Carroll, Christopher, David Weil, and Lawrence H. Summers. 1993. "Savings and Growth: A Reinterpretation." Paper presented at the Carnegie-Rochester Public Policy Conference, Bradley Policy Research Center, April 23–24.

Chan, Steve, and Cal Clark. 1992. *Flexibility, Foresight and Fortune in Taiwan's Development: Navigating between Scylla and Charybdis.* London: Routledge.

Chant, John, and Mari Pangestu. Forthcoming. "An Assessment of Financial Reform in Indonesia: 1983–90." In Gerard Caprio, Jr., Izak Atiyas,, and James Hanson, eds., *Financial Reform: Theory and Experience.* Cambridge: Cambridge University Press.

Chen, Edward K.Y. 1979. *Hypergrowth in Asian Economies: A Comparative Survey of Hong Kong, Japan, Korea, Singapore and Taiwan.* London: Macmillan.

Chen, Kang, Gary H. Jefferson, and Inderjit Singh. 1992. "Lesson from China's Economic Reform." *Journal of Comparative Economics* 16: 201–25.

Chenery, Hollis B. 1959. "The Interdependence of Investment Decisions." In Moses Abramovitz, ed., *The Allocation of Economic Resources.* Stanford, Calif.: Stanford University Press.

___. 1960. "Patterns of Industrial Growth." *American Economic Review* 50(4): 624–54.

___. 1986. "Growth and Transformation." In Hollis B. Chenery, Sherman Robinson, and Moshe Syrquin, eds., *Industrialization and Growth: A Comparative Study.* New York: Oxford University Press.

Cheng, Hang-Sheng, ed. 1986. *Financial Policy and Reform in Pacific Basin Countries.* Lexington, Mass.: Lexington Books.

Chia, Ngee Choon, and John Whalley. Forthcoming. "Patterns in Investment Tax Incentives among Developing Countries." In Anwar Shah, ed., *Fiscal Incentives for Investment in Developing Countries.* New York: Oxford University Press.

Chia, Siow Yue. 1992. "The Role of Institutions in Singapore's Economic Success." Background paper for *The East Asian Miracle.* World Bank, Policy Research Department, Washington, D.C.

Chiu, Paul C. H. 1992. "Money and Financial Markets: The Domestic Perspective." In *Taiwan from Developing to Mature Economy.* Colorado: Westview.

Cho, Yoon Je, and Thomas Hellmann. 1993. "Government Intervention in Credit Market: An Alternative Interpretation of Japanese and Korean Experiences from the New Institutional Economics Perspective." Paper prepared for a World Bank research project on The Effectiveness of Credit Policies in East Asia. World Bank, Financial Sector Development Department, Washington, D.C.

Cho, Yoon Je, and Deena Khatkate. 1989. *Lessons of Financial Liberalization in Asia: A Comparative Study.* World Bank Discussion Paper 50. Washington, D.C.

Cho, Yoon Je, and Joon-Kyung Kim. 1993. "Credit Policies and Industrialization of Korea." World Bank, Financial Sector Development Department, Washington, D.C. February.

Christensen, Scott R., David Dollar, Ammar Siamwalla, and Pakorn Vichyanond. 1993. *Institutional and Political Bases of Growth-Inducing Policies in Thailand. Lessons of East Asia.* World Bank Country Study. Washington, D.C.

Clarke, George. 1992. "More Evidence on Income Distribution and Growth." Policy Research Working Paper 1064. World Bank, Policy Research Department, Washington, D.C.

Cohen, S. I. 1985. "A Cost-Benefit Analysis of Industrial Training." *Economics of Education Review* 4(4): 327–39.

Collins, Susan M., and Won-Am Park. 1989. "External Debt and Macroeconomic Performance in South Korea." In Jeffrey D. Sachs and Susan M. Collins, eds., *Developing Country Debt and Economic Performance,* vol. 3. Chicago: University of Chicago Press.

Collins, Susan M., and Dani Rodrik. 1991. *Eastern Europe and the Soviet Union in the World Economy.* Washington, D.C.: Institute for International Economics.

Corbo, Vittorio, and Klaus Schmidt-Hebbel. 1991. "Public Policy and Savings in Developing Countries." *Journal of Development Economics* 36(1): 89–115.

Corden, W. Max. 1971. *The Theory of Protection*. London: Oxford University Press.

___. 1974. *Trade Policy and Economic Welfare*. London: Oxford University Press.

___. 1993. "Seven Asian Miracle Economies: Overview of Macroeconomic Policies." Background paper for *The East Asian Miracle*. World Bank, Policy Research Department, Washington, D.C.

Dahlman, Carl J. 1990. "Technology Strategy in the Economy of Taiwan: Exploiting Foreign Linkages and Investing in Local Capability." World Bank, Private Sector Development Department, Washington, D.C.

Dahlman, Carl J., and Peter Brimble. 1990. "Technology Strategy and Policy for Industrial Competitiveness: A Case Study in Thailand." Industry Series Paper 24. World Bank, Industry and Energy Department, Washington, D.C.

Dahlman, Carl J., and Valdares Fonseca. 1987. "From Technological Dependence to Technological Development: The Case of the Usiminas Steel Plant in Brazil." In Jorge Katz, and others, eds., *Technology Generation in Latin American Manufacturing Industries*. London: Macmillan.

Dahlman, Carl J., and Ousa Sananikone. 1993. *Economic Policies and Institutions in the Rapid Growth of Taiwan, China. Lessons of East Asia*. World Bank Country Study. Washington, D.C.

Dasgupta, Partha, Amartya Sen, and Stephen Marglin. 1972. *Guidelines for Project Evaluation*. New York: United Nations Industrial Development Organization.

De Long, J. Bradford, and Lawrence H. Summers. 1991. "Equipment Investment and Economic Growth." *Quarterly Journal of Economics* 106(2): 445–502.

___. 1993. "How Robust Is the Growth-Machinery Nexus?" Paper presented at a conference on How Do National Policies Affect Long-Run Growth? World Bank, Washington, D.C., February.

de Melo, Jaime, Carl Hamilton, and L. Alan Winters. 1990. "Voluntary Export Restraints: A Case Study Focusing on Effects in Exporting Countries." Paper 464, Institute for International Economic Studies, Stockholm.

de Melo, Jaime, and Sherman Robinson. 1992. "Productivity and Externalities: Models of Export-Led Growth." *Journal of International Trade and Economic Development* 1: 41–69.

Deaton, Angus, and Christina Paxson. 1992. "Savings, Growth, and Aging in Taiwan." Paper presented at an NBER Conference on Aging, Caneel Bay, U.S. Virgin Islands, May 7–10.

Dekle, Robert. 1988. "Do the Japanese Elderly Reduce Their Total Wealth?" Reischauer Institute of Japanese Studies, Harvard University, Cambridge, Mass.

___. 1993. "Raising Saving Rates: Lessons from the Japanese Experience." Background paper for *The East Asian Miracle*. World Bank, Policy Research Department, Washington, D.C.

Dollar, David. 1990. "Outward Orientation and Growth: An Empirical Study Using a Price-Based Measure of Openness." World Bank, East Asia and Pacific Region, Country Department I, Washington, D.C.

___. 1992. "Outward-Oriented Developing Economies Really Do Grow More Rapidly: Evidence from 95 LDCs, 1976–1985." *Economic Development and Cultural Change* 40(3): 523–44.

Dollar, David, and Kenneth Sokoloff. 1990. "Patterns of Productivity Growth in South Korean Manufacturing Industries, 1963–79." *Journal of Development Economics* 33(2): 309–27.

Dornbusch, Rudiger, and Stanley Fischer. 1993. "Moderate Inflation." *World Bank Economic Review* 7(1): 1–44.

Easterly, William. 1993. "Explaining Miracles: Growth Regressions Meet the Gang of Four." Paper presented at the NBER's Fourth Annual East Asian Seminar on Economics, San Francisco, June 17–19.

Easterly, William, Michael Kremer, Lant Pritchett, and Lawrence H. Summers. 1993. "Good Policy or Good Luck? Country Growth Performance and Temporary Shocks." Paper presented at a conference on How Do National Policies Affect Long-Run Growth? World Bank, Washington, D.C., February.

Easterly, William, and Sergio Rebelo. 1993. "Fiscal Policy and Economic Growth: An Empirical Investigation." Paper presented at a conference on How Do National Policies Affect Long-Run Growth? World Bank, Washington, D.C., February.

Easterly, William, and Klaus Schmidt-Hebbel. Forthcoming. "The Macroeconomics of Public Sector Deficits: A Synthesis." In William Easterly, Carlos Rodriguez, and Klaus Schmidt-Hebbel, eds., *Public Sector Deficits and Macroeconomic Performance*. New York: Oxford University Press.

Edwards, Chris. 1990. "Protection and Policy in the Malaysian Manufacturing Sector." *Policy Assessment of the Malaysian Industrial Policy Study (MIPS) and the In-*

dustrial Master Plan (IMP), Volume 3. Vienna: United Nations Industrial Development Organization.

Edwards, Sebastian. 1988. *Exchange Rate Misalignment in Developing Countries.* Baltimore, Md.: Johns Hopkins University Press.

___. 1992. "Trade Orientation, Distortions and Growth in Developing Countries." *Journal of Development Economics* 39(1): 31–57.

Elias, Victor J. 1990. "The Role of Total Factor Productivity on Economic Growth." Background paper for the *World Development Report 1991.* World Bank, Office of the Vice President, Development Economics, Washington, D.C.

Erzan, Refik, Kiroaki Kuwahara, Serafino Marchese, and Rene Vossenar. 1989. "The Profile of Protection in Developing Countries." *UNCTAD Review* 1: 29–73.

Fanelli, José Maria, Roberto Frenkel, and Lance Taylor. 1992. "The World Development Report 1991: A Critical Assessment." Prepared as part of an UNCTAD-executed project to assist the Intergovernmental Group of Twenty-Four.

Far Eastern Economic Review. Various issues.

Farrell, M. J. 1957. "The Measurement of Productive Efficiency." *Journal of the Royal Statistical Society, Series A* 120 (part 3): 253–81.

Fecher, M., and S. Perelman. 1992. "Industrial Efficiency in OECD Countries." In R. Caves, ed., *Industrial Efficiency in Six Nations.* Cambridge, Mass.: MIT Press.

Federation of Bankers Association of Japan. 1991. "Japanese Banks."

John Fei, Shirley W. Y. Kuo, and Gustav Ranis. 1981. *The Taiwan Success Story: Rapid Growth with Improved Distribution in the Republic of China, 1952–79.* Boulder, Colo.: Westview.

Fields, Gary S. 1992. "Changing Labor Market Conditions and Economic Development in Hong Kong, Korea, Singapore, and Taiwan, China." Background paper for *The East Asian Miracle.* World Bank, Policy Research Department, Washington, D.C.

Fischer, Stanley. 1993. "Macroeconomic Factors in Growth." Paper presented at a conference on How Do National Policies Affect Long-Run Growth? World Bank, Washington, D.C., February.

Foundation for Advanced Information Research. 1991. "The Development of Financial and Capital Markets in the Asia-Pacific Region." Tokyo, Japan. September.

Freeman, Richard. 1992. "Does Suppression of Labor Contribute to Economic Success? Labor Relations and Markets in East Asia." Background paper for *The East Asian Miracle.* World Bank, Policy Research Department, Washington, D.C.

Freeman, Richard, and Martin L. Weitzman. 1987. "Bonuses and Employment in Japan." *Journal of Japanese and International Economics* 1(2): 168–94.

Frischtak, Claudio R., Bita Hadjimichael, and Ulrich Zachau. 1989. *Competition Policies for Industrializing Countries.* World Bank Policy and Research Series Paper 7. Washington, D.C.

Fry, Maxwell J. 1988. *Money, Interest, and Banking in Economic Development.* Baltimore, Md.: Johns Hopkins University Press.

Fukasaku, Kiichiro. 1992. "Economic Regionalization and Intra-Industry Trade: Pacific-Asian Perspectives." Technical Paper 53, OECD Development Centre, Paris.

Gelb, Alan H. 1989. "Financial Policies, Growth and Efficiency." PRE Working Paper 202. World Bank, Washington, D.C.

Gelb, Alan H., John Knight, and Richard H. Sabot. 1991. "Public Sector Employment, Rent Seeking and Economic Growth." *Economic Journal* 101(408): 1186–99.

Gerschenkron, Alexander. 1962. *Economic Backwardness in Historical Perspective.* Cambridge, Mass.: Harvard University Press.

Ghose, T. K. 1987. "The Banking System of Hong Kong." Butterworth (Asia) Ltd.

Giovannini, Alberto. 1983a. "Essays on Exchange Rates and Asset Markets." Ph.D. diss., Massachusetts Institute of Technology (MIT), Cambridge, Mass.

___. 1983b. "The Interest Elasticity of Savings in Developing Countries: The Existing Evidence." *World Development* 11(7): 601–07.

Gordon, David L. 1983. *Development Finance Companies, State and Privately Owned: A Review.* World Bank Staff Working Papers 578. World Bank, Washington, D.C.

Goto, Akira, and Ryuhei Wakasugi. 1988. "Technology Policy." In Ryutaro Komiya, Masahiro Okuno, Kotaro Suzumura, eds., *Industrial Policy of Japan.* New York: Academic Press, Inc.

Granger, Clive W. J. 1969. "Investigating Causal Relations by Econometric Models and Cross-Spectral Methods." *Econometrica* 37: 428–38.

Greenwald, B., and Joseph E. Stiglitz. 1986. "Externalities in Economies with Imperfect Information and Incomplete Markets." *Quarterly Journal of Economics* 101(2): 229–64.

___. 1988. "Pareto Inefficiency of Market Economies: Search and Efficiency Wage Models." *American Economic Review* 78(2): 351–55.

Gregory, Peter, and Deepak Lal. 1977. "Demand, Supply, and Structure: A Cross-Sectional Analysis of Manufacturing Wages." World Bank, Employment and Rural Development Division Working Paper, Washington, D.C.

Grossman, Gene, and Elhanan Helpman. 1991. *Innovation and Growth in the Global Economy.* Cambridge, Mass.: MIT Press.

Gupta, Kanhaya L. 1984a. *Finance and Economic Growth in Developing Countries.* London: Croom Helm.

___. 1984b. "Financial Liberalization and Economic Growth: Some Simulation Results." *Journal of Economic Development* 9(2): 25–34.

Haddad, Mona, and Ann E. Harrison. 1991. "Are There Dynamic Externalities from Direct Foreign Investment? Evidence From Morocco." Industry Series Paper No. 48. World Bank, Industry and Energy Department, Washington, D.C.

___. Forthcoming. "Are There Positive Spillovers from Direct Foreign Investment? Evidence from Panel Data for Morocco." *Journal of Development Economics.*

Haggard, Stephan. 1990. *Pathways from the Periphery.* Ithaca, N.Y.: Cornell University Press.

Halvorsen, Robert. Forthcoming. "Fiscal Incentives for Investment in Thailand." In Anwar Shah, ed., *Fiscal Incentives for Investment in Developing Countries.* New York: Oxford University Press.

Hamilton, Carl B. 1989. "The Political Economy of Transient 'New' Protectionism." *Welwirtschafliches Archive, Review of World Economics* 125: 522–46.

___, ed. 1990. *Textiles Trade and the Developing Countries: Eliminating the Multi-Fiber Arrangement in the 1990s.* Washington, D.C: World Bank.

Hanson, James, and Roberto Rocha. 1986. "High Interest Rates, Spreads, and the Costs of Intermediation: Two Studies." Industry and Finance Series 8. World Bank, Washington, D.C.

Hanushek, Eric A., and Richard H. Sabot. 1991. "Notes on Changes in Educational Performances." A paper prepared for PEER Meetings. Boston, Mass.

Harris, John, Fabio Schiantarelli, and Miranda G. Siregar. 1992. "The Effort of Financial Liberalization on Firms' Capital Structure and Investment Decisions: Evidence from a Panel of Indonesia Establishments, 1981–88." Paper presented at a conference on the Impact of Financial Reform, World Bank, Washington, D.C., April 2–3.

Harrison, Ann E. 1991. "Openness and Growth." PRE Working Paper 809. World Bank, Washington, D.C.

Hendrie, Anne. 1986. "Banking in the Far East: Structures and Sources of Finance." Financial Times Business Information, London.

Hill, Anne M., and Elizabeth King, eds. 1991. "Women's Education in Developing Countries: Barriers, Benefits, and Policy." PHREE Background Paper Series. World Bank, Washington, D.C.

Hon, Wong Seng. 1992. "Exploiting Information Technology: A Case Study of Singapore." *World Development* 20(12): 1817–28.

Hong, Won-Tak. 1989. "Korean Economy at Crossroads." *Sasang Quarterly* 1 (Summer).

Horioka, Charles Yuji. 1990. "Why Is Japan's Household Savings Rate So High? A Literature Survey." *Journal of Japanese and International Economics* 4: 49–92.

___. 1991. "The Determinants of Japan's Savings Rate: The Impact of the Age Structure of the Population and Other Factors." *The Economic Studies Quarterly* 2(3): 237–53.

Horiuchi, Akiyoshi, and Qing-Yuan Sui. 1992. "The Influence of the Japan Development Bank Loans on Corporate Investment Behavior."

Hou, Chi-Ming, and Gee San. 1990. "National Systems Supporting Technical Advance in Industry: The Case of Taiwan." Taipei, Taiwan, China.

Hughes, Helen. 1992. "East Asian Export Success." Research School of Pacific Studies, Australian National University.

Hulten, Charles Jr. 1989. "The Embodiment Hypothesis Revisited." University of Maryland, College Park, Md.

Huseinga, Mark, and Christos Kostopolous. 1992. "Options for Reform of the Business Regulation System: Nepal." Country Report 8, Center for Institutional Reform and the Informal Sector, College Park, Md.

Hwang, Y. Dolly. 1991. *The Rise of a New World Economic Power: Postwar Taiwan.* New York: Greenwood.

Imai, Ken'ichi. 1988. "Industrial Policy and Technological Innovation." In R. Komiya, M. Okuno, and K. Suzumura. 1988. *Industrial Policy of Japan.* New York: Academic Press.

India. Various issues. *Reserve Bank of India Bulletin.*

Indonesia. Various issues. *Indonesian Financial Statistics.* Jakarta: Bank of Indonesia.

Ingram, James C. 1971. *Economic Change in Thailand, 1850–1970.* Stanford, Calif.: Stanford University Press.

Inoki, Takenori. 1993. "Retirement Behavior of Japanese Bureaucracies and the Role of Public Corporations: An Economic Interpretation of Human Resources' Mobility from Central Government to Public Corporation." World Bank, Economic Development Institute Working Paper, Washington, D.C.

IMF (International Monetary Fund). 1993. *World Economic Outlook.* Washington, D.C., May.

International Road Federation. Various years. *World Road Statistics.* Washington, D.C.

ISEI (Indonesian Economists' Association). 1990. *The Understanding of Economic Democracy.* Jakarta.

Ishikawa, T. 1987. "Savings: Structural Determinants of Household Saving and the Financial and Tax Systems." In Koichi Hamada, Makato Kuroda, and Akiyoshi Horiuchi, ed., *Macroeconomic Analysis of the Japanese Firm.* Amsterdam: North Holland.

Ito, Takatoshi. 1992. *The Japanese Economy.* Cambridge, Mass.: MIT Press.

____. 1993. "Industrial Policy for Development: Japanese Experience and Replicability." John F. Kennedy School of Government, Harvard University, Cambridge, Mass.

Itoh, Motoshige, and Kazuharu Kiyono. 1988. "Foreign Trade and Direct Investment." In Ryutaro Komiya, Masahiro Okuno, Kotaro Suzumura, eds., *Industrial Policy of Japan.* New York: Academic Press.

Itoh, Motoshige, Kazuharu Kiyono, Masahiro Okuno-Fugiwara, and Kataro Suzumura. 1988. "Industrial Policy as a Corrective to Market Failures." In Ryutaro Komiya, Masahiro Okuno, and Kotaro Suzumura, eds., *Industrial Policy of Japan.* New York: Academic Press.

____. 1991. *Economic Analysis of Industrial Policy.* New York: Academic Press.

Itoh, Motoshige, and S. Urata. 1993. "Small and Medium-Size Enterprise Support Policy of Japan." World Bank, Policy Research Department, Washington, D.C.

Jaffe, Adam B. 1986. "Technological Opportunity and Spillovers of R&D: Evidence from Firms' Patents, Profits and Market Value." *American Economic Review* 76(5): 984–1001.

JDB/JERI (Japan Development Bank and Japan Economic Research Institute). 1993. "Policy-Based Finance: The Experience of Postwar Japan." Tokyo.

Japan. Various years. *Economic Statistics Annual.* Tokyo: Bank of Japan.

____. *National Income Accounts of Japan.* Tokyo: Japanese Economic Planning Agency.

Jitsuchon, Somchai. 1991. "Retrospects and Prospects of Thailand's Economic Development." Working Paper 2, Japanese Economic Planning Agency, Tokyo.

Johnson, Chalmers. 1982. MITI *and the Japanese Miracle.* Stanford, Calif.: Stanford University Press.

Jones, Leroy, and Fadil Azim Abbas. 1992. "Malaysia: Background, Malaysian Airlines, Kelang Container Terminal, Sports Toto." Paper presented at a World Bank Conference on The Welfare Consequences of Selling Public Enterprises, Washington, D.C., June 11–12.

Jorgenson, Dale W., Masahiro Kuroda, and Mieko Nishimizu. 1987. "Japan-U.S. Industry-Level Productivity Comparisons, 1960–70." *Journal of Japanese and International Economics* 1(1).

Katseli, Louka T. 1992. "Foreign Direct Investment and Trade Interlinkages in the 1990s: Experience and Prospects of Developing Countries." Background paper for United Nations Symposium on Globalization and Developing Countries, The Hague. (Reprinted as Center for Economic Policy Research Discussion Paper 687, London, July 1992.)

Katz, Jorge, ed. 1987. *Technology Generation in Latin American Manufacturing Industries.* London: Macmillan.

Kaufman, George G. 1992. *Banking Structures in Major Countries.* Boston: Kluwer Academic Publishers.

Kawaura, Akihiko. 1991. "Identification of the Size and Direction of the Post-War Credit Allocation in Japan." World Bank, Financial Sector Development Department, Washington, D.C.

Kim, C. 1990. "Labor Market Development." In Jene K. Kwon, ed., *Korean Economic Development.* New York: Greenwood.

Kim, Chang-Shik. 1993a. "Government-Business Relationship in Korea: Selective Case Studies." Background paper for *The East Asian Miracle.* World Bank, Policy Research Department, Washington, D.C.

____. 1993b. "Trade Policy and Industrial Transformation in Korea." Background paper for *The East Asian Miracle.* World Bank, Policy Research Department, Washington, D.C.

Kim, Ji Hong. 1990. "Korean Industrial Policy in the 1970s: The Heavy and Chemical Industry Drive." Working Paper 9015. Korean Development Institute, Seoul, Korea.

Kim, Jong-Il, and Laurence J. Lau. 1993. "The Sources of Economic Growth of the East Asian Newly Industrialized Countries." Paper presented at a Conference on the Economic Development of the Republic of China and the Pacific Rim in 1990 and Beyond, Stanford University, Stanford, Calif., April.

Kim, K., and J. K. Park. 1985. *Sources of Economic Growth in Korea*. Seoul: Korea Development Institute.

Kim, Kihwan, and Danny Leipziger. 1993. *Korea: A Case of Government Led Development. Lessons of East Asia.* World Bank Country Study, Washington, D.C.

Kim, L., and J. Nugent. 1993. "Korean SMEs and Their Support Mechanisms: An Empirical Analysis of the Role of Government and Other Non-Profit Organizations." World Bank, Policy Research Department, Washington, D.C.

Kim, S. 1987. *In Service Training as an Instrument for the Development of Human Resources in Korea.* Paris: OECD Development Center.

___. 1988. *Japan's Civil Service System: Its Structure, Personnel and Politics.* New York: Greenwood.

Kim, Y. C., and J. K. Kwon. 1977. "The Utilization of Capital and the Growth of Output in a Developing Economy: The Case of South Korean Manufacturing." *Journal of Development Economics* 9: 265–78.

King, Elizabeth, Katherine Anderson, and Yan Wang. 1993. "Feedback Effects on the Labor Market on Schooling Choice in Malaysia." Paper presented at the April 1992 Meetings of the Population Association of America, Cincinnati, Ohio.

King, Robert, and Ross Levine. 1993. "Finance, Entrepreneurship and Growth." Paper presented at a conference on How Do National Policies Affect Long-Run Growth? World Bank, Washington, D.C., February.

Knight, John, and Richard H. Sabot. 1991. *Education, Productivity, and Inequality.* New York: Oxford University Press.

Komiya, Ryutaro. 1990. *The Japanese Economy: Trade, Industry, and Government.* Tokyo: University of Tokyo Press.

Komiya, Ryutaro, Masahiro Okuno, Kotaro Suzumura, eds. 1988. *Industrial Policy of Japan.* New York: Academic Press.

Konishi, Y. 1989. *A Quantitative Analysis of Educational Policies in Postwar Japan.* Research Institute for Economics and Business Administration, Kobe University, Kobe, Japan.

Korea, Republic of. Various years. *Economic Statistics Yearbook.* Seoul: Bank of Korea.

___. Various issues. *The Financial System in Korea.* Seoul: Bank of Korea.

___. 1978. *Major Statistics of the Korean Economy.* Seoul: Economic Planning Board.

Krueger, Anne O. 1978. "Alternative Trade Strategies and Employment in LDCs." *American Economic Review.* 68(2): 270–74.

___. 1984. "Comparative Advantage and Development Policy Twenty Years Later." In Moshe Syrquin, Lance Taylor, and Larry E. Westphal, eds., *Economic Structure and Performance.* New York: Academic Press.

___. 1993. "East Asia: Lessons for Growth Theory." Paper presented at the Fourth Annual East Asian Seminar on Economics, National Bureau of Economic Research, San Francisco, Calif., June 17–19.

Krueger, Anne O., and Jagdish Bhagwati. 1973. "Exchange Control, Liberalization Attempts, and Economic Development." *American Economic Review* 63(2): 419–27.

Krugman, Paul R. 1986. "Introduction: New Thinking about Trade Policy." In Paul R. Krugman, ed., *Strategic Trade Policy and the New International Economics.* Cambridge, Mass.: MIT Press.

Kumar, Nagesh. 1985. "Cost of Technology Imports: The Indian Experience." *Economic and Political Weekly* 20: M103–114.

Kunio, Y. 1988. *The Rise of Ersatz Capitalism in South East Asia.* New York: Oxford University Press.

Kuo, S. 1983. *The Taiwan Economy in Transition.* Boulder, Colo.: Westview.

Kuo, Wan-Yong. 1976. "Income Distribution by Size in Taiwan Area: Changes and Causes." *Industry of Free China* 45.

Kuznets, Simon. 1955. "Economic Growth and Income Inequality." *American Economic Review* 45(1): 1–28.

___. 1959. *Six Lectures on Economic Growth.* Glencoe, Ill.: Free Press.

___. 1966. *Modern Economic Growth.* New Haven, Conn.: Yale University Press.

Lall, Sanjaya, and G. Wignaraja. 1992. "Foreign Involvement by European Firms and Garment Exports by

Developing Countries." Development Studies Working Paper 54, Queen Elizabeth House, Oxford/Centro Studi Luca d'Agliano, Torino, Italia.

Lanyi, Anthony, and Rusdu Saracoglu. 1983. "Interest Rate Policies in Developing Countries." Occasional Paper 22. International Monetary Fund, Washington, D.C.

Lawrence, Robert Z. 1991. "Scenarios for the World Trading System and Their Implications for Developing Countries." Technical Paper 47, OECD Development Center, Paris. (Paper prepared for the Research Program on Globalization and Regionalization.)

___. 1993. "The Global Environment for the East Asian Model." John F. Kennedy School of Government, Harvard University, Cambridge, Mass.

Lee, Chinaboon. 1985. "Financing Technical Education in LDCs: Economic Implications from a Survey of Training Modes in the Republic of Korea." Education and Training Series 6. World Bank, Education and Training Department, Washington, D.C.

Lees, Francis A., James Botts, and Rubens Penha Cysne. 1990. *Banking and Financial Deepening in Brazil.* New York: St. Martin's Press.

Leipziger, Danny. 1987. *Korea: Managing the Industrial Transition.* Washington, D.C.: World Bank.

Leipziger, Danny, David Dollar, Anthony F. Shorrocks, and Su-Yong Song. 1992. *The Distribution of Income and Wealth in Korea.* Washington, D.C.: World Bank.

Levy, Brian. 1993. "Obstacles to Developing Indigenous Small and Medium-Size Enterprises: An Empirical Assessment." *World Bank Economic Review* 7(1): 65–85.

Lewis, W. Arthur. 1954. "Economic Development with Unlimited Supplies of Labor." *Manchester School of Economics and Social Studies* 22(2): 139–91.

Li, K. T. 1989. *The Evolution of Policy Behind Taiwan's Development Success.* New Haven, Conn.: Yale University Press.

Liddle, William. 1991. "The Relative Autonomy of the Third World Politician: Soeharto and Indonesian Economic Development in Comparative Perspective." *International Studies Quarterly* 35: 403–27.

Lim, Chee Peng. 1992. "Managing Structural Change and Industrialization—Heavy Industrialization: The Malaysian Experience." Paper presented at the ISIS-HIID Conference on the Malaysian Economy, Kuala Lumpur. Institute of Strategic and International Studies. June 1–3.

Lim, Linda Y. C., and Pang Eng Fong. 1991. *Foreign Direct Investment and Industrialization in Malaysia, Singapore, Taiwan and Thailand.* OECD, Paris.

Lim, Youngil. 1991. "Upgrading Industrial Base and Trade: The Role of Government Policy in Korea." United Nations Industrial Development Organization, New York.

Lindauer, David L., and Barbara Nunberg, eds. 1993. "Rehabilitating Government: Pay and Employment Reform in Sub-Saharan Africa." World Bank, Policy Research Department, Washington, D.C.

Little, Ian M. D. 1979. "The Experience and Causes of Rapid Labor-Intensive Development in Korea, Taiwan, Hong Kong, and Singapore, and the Possibilities of Emulation." Working Papers, Asian Employment Programme, ILO-ARTEP, Bangkok.

___. 1982. *Economic Development.* New York: Basic Books.

Little, Ian M. D., Richard N. Cooper, W. Max Corden, and Sarath Rajapathirana. Forthcoming. *Boom, Crisis, Adjustment: The Macroeconomic Experience of Developing Countries.* New York: Oxford University Press.

Little, Ian M. D., Tibor Scitovsky, and Maurice FG. Scott. 1970. *Industry and Trade in Some Developing Countries.* London: Oxford University Press.

Liu, Alan P. L. 1987. *Phoenix and the Lame Lion: Modernization in Taiwan and Mainland China, 1950–80.* Stanford, Calif.: Hoover Institution Press.

Liu, Lili. 1991. "Entry-Exit: Learning and Productivity Change—Evidence from Chile." Policy Research Working Paper 769. World Bank, Country Economics Department, Washington, D.C.

Lockheed, Marlaine, and Adriaan Verspoor. 1991. *Improving Primary Education in Developing Countries.* New York: Oxford University Press.

Lockwood, William W. *The Economic Development of Japan: Growth and Structural Change, 1868–1938.* Princeton: Princeton University Press.

Long, Millard, and Dimitri Vittas. 1991. "Changing the Rules of the Game." Policy Research Working Paper 803. World Bank, Policy Research Department, Washington, D.C.

Maisom, Abdullah. 1992. "Patterns of Total Factor Productivity Growth in Malaysian Manufacturing Industries, 1973–89." Paper presented at ISIS-HIID Workshop on the Malaysian Economy, Kuala Lumpur, September.

Maki, Atsushi. 1993. "The Relation between Household Saving Rate and Economic Growth: Consumers' Stimulus to Purchase Durable Goods." Paper prepared for a World Bank Asian Miracle Project Workshop, Tokyo, Feb. 1–2.

Malaysia. 1990. *Quarterly Bulletin.* Kuala Lumpur: Bank Negara. March–June.

Mankiw, N. Gregory, David Romer, and David Weil. 1992. "A Contribution to the Empirics of Economic Growth." *Quarterly Journal of Economics* 107(2): 407–38.

Mayer, C. 1987. "The Assessment: Financial Systems and Corporate Investment." *Oxford Review of Economic Policy* 3(4): i–xvi.

Mazumdar, Deepak. Forthcoming. "Labor Markets and Adjustment in Open Asian Economies: The Republic of Korea and Malaysia." *World Bank Economic Review.*

McKinnon, Ronald I. 1973. *Money and Capital in Economic Development.* Washington, D.C.: Brookings Institution.

Mellor, John, ed. 1993. "Agriculture on the Road to Industrialization." International Food Policy Research Institute, Washington, D.C.

Middleton, J., A. Ziderman, and A. van Adams. Forthcoming. *Skills for Productivity.* Baltimore, Md.: Johns Hopkins University Press.

Modigliani, Franco. 1970. "The Life Cycle Hypothesis of Savings and Intercountry Differences in the Savings Ratio." In W. A. Eltis, Maurice FG. Scott, and J. N. Wolfe, eds., *Induction Growth and Trade: Essays in Honor of Sir Roy Harrod.* Oxford: Clarendon Press.

Mody, Ashoka, R. Suri, and J. Sanders. 1992. "Keeping Pace with Change: Organizational and Technological Imperatives." *World Development* 20(12): 1797–816.

Monetary Authority of Singapore. 1991. "Savings-Investment Balances in Singapore: Determinants and Medium-Term Outlook." Singapore: Economics Department.

Morris, Felipe, Mark Dorfman, José Pedro Ortiz, and Maria Claudia Franco. 1990. *Latin America's Banking Systems in the 1980s: A Cross-Country Comparison.* World Bank Discussion Paper 81. Washington, D.C.

Mukai, Yurio. 1963. "Development of Postal Savings and Its Factors." In Japanese. *Kinyu Keizai,* no. 83. December.

Munasinghe, Mohan. 1987. *Rural Electrification for Development: Policy and Analysis and Applications.* Boulder, Colo.: Westview.

Murdock, K., and Joseph E. Stiglitz. 1993. "The Effect of Financial Repression in an Economy with Positive Real Rates." Background paper for *The East Asian Miracle.* World Bank, Policy Research Department, Washington, D.C.

Murphy, Kevin, Andre Shleifer, and Robert Vishny. 1989. "Industrialization and the Big Push." *Journal of Political Economy* 97(5): 1003–26.

Mutoh, Hiromichi. 1988. "The Automotive Industry." In Ryutaro Komiya, Masahiro Okuno, and Kotaro Suzumura, eds., *Industrial Policy of Japan.* New York: Academic Press.

Mytelka, Lynn. 1978. "Licensing and Technology Development in the Andean Group." *World Development* 6(4): 447–60.

Nagaoka, Sadao. 1989. "Overview of Japanese Industrial Technology Development." Industry Series Paper 6. World Bank, Industry and Energy Department, Washington, D.C.

Nalebuff, B. 1983. "Information, Competition and Markets." *American Economic Review* 72(2): 278–84.

Nalebuff, B., and Joseph E. Stiglitz. 1983. "Prizes and Incentives: Towards a General Theory of Compensation and Competition." *Bell Journal of Economics* 14(1): 21–43.

Nam, Sang-Woo. Undated. "Korea's Financial Reform since the Early 1980s." Korea Development Institute, Seoul.

Neal, Craig R. 1990. "Macrofinancial Indicators for 117 Developing and Industrial Countries." PRE Working Paper 58. World Bank, Office of the Vice President, Development Economics, Washington, D.C.

Nehru, Vikram, and Ashok Dhareshwar. 1993. "A New Database on Physical Capital Stock: Sources, Methodology, and Results." World Bank, International Economics Department, Washington, D.C.

Nelson, Richard R. 1973. "Recent Exercises in Growth Accounting: New Understanding or Dead End?" *American Economic Review* 63(3): 462–8.

Nishimizu, Mieko, and John M. Page, Jr. 1982. "Total Factor Productivity Growth, Technological Growth, and Technical Efficiency Change: Dimensions of Productivity Change in Yugoslavia, 1965–78." *Economic Journal* 92(368): 920–36.

___. 1987. "Economic Policies and Productivity Change in Industry: An International Comparison." Paper for a World Bank research project on Productivity Change in Infant Industry. World Bank, Policy Research Department, Washington, D.C.

___. 1991. "Trade Policy, Market Orientation, and Productivity Change in Industry." In Jaime de Melo and Andres Sapir, eds., *Trade Theory and Economic Reform: North, South and East—Essays in Honor of Bela Balassa.* Oxford: Blackwell.

Noguchi, Y. 1985. "Nenkin, zeisei to kokumin no chochiku kodo [Pensions, the tax system, and the saving behavior of the people]." In *Kenkyu Hokoku Gaiyo [Summary of Research Findings].* Kokuei Nin'i Seimei Hoken no Shorai Tenbo ni kansuru Chosa Kenkyukai [Research project on the Future Prospects of Government-Managed Voluntary Life Insurance], Tokyo.

North, Douglas C., and R. Thomas. 1973. *The Rise of the Western World: A New Economic History.* Cambridge, U.K.: Cambridge University Press.

Ogura, Seiritsu, and Naoyuki Yoshino. 1988. "The Tax System and Fiscal Investment and Loan Program." In Ryutaro Komiya, Masahiro Okuno, and Kotaro Suzumura, eds., *Industrial Policy of Japan.* New York: Academic Press.

Okimoto, Daniel. 1989. *Between MITI and the Market: Japanese Industrial Policy for High Technology.* Stanford, Calif.: Stanford University Press.

Ono. 1992. *Jissenteki Sangyo Seisakuron.* In Japanese. Tsusho Sangyo Chosakai.

Pack, Howard. 1971. *Structural Change and Economic Policy in Israel.* New Haven, Conn.: Yale University Press.

___. 1988. "Industrialization and Trade." In Hollis B. Chenery and T. N. Srinivasan, eds., *Handbook of Development Economics,* vol. 1. Amsterdam: North Holland.

___. 1992. "Learning and Productivity Change in Developing Countries." In Gerald K. Helleiner, ed., *Trade Policy Industrialization and Development.* Oxford: Clarendon Press.

___. 1993a. "Exports and Externalities: The Source of Taiwan's Growth in Taiwan." University of Pennsylvania, Philadelphia, Pa.

___. 1993b. "Industrial and Trade Policies in the High-Performing Asian Economies." Background paper for *The East Asian Miracle.* World Bank, Policy Research Department, Washington, D.C.

___. 1993c. "Technology Gaps between Industrial and Developing Countries: Are There Dividends for Latecomers?" In *Proceedings of the World Bank Annual Bank Conference on Development Economics, 1992.* Washington, D.C.: World Bank.

Pack, Howard, and John M. Page, Jr. 1993. "Accumulation, Exports, and Growth in the High-Performing Asian Economies." Background paper for *The East Asian Miracle.* World Bank, Policy Research Department, Washington, D.C.

Pack, Howard, and Larry E. Westphal. 1986. "Industrial Strategy and Technological Change: Theory vs. Reality." *Journal of Development Economics* 22(1): 87–128.

Packer, Frank. 1992. "The Role of Long-Term Credit Banks within the Japanese Main Bank System." Columbia University, New York.

Page, John M., Jr. 1990. "The Pursuit of Industrial Growth: Policy Initiatives and Economic Consequences." In Maurice FG. Scott and Deepak Lal, eds., *Public Policy and Economic Development: Essays in Honor of Ian Little.* Oxford: Clarendon Press.

Page, John M., Jr., and Peter A. Petri. 1993. "Productivity Change and Strategic Growth Policy in the Asian Miracle." Background paper for *The East Asian Miracle.* World Bank, Policy Research Department, Washington, D.C.

Panagariya, Arvind. 1993. "Unraveling the Mysteries of China's Foreign Trade Regime." *World Economy* 16(1): 51–8.

Pempel, T. J. 1984. "The Japanese Bureaucracy and Economic Development: Can the Model be Copied?" Economic Development Institute, World Bank, Washington, D.C.

Perry, Guillermo, and Ana Maria Herrera. 1993. "Finanzas Públicas, Estabilización y Reforma Estructural en América Latina." Working Paper Series 165. Inter-American Development Bank, Washington, D.C.

Petri, Peter A. 1988. "Korea's Export Niche: Origins and Prospects." *World Development* 16(1): 47–64.

Pfeffermann, Guy P., and Andrea Madarassy. 1992. *Trends in Private Investment in Developing Countries. 1992 Edition.* IFC Discussion Paper 14. Washington, D.C.: World Bank and IFC.

Psacharopoulos, George. 1993. "Returns to Investment in Education: A Global Update." Policy Research Working Paper 1067. World Bank, Latin America and the Caribbean Region, Washington, D.C.

Psacharopoulos, George, Jee-Peng Tan, and Emmanuel Jimenez. 1986. *Financing Education in Developing Countries: An Exploration of Policy Options.* Washington, D.C.: World Bank.

Ranis, Gustav. 1973. "Industrial Sector Labor Absorption." *Economic Development and Cultural Change* 21(3): 387–408.

___. 1979. "Industrial Development." In W. Galenson, ed., *Economic Growth and Structural Change in Taiwan.* Ithaca, N.Y.: Cornell University Press.

___, ed. 1992. *Taiwan: From Developing to Mature Economy.* Boulder, Colo.: Westview.

___. 1993. "Labor Markets, Human Capital, and Development Performance in East Asia." Background paper for *The East Asian Miracle.* World Bank, Policy Research Department, Washington, D.C.

Ranis, Gustav, and John Fei. 1961. "A Theory of Economic Development." *American Economic Review* 51(4): 533–65.

Ranis, Gustav, and Chi Schive. 1985. "Direct Foreign Investment in Taiwan's Development." In Walter Galenson, ed., *Foreign Trade and Investment: Economic Development in the Newly Industrializing Asian Countries.* Madison, Wis.: University of Wisconsin Press.

Ranis, Gustav, and Frances Stewart. 1987. "Rural Linkages in the Philippines and Taiwan." In Frances Stewart, ed., *Macro-policies for Appropriate Technology in Developing Countries.* Boulder, Colo.: Westview.

Rebelo, Sergio. 1991. "Long Run Policy Analysis and Long Run Growth." *Journal of Political Economy* 99(3): 500–21.

Reid, Gary. 1992. "Civil Service Reform in Latin America: Lessons of Experience." Occasional Paper 6. World Bank, Latin America Technical Department, Washington, D.C.

Remolona, E., and M. Lamberte. 1986. "Financial Reforms and the Balance of Payments Crisis: The Case of the Philippines, 1980–83." Working Paper 86-02. Philippine Institute of Development Studies, Manila.

Revell, Jack. 1987. "Mergers and the Role of Large Banks." Institute of European Finance, University College of North Wales, Bangor, Wales.

Rhee, Yung Whee. 1989a. "Managing Entry into International Markets: Lessons from the East Asian Experience." Industry Series Working Paper 11. World Bank, Industry and Energy Department, Washington, D.C.

___. 1989b. "Trade Finance in Developing Economies." Policy Research Series 5. World Bank, Washington, D.C.

Rhee, Yung Whee, and Larry E. Westphal. 1977. "A Microeconomic Investigation of Choice of Technique." *Journal of Development Economics* 4: 205–38.

Riedel, James. 1988. "Demand for LDC Exports of Manufactures: Estimates from Hong Kong." *Economic Journal* 98(389): 138–48.

Rob, Rafael. 1990. "The Evolution of Markets under Demand Uncertainty." University of Pennsylvania, Philadelphia, Pa.

Romer, Paul M. 1993. "Two Strategies for Economic Development: Using Ideas and Producing Ideas." *In Proceedings of the World Bank Annual Bank Conference on Development Economics, 1992.* Washington, D.C.

Rosenberg, Nathan. 1976. *Perspectives on Technology.* Cambridge, U.K.: Cambridge University Press.

Sabot, Richard H. 1979. *Economic Development and Urban Migration.* London: Oxford University Press.

Sakakibara, E., R. Feldman, and Y. Harada. 1982. *The Japanese Financial System in Comparative Perspective.* Washington, D.C.: Joint Economic Committee, Congress of the United States.

Sakong, I. 1993. *Korea in the World Economy.* Washington, D.C.: Institute for International Economics.

Salleh, Ismael. 1991. "The Privatisation of Public Enterprises: A Case Study of Malaysia." In Geeta Gouri, ed., *Privatisation and Public Enterprise.* New Delhi: Oxford University Press and IBH Publishing Company.

Salleh, Ismael, Kim Leng Yeah, and Saha Dhevan Meyanathan. 1993. *Growth, Equity, and Structural Transformation in Malaysia: The Role of the Public Sector. Lessons of East Asia.* World Bank Country Study, Washington, D.C.

Samudavanija, Chaianan. 1992. "High Speed Growth and High Performance in a Technocratic Polity: The Thai Case." Background paper for *The East Asian Miracle.* World Bank, Policy Research Department, Washington, D.C.

San, G. 1990. "Enterprise Training in Taiwan: Results from the Vocational Training Needs Survey." *Economics of Education Review* 9(4): 411–8.

Saxonhouse, Gary. 1983. "What Is All This about Industrial Targeting in Japan?" *World Economy* 6(3): 253–73.

Schiff, Maurice. 1993. "Agriculture Pricing Policy and Growth in Asia." World Bank, Policy Research Department, Washington, D.C.

Schiff, Maurice, and Alberto Valdés. 1992. *The Political Economy of Agricultural Pricing Policy, Volume 4: A Synthesis of the Economics in Developing Countries.* Baltimore, Md.: Johns Hopkins University Press.

Schultz, T. Paul. 1988. "Education Investment and Returns." In Hollis B. Chenery and T. N. Srinivasan, eds., *Handbook of Development Economics*, vol. 1. Amsterdam: North Holland.

Scitovsky, Tibor. 1954. "Two Concepts of External Economies." *Journal of Political Economy* 62(2): 143–51.

Scott, Maurice FG. 1979. "Trade." In W. Galenson, ed., *Economic Growth and Structural Change in Taiwan.* Ithaca, N.Y.: Cornell University Press.

Scully, Michael T., and George J. Viksnins. 1987. *Financing East Asia's Success: Comparative Financial Development in Eight Asian Countries.* London: Macmillan.

Shah, Anwar, ed. Forthcoming. *Fiscal Incentives for Investment in Developing Countries.* New York: Oxford University Press.

Shah, Shekhar, and Subodh C. Mathur. 1992. "Sources of Labor Market Flexibility in East Asia: A Review of Selected Issues." Background paper for *The East Asian Miracle.* World Bank, Policy Research Department, Washington, D.C.

Shapiro, Helen, and Lance Taylor. 1990. "The State and Industrial Strategy." *World Development* 18(6): 861–78.

Shea, J. D. Forthcoming. "Development and Structural Change of the Financial System." In Patrick Hugh and Yung Chul Park, eds., *Financial Development: Japan, Korea, and Taiwan.* New York: Oxford University Press.

Sheng, Andrew. 1989. "Bank Restructuring in Malaysia, 1985–88." PRE Working Paper 54. World Bank, Financial Sector Development Department, Washington, D.C.

___. 1990. "The Art of Bank Restructuring: Issues and Techniques." World Bank, Financial Sector Development Department, Washington, D.C.

Shouda, Yasutoyo. 1982. "Effective Rates of Protection in Japan." *Nihon Keizai Kenkyu* 11 (March).

Shoven, John. 1988. *Government Policy Towards Industry in the United States and Japan.* Cambridge, U.K.: Cambridge University Press.

Singapore. Various years. *Yearbook of Statistics and an Economic Survey of Singapore.* Singapore: Department of Statistics.

___. 1983. *Economic and Social Statistics 1960–1982.* Singapore: Department of Statistics.

Singh, Ajit. 1992. "'Close' vs. 'Strategic' Integration with the World Economy and the 'Market-Friendly Approach to Development' vs. an 'Industrial Policy': A Critique of the *World Development Report 1991* and an Alternative Policy Perspective." Faculty of Economics, University of Cambridge, Cambridge, England.

Singh, Ajit, and Javed Hamid. 1992. "Corporate Financial Structures in Developing Countries." Technical Paper 1. International Finance Corporation, Washington, D.C.

Solow, Robert M. 1956. "A Contribution to the Theory of Economic Growth." *Quarterly Journal of Economics* 70(1): 65–94.

___. 1957. "Technical Change and the Aggregate Production Function." *Review of Economics and Statistics* 39(3): 312–20.

Soon, Tek-Wong, and Suan Tan. 1992. "Public Policy and Economic Development in Singapore." Manuscript prepared for a World Bank Conference on the Role of Government and East Asian Success, Washington, D.C.

Spence, M. 1981. "The Learning Curve and Competition." *Bell Journal of Economics* 12(1): 49–70.

Squire, Lyn. 1981. *Employment Policy in Developing Countries: A Survey of Issues and Evidence.* New York: Oxford University Press.

Srinivasan, T. N. 1992. "Database for Development Analysis: An Overview." Paper presented at a Conference on Data Base of Development Analysis, Yale University, New Haven, Conn., May.

Stern, Joseph, Ji-Hong Kim, Dwight Perkins, and Jung-Ho Yoo. 1992. "Industrialization and the State: The Korean Heavy and Chemical Industry Drive." Research report. Harvard Institute for International Development, Cambridge, Mass., and Korea Development Institute, Seoul.

Stevenson H., and J. Stigler. 1992. *The Learning Gap.* New York: Summit.

Stewart, Francis, and Ejaz Ghani. 1991. "How Significant Are Externalities for Development?" *World Development* 19(6): 569–94.

Stiglitz, Joseph E. 1993a. "The Role of the State in Financial Markets." Paper prepared for the Annual Bank Conference on Development Economics, World Bank, Washington, D.C.

———. 1993b. "Some Lessons from the Asian Miracle." Background paper for *The East Asian Miracle*. World Bank, Policy Research Department, Washington, D.C.

Summers, Lawrence H. 1985. "Issues in National Savings Policy." NBER Working Paper 1710, Cambridge, Mass.

Summers, Lawrence H., and V. P. Summers. 1989. "When Financial Markets Work Too Well: A Cautious Case for a Securities Transaction Tax." In *Regulatory Reform of Stock and Futures Markets*, a special issue of the *Journal of Financial Services Research*. Boston: Kluwer Academic Publishers.

Summers, Robert, and Alan Heston. 1988. "A New Set of International Comparisons of Real Product and Prices: Estimates for 130 Countries." *Review of Income and Wealth* 34(1): 1–25.

———. 1991. "The Penn World Tables (Mark 5): An Expanded Set of International Comparisons, 1950–88." *Quarterly Journal of Economics* 105(2).

Sun, C., and M. Liang. 1982. "Savings in Taiwan, 1953–1980." In Kwoh-Ting Li and Tzong-Shian Yu, eds., *Experiences and Lessons of Economic Development in Taiwan*. Taipei: Institute of Economics, Academia Sinica.

Sundavarej, Tipsuda, and Trairatvorakul, Prasarn. "Experiences of Financial Distress in Thailand." PRE Working Paper 283. World Bank, Office of the Vice President for Development Economics, Washington, D.C.

Sussangkarn, Chalongphob. 1988. "Production Structures, Labor Markets and Human Capital Investments: Issues of Balance for Thailand." Thailand Development Research Institute, Offprint #7, Bangkok.

Suzuki, Yoshio. 1987. *The Japanese Financial System*. Oxford: Clarendon Press.

Syrquin, Moshe, and Hollis B. Chenery. 1989. *Patterns of Development, 1950 to 1983*. World Bank Discussion Paper 41. Washington, D.C.

Taiwan, China. Various issues. *Financial Statistics Monthly*. Taipei: Central Bank of China.

———. Various years. *Statistical Yearbook of the Republic of China*. Taipei: Directorate General of Budget, Accounting, and Statistics.

———. 1988. *Statistical Yearbook of the Republic of China*. Taipei.

———. 1992a. *Statistical Yearbook of the Republic of China*. Taipei.

———. 1992b. *Statistics of Small and Medium Business in Taiwan, Republic of China*. Taipei: Ministry of Economic Affairs.

Tan, Jee-Peng, and Alain Mingat. 1992. *Education in Asia: A Comparative Study of Cost and Financing*. Washington, D.C.: World Bank.

Tanaka, Naoki. 1988. "Aluminum Refining Industry." In Ryutaro Komiya, Masahiro Okuno, and Kotaro Suzumura, eds., *Industrial Policy of Japan*. New York: Academic Press.

Tanzi, Vito, and Parthsarathi Shome. 1992. "The Role of Taxation in the Development of East Asian Economies." In Takatoshi Ito and Anne O. Krueger, eds., *The Political Economy of Tax Reform*. Chicago: University of Chicago Press.

Teranishi, Juro. 1986. "Economic Growth and Regulation of Financial Markets: Japanese Experience during the Postwar High Growth Period." *Hitotsubashi Journal of Ecnomics* 27: 149–65.

Thailand. Various issues. *Quarterly Bulletin*. Bangkok: Bank of Thailand.

Thomas, Vinod, and Yan Wang. 1993. "Government Policies and Productivity Growth: Is East Asia an Exception?" Background paper for *The East Asian Miracle*. World Bank, Policy Research Department, Washington, D.C.

Thurow, Lester. 1992. *Head to Head: The Coming Economic Battle Among Japan, Europe, and America*. New York: Morrow.

Trela, Irene, and John Whalley. Forthcoming. "Taxes, Outward Orientation and Growth Performance in the Republic of Korea." In Anwar Shah, ed., *Fiscal Incentives for Investment in Developing Countries*. New York: Oxford University Press.

Trezise, P. H. 1983. "Industrial Policy Is Not the Major Reason for Japan's Success." *Brookings Review* 1(3): 13–8.

Tullock, Gordon. 1988a. "Why Did the Industrial Revolution Occur in England?" In C. Rowley, R. Tollison, and G. Tullock, eds., *The Political Economy of Rent-Seeking*. Boston: Kluwer Academic Publishers.

___. 1988b. "Rents and Rent-Seeking." In C. Rowley, R. Tollison, and Gordon Tullock, eds., *The Political Economy of Rent-Seeking*. Boston: Kluwer Academic Publishers.

Turnham, David. 1993. *Employment and Development in New Review of Evidence*. Paris: Development Center, OECD.

Ueda, Kazuo. 1992. *Institutional and Regulatory Frameworks for the Main Bank System*. Tokyo: University of Tokyo.

UNESCO. Various years. *Statistical Yearbook*. Paris.

United Nations. Various years, a. *Demographic Yearbook*. New York.

___. Various years, b. *Energy Statistics Yearbook*. New York.

___. 1976. *World Energy Supplies 1950–74*. New York.

___. 1992. *World Economic Survey: Current Trends and Policies in the World Economy*. New York.

UNDP (United Nations Development Programme). 1991. *Human Development Report*. New York: Oxford University Press.

Van Adams, A. 1989. "A Study of the Economic Environment's Influence on Human Capital Formation in Korea and Egypt." George Washington University, Washington, D.C.

Viner, Aron. 1988. *Inside Japanese Financial Markets*. Homewood, Ill.: Dow Jones–Irwin.

Vittas, Dimitri. 1991. "Measuring Commercial Bank Efficiency: Use and Misuse of Bank Operating Ratios." Policy Research Working Paper 806. World Bank, Country Economics Department, Washington, D.C.

___. 1992. "Policy Issues in Financial Regulation." World Bank, Country Economics Department, Washington, D.C. April.

Vogel, Ezra F., and David Lindauer. 1991. "Toward a Social Compact for Korean Labor." In David Lindauer, Jong-Gie Kim, Joung-Woo Lee, Hy-Sop Lim, Jae-Young Son, and Ezra F. Vogel, eds., *Korea: The Strains of Economic Growth*. Cambridge, Mass.: Harvard Institute for International Development.

Wade, Robert. 1989. "What Can Economies Learn from East Asian Success?" *Annals of the American Academy of Political Science* 505: 68–79.

___. 1990. *Governing the Market: Economic Theory and the Role of the Government in East Asian Industrialization*. Princeton, N.J.: Princeton University Press.

The Wall Street Journal. 1990. "Taiwan, Long Noted for Cheap Imitations, Becomes an Innovator." June 1.

Wang, Fang-Yi. 1990. "Reconsidering the 'East Asian Model of Development': The Link between Exports and Productivity Enhancement, Evidence from Taiwan, 1950–87." Ph.D diss. University of California at Los Angeles.

Warr, Peter G., and Bhanupong Nadhiprabha. 1993. "Macroeconomic Policies, Crisis, and Growth in the Long Run: Thailand." Background paper prepared for Little, Ian M. D., Richard N. Cooper, W. Max Corden, and Sarath Rajapathirana, eds., *Boom, Crisis, Adjustment: The Macroeconomic Experience of Developing Countries*. New York: Oxford University Press.

Wei, Shang-Jin. 1993. "Open Door Policy and China's Rapid Growth: Evidence from City-Level Data." Prepared for the Fourth Annual East Asian Seminar on Economics, National Bureau of Economic Research, Cambridge, Mass.

Westphal, Larry E. 1978. "The Republic of Korea's Experience with Export Led Development." *World Development* 6: 347–82.

Westphal, Larry E., Yung Whee Rhee, and Garry Pursell. 1988. *Korean Industrial Competence: Where It Came From*. World Bank Staff Working Paper 469. Washington, D.C.

Whalley, John. 1990. "Non-Discriminatory Discrimination: Special and Differential Treatment under the GATT for Developing Countries." *Economic Journal* 100(403): 1318–28.

Wiboonchutikula, Paitoon. 1987. "Total Factor Productivity Growth of Manufacturing Industries in Thailand." In *Productivity Changes and International Competitiveness of Thai Industries*. Bangkok: Thailand Development Research Institute.

Winkler, Donald R. 1990. *Higher Education in Latin America: Issues of Efficiency and Equity*. World Bank Discussion Paper 77. Washington, D.C.

Wolf, Charles. 1988. *Markets or Governments: Choosing between Imperfect Alternatives*. Cambridge, Mass: MIT Press.

World Bank. 1983. "Special Economic Report: Policies for the Financial Sector." Europe, Middle East, and North Africa Region, Washington, D.C.

___. 1987a. *Korea: Managing the Industrial Transition*. 2 vols. Washington, D.C.

___. 1987b. *World Development Report 1987*. New York: Oxford University Press.

___. 1989a. "Indonesia: Strategy for Growth and Structural Change." Country Department V, Washington, D.C.

___. 1989b. *Malaysia: Matching Risks and Rewards in a Mixed Economy.* Washington, D.C.

___. 1989c. *World Development Report 1989.* New York: Oxford University Press.

___. 1990a. *Indonesia: Strategy for a Sustained Reduction in Poverty.* Washington, D.C.

___. 1990b. *World Development Report 1990.* New York: Oxford University Press.

___. 1991a. *Colombia: Industrial Competition and Performance.* Washington, D.C.

___. 1991b. *World Development Report: The Challenge of Development.* New York: Oxford University Press.

___. 1992a. "China: Reform and the Role of the Plan in the 1990s." East Asia and the Pacific Regional Office, Washington, D.C.

___. 1992b. *Global Economic Prospects and the Developing Countries.* Washington, D.C.

___. 1992c. *World Bank Support for Industrialization in Korea, India, and Indonesia.* Washington, D.C.

___. 1992d. *World Development Report 1992.* New York: Oxford University Press.

___. 1993a. *Global Economic Prospects and the Developing Countries.* Washington, D.C.

___. 1993b. *World Development Report 1993: Investing in Health.* New York: Oxford University Press.

World Economic Forum. 1992. *World Competitiveness Report.* Geneva.

Yamamura, Kozo. 1986. "Caveat Emptor: The Industrial Policy of Japan." In Paul Krugman, ed., *Strategic Trade Policy and the New International Economics.* Cambridge, Mass.: MIT Press.

___. 1985. *The Political Economy of Japan.* Stanford, Calif.: Stanford University Press.

Yamawaki, Hideki. 1988. "The Steel Industry." In Ryutaro Komiya, Masahiro Okuno, and Kotaro Suzumura, eds., *Industrial Policy of Japan.* New York: Academic Press.

Yamazawa, Ippie. 1988. "The Textile Industry." In Ryutaro Komiya, Masahiro Okuno, and Kotaro Suzumura, eds., *Industrial Policy of Japan.* New York: Academic Press.

Yan, Lin See. 1991. "Savings Investment Gap, Financing Needs and Capital Market Development." Bank Negara, Malaysia. September.

Yaron, Jacob. 1992. *Successful Rural Finance Institutions.* World Bank Discussion Paper 150. Washington, D.C.

Yonezawa, Yoshie. 1988. "The Shipbuilding Industry." In Ryutaro Komiya, Masahiro Okuno, and Kotaro Suzumura, eds., *Industrial Policy of Japan.* New York: Academic Press.

Yoshino, Naoyuki. 1993. "The Low Interest Rate Policy and Economic Growth of Japan." Department of Economics, Keio University, Tokyo, Japan.

Young, Alwyn. 1992. "A Tale of Two Cities: Factor Accumulation and Technical Change in Hong Kong and Singapore." Paper presented at a World Bank seminar. February.

Yusof, Z. A., A. A. Hussin, I. Alowi, S. Singh, and L. C. Sing. Forthcoming. "The Impact of Financial Reform in Malaysia." In Gerard Caprio Jr., Izak Atiyas, and James Hanson, eds., *Financial Reform: Theory and Experience.* Cambridge: Cambridge University Press.